CULINARY
CAREERS

CULINARY CAREERS

HOW TO GET YOUR DREAM JOB IN FOOD
WITH ADVICE FROM TOP CULINARY PROFESSIONALS

RICK SMILOW

PRESIDENT AND CEO OF
THE INSTITUTE OF CULINARY EDUCATION

and ANNE E. McBRIDE

CLARKSON POTTER/PUBLISHERS
NEW YORK

Grateful acknowledgment is made to Broadway Books for permission
to reprint an excerpt from *The United States of Arugula: How We Became
a Gourmet Nation* by David Kamp, copyright © 2006 by David Kamp.
Reprinted by permission of Broadway Books, a division of Random
House, Inc.

Library of Congress Cataloging-in-Publication Data
Smilow, Rick.
Culinary careers / Rick Smilow and Anne E. McBride. — 1st ed.
      p. cm.
Includes index.
1. Food service—Vocational guidance.   2. Cooks—Vocational guidance.
3. Cookery—Vocational guidance.   I. McBride, Anne E.   II. Title.
TX911.3.V62S62 2010
647.95023—dc22   2009033588

ISBN 978-0-307-45320-4

Printed in the United States of America

Design by Stephanie Huntwork

10 9 8 7 6 5 4 3 2

First Edition

CONTENTS

INTRODUCTION

Working in the food industry is no longer only a plan B—it has become a career of *choice*. You can proudly walk up to your parents and tell them that you are going to culinary school—they might even pay for it. You can let go of your corporate job to work in a restaurant and have the support, and even the envy, of your friends.

Your signature recipe can become a product sold in every supermarket. The new celebrities are found not on sitcoms but on televised cooking shows. Dining out rivals the theater as a stand-alone leisure activity. Food personalities have become moguls of multimedia empires. Food movies like *Ratatouille* and *Julie & Julia* are as important to Hollywood as action flicks and romantic comedies. In such a wide-open field, there truly are no limits to what you can accomplish and to how many people can accomplish it.

All these developments mean that you can follow a plethora of career paths if you want to work in a food-related field, regardless of the level at which you wish to enter the industry or switch jobs. But the options are not always obvious. Food plays a role in so many areas that it can be hard to find out exactly what job would be best for you and how to go about obtaining it. What degrees do you need? What will be your first job? What do you do in a certain job?

From my position as president of the Institute of Culinary Education (ICE) in New York City, I have a bird's-eye view of the spectrum of jobs, activity, and development in America's culinary scene. ICE offers a vast array of courses and programs; throughout the year, I meet chefs, chocolatiers, caterers, beverage managers, restaurant owners, cheesemakers, private chefs, sommeliers, food journalists, and on and on who come to ICE to teach or

> Our culinary elites—the chefs, cookbook authors, cooking-school instructors, purveyors, and food writers who lead the way—are suffused with feelings of boundless possibility, having liberated themselves from the old strictures and prejudices that hemmed in their predecessors.
>
> —DAVID KAMP,
> *The United States of Arugula*

America's Love Affair with Food—Some Milestones

1959 The Four Seasons opens in New York, NY

1961 Julia Child's *Mastering the Art of French Cooking,* volume one, is published

1963 WGBH in Boston airs Julia Child's *The French Chef*

1966 Julia Child appears on the cover of *Time*

1971 Alice Waters opens Chez Panisse in Berkeley, CA

1971 The Culinary Institute of America starts offering associate's degrees

1972 *James Beard's American Cookery* is released

1973 The Cuisinart is introduced in the United States

1975 Peter Kump begins teaching cooking classes in New York, starting what would become Peter Kump's New York Cooking School and, later, ICE

1976 The American Culinary Federation successfully lobbies to have the title of executive chef moved from the service to the professional category in the U.S. Department of Labor's *Dictionary of Occupational Titles*

1976 California wines win against French wines in the Judgment of Paris competition

1979 The first Zagat survey is published

1980 The first Whole Foods Market opens in Austin, TX

1981 Julia Child and Robert Mondavi launch the American Institute of Wine and Food

1982 Martha Stewart's *Entertaining* is published

1982 Wolfgang Puck opens Spago in Beverly Hills, CA

1982 *The Silver Palate* is published

1986 Julia Child and Peter Kump launch the James Beard Foundation

1991 First James Beard Foundation Awards

1993 The Food Network begins airing—the first all-food cable channel

speak, or for a cornucopia of other reasons. Meanwhile, our graduates have gone on to hold all sorts of coveted food jobs, from the assistant director of operations at Daniel Boulud's global company Dinex Group to a producer at Martha Stewart Living Omnimedia. From talking to professionals in all aspects of the industry—asking them to tell us about their education, career path, and day-to-day activities in their current job—Anne and I have gathered a wealth of information to share with those interested in pursuing cooking and food. *Culinary Careers* is a comprehensive guide to help you—students, career changers, prep cooks looking to move up, weary chefs in need of a new way to use their skills, budding food writers, or aspiring winemakers—go about your job search and learn more about the industry as a whole.

A common story when talking to people in the food industry is that they got their job "by chance." Many of the people who are profiled in this book said something along the lines of: "My story isn't typical because I just got lucky." What they didn't realize is that they are not alone in that situation. And that is true of most careers; a large part of why you do what you do happens by chance. Maybe what used to be a summer job while in high school turned into a career because you had the right mentors. Or a career change happened because you were sitting next to the right person at an industry event one night. Or your neighbor knows the person who can give you your next big break. So perhaps chance is what it takes to succeed. But this isn't to say that luck only happens to a few and that you'll never make it if you think you are not a lucky individual. It's all about placing yourself in the way of luck by using the qualities, skills, and connections you already possess and developing the ones that you don't own quite yet. This book will help you do that.

Another repeated refrain in discussions of culinary careers is that you need plenty of passion to make it in this field. Passion comes in many flavors, but three particularly stand out when it comes to choosing a culinary career: Passion for food is first, of course, and it can manifest itself in many different ways, some more hands-on and creativity based, which would be best suited for a restaurant kitchen, and others that are more intellectual and might be developed by focusing on culinary history or teaching. Second is passion for hospitality, which centers on pleasing people and seeing them enjoy eating your food or using your products. Passion for action and fast pace is the third; time moves fast at a busy restaurant, catering job, or bar, and all of the parts of the business need to work together. One of these passions might be what draws you into the culinary field. But you'll see that to advance, you will need to appreciate all of them.

Over the past fifteen years, I have had the opportunity to meet a healthy percentage of America's most famous culinary

Food Magazines—A Timeline

1941 *Gourmet* (2009)
1956 *Bon Appétit*
1967 *Nation's Restaurant News*
1976 *Wine Spectator*
1978 *Food & Wine*
1987 *Cooking Light*
1988 *Food Arts*
1991 *Martha Stewart Living*
1994 *Saveur*
1994 *Fine Cooking*
2001 *Gastronomica*
2003 *Everyday Food*
2005 *Every Day with Rachael Ray*
2008 *Food Network Magazine*

personalities, including Thomas Keller, Wolfgang Puck, Emeril Lagasse, Daniel Boulud, Charlie Trotter, Lidia Bastianich, Tom Colicchio, Mario Batali, Rick Bayless, and so on. They share qualities that include intelligence, determination, a strong work ethic, curiosity, and charisma, combined with an extraordinarily hardworking personality and a dosage of good luck. If you want to make it to the top of any area in the culinary field, you will need the same qualities.

Common Characteristics in Culinary Careers

Throughout our research and interviews, we found many common traits among successful culinary professionals. Here are some of those key findings.

What they like most:
Making people happy
That no two days are the same
The instant gratification of seeing the result of their work
The freedom of being their own boss

What they like least:
The sacrifices related to their schedules
The administrative duties
Having to be "always on"
Personnel issues

The skills they need to do their job well:
Passion for and dedication to their work and the industry

Commitment to quality
Culinary skills—which goes without saying
Creativity
Leadership and management skills

The skills they'd like to have to further their careers:
Broader and deeper business experience and training
Knowledge of more, different cuisines and techniques

Their long-term goals include:
Opening their own business
Expanding their businesses
Achieving more work-life balance

They achieve somewhat of a work-life balance by:
Training their staff to work well without the boss there
Switching to a job that has different, fewer, or more flexible hours
Having an understanding and supportive spouse or partner

When hiring, they look for:
Passion
Dedication
Willingness to learn
Open-mindedness
Personality
Positive attitude

When it comes to food, ICE, Anne, and I are all drawn to "chef-driven" concepts. Chef-driven means that someone with an appreciation and knowledge of good ingredients, cooking technique, flavor, and presentation puts his or her passion into what they serve. That may happen at your local diner, but it will not happen at your local fast-food restaurants (where nobody has the title of "chef"). We believe that all the profiles in this book are of people who appreciate and practice chef-driven thinking, even if their job keeps them far away from the kitchen.

Part I of *Culinary Careers* covers industry issues and will help you make career decisions, with information on the educational options that are available around the country, the types of degrees that food professionals typically pursue—from culinary diplomas to PhDs—and the specialized certifications that are available in various fields. You'll find material that will help you with your very first job interview and with the opening of your own company, and at every step along the way.

Part II offers specific information for each subfield of the food industry, with the perspectives of daily practitioners. If you want quick information on select professions, you can focus your time on these job overviews and never-before-published profiles. My coauthor Anne and I interviewed more than one hundred people around the country, in all types of professions and operations, to provide an idea of the possibilities that exist and how each person arrived at his or her current position. Hear straight from people who work daily in the same job you might want to have one day. While this book covers a vast range of positions available in the culinary industry, it certainly does not encompass all of them. Each chapter's introduction gives specific information as to the types of titles, career paths, jobs, education, possibilities, challenges, and more that are out there.

The chapter introductions also cover the subject of salaries, but they generally do not take into account the difference in cost of living between large and small cities. To get more specific information, we asked each profile subject to give us comments on salaries. Some people decided to give us their own salaries, others that of their staff, while others still talked about the industry in general in their city or region. While not definitive, this combination of sources will provide you with a representative idea of what to expect in various positions.

The valuable appendices will give you all the resources you need to join organiza-

> **Top culinary professionals share qualities that include intelligence, determination, a strong work ethic, curiosity, and charisma, combined with an extraordinarily hardworking personality and a dosage of good luck.**

tions, find the right schools, and locate scholarships.

Whether you want to spend time learning about the food industry or quickly acquire information before a job interview, this book will ensure that you get what you need in as little or as much time as desired. I hope that you will use and reuse *Culinary Careers* as your career progresses, either going back to a specific chapter or looking up different profiles when you want to move up or change careers in the food industry.

With such a wide range of opportunities becoming available in the food world, and with the increasing popularity of the industry, I'm thrilled to share the knowledge and experience of chefs, entrepreneurs, and other professionals who have found success working in food. Anne and I hope that *Culinary Careers* will become an indispensable resource for you as you launch or further your own career in the food industry.

—RICK SMILOW

PART I

What You Need to Know

Getting Started
and Training

★

Career
Development and
Growth

★

Ownership and
Entrepreneurship

★

Lessons from the
Stratosphere

1. GETTING STARTED AND TRAINING

Whether you are just about to finish high school and looking for the best way to start a career in the food industry, a college graduate finally able to do what you want now that you received the degree your parents wanted, or a career changer seeking ways to market previous experience into something compatible with a

food-centric life, determining what sort—if any—of formal training or culinary education you need to make it in the culinary world will be a question. Should you go to culinary school to become a food writer? Do you need an MBA to own and run your own business? Should you get an associate's degree or will a certificate be enough to become a professional cook? What is the best path for you based on what you want to do? We hear questions like these all the time, whether formally when a prospective student tours ICE or in casual conversations with people of all ages considering their career options. There is no right or wrong answer; you will find people in the food industry who have all types of backgrounds. You will meet chefs who earned an associate's degree at the Culinary Institute of America in their midtwenties and others who did not go to culinary school,

writers with journalism degrees and others who went to law school or used to be line cooks, restaurant publicists with master's degrees in food studies and others with experience representing musical performers. There seems to be no set mold, only a common passion for food. However, certain paths will make it easier for you to reach your goal.

> The more people watch food, think about food, the better it is. And I don't care what it is that people are watching. The fact that people are thinking about food, I think, is good for the industry and good for the world.
> —RUTH REICHL,
> *author and former editor in chief of* Gourmet, *from* The Main Course (ICE's newsletter), 2006

One first step toward figuring out what route to take is to assess your learning style. If you work best on your own and have the discipline to read professional culinary or pastry textbooks and as many cookbooks as you can get your hands on while also working in a restaurant to learn the speed required in a professional kitchen, you might not need to go to school to become a chef. But if you are the type who has or would benefit from a more traditional, structured education program, culinary school will introduce you to the basics of cooking techniques, ingredients, tools, theory, timing, and taste before you go on to make a living in the field. As a student, your main job is to learn, while as an employee, your education will not be your employers' primary goal.

As a career changer, you might not want to go back to school, particularly if you have already invested a large amount of time training for what will now be your past life. Depending on the stage you reached before your switch, you might already have acquired leadership, marketing, or writing skills, for example. If you were a team manager in retail, you should be able to transition into restaurant management without having to pursue a hospitality degree. You might take an internship, if you have the time for it and money to afford it, or find an entry-level job in the field you wish to enter. As a journalist in a nonfood field, you can find positions in restaurant public relations or as an assistant to a chef without going to culinary school, or you could start working on the feature side of a food magazine rather than in the test kitchen.

Many types of culinary education exist around the nation, so there are plenty of options to choose from. An important question to consider is what credentials you are looking to gain and what door you think each option will open. These include a bachelor's or associate's degree, a diploma, a certificate, or none at all. The largest distinction between programs is the length of time that each will take to achieve: You will likely earn a bachelor's degree in cooking in four years, an associate's in two years, a diploma in eight to twelve months, and a certificate in one to four months. In many aspects of the culinary world, particularly as a cook in the kitchen, you will likely be hired for the same job or position regardless of which credentials you achieve. Longer programs have the inconvenience of being just that—longer. They will give you opportunities to take general-education courses and electives in subject areas that might be of interest to you in either your career or your personal life. These programs also often offer the advantage of a campus life, with dorms, a gym, and communal activities. They generally cost more than shorter ones. That said, you may be exposed to a broader range of learning and have more opportunities to practice under the guidance of chef-instructors in a longer program.

should you go to culinary school?

Do you need a formal culinary education in order to work as a cook, pastry assistant, food writer, or food stylist? The true answer is that there is no rule about it. There are many noted examples of very successful chefs who did not go to culinary school, such as Charlie Trotter and Thomas Keller (page 76). Many restaurants will take on apprentices, or *stagiaires*, with little to no experience if they demonstrate a strong desire to learn and the willingness to start at the bottom of the ladder. You will be able to become a cook even if you start with the most basic skills, but taking a few classes can boost your confidence. Today, however, more people than ever are going to culinary school, so the lack of formal culinary training may be more of a limitation than it was twenty years ago. Keller

and Trotter were also fortunate to have the right mentors; if you choose not to go to culinary school, make sure that you work places where you can forge such essential mentor/mentee relationships yourself.

Certain positions, such as those in test kitchens and culinary production, will require that you have formal culinary training. Employers feel that those degrees show that you know the basics of cooking and that they might not have to teach you everything from scratch, thus saving training time. If you have extensive cooking experience and other skills that you can market for those positions or are able to obtain an interview because of your network, you might be able to get around that

Do You Need to Know How to Cook?

There are plenty of positions in the food industry where you won't need to cook like a pro. If you want to work in a restaurant but have no desire to cook, go for front-of-the-house or office positions. Marketing and communication jobs are also usually free of hands-on cooking requirements, as are many sales positions. Generally, you can work any and all administrative positions without cooking skills or experience. If you are interested in those careers, going to culinary school might not be the best option for you. Part II will tell you in detail what cooking skills are expected in each sector.

However, what you will notice is that many of the people who hold a position that does not require hands-on cooking knowledge or experience actually do possess it. They might have come to their job from a professional cooking background after getting tired of the kitchen, for example. Or they went to culinary school but realized they wanted weekday, daytime hours as well as benefits. They might simply be experienced home cooks who live and breathe food, not just for their job but as a lifestyle. In most food-related work environments, even if you never touch food, you will be constantly thinking, talking, and hearing about it. At a minimum, even if you don't know how to cook and have no intention of learning, you better be interested in eating!

Good schools will also expose you to local and national culinary leaders, new technologies, and unusual ingredients through seminars, demonstrations, and hands-on supplemental classes.

requirement, but you will need serious cooking chops to make up for the lack of a degree (even if that is just a perception in the eyes of the employer).

You will be able to excel at other positions, in marketing, media on the features side, sales, and publicity, for example, without a culinary degree, as long as you have the food and industry knowledge required of the position. Understanding how a professional kitchen functions will go a long way if you write about the work of chefs. But you can acquire much of that awareness by spending a lot of time observing kitchens.

Many potential employers will look favorably on a culinary degree because it shows a commitment to the industry and knowledge of the basics, such as knife skills or culinary terms. Going to school

also shows a willingness to make a career out of working in the food industry, rather than stumbling upon it while trying to be an actor, for example. Because even the shortest vocational culinary program requires a commitment of both time and money, it implies seriousness in graduates.

What a culinary school offers is broad exposure to countless different techniques, recipes, ingredients, tools, flavors, and instructors in a short period of time. You will learn about many types of cuisine, from classic French to contemporary American to Asian, in one place. Acquiring that experience hands-on would mean that you'd have to spend time in many different restaurants before perhaps discovering the type of cuisine that you prefer cooking. In school, instructors will take the time to explain to you how and why you need to do something—because that's their job. Good chefs will also do that in a kitchen but may not always have the time or patience to repeat it more than once. School is your opportunity to ask all the questions that come to mind. On the job, there may be less time to do so.

Good schools will also expose you to local and national culinary leaders, new technologies, and unusual ingredients through seminars, demonstrations, and hands-on supplemental classes. When you research a school, make sure to look at these aspects of its curriculum to ensure that you will gain many opportunities to learn much more than what's in a textbook. Likewise, instructors should also be interested in learning more—taking classes, attending seminars and industry events,

Leading Chefs Without Formal Culinary Training

Rick Bayless	Gordon Hamersley
Lidia Bastianich	Paul Kahan
David Bouley	Thomas Keller
Tom Colicchio	Bob Kinkead
Traci Des Jardins	Mark Miller
Tom Douglas	Charlie Trotter

and even spending time in restaurants to keep their knowledge on par with that of the best chefs—and be up-to-date on industry trends.

The placement or career service department of a culinary school is an essential component to consider. They are the ones who will help you find trails (one or several shifts spent in a kitchen observing and, at times, working), internships, and jobs. Most schools offer those services for as long as you work in the industry— make sure to ask whether this is the case at the school(s) you are considering. Ask about the career-placement staff's background. Have they held positions that give them insights into the culinary field? What is their placement rate? Ask about the school's alumni to know what network you will be joining by putting the same affiliation on your résumé. Talk to current students. You likely will be able to sit in on classes during your admission process; use that opportunity to ask students why they chose that particular school, what they like and dislike about the program, and what they expect to do upon graduation. But don't just rely on what you are told during your visit; spend time online researching mentions of the school in the media to see what the general commentary on its program and alumni is.

We hear of one downside about culinary education from established professionals: It can make students and graduates feel entitled. This is the number one complaint from chefs and other culinary professionals: Some graduates show a tendency not to want to pay their dues and work their way

up in a kitchen. Some think that the six months to two years spent in school have taught them everything they need to know and that they are fully trained. Most chefs will say that culinary school makes you a cook, not a chef, and to never forget that distinction. There is no substitute for the years it takes to master the craft of cooking. Oftentimes, culinary school also teaches you one way of doing something. The chef you later work for might have a different method or entirely different culinary philosophy altogether. But if you approach your career with an open mind and show your employer, be it a chef, culinary producer, or editor, that you are willing to learn and are humble about your skills and experience, you will turn your culinary school experience into a valuable asset to your career.

working in the field before going to school

Gaining some practical experience before going to culinary school is often recommended. Not only will you know that you

You can also set up a stage—an internship that would likely be unpaid—if you want to gain experience at a specific restaurant that might not currently be hiring but would be your number one choice to gain experience.

Gaining some practical experience before going to culinary school is highly recommended. Not only will you know that you will be truly committed to your education and have some basic knowledge of the industry before starting, but most important, you'll know what you're in for before committing to a program.

will be truly committed to your education and have some basic knowledge of the industry before starting, but most important, you'll know what you're in for before committing to a program. Chefs in particular recommend this approach to anyone looking to spend significant time and money on culinary training. Because the work is hard and the lifestyle potentially grueling, spending a few months in a kitchen before enrolling in school will ensure that you are making the right decision for yourself. You might realize after a couple of weeks that you are not cut out for that lifestyle. There is no shame in that. You might also realize that you really enjoy working with food and want to work in this industry—just not in the kitchen. Entering culinary school with this knowledge means that you will be able to take on internships and extracurricular activities that are right in line with your career goal. You might also decide not to go to culinary school and rather that you'd prefer to keep working in restaurants, making money and gaining hands-on experience while

studying something else that will be more useful to your career in the long run. If you want to work as a food photographer, a photography or arts degree might be ideal. If you want to work on the editorial side of a food magazine, restaurant experience and a degree in communications or other liberal arts studies will give you the skills sought after by publications.

To find opportunities for short-term work in kitchens, look for open positions at restaurants around you through the traditional channels of ads and word of mouth, or by contacting restaurants directly. You can also set up a stage, an internship that would likely be unpaid, if you want to gain experience at a specific restaurant that might not currently be hiring but would be your number one choice to gain experience. If you are looking for a job or a stage (pronounced stahje) without knowing that one is available, it is best to contact the restaurant directly. Larger operations will have a human resources department, which you can call for more information or send your résumé and cover letter (via e-mail is typically best). Call smaller operations directly, outside of their hours of service (the middle of the afternoon is usually good if they have lunch and dinner service), and ask to whom you might send a résumé. You can also e-mail them (most restaurants have websites today, with a general e-mail address if none is specified for employment queries) or, depending upon the establishment, drop by in person.

choosing the right school (and paying for it)

The first thing you want to consider is the type of degree that you need or want. Do you want to spend six months, two years, four years, or more in school? This will help you narrow your options to programs that fit your needs. Then examine your local options. Do you live near a school that has a high reputation, a strong placement network, and successful alumni? Do they teach what you want to learn? What are their strengths and weaknesses? Where will you be able to work when you graduate? Is the school's program too long or too short for what you need? Does it have schedule options that fit your life? Is it your best option from a financial perspective? Once you've considered those questions, you may see that you will need to move to attend a program that meets your needs. Moving to a new city to attend school is a great way to get a start in a new place within the comfort of a community. You will benefit from the school's assistance with accommodations, will instantly have a new circle of friends in your classmates, and will be able to find volunteering or job opportunities thanks to the school's listings. So if you have been aching for a fresh start somewhere, school is a great way to get it.

New York, Chicago, and San Francisco are examples of such cities. They have vibrant culinary scenes but also countless food-related jobs in media, technology, design, retail, production, and more. The restaurants that you find in metropolitan centers in general also tend to offer more diverse cuisines, which opens up your training opportunities. Conversely, a school in a smaller town might offer opportunities to work with artisanal food producers or on farms, if you are interested in how food grows and want that to be the focus of your career or culinary philosophy.

The cost of a school is another thing that will heavily factor into your decision. When you explore your options, even before you talk to the schools that interest you, examine the financial aid options they might list on their website. Ask to talk to the financial aid adviser when you visit the school, and inquire as to the types of loans available, interest rates, monthly payments, and typical length of repayment. Be realistic. Taking out $50,000 in loans might not be ideal if you want to work in restaurant kitchens or in media. Your starting salary in those types of careers will float around $30,000 a year, meaning that it will take you a very, very long time to repay your loans. You might be fine with that decision—but it is one you need to have

Moving to go to school is also an opportunity to get your foot in the (kitchen) door of a city with a large, sophisticated culinary scene. The more food industry jobs there are in one location, the more options you will have for both stages and jobs.

fully considered. If you want to pay for school completely out of pocket, decide what you can afford up front and how much you will need to work during school to make that possible. Attending a less expensive community college program in your area that would allow you to live at home might be a better alternative.

Scholarships are a way to cover some of your tuition expense. Generally, however, the number of scholarships available in the culinary field is limited. Ask for a list of the available scholarships for your program, and look at their deadlines. If you have just missed any, you might have to wait a year before enrolling. In this book, look for a list of the main scholarships available for schools in the appendix (see page 351).

Several print and online directories list culinary, hospitality, and restaurant-management programs around the nation.

Two sources are ShawGuides (shawguides .com) and Peterson's (petersons.com). These websites are useful in providing you with information about a variety of programs but are only part of the search for the right training. Be mindful of the fact that often schools can pay to be featured more prominently in rankings or lists. Accordingly, you want to conduct a thorough and comprehensive search, relying on the school's official website, alumni, media, and current students.

CULINARY AND PASTRY EDUCATION PROGRAMS

As noted above, you will get to choose from a wide range of culinary programs that vary in duration and scope, from a diploma that will take six months to complete to a bachelor's degree that will take four years.

Fifteen Questions to Ask Your Admissions Representative

1. What is a typical day in class like?

2. How many students are there in a typical class?

3. How would you define the school's culinary philosophy?

4. What accreditation(s) do you have?

5. How often do you update the curriculum?

6. What extracurricular classes and demonstrations take place here?

7. What is the background of your chef-instructors and what continuing education programs do they attend?

8. What types of students will I be in class with?

9. What financing options do you offer and what scholarships are available to incoming students?

10. What is the career path of a typical graduate?

11. In how many different establishments did you place externs in the last year?

12. Do you place your graduates or externs in your city's most prestigious restaurants?

13. Can your placement department help me get a position in other parts of the country?

14. What services do you offer your alumni?

15. How does your school compare to other options?

The two basic tracks available in culinary schools are culinary arts and pastry and baking. Some programs include general-education classes in subjects such as math and English, while others do not. Significantly, you will find that different schools have different personalities; use tours and research to find the school with the personality that suits you best.

Many community and junior colleges offer associate's degrees in culinary arts, which take about two years to complete. Once you obtain an associate's degree, you can transfer to a college that offers a bachelor's program in culinary arts and complete the last two years of your education there. These types of degrees offer hands-on culinary and/or pastry training, along with classes in business and organizational skills, management, operations design, marketing, and more. They vary widely in cost, from a couple of thousand dollars a semester to more than $30,000 a year.

Culinary schools across the country offer certificate or diploma programs in culinary arts and pastry and baking that typically last less than a year (from six to twelve months, depending upon full- or part-time attendance), and offer flexible schedules, including evening and weekend classes, for students who work full-time while in school. Some include an internship in an outside restaurant, others internships at an on-campus facility, and yet others do not require internships to graduate. These programs are generally hands-on only. Some schools also offer extracurricular demonstrations, hands-on classes, and lectures or workshops. The key with these programs is to choose established, accredited ones that not only offer solid programs with experienced instructors but also have a well-organized, and well-connected, career service or placement department. You want to make sure that the investment of money and time you will make in those programs will pay off with job leads and other assistance for the duration of your career. Many schools organize job fairs and other events that are available at reduced or no cost to their alumni as well as their students, for example.

Below are representative schools in five categories of culinary-training institutions.

The Culinary Institute of America (www.ciachef.edu)

The Culinary Institute of America was the country's first large culinary institute. At its Hudson Valley campus in Hyde Park, NY, the CIA offers bachelor's degrees of professional studies (BPS) in culinary arts management and in pastry and baking arts that take thirty-eight months to complete and include an eighteen-week paid externship. The associate's degrees in occupational studies (AOS) in culinary arts and in baking and pastry arts require twenty-one months of study and a similar externship. These four programs take place at the school's flagship campus in Hyde Park, NY. Pastry students spend time working in the school's Apple Pie Bakery Café as part of their curriculum. Students can also complete an AOS in culinary arts at the Greystone, CA, campus. Experienced culinary professionals can take advantage of an

Five Categories of Culinary Schools

While not all schools fit neatly into these, culinary schools can generally be grouped into five categories:

1. **Large campus-based schools with longer programs and a majority of students living in dormitories.** Examples: the Culinary Institute of America (Hyde Park, NY), Johnson & Wales (Providence, RI; Charlotte, NC; Denver, CO; and North Miami, FL), and the New England Culinary Institute (Montpelier, VT).

2. **Urban culinary institutes with medium-to-long programs, owned and operated by national chains and located around the country. These schools use a rolling admission system, allowing you to start a program any month of the year.** Examples: the Interna-tional Culinary Schools at the Art Institutes and the American Cordon Bleu programs (such as the California Culinary Academy).

3. **Urban culinary institutes with short-to-medium programs that are independently owned and operated.** Examples: the Institute of Culinary Education (New York, NY), Cooking School of the Rockies (Boulder, CO), the Cambridge School of Culinary Arts (Cambridge, MA), L'Académie de Cuisine (Gaithersburg, MD), and the French Culinary Institute (New York, NY).

4. **Four-year colleges with culinary programs as a small part of their overall academic mix.** Examples: Culinard—the Culinary Institute of Virginia College (Birmingham, AL), the University of Nevada–Las Vegas, and Nicholls State University (Thibodeaux, LA).

5. **Community colleges and technical schools with short to long programs.** Examples: Bucks County Community College (PA), Northern Virginia Community College, and New York City College of Technology–CUNY.

associate's program designed specifically for their needs and interests, which lasts fifteen months. The bachelor's program consists of hands-on classes that cover various cuisines, along with courses in culture and history, finance, management, marketing, communications, food costs, and more.

Johnson & Wales University (www.jwu.edu)

Johnson & Wales University, which has campuses in Providence, RI; Charlotte, NC; North Miami, FL; and Denver, CO, offers associate's degrees in culinary arts and pastry and baking and joint bachelor's degrees in culinary or pastry and hospitality management at all four locations. The Providence campus—the school's original location—offers bachelor's degrees in baking and pastry arts, food-service entrepreneurship, culinary nutrition (also available in Denver), and food marketing (also available in North Miami). Students receive first-level certification from the American Culinary Federation upon completion of their associate's degree. As with other two- and four-year programs, Johnson & Wales's curricula combine hands-on training with classroom education.

Bachelor's degrees in hotel and lodging management; international hotel and tourism management; restaurant, food, and beverage management; sports, entertainment, and event management; and travel, tourism, and hospitality management are available at Johnson & Wales Hospitality College. Students can also earn joint degrees with the College of Culinary Arts in baking and pastry arts and food-service management and culinary arts and food-service management. An MBA in hospitality is also available at the Providence campus, with concentrations in accounting, financial management, international trade, marketing, organizational leadership, event leadership, and finance.

New England Culinary Institute (www.neci.edu)

The New England Culinary Institute in Montpelier, VT, offers bachelor's degrees in culinary arts and in hospitality and restaurant management, with specializations in sustainability, wine and beverages, and baking and pastry. Its other educational options in the management track are associate's degrees in hospitality, which take fifteen months to complete, and restaurant management, and an online bachelor's degree in the same field. The school also offers a thirty-nine-month bachelor's degree in culinary arts, during which students are required to complete three six-month externships away from campus. Students can also elect to focus on one of the program's three specializations: wine and beverage studies, sustainability, and baking and pastry arts. NECI's AOS degree in culinary arts takes twenty-four

months to complete, with two six-month externships.

The International Culinary Schools at the Art Institutes (www.artinstitutes.edu)

The International Culinary Schools at the Art Institutes—owned and operated by a company called Education Management Corporation—has more than thirty locations around the country and offers diplomas or certificates, associate's degrees, and bachelor's degrees in culinary arts; bachelor's degrees in culinary management, hospitality management, and food and beverage management; certificates or diplomas and associate's degrees in pastry and baking; and associate's degrees in wine, spirits, and beverage management. Not all programs are available in each location, but each school has its own website, which explains clearly which degree(s) students can obtain there.

Le Cordon Bleu Schools North America (www.chefs.edu)

Many of America's formerly independent culinary schools were acquired—and are now owned and operated—by Career Education Corp. CEC has licensed Le Cordon Bleu's name for use throughout the country, so Cordon Bleu programs are now offered at schools such as the California School of Culinary Arts (www.csca.edu), the Orlando Culinary Academy (www.orlandoculinary.com), and the California Culinary Academy (www.baychef.com). The California School of Culinary Arts' Pasadena location offers a fifteen-month AOS program, during which students spend twelve months in class and three months in an externship, for both culinary arts and pastry and baking; an AOS in hospitality and restaurant management that lasts sixty weeks with an internship; and a pastry diploma that takes thirty to forty-two weeks to complete. At the Orlando Culinary Academy, AOS degrees in culinary arts and pastry and baking are offered, along with a culinary arts diploma taught in either English or Spanish. In San Francisco, the California Culinary Academy offers two Cordon Bleu programs: an associate's degree in culinary arts, which requires sixty weeks of courses and a twelve-week internship; and a pastry and baking certificate, which takes forty weeks.

The Institute of Culinary Education (www.iceculinary.com)

Our school, based in New York City, offers diplomas in culinary arts, pastry and baking, and culinary management that take seven to twelve months to complete. A hospitality management program launched in 2010. Options include morning, afternoon, evening, and weekend classes. The culinary and pastry programs require students to complete a 210-hour externship, which they typically do in restaurants, pastry shops, hotels, catering companies, and media companies. Students are assigned externship advisers, who will help place them in the site that will best suit their career aspiration. Students simultaneously enrolling in the culinary management program receive a 20 percent discount on that tuition, and schedules are designed to facilitate this double major.

Culinary arts classes are intimate, limited to twelve to sixteen students. The diverse student body comes from all over the United States, as well as more than thirty countries, such as Brazil, the Philippines, Israel, Mexico, and Russia. The school has a range of housing options available for students seeking a one-year stay in New York. A wide range of guest speakers, demonstrations, and volunteer opportunities is offered. ICE students can choose from more than 1,500 elective classes taught by celebrated chef-instructors to supplement their education. Topics range from Tuscan, Vietnamese, and Caribbean cuisine to artisinal breads and Italian wine. ICE also houses two specialized centers: the Center for Advanced Pastry Studies (CAPS), which offers three-day courses with worldwide experts to pastry professionals; and the Center for Food Media, which features classes in all aspects of the media world as it pertains to food, including recipe development and writing, cookbook writing, food styling, and podcasting.

The French Culinary Institute (www.frenchculinary.com)

The French Culinary Institute, at the International Culinary Center in New York, NY, also offers diplomas in culinary and pastry arts, which each take six hundred hours to complete. Students can choose between daytime and evening schedules. Culinary arts students spend time working in the school's restaurant, L'Ecole, alternating between front-of-the-house and back-of-the-house positions. The school also offers a 1,057-hour program in Italian cooking, during which students take classes in New York and in Parma, Italy, and then complete an externship in Italy.

Cooking School of the Rockies (www.culinaryschoolrockies.com)

At the Cooking School of the Rockies, in Boulder, CO, students can take on a six-month full-time program in the culinary arts, which also requires them to complete a one-month farm-to-table externship with Colorado farmers. The full-time program starts twice a year. A part-time "chef track" is also available, which lasts eighteen weeks and takes place in the evening. The school also offers two pastry programs: the full-time one, available twice a year, lasts five weeks, while the part-time, fifteen-week program begins once a year.

The Cambridge School of Culinary Arts (www.cambridgeculinary.com)

The Cambridge School of Culinary Arts in Cambridge, MA, offers professional culinary and pastry programs that last thirty-seven weeks as well as sixteen-week certificate programs in both fields. During any of these programs, students take part in two eight-hour labs and one three-hour evening seminar a week.

Culinard—The Culinary Institute of Virginia College (www.culinard.com)

At Culinard, which is part of Virginia College in Birmingham, AL, students can earn diplomas in culinary or pastry arts in thirty-six weeks that follow the American Culinary Federation Accrediting Commission's guidelines. Students who already possess a diploma—from Culinard or a similar school—can earn an associate's degree online through Virginia College Online.

Bucks County Community College (www.bucks.edu)

The department of business studies at Bucks County Community College in Newtown, PA, offers associate degrees that take the form of what it calls chef apprenticeships, with food or pastry emphases. These two majors, which the school states focus on "job preparedness," require the completion of six thousand hours of on-the-job training in addition to coursework. The department also offers a tourism and hospitality associate's degree, which can be completed in two years of full-time studies, along with a summer internship. Because these are all occupational majors, the school recommends that students who wish to then transfer to bachelor-granting programs ensure that all their credits count early in their courses.

HOSPITALITY AND RESTAURANT MANAGEMENT PROGRAMS

Hospitality management programs offer everything from certificates to graduate degrees. They prepare you for the business and service side of the hospitality world, to be managers or owners and deal with the financial aspects of running or managing a business, large or small. Career tracks for graduates of such programs usually include high-level management in

Some hospitality management programs may be most closely focused on careers in the hotel and lodging field, while at other schools, the same program may be broader and prepare people for many sectors, including restaurants and corporate and contract food service.

hotels, resorts, restaurants, institutional food service, tourism, catering, as well as entrepreneurial pursuits in any of those areas. Some hospitality management programs may be most closely focused on careers in the hotel and lodging field, while at other schools, the same program may be broader and prepare people for many sectors, including restaurants and corporate and contract food service. Some schools include hands-on cooking as part of their required courses, but in general, hospitality programs offer much less hands-on cooking than full-fledged culinary institutes. The longer programs usually require that students complete an internship of varying length over the course of their studies.

Associate's and bachelor's degree programs exist in many large universities around the country. Associate's degrees are most likely to be available at community and junior colleges and take about two years to complete for full-time students. Bachelor's degrees usually take four years to earn. If you are not immediately familiar with the options that are available close to where you live and do not wish to move, spend time online researching to find the program that will best suit your needs. Find out where local chef-owners, food business owners, and hospitality managers went to school by asking them, reading bios on their companies' websites, or doing a search in your local paper's archives.

The Cornell School of Hotel Administration (www.hotelschool.cornell.edu)

The Cornell School of Hotel Administration, in Ithaca, NY, is undoubtedly the most prestigious hospitality management program in the country. It offers a BS in hotel administration, a master of management in hospitality (MMH), and master's and doctoral degrees in hotel administration. The four-year program provides a traditional business-focused education and hospitality-focused electives that cover everything from law and real estate to finance and information systems as well as facilities, food, and beverage management. The MMH is completed in one year and offers study tracks in human resource management, marketing management, operations and revenue management, and real estate finance and investments. MS and doctoral candidates have to spend at least two and three years, respectively, on campus at Cornell to complete their course work and work toward a master's thesis or a dissertation.

The Penn State School of Hospitality Management (www.hhdev.psu.edu/shm)

The Penn State School of Hospitality Management, in State College, PA, is another reputed program that offers undergraduate (associate's and bachelor's) and graduate (MS and PhD) degrees. Its bachelor's degree program offers two options: hotel, restaurant, and institutional management, which has a broader focus, and management dietetics, which more specifically addresses the interests of students who want to work in institutional food-service operations and might also obtain their registered dietitian designation.

Les Roches School of Hospitality Management at Kendall College (hospitality.kendall.edu)

The Les Roches School of Hospitality Management at Kendall College, in Chicago, provides seven different management tracks: hotel, restaurant, event, asset, club, casino, and sports. These educational tracks are designed to be completed over fourteen quarters with online and weekend options for people who are not able to attend school full-time.

Shorter programs—which may be ideal for career changers or people who already hold a bachelor's degree—grant a certificate or diploma and are available at many colleges that offer two- or four-year program options, as well as in a number of established culinary schools. For example, ICE offers a twenty-eight-week culinary management diploma program, which is divided into thirteen courses that cover concept development, purchasing and cost control, service management, facilities and design, marketing, and food-service law, among other topics. This program is structured and timed to help

students earn a double diploma, in culinary or pastry arts and culinary management, at the same time.

Other Options

Other examples of shorter programs include a one-year certificate in restaurant and hospitality supervision at the Bucks County Community College (www.bucks .edu/catalog/3073.php) in Newtown, PA, and a one-year certificate in hospitality operations offered by Monterey Peninsula College (www.mpc.edu/academics/life-science/Hospitality) in Monterey, California. Often, classes in programs like these are held at night or on weekends so that students can hold a full-time job while pursuing job-enhancing education.

VITICULTURE AND AGRICULTURE PROGRAMS

The world of food isn't just one of kitchens and offices. It starts with what we grow, before we even consider cooking or eating. Each state has at least one of those universities, which offer a wide range of degrees in nonagricultural fields—they often are part of the state's university system, such as Rutgers University in New Jersey or the University of Wisconsin–Madison—as well as the degrees of interest here. Students thus get a general liberal arts or science education along with their specific course work. In addition to training students and providing a place of research for professors, these universities usually have an extension office through which they work with the local community, assisting

If you want to pursue a career in farming or winemaking, whether as an entrepreneur or as a researcher, educator, or consultant, look into agriculture and viticulture programs. Those predominantly take place at land-grant universities.

farmers, beekeepers, winemakers, etc. with questions related to their work.

The length of agriculture and viticulture programs ranges from two-year associate's degrees to four-year bachelor's degrees to doctoral degrees that can take six or so years. Majors include dairy science, agricultural economics, agronomy, food science, soil science, genetics, nutritional science, animal science, viticulture and enology, and many others. Cornell University, listed above for its hospitality program, also has the third-largest college of agriculture and life science in the country. You can obtain bachelor's and master's degrees in enology and viticulture there, at the University of California–Davis, or at Washington State University, for example. Those programs tend to have an agricultural science focus and prepare students for careers in the winemaking industry, research, education, and consulting.

University of California–Davis (caes.ucdavis.edu)

The University of California–Davis's College of Agricultural and Environmental Sciences offers bachelor's, master's, and doctoral degrees in twenty-one different departments, which cover subjects such as animal science; viticulture and enology; plant sciences; wildlife, fish, and conservation biology; nutrition; and agricultural and resources economics. The school also hosts a large number of centers and institutes as well as research projects both nationally and internationally, which allows students to work on a variety of projects based on their specific interests.

University of Wisconsin–Madison (www.cals.wisc.edu)

Unlike UC–Davis, the University of Wisconsin–Madison does not offer a viticulture program. Its College of Agricultural and Life Sciences' nineteen departments include dairy science, life science communication, rural sociology, agronomy, food science, and soil science. Degrees from bachelor's to doctorate are available in almost all of those disciplines.

Washington State University (www.cahe.wsu.edu)

The College of Agricultural, Human, and Natural Resource Sciences at Washington State University in Pullman, WA, includes departments such as agricultural and food systems, crop and soil science, food science, and natural resource sciences. The department of horticulture and landscape architecture offers undergraduate programs in fruit and vegetable horticulture and viticulture and enology. Students can pursue viticulture and enology at the graduate level through some of the other departments in the college, depending on the area on which they want to focus their research.

FOOD STUDIES AND GASTRONOMY PROGRAMS

Some universities have developed academic programs in food studies and gastronomy for students who wish to study food from an academic perspective in lieu of or as a complement to formal culinary training. The undergraduate programs involve classic liberal arts courses and university-wide requirements. Students then pursue majors that focus on food from a historical, sociological, cultural, and anthropological perspective. These programs typically involve a few hands-on cooking courses, but their goal is not to prepare students for cooking careers per se—even though many end up in a cooking career, or come to school with a food background.

New York University (steinhardt.nyu.edu/foodstudies)

New York University offers bachelor's, master's, and doctoral degrees in food studies. Students in the undergraduate program must complete sixty credits of liberal arts courses, eighteen credits of core food studies courses, twenty-five credits of specialization courses, and twenty-five credits of electives. Courses include food history, food and pop culture, food issues in contemporary society, global issues in nutrition, production and management, sanitation, finance, marketing, communications, and international cuisines. Graduate students must take forty credits' worth of classes, mostly in food studies but with the opportunity to take electives in other departments, including performance studies and business. Course topics include food and culture, food markets, food systems, food writing, theoretical perspectives in food, and food issues. With a culinary or pastry degree already under your belt, the required number of credits for completion goes down to thirty-four. That program takes two to three years to complete, depending on how many courses you take each semester. Graduates of both the bachelor's and the master's degrees go on to careers in food media, the nonprofit sector, sustainability, public relations and marketing, hospitality, or education, or open their own businesses. The doctoral program admits one or two students a year, who will take some of these same food studies courses, along with theoretical and research courses in other departments, according to their field of interest.

Boston University (bu.edu/met/gastronomy)

Boston University offers a master's degree in gastronomy, which is also interdisciplinary. Students must take forty credits and complete a master's thesis in order to obtain their degree. Courses include food history, anthropology of food, theory and methodology, food writing, food and the visual arts, culture and cuisine of various countries, history of wine, and sociology of food. They pursue a concentration in one of four areas: business, communication, food policy, or history and culture. Career opportunities are similar to those of the NYU program.

OVERSEAS PROGRAMS

Schooling options for culinary, pastry, management, liberal arts, and agricultural science degrees abound around the world. France and Italy seem to hold a particular appeal for students who want to learn about the cuisine of these countries in culinary schools there; these countries have many culinary programs that take a few months to complete and are ideal if you already have another type of degree. Cooks have started to train in Asia to learn about the specific techniques of the local cuisines. Living and studying overseas will bring you a lifetime's worth of enrichment and knowledge as well as much fun and excitement. The advantage for your career might not be great, however, if the school you choose does not have a placement department with a strong U.S. record, should you decide to move back. Be sure to consider that important factor as you decide on which school to attend, particularly because they tend to be expensive for foreigners, with little to no financial aid available.

International programs in hospitality management are found throughout the world. Many are taught in English, but others are only offered in the country's main language. Some of the most prestigious ones are found in Switzerland and include IMI-Luzern (International Hotel, Tourism, and Events Management Institutes; www.imi-luzern.com), Swiss Hotel Management School (www.shms .com), Les Roches International School of Hotel Management (www.lesroches.edu), Ecole Hôtelière de Lausanne (www.ehl .edu), and the Glion Institute of Higher Education (www.glion.ch). Oxford Brookes University (www.business.brookes.ac.uk/ bs/departments/hltm) in England and Hotelschool The Hague (www.hotelschool .nl) in the Netherlands are other high-level international schools. Most of these programs send graduates to positions in international hotel or restaurant companies, resorts, tourism, or similarly high-level management careers.

Le Cordon Bleu (www.cordonbleu.edu)

Le Cordon Bleu offers programs in Paris, London, Ottawa, Seoul, Kobe, Tokyo, Adelaide, and Sydney. Le Cordon Bleu programs in the U.S. are run by Career Education Corporation. Its most prestigious program is Le Grand Diplôme Le Cordon Bleu, which takes about a year to complete and combines both culinary and pastry training. Its two components, le diplôme de cuisine and le diplôme de patisserie, are also offered separately.

Ecole Ritz Escoffier (ritzparis.com)

The Ecole Ritz Escoffier is part of the magnificent Ritz hotel in Paris, France. In addition to one-day classes and short-term (from a couple of days to three or six weeks) programs in culinary and pastry arts, the school offers a fifteen-week Superior Diploma. The chefs who teach the classes do so in French, with bilingual assistants who translate everything into English.

At-Sunrice GlobalChef Academy (www.at-sunrice.com)

At-Sunrice in Singapore works in partnership with Johnson & Wales in the United

States. Its Advanced Culinary Placement Diploma takes twenty-four months to complete, during which students alternate between one month in school and three months in paid externships. They can then go on to earn a degree from Johnson & Wales in the United States or the William Angliss Institute in Australia. The school also offers diplomas in culinary arts and pastry and baking, with the same options for further studies. During the first term of those programs, students are in class and in the school's kitchens. They divide their second term between two classroom days and four paid apprenticeship days. For the culinary arts program, students spend six months each at a Western and at an Asian restaurant.

BACHELOR'S DEGREES IN NONCULINARY FIELDS

As you will see from countless profiles in later chapters, a liberal arts education is a perfect entryway to the food industry—or to anything else for that matter. Some people start working in restaurants while in college and realize that they don't want to go into the field of their education but prefer to stay in the food industry. Others might obtain a bachelor's degree before pursuing their passion for food. This is true of both front- and back-of-the-house personnel; we know countless examples for each, and you probably do too. The right decision for you might be to obtain a bachelor's or associate's degree before you go on to a career in the food industry, whether you want to cook or do something else food related. That will always give you some-

thing to fall back on should you decide not to be in the kitchen after all. A communications or English degree will be helpful if you want to work in food media, for example. Combining such an education with working in restaurants throughout school should be enough to open the right doors to you after graduation without the need for a formal culinary degree as a supplement. This decision will depend on the grades you obtained in high school and should be based on a general interest in academics. If you don't like to read books and write papers, spending four years working on an art history or physics degree might not be the best choice. But if you have that intellectual curiosity and feel that this education will benefit your work in food, make it your first option.

Most universities do not offer food studies as a liberal arts or humanities field of study. However, food-related courses are appearing in many universities, thanks to the ever-growing popularity of chefs and the increasing general interest in eating better. You might thus pursue a bachelor's degree in an unrelated field but still be able to take classes about food. History departments might offer general food-history courses or even classes that specialize in the food of a specific country or time period. A sociology department might offer classes in sociology of food or

The Institute of Food Technologists' website (www.ift.org) features a list of approved undergraduate food science programs. The Association for the Study of Food and Society lists a set of food-course syllabi on its website, www.food-culture.org.

agriculture, while a food and culture course might be found in anthropology. Other popular food-related courses include examinations of local and global food systems, sustainability, nutrition, agriculture, food in literature, and food in film. Some universities also offer food-writing courses as part of their general writing requirements. Summer and study-abroad programs have also started to include food courses in their curricula because of their popularity with students. You could certainly craft your seminar thesis around an interest in food.

Food science is a field that requires a specialized bachelor's degree. As its name indicates, this field requires a solid knowledge of science, reflected in the inclusion of courses such as organic chemistry, microbiology, and biochemistry, in addition to nutrition and lab courses and other fundamental courses required for each undergraduate student in the university where the studies take place. Those programs are heavily quantitative in nature and typically prepare students for careers in large corporations, where they will design food products such as pasta sauces, ice creams, candies, prepared foods, and more. Pennsylvania State University, Rutgers University, Cornell, the University of Massachusetts–Amherst, Purdue University, and the University of California–Davis are among the schools that provide programs. Master's and doctoral degrees are also available in food science. If you want to work in corporations' labs rather than in product development, an advanced degree in chemistry is a desirable course of study.

apprenticeships

Many chefs who came to the United States from Europe in the 1980s and reached culinary heights here started their careers as apprentices in their early teens. Formal programs of this kind never developed in this country on the same scale, however. You can apprentice in a restaurant with no formal structure, working your way up the line, but will not receive any in-class training when doing so. The American Culinary Federation (www.acfchefs.org), the largest professional organization for chefs and cooks in this country, with more than 22,000 members, offers two- or three-year apprenticeships, which combine hands-on experience with 576 hours of classroom education. While working full-time in a kitchen, ACF apprentices are required to attend at least twelve courses, with some programs leading to an associate's degree. ACF states that this program prepares apprentices to take the ACF certification examinations. Apprentices are usually paid and might be provided room and board (often at their own expense) in programs where that is possible. ACF offers four models of apprenticeships, according to its website: (1) An apprenticeship coordinated by a local chapter. (2) One that takes place in an institution that has an approved supervisor. (3) One offered by a large employer. (4) One that is strictly for corporations or large employers that have no ACF affiliation. The apprenticeship program is available in twenty-eight states; several of those states have multiple locations from which apprentices can choose.

finding your first job

If you are enrolled in school, take advantage of your career services department. Read the listings that they send via e-mail or post on bulletin boards to see what is available even before you graduate. Make a point of visiting your career counselor regularly as you decide on your post-school plans, whether you are looking for an internship or an actual job. Starting your research online means that you can do it whenever you want or can, without the excuse that your classes or day job get in the way of you finding a culinary position. Newspaper classifieds are still a source of job listings, but the Internet has been taking over for years now and is likely to be where you will find jobs listed. Web-

sites like starchefs.com list culinary jobs around the country, while mediabistro. com offers media jobs that include food-related openings. Most large food corporations and restaurant groups have a career section on their website. Many privately owned restaurants have started to do the same. Blogs that are local to your city or area, like the Strong Buzz in New York, also include classifieds—don't forget to read those.

And perhaps even more so than in any other industry, word of mouth and networking are the most efficient ways to find out about openings. Is one of your classmates working at a company that has an opening? Does your instructor know someone in your dream restaurant? Don't ever be afraid to ask people around you and to make it known that you are looking for a job. Take on every volunteer opportunity that you can to meet chefs and other culinary professionals, work with them, and find out about their openings. Job listings are also a good reason to join a local professional organization. You might hear about an opening while attending a meeting or read about it on an organization's website or in their newsletter.

> Your résumé needs to be visually clear and appealing. It's sometimes as much about the package as about the contents, particularly when an employer might be sifting through several hundred résumés after posting an ad.

Job fairs offer terrific opportunities to meet face-to-face with someone from a company you want to work for, find out about their current or upcoming openings, and learn the names and contact information for these positions.

WRITING A RÉSUMÉ AND COVER LETTER

Your résumé and cover letter are sales tools. They tell prospective employers how you will be able to help their company and why you are the best person for the job. They complement each other: Specific career details are clearest when presented in a bullet-point format on the résumé itself; expressing how your involvement in a particular project corresponds exactly to the requirements of a position as highlighted in an ad is best done in a cover letter. Each requires hours of work and careful editing to make sure that it presents you in the best light.

When starting a career, it can be hard to think of yourself as a product that needs to be sold, requiring attractive branding and packaging. It sounds crass, even. You want to do something beautiful and noble with food, and yet you have to think about your selling points? Yes, actually, you do. Start by making a list of the key points that you want to come across to a prospective employer. These points can be adjectives, such as "dedicated," "driven," "hardworking," "team player," or "positive." They can also take the form of specific performance-related points: "scheduled staff of twelve

servers," "edited ten daily submissions from pool of thirty freelancers for launch of website," or "line cook at two-hundred-seat restaurant."

The second step, once you have made that list of your selling points, is to make sure that they are reflected in your résumé. Start by listing every job you have held that is relevant to the position you are seeking. For each position, list your title, the name and location of your employer, and the time spent at the location. Then list your accomplishments at each with bullet points or in paragraph format. Once you are done with all your jobs, education, and special skills (languages, computer programs, specialized training), look at your résumé and see if it conveys those selling points you listed initially. It is particularly important to quantify your experience. Look at your descriptions and see where you can add numbers, which will give an employer a better idea of what you've done before. You might have been an intern at an event-planning firm and performed typical tasks like making copies in the office and handing out gift bags at an event. But if you change that to "provided administrative support to staff of twelve planners" and "assisted in the planning and running of seven galas for eight hundred people," a prospective employer will have a better idea of the scale of your experience.

Your résumé needs to be visually clear and appealing. It's sometimes as much about the package as about the contents, particularly when an employer might be sifting through several hundred résumés after posting an ad. Yours needs to stand out from the rest of the pile. Use a boldface font for the main categories of your résumé and for your job titles. If the only position you've held was intern but you interned at several companies whose names will appeal to a prospective employer, you can highlight those instead of the title you held by placing them first and bolding those names. That way an employer will immediately see where you've worked. Your résumé should not be longer than a page, particularly when you start your career. This is where the editing process comes in. Keeping it to one page does not mean that you should use an eight-point font size and crunch everything in. Rather, it means that you cannot afford to waste a single line and need to ensure that every item on your résumé conveys how you are best suited for the position you want. If you have or are finishing a bachelor's or associate's degree, there's no need to include your high school information. If you're listing every job you've ever had, starting with babysitting in your teens, keep yourself to jobs that are most relevant to your current aspirations. If you don't have much experience and need to keep a summer camp counselor or lifeguard job on your résumé, relate the skills you acquired in those positions to what the position you want requires. What leadership roles did you take on? How many people did you work with or supervise? Talk about the quick thinking and decision making one job required or how you had to multitask at another. The positions themselves might not be related to the line cook or account coordinator position you are applying for today, but the skills and tasks

likely are. A clear and concise résumé will allow an employer to see that.

A cover letter is meant to catch a prospective employer's attention so that he or she will look at your résumé and want to interview you. The first paragraph is crucial, because if it is not catchy enough or is riddled with typos, the employer might not read further. You might be one of several hundred sending in your application. Or if you are contacting an employer without responding to an ad—cold-calling, essentially—you want to make a great impression so that he or she will want to meet with you.

Keep your cover letter brief; three or four paragraphs are enough. Use the first paragraph to provide some context: mention where you heard about the job, any potential connection you might have with the person ("So and so suggested that I contact you"), and why you are contacting them. The second paragraph should highlight why you would be ideal for the position. Do not use it to repeat your résumé; specifically emphasize what in your previous experiences makes you the best candidate. In the last paragraph list your contact information and any follow-up you plan on doing.

AT THE JOB INTERVIEW

Once your strong cover letter and impressive résumé get you an interview, it's time to prepare. Spend some time on the company's website to familiarize yourself with its history, its main players, its products, its recent news, and any other relevant information that you will find there. Look at a restaurant's menus and reviews. Read a magazine's masthead and make sure you understand its voice and what distinguishes it from its competitors (media kits for advertisers usually have a lot of information on a magazine's audience—read those too). Use Google as well for news that might not be posted on the company's site (rumors of closure or a merger, for example).

A job interview for a food industry job might be like any other interview you've ever had—or completely different. It goes without saying that you should be there on time, with a couple of clean copies of your résumé and your references on hand. If you are interviewing for an office or management position, wear a suit with clean, polished shoes. However, when interviewing for a media position or in creative fields in general, particularly in New York, a suit might make you look too uptight, and perfectly pressed, stylish separates might be more appropriate. When interviewing for a cooking position, wear slacks and a button-down shirt (or even a jacket if interviewing at a four-star restaurant) if you are a man, and a skirt or tailored pants with a businesslike top and a jacket if you are a woman. You don't need a suit for those interviews, but you do need to look professional and polished. If you look sloppy, you might give an employer the impression that your cooking will be sloppy too. Wearing your uniform might be appropriate for cooking jobs if you know you will have to take a cooking test as part of the interview. Ask the person who schedules your interview what you should wear if you are

not sure. Pay the same attention to it as you would a street outfit, and make sure that your uniform is perfectly pressed and cleaned with no buttons missing, that your pants are tailored, and that your clogs are clean.

Students often worry about being overdressed. It is true that you might interview with a GM who has not yet changed into his suit and will be in a T-shirt and jeans. But remember that he already has the job. You want them to look at you the way a diner would look at you in the dining room or a partner might look at you in a meeting. It is better to be overdressed than underdressed.

For a cooking job, you might be asked to cook a dish as part of your job interview. This will certainly be the case as you rise up the ranks and go for positions at higher levels, but even entry-level positions can require a test of your prepping skills. Bring a notepad so that you can take notes as the chef or interviewer tells you about tasks he or she will want you to accomplish. You will also likely be asked to trail for a shift: after interviewing, you will go to the kitchen and do some prep work, so that the chef can observe your knife skills and work ethic. A trail is very common and functions like an audition that allows an employer to observe your attitude, knife skills, sanitation, the questions you ask, and how well you fit within the kitchen. It is also an opportunity for you to see if you like that restaurant, its employees and their work ethic and attitude, and the general work environment. Don't obsess over that part of the interview, but go in ready to perform in the kitchen with some ideas about what you'll cook. Candidates for a teaching position at ICE have to pass what we call the "trial by chicken." They have to cook a chicken while explaining every step of the process so that we can judge their teaching abilities. A prospective pastry instructor has to make a chocolate mousse and prepare a fifteen-to-thirty-minute lesson on an assigned subject, which he or she will present to other faculty members. For an executive chef position, you will likely be asked to prepare several signature dishes or tastings and to present a sample menu for the restaurant with which you are interviewing.

For several types of positions, you will need to show a portfolio of your work during an interview. Having that information readily available on a website is also valuable, since it means that a potential employer can have an idea of your style and philosophy before even meeting you. For cooking positions, bring photos of dishes and sample menus you have created. It's better to show fifteen great photos than fifty poorly lit, poorly shot ones, so choose carefully when you organize them. If your photography skills are lacking, find a friend who is better at it than you and trade a couple of great meals you'll cook in exchange for photos. When interviewing for a position that will require you to create recipes, such as corporate or research chef positions, bring sample recipes. Ask a friend who is a good writer or has an eagle eye to proofread those for you. Depending on your experience, your portfolio might even include media mentions, such as ar-

Common Interview Questions

Tell me about yourself.

Why do you want to work here?

Why did you get into cooking?

What cookbooks are you reading?

What are your favorite foods?

Why are you leaving your current job?

What do you know about our company?

Who do you consider our competitors to be?

Tell me about a challenging situation you've experienced and how you resolved it.

Why should we hire you?

What do you find rewarding/challenging about your job?

What have you most enjoyed doing so far in your career?

How do you work with a team?

What is your preferred work environment?

Where do you see yourself in five years?

ticles about your work, reviews, or recipes you might have published in a magazine, in a newspaper, or on a website.

As a photographer or stylist, you will need a portfolio that shows your skills. If your work has been published, include copies of the publication in your portfolio, but otherwise your own pictures will be fine. Such a portfolio can be costly to assemble, so having photographs available on your website will allow an employer to go and look back at your work at a later date if they want to do so without requiring you to leave copies with them. It is, however, a good idea to have postcards made with a photo that you find particularly striking.

Include your contact information on the back, and leave that with the employer at the end of your interview. If they like it enough to pin it to a bulletin board, for example, that postcard will be a daily reminder of how talented you are and make them more likely to call you on the spot when they need someone. Postcards are cheap to produce, so consider it a professional investment. Include a recipe, if you have one, that you know is perfectly developed, tested, and written.

If you write, bring sample articles with you to an interview. Have enough copies that you can leave them with the person who interviews you. The employer might ask to see those as part of the application process, so make sure that you always have a repertoire of recent clips that best demonstrate what you can do. As mentioned above for photographers and stylists, a postcard with a great recipe is a good thing to leave behind with your interviewer.

HAVING THE RIGHT ATTITUDE

The single most common answer we received when asking people what they look for when hiring staff is "the right attitude." You can learn new skills and gain experience as you go. But approaching a situation with the right attitude comes from the inside, from something much more intangible. You will see as you read their answers: Chefs, managers, and business owners all look for someone who is hungry to learn, has a passion for the food industry, and will put their head down and do what is asked of him or her.

Having the right attitude does not mean that you merely execute what is asked of you without asking questions or offering ways to do things differently once you get more comfortable. It means having an open mind so that you can listen to, and *hear,* what your chef or your boss tells you. It means being anxious to get to work because you are doing something that you are passionate about and want to know more about every day. You arrive with a smile on your face, eager to do what is expected of you and go beyond that if the day allows. It means being a person who is positive and doesn't get bogged down by things like the occasional mistake. Rather, you always seek to move forward and inspire those around you to do the same. Your positive attitude, which makes you look at problems as challenges, not obstacles, inspires you to conquer problems and improve the way things work. You engage in constructive dialogues with your peers and superiors but do not talk back when asked to perform a task. You have a team-oriented attitude, so you'll pitch in regardless of who needs your help and for what task.

Demonstrating that you are this kind of person will go a long way in moving you along your career path. If you are not someone who is typically perceived as having the right attitude, it is never too late to change. Perhaps a bad attitude simply stems from not being happy at your current job. If that's the case, promptly look for a new one and make a fresh start, one that will showcase your best, most positive side and allow you to use your existing skills and learn new ones.

2. CAREER DEVELOPMENT AND GROWTH

I t doesn't matter if you are just starting your career, in the middle of it, or perhaps still deciding on what type of school to attend; it is never too early to think about long-term goals and envision the path you want to follow five or ten years down the line, or to explore the options you have at your current stage to take the next step in your

career. You might decide right away that attending school for two or four years is not enough and that you want to pursue advanced studies. Or you may realize after two years as a public relations account executive that knowing more about wine will help you move toward gaining wine and spirits clients. The ways to expand your culinary knowledge, grow as a professional, and develop your career are endless. The routes are as diverse as the industry is, but the good news is that many of those cross over one another, so picking one path or obtaining one type of advanced degree will not pigeonhole you into one job.

The food industry is also one in which you never stop learning, regardless of where you are or what you do. A day out of town will give you plenty of opportunities to sample different foods. A birthday dinner is the occasion to try a new restaurant. Cocktails with friends is an opportunity to learn more about artisanal spirits producers. You could constantly increase your knowledge and love of food without ever working a single day in the food industry, thanks to the myriad activities that focus on food outside of our three meals a day.

Your culinary education, whether you work in a kitchen or at a desk, is never over. Even the greatest chefs speak of the continuous excitement of learning about new ingredients and tasting new dishes.

In this chapter, we provide you with many ways to go about developing yourself professionally and personally as a food lover and food worker. From classes to trips, from conferences to websites, you will learn what tools to use to further your career and become a more accomplished culinary professional.

traveling, eating, staging

Your culinary education, whether you work in a kitchen or at a desk, is never over. Even the greatest chefs speak of the continuous excitement of learning about new ingredients and tasting new dishes. From a hole-in-the-wall in town to the finest restaurants halfway across the globe, eating is not only the simplest way to develop your palate, it's the most enjoyable too. It also has the advantage of being tailorable to your budget, from eating out to choosing which dishes to cook at home.

Eating and cooking at home is the easiest—and potentially cheapest, depending on what you cook—way to experience new dishes and ingredients, because you can decide what to cook when, how much of it to eat, and what to pair it with, and really create a menu that reflects exactly what you are looking to learn. You can challenge yourself by making a new dish every night or a new dessert every weekend. You can methodically explore the regional cuisines of a particular country, spending months on the process. You can decide to cook your

way through a cookbook, recipe after recipe, as blogger Carol Blymire did with *The French Laundry Cookbook* and *Alinea*.

Seek out markets, both at home and wherever you travel. Most large cities now have at least a weekly farmers' market, and when you visit one while traveling, you will be able to taste fruits and vegetables, along with local prepared foods, that might not be available in your region. If you hail from the East Coast, a visit to San Francisco in late December will reveal dozens of varieties of citruses that you have never tasted nor will ever see in a local supermarket. A journey through the stalls of the market in Oaxaca will forever change the way you think about Mexican food (particularly once you have snacked on fried grasshoppers). If you can't cook while traveling because of your accommodations, buy ingredients in dried or jarred form that you can take home. Ask merchants, chefs, and locals with whom you strike up a conversation for recipes and restaurant recommendations so that you can enjoy traditional foods both there and when back at home.

Staging is another way to develop your culinary knowledge and your palate (see page 14 for information on how to obtain a stage). Derived from the French word for apprentice, *stagiaire*, staging means working for free in a restaurant in order to gain valuable experience. Even if you don't work in a restaurant kitchen, staging a day here and there, or even as regularly as one day a week for example, is a great way to acquire skills and ideas for the aspect of your job that deals with food. You will gain insight into the life of professional cooks but also learn new flavor combinations, techniques, and ingredients. If you already work as a cook, or even as a chef somewhere, you can choose to stage at other restaurants in town on your day off. If you work mostly with meats, for example, you will learn a lot from staging at a seafood restaurant. Staging is also an opportunity to enter an establishment that might be of higher standing than your current place of employ. You could stage at a four-star restaurant with the hope of one day working there. Staging also refreshes your mind and gives you a new perspective on the routine of your day-to-day life in "your" kitchen. Michael Laiskonis, pastry chef at Le Bernardin in New York, blogged about a young pastry cook whom he felt was becoming somewhat bored in his position. The cook spent one of his days off staging in another kitchen and came back full of ideas he wanted to develop. That one shift was enough to awaken his creative senses and make him feel passionate about his profession again.

Whether you spend a week in Spain and are able to stage just one day or decide to spend six months traveling and staging throughout Asia, you will find the experience priceless in terms of knowledge acquired. Those stages go beyond providing you with new skills and ingredient knowledge; they teach you about different ways of running a business, treating customers, and building a wine or cocktail list. More broadly, but perhaps more important, they also build in you a new appreciation for what cooking and food represent to people around the world by letting you into their cultures via their kitchens.

changing jobs

It is less the case with office jobs in the culinary world, but if you are working in the kitchen or aspire to, you may hear that early in your career, you should switch jobs every year or two in order to learn as much as possible from as many people as possible. The benefit of such transience most often cited is that each chef has his or her own way to cook a certain dish or use a specific cooking technique, and by spending time in different kitchens, a young cook will be able to learn all these different skills and add them to his or her repertoire. Once you reach a certain level, however, moving around too much takes on negative connotations. At that point, remaining in one position for a few years—particularly if it is in a top kitchen—is more valuable.

How do you know when it is time to move on to another job? One answer is when you have reached the highest level you can (if there is very little turnover in the staff, for example—although that is rare

> How do you know when it is time to move on to another job? One answer is when you have reached the highest level you can. But the simplest answer is when you have stopped learning.

Using Recruiters

Once you gain some experience in the food industry, you might decide to use a recruiter to find your next job—or be approached by one who wishes to interview you for his or her clients. The use of recruiters is more common for mid- and upper-level jobs and occurs for both cooking and management positions. Many recruiters specialize in larger operations, but most major restaurant cities, such as New York, San Francisco, and Los Angeles, also have recruiters who specialize in independent and fine-dining operations. Here is a recruiter's perspective on the process.

JO-LYNNE LOCKLEY, Owner, Chefs' Professional Agency, San Francisco, CA

Jo-Lynne Lockley's mother started Chefs' Professional Agency in 1960. It is the oldest recruiting agency in the country that specializes in restaurants. Ms. Lockley herself has been involved with the company for more than twenty-five years. She works with high-end independent restaurants, "very good little ones too," and with some hotels and hotel groups. While most of the positions she fills are for chefs and managers, she also works with pastry chefs and occasionally with sous chefs. Chefs' Professional Agency does not represent candidates and is not a headhunter but instead works for companies that have specific openings and need Ms. Lockley's services to fill them.

Ms. Lockley states that restaurants, not the candidates themselves, pay recruiters. When candidates send her their résumés, she either works with them if they are immediately a match for a position or keeps them in her database if she sees potential for a long-term professional relationship. She also uses her contacts and personal referrals to find suitable candidates for her clients. She rigorously checks the backgrounds of the candidates she deals with to ensure that they are truthful about their experience.

"A good recruiter's first concern is for the welfare of the clients," she says. "We are not advocates for our candidates. It has to be a win-win situation, though. If I send a good person to a bad job, I lose access to good people."

When identifying suitable candidates, Ms. Lockley looks for the right career development ("provenance"), sense of focus, stability, commitment, quality, clear-eyed vision, talent, and professional rigor. "It's hard to subordinate yourself to the discipline—the attention to detail—of a great kitchen without much recognition. But if you are dedicated to your career you will get it," she stresses. She also keeps watch for negative characteristics such as arrogance, foolishness, self-importance, or dishonesty.

Candidates and companies should look for smaller recruiters who can provide one-on-one service, she advises, to make sure that the match made is ideal and that the information provided about an opening remains confidential, which she says is harder to track with a large recruiting firm that might be dealing with hundreds of jobs. "A good agency has to be a firewall. If a company calls me and says they want a new chef, I can't tell the chef. If the chef calls and says he wants a new job, I can't tell the company," she adds.

In the types of businesses she works with, Ms. Lockley currently sees salaries for executive chefs that range from $70,000 to a maximum of $140,000 and around $45,000 to $50,000 for sous chefs. A chef with an established brand can expect to receive 30 percent more than someone else who does not benefit from such a reputation, when going for the same position.

in a restaurant kitchen). But the simplest answer is when you have stopped learning. Learning is twofold and consists of immediate knowledge and knowledge-building toward your greater goal. "Immediate knowledge" refers to the skills you have acquired and the new dishes you now know how to make. If that well is dry, or you at least feel that it is, it's time to move on. But learning is also about reaching a goal in your career. If you want to open a restaurant one day, does the one where you currently work offer you the perfect place to learn how to do that? Is the owner about to open another place, where you could work and follow the opening process? Or would you be better off going to a different type of place that would bring you closer to your goal, such as a slightly bigger or smaller operation, a multiunit restaurant, or even a chain? Those are among the questions to consider when deciding if it is time to move or not. All this said, you do not want to change jobs so often that you'd appear unreliable or unfocused.

Changing jobs is also about charting your specific path. Are you working at the best restaurant you possibly can? With which chefs have you worked? If you want to work at a four-star restaurant, are you building your résumé toward that? If you want to open your own place, it will help if you've worked with prestigious chefs whose names will make customers want to try your cooking and investors trust you with their money. Or, taking the opposite route, you might decide to only work at small, individually owned restaurants that mirror the one you want to open.

If you do not work in a restaurant kitchen, some of these points are good to keep in mind, but with a slightly extended time frame. Most employers do not want to see that you make a habit of changing jobs every few months. So plan on staying a couple of years each at jobs that require you to use a computer rather than a knife, even as you build your career. When looking for a new position, follow the same rules of résumé-building and looking for the right experience to achieve your career goal. If you get to the level of assistant account director at one public relations agency, moving to another one might allow you to obtain a job as account director. Working for a large, well-known company will carry a lot of weight should your goal be to become a consultant and establish your own business.

Changing jobs also allows you to make more money in each new position. Assuming you change jobs and/or companies to take on greater responsibilities, a higher income will be part of the new position you are seeking. Keep that in mind when applying and interviewing, so that you can earn what you are worth as you move on. Money is also often the reason why people move to another company: They may like what they do and still be learning a lot, but if they know they can make more money elsewhere, they will eventually leave that position.

inspiration and creativity

Being creative has many meanings in the food industry. You may have been an art major in college who now creates fantasy-like desserts with extraordinary plating. You might be inspired by everything around you—the color of the sky, the sound of tires on the pavement, the sandwich you had for lunch—and constantly in need of ways to channel those stimulations into an actual product. That will make you great at thinking of new dishes.

Many chefs told us that they start creating a dish on paper, whether with words or with diagrams. They write down everything that comes to mind when thinking of a particular time of year, flavor, or ingredient. That's one of the early phases of their creative process, before they ever think about cooking anything. If you find that thinking about a source of inspiration does not come naturally to you, practice it. When you come back from the market with thoughts for an ingredient you would like to use, whether it's in a dish, a product, or

You can be inspired by the world's most famous food just as you can be by the great pasta dish of your neighborhood trattoria. Use flavors from these dishes, combination ideas, or one element you liked in the design of a store as a point of departure for your own dish, product, or company.

an article, sit down and start writing. At first it will be hard to let words flow if you are not used to it, but soon you will realize that you are beginning to think about your creative process on paper, which will make you a better, more efficient cook because you'll have a starting point when you get to the kitchen.

Inspiration also comes from other people in your field, or in the food world in general. Your mentors, whose career path represents the ideal one you wish for yourself, might inspire your creative process but also your daily life. They might have told you something really special one day, a priceless piece of advice, that still inspires you today to the point that you carry it on a slip of paper in your wallet or had it carved on a knife handle. Beyond your personal mentors, think of people in the industry who inspire you, anywhere around the country or the world. Thanks to the Internet, you know what the food at El Bullì or French Laundry looks like without ever having to set foot in the restaurant. You will find complex descriptions of dishes on forums and blogs and in magazines, sometimes accompanied by recipes, if they are not already in cookbooks. You can be inspired by the world's most famous food just as you can be by the great pasta dish of your neighborhood trattoria. Use flavors from these dishes, combination ideas, or one element you liked in the design of a store as a point of departure for your own dish, product, or company. The key point is that they are sources of inspiration, not things to copy exactly. Crossing that line is not only plagiarism, which can be hard to define when it comes to dishes, but it is the antithesis of culinary creativity. You need to make whatever inspires you your own, give it some of your essence, some of your background, some of your aspirations.

cooking- and food-knowledge-based certifications

You might have noticed that some chefs' names, on their jackets, on television during interviews, or in articles, are followed by a myriad of initials. These indicate the certifications that they have acquired through the years after passing rigorous exams. The goal of these certifications is to ascribe standards to the profession. A colleague will instantly know your level of expertise, what you know how to do, the rank that you have achieved in a kitchen, by looking at those abbreviations. They also mean that you abide by a certain code of knowledge, since you have had to reach a certain skill level and studied certain topics common to all those who took the test in order to receive your certification.

In America, you will be more likely to find chefs with such certifications in institutional dining, hotels, casinos, private clubs, and teaching positions than you will among chef-owners who have one or two restaurants. Studying for certifications, and then taking the examination, requires a lot of time, which chef-owners do not generally have. For many chefs, having certifications is also not as important in their pedigree as having learned from and

ACF CERTIFICATIONS

ACF certifications are broken down into cooking professional, personal cooking professional, pastry and baking professional, culinary administrator, and educator categories and are as follows:

Certified Culinarian (CC)

Certified Sous Chef (CSC)

Certified Chef de Cuisine (CCC)

Certified Executive Chef (CEC)

Certified Master Chef (CMC)

Personal Certified Chef (PCC)

Personal Certified Executive Chef (PCEC)

Certified Pastry Culinarian (CPC)

Certified Working Pastry Chef (CWPC)

Certified Executive Pastry Chef (CEPC)

Certified Master Pastry Chef (CMPC)

Certified Culinary Administrator (CCA)

Certified Secondary Culinary Educator (CSCE)

Certified Culinary Educator (CCE)

worked with top chefs around the country or the world. Whether you decide you want to obtain those types of certifications may be more about personal growth and achievement than career advancement.

American Culinary Federation (www.acfchefs.org)

The largest certifying body is undoubtedly the American Culinary Federation (which states on its website that it is also "the only chef organization that has a certification program that is recognized by the U.S.

Department of Labor as a trade/profession"). ACF offers fourteen different certifications, based on the chef's field and level of expertise. Each certification has its own page on the organization's website, which includes the application form, requirements, guidelines for the examination, and study material.

Graduates of ACF-accredited schools (which include community colleges, technical schools, and some Art Institute and Cordon Bleu programs) automatically receive their Certified Culinarian certification. Each additional certification gradually requires more skills and responsibilities. The highest level a chef can achieve is that of Certified Master Chef or Certified Master Pastry Chef, which is reached after passing an eight-day exam and spending several thousand dollars in exam-related expenses. As of summer 2009, there were only fifty-nine Certified Master Chefs in America.

You will need to renew your certification every five years. In order to do so, you will need to show that you took eighty hours of continuing-education classes, including requisite refresher courses in nutrition, food safety and sanitation, and supervisory management. Trade shows (see page 52) usually offer courses that qualify for ACF continuing education credits. ACF offers lists of regional events and other activities that qualify as credits.

ProChef—Culinary Institute of America (www.ciachef.edu)

The Culinary Institute of America has developed a certification program in partnership with ACF, which consists of three categories: ProChef Level I (certified culinarian); ProChef Level II (certified chef de cuisine); and ProChef Level III (certified executive chef). Each of those provides you with a dual certification from CIA and ACF. These certifications are not as widely represented in the industry as the ACF ones, however.

International Association of Culinary Professionals (www.iacp.com)

The International Association of Culinary Professionals offers a certified culinary professional (CCP) certification, which does not differentiate between educators, chefs, or any other type of culinary profession. Before being allowed to take the certification exam, which takes place at the IACP's annual conference, applicants must submit a file that demonstrates that they have acquired the requisite number of points to be allowed to take the exam, based on participation in events, attendance at conferences, number of years spent working in the food industry, and more.

specialized pastry training

Pastry is not one uniform category; many professionals decide to specialize in a particular area of the industry, such as making chocolates, sugar work, cake designing, or breadmaking skills. Restaurant pastry chefs will work with plated desserts, while bakery owners will make treats that can be eaten on the go or sold for wholesale distribution. They generally follow the same basic training and then go on to specialize through on-the-job training, but they can also take classes at a number of establishments around the country. Some of the hands-on continuing-education courses have minimum requirements for admission, such as having spent a number of years in the industry, to ensure that students share basic skills and are ready and able to learn the more advanced techniques presented in those workshops. Demonstration courses generally do not have such requirements. If you want to learn about pulled sugar but have never worked in the medium before, it might be useful to start with a demonstration or a one-day course before diving into a week-long specialized course.

The World Pastry Forum (see page 53) also offers a wide range of workshops as part of its events, making it a unique opportunity to work with international stars like Albert Adrià. Many professionals, such as cake designer Elisa Strauss (page 163), also take on students for one-on-one or small group training.

The Center for Advanced Pastry Studies (CAPS) at the Institute of Culinary Education in New York; the Notter School of Pastry Arts in Orlando, FL; the Culinary Institute of America in Hyde Park, NY, and Greystone, CA; and the French Pastry School in Chicago are among the schools that provide advanced courses in specific pastry skills. Many of the renowned pastry professionals who teach do so at schools around the country but might have certain workshops available only in one location. What you can learn from one person in New York might not be available in Chicago, for example, which should motivate you to travel around the country to attend classes if you are able to do so. Most of the courses focus on specific aspects related to working with sugar, chocolate, wedding or sculpted cakes, boulangerie and viennoiseries, specialized pastries, plated desserts, confectionery, and showpieces. Each instructor offers his or her own nuances to the material learned, however, so one topic taught by two different people will reveal new forms of knowledge and varied techniques.

Center for Advanced Pastry Studies (www.iceculinary.com/caps)

CAPS offers three-day workshops for working pastry professionals and graduates of accredited pastry programs, all taught by experts from around the United States and Europe. Past courses have focused on sculpted cakes, pulled sugar, chocolate showpieces, sugar dough, hydrocolloid uses, French pastry, and plated desserts.

The Notter School (www.notterschool.com)

The Notter School provides continuing-education courses on various sugar, chocolate, cake, confectionery, and viennoiserie topics, also taught by international experts. It also offers a twenty-four-week European pastry and baking diploma, which is more akin to the basic curriculum of the pastry programs detailed in this chapter. The school is owned by Ewald Notter, an accomplished pastry chef who has won countless national and international competitions, who is also its lead instructor.

The French Pastry School (www.frenchpastryschool.com)

The French Pastry School's continuing-education courses typically last three days and focus on topics similar to those detailed above. The school also invites international experts like Pierre Hermé and Oriol Balaguer for special workshops.

Albert Uster Imports (www.auiswiss.com)

Albert Uster Imports in Maryland also sponsors dozens of continuing-education courses and demonstrations around the country (several in partnership with the Notter School) every year.

wine education

Wine education can take many forms. If you want to write about wine, for example, or become a sommelier down the line, starting by working at a wine store a few hours a week is a simple way to learn about grape varietals, producers, countries, and regions, and about which wines you like and don't like. Joining the waitstaff of a restaurant whose sommelier and wine staff have a great reputation is another— the sommelier will likely provide tastings and notes during pre-service meetings to help you sell wines to your customers. A next step could be to sign up for classes at a local school or at a store that offers them. You will find classes that last for a couple of hours all the way to certifications that take years to complete. Even if you have no aspiration to become a master sommelier, you can take one or two levels of the courses offered toward those certifications. In the culture and business of wine, advanced certifications do garner respect and aid career advancement. Here are a few of the most prestigious available.

Wine and Spirit Education Trust (wsetglobal.com)

The Wine and Spirit Education Trust (WSET) is an organization based in England that provides wine education programs in forty-seven countries. You must take the WSET courses and examinations in an approved facility, which are found around the world and listed on the organization's website. Students range from professionals in the wine industry (service or retail) to people working on wine and spirits communication (editorial, public relations, marketing) to wine enthusiasts. The series of courses starts with Level 1: Foundation Wine, which will give you a basic understanding of grape and wine types and service. WSET recommends this one-day course for people in their first wine sales or service position. Level 2: Intermediate in Wine and Spirits, is a much more thorough introduction and lasts sixteen hours, during which you will learn about the major wine-producing regions of the world and about spirits categories. (Level 1 and 2 Spirits courses are also available.)

The advanced certificate that you obtain in level 3 is required in order to be awarded the diploma. WSET suggests it for professionals who hold positions as supervisors in wine service or sales. The course itself lasts twenty-eight hours, with an additional fifty-six in individual study before taking the exam. Level 4 requires both course work and independent study. Students who take the course at the International Wine Center in New York are registered for three years, which is the maximum time students have to complete and pass the course, but the school states that most students finish in two. The diploma allows its recipients to take on studies to obtain master of wine degrees. Diploma holders can work on an independent research project to qualify for an honors diploma. Each level is a prerequisite to the next and includes a written examination.

The Court of Master Sommeliers (www.mastersommeliers.org)

The Court is another UK-based organization that offers its certification around the world. The courses and certification target wine service professionals. Its four levels are the Introductory Sommelier Course, Certified Sommelier Exam, Advanced Sommelier Course and Exam, and Master Sommelier Diploma Exam. The introductory level requires two days of course work followed by the one-day exam leading to the certified sommelier certification. It is a prerequisite to reaching the advanced level. The Advanced Sommelier Course takes three days to complete and is followed by a three-part exam that consists of

"practical knowledge and salesmanship, knowledge of the Sommelier, written questions and answers, and practical tasting of six wines." Students who successfully answer 60 percent of the questions receive a certificate and qualify for the master exam. No additional course work is required for the master exam, and it is similar in content to the advanced sommelier exam, the organization states, but students must pass with a minimum of 75 percent correct answers. If they do not pass the three parts of the exam on the first try (which very few candidates manage to do), they have two years to retake the parts that they failed.

Wine professionals who have passed the last stage of examination get to append the initials MS after their name. Diploma holders must also sign a code of ethics, which requires them to abide by standards set by the organization.

The Society of Wine Educators (www.societyofwineeducators.org)

The Society of Wine Educators offers three different levels of certification: certified specialist of wine (CSW), certified wine educator (CWE), and certified specialist of spirits (CSS). Preparation for each exam includes an extensive study guide that covers viticulture, grape varieties, wine production, wine regions, and wine appreciation. Studying is done independently. Candidates must pass the CSW and CSS exams with 75 percent correct answers and the CWE exam with 80 percent. The CWE exam also includes two sensory evaluation sections in addition to the written component, which consists of eighty-five

> Working at a wine store a few hours a week is a simple way to learn about grape types, producers, countries, and regions, and about which wines you like and don't like.

multiple-choice questions and one essay question. The other two exams consist of a multiple-choice written test.

Institute of Masters of Wine (www.mastersofwine.org)

The master of wine is a certification held by 275 people worldwide as of spring 2009. The organization that administers it, the Institute of Masters of Wine, requires that students take at least two years to study, with one week a year spent "in residency" in the United States, Europe, and Australia before sitting down to take the practical and theory portions of the exam. They then have a year to write a ten-thousand-word dissertation on a wine-related topic. Throughout the duration of their preparation, students work with current MWs (the usual appellation for holders of this degree).

food media

If you want to be a food writer, being a talented writer will go a long way. You can know a lot about food, but if you don't know how to communicate that knowledge well, you will have a hard time being successful at food writing. This isn't to say that you need to enroll in a journalism program.

Hundreds of very accomplished food writers have reached their status without formal writing training. But it does help to know the basic structure of a news story and what elements contribute to a solid feature piece.

Schools in most cities offer short writing courses that last from a couple of hours to a few weeks. They may not be specialized in food writing, but good writing is good writing regardless of the topic. More and more specialized food-writing courses are available too, both in person and online, through outlets such as ICE in New York and mediabistro.com, which offers in-person classes in New York, Los Angeles, Chicago, and Boston as well as online. They are usually taught by experienced food writers or magazine editors who will tell you how they were able to get published in magazines, newspapers, or websites and perhaps even share an editor's contact information with you. Google the instructors to make sure that those writing credits are current, and visit their personal websites. If you are impressed by their credentials, you are more likely to sign up for the class, first and foremost, but also to approach the person with a level of respect that will make you take the course more seriously.

Taking a writing class that lasts a few weeks typically means that the instructor will give you various assignments followed by feedback on each piece. The advantage of taking a food-writing class is that the six or eight pieces you'll write will be food related and hopefully ready to be sent out to an editor. While most publications do not take pieces "on spec," meaning already written, you can always send out a pitch—a short paragraph that aims to sell the editor on your idea—for something that you workshopped in a writing course.

Working in food media is not just about writing. Educational programs and organizations exist that focus on publicity, marketing, photography, styling, and broadcasting, for example. While they typically are not food focused, they nonetheless offer professional credentials, networks, and education that will help you further a career in food media. Your chapter of the Public Relations Society of America (www.prsa.org) might organize a panel that focuses on working with food businesses, while the communications program of a local university might arrange a panel with television culinary producers. Attending such events will not provide you with an advanced degree, but you will gain useful skills and resources.

Certain professional media-related organizations offer accreditations for their members. The PRSA gives its members the opportunity to add the APR (accredited in public relations) designation after their name. Those types of accreditations, like the IACP's CCP, are designed to prove that their members are skilled professionals, but they also serve to establish the validity of the profession itself. Because accreditations represent standards by which professionals must abide, setting those standards for an industry instantly elevates it. At PRSA, the APR designation is earned once the approved applicant has passed an in-person review with three professionals who are already APR, completed a "Readiness Review Questionnaire," and passed a comprehensive examination.

advanced degrees

Most careers in the food industry do not require an advanced college degree. But if you wish to follow certain paths, a master's or doctoral degree or an MBA will go a long way toward ensuring you reach your goal. In the previous chapter, we covered the major schools that offer advanced degrees in hospitality management. Here are some other options.

MBAs are of particular use if you are entrepreneurially minded and want to open your own business. Many of the owners and high-level managers whom we interviewed for this book expressed a desire to increase their business knowledge, and some went as far as recommending obtaining an MBA over degrees with a greater hospitality focus. MBA programs will not focus on food, but your course work will allow you to develop a business plan and to explore case studies that relate to the area of the food industry that most interests you. It is also likely that at least one of your professors will have experience with food businesses, even if it's just from studying them and not from actively working in one, and you might not be the only one in your class interested in this line of work. Even if you do not wish to own a business, you will learn managerial and financial skills in an MBA program that will prove invaluable to whichever management position you later hold, in companies large or small.

With a master's degree, you will be able to teach as an adjunct at most universities and community colleges, and in certain cases also in tenure-track positions. Many of the full-time faculty members in professional studies departments do not have doctoral degrees and yet are tenured. They are, however, encouraged, and in some cases required, to publish articles in scholarly journals and to present their work at academic conferences. If you want to teach and do research, the time and money invested in a graduate degree will be well spent. With a master's degree, you can teach management and liberal arts courses (on gastronomy, food history, food culture, and the like) at culinary schools that offer them. Some of the smaller schools might not have a full-time program but might be open to you offering a weekend course a few times a year.

A master's degree in food studies can be obtained at New York University, while Boston University offers a master's in gastronomy (see page 25 for more information on those schools' programs). NYU also has a doctoral program in food studies, which prepares students for a life in academia. Its graduates work in four-year colleges and universities, in hospitality or food and nutrition programs, or as adjuncts while pursuing a full-time career in the food industry. A PhD program in the anthropology of food is also available at Indiana University–Bloomington. In Europe, the University of Gastronomic Sciences in Bra, Italy, offers a master's degree in food culture and communication.

mentors

Throughout your career, a select number of people will become essential components of who you are as a food industry professional, thanks to the guidance, inspiration, encouragement, criticism, and friendship they provide along the way. Thomas Keller still speaks of his first mentor, Roland Henin (page 76), while John Besh found some of his mentors while cooking in Germany early in his career (page 83). Mentors are more than part of your network; you will surely rely on them for work-related questions or leads, but the relationship with someone you consider your mentor will be deeper than that. A mentor is part teacher, part leader, part friend, part family—someone whose advice you trust completely, because he or she always has your best interest at heart.

You might find your mentors at work or through repeated contacts at industry events, as you share your projects and experiences with them. They might be your direct supervisor, a colleague, or your company's owner. But not every person you work for will become a mentor. You might respect someone without wanting to push the relationship further.

You don't ask someone to become your mentor; it happens organically, through mutual respect and exchange. That ex-

> MBA programs will not focus on food, but your course work will allow you to develop a business plan and to explore case studies that relate to the area of the food industry that most interests you.

change is initially unbalanced: you have everything to learn and cannot provide much advice in exchange for all the ideas that your mentor might give you. At some point, however, you will be able to give something back, thanks to new ideas you are developing or seeing in the industry. You will always think of these people as mentors, but over time they turn into colleagues, and you in turn will become the mentor of young industry professionals.

volunteering

Volunteering is one of the most efficient ways to get to know the culinary scene in your city and work with a variety of professionals. Early in your career, it is also a way to attend lots of events for free, in exchange for your labor. Volunteering opportunities are endless, from teaching basic nutrition to kids or plating dishes at a gala to stuffing envelopes for a fund-raising drive or blogging on behalf of an organization. Volunteering is something that you can, and should, do throughout your career, not only because it will allow you to meet people and make use of your skills, but because it is a truly essential component of working in the culinary and hospitality world. Most charitable organizations would not be able to function if not for the volunteers they attract every year, who help with everything from day-to-day operations to special events.

Aside from the philanthropic aspect, volunteering also allows you to gain behind-the-scenes access to your favorite organizations and events. Most "Taste of" types of events and large food-related galas require volunteers to work with chefs, helping them prep, plate, and serve their dishes, for example. If you are currently in culinary school, you will be able to work with a variety of chefs, which will be helpful in selecting the site of your internship or first job or will give you the opportunity to work with an out-of-town chef whose work you admire. Organizations, such as the James Beard Foundation in New York, might also offer dinners for which they need prep cooks and other assistant types. Depending on the organization's needs, the type of work required, and your availability, volunteering can last from one day to several years.

How do you start volunteering? If you are in school (culinary or otherwise), look for announcements on your school's bulletin board or on the e-mail list that the school uses to communicate with you. For- and not-for-profit companies alike know to reach out to students when looking for volunteers; they know that students seek experience to add to a résumé and want to gain invaluable contacts among current industry professionals who could be sources of employment. Another way is to contact organizations, individuals, and companies directly. If you see an event that you would like to attend but cannot afford, for example, contact the organizers to see if they need more volunteers.

networking

Being a good networker is a talent required regardless of your field. But it seems that in the food industry in general, networking is how many jobs are obtained and knowledge is acquired. From finding a school to finding a stage or internship and finding a job, your network—friends, family, bosses past and present, colleagues, acquaintances, strangers—is part of what will make you a successful professional. When you start your career, you might find it difficult to think of a network, or even to know how to tap into it. Your network is anyone who can be in a position to help you because they know how talented you are. People who have worked with you, in any position, or who have taught you are people who can refer you to others because they know a particular position would be the perfect fit for you. A stranger you met because he or she sat next to you at a party or at a restaurant bar might have just heard of a job lead. In that case, they might not be able to pass along more than a contact name to you, but it's still one thing you didn't have before meeting them. Your parents might have colleagues who know people in the food industry who could have a job for you. Your current boss might be happy to recommend you for another position once you both feel it's time to move on. A friend might have too much to do and need some freelance help. As a company owner, your network can bring you anything from business leads to ways to solve problems.

Thinking about all these people is the first step to building a network. As you go on with your career, you will join organizations, attend professional conferences and events, and make business deals with more and more people, which will expand your network. These days, you can also build a network online, thanks to websites such as LinkedIn, for example (see page 57). On a more traditional note, networking for young cooks often takes place at the local late-night watering holes the industry favors. You might have subnetworks, depending on what you need your connections for. Some of those relationships will remain strictly professional, while other people who started as acquaintances will become close friends over the course of your career.

Do not be afraid to contact your network. It can be hard, as a student about to graduate, for example, to dare to contact people to tell them that you are looking for a job, or, once you've been in a position for a couple of years, to tell people who might have job leads for you that you are on the job market. Do not hesitate to do it, however, because you will be amazed at the

> Your network is anyone who can be in a position to help you because they know how talented you are. People who have worked with you, in any position, or who have taught you are people who can refer you to others because they know a particular position would be the perfect fit for you.

results obtained by sending a simple e-mail. Do not be too demanding—state that you are looking for a job/recommendation/connection/advice, and ask if they can keep you in mind should they hear of a job/recommend you for a position/make an introduction/answer a question at their convenience. The worst that can happen is that someone does not get back to you or tells you that they cannot be of help. Remember to always thank someone who provides a lead and let them know if it turns into an interview or a job. Don't hesitate to send an e-mail every once in a while updating some key people in your network about your whereabouts so that they can keep up with your career.

organizations

Joining professional organizations is among the easiest ways to develop your network and gain educational and employment opportunities in your field. You will find national culinary organizations, regional chapters of national organizations, and local organizations in most major cities in the country. From wine to public relations to business ownership to writing to cooking, each field has a wide variety of organizations to choose from. Some will be food specific, like the Association of Food Journalists, the Research Chefs Association, the Club Managers Association of America, or the IACP. Others will be general organizations, be they the local chamber of commerce or the Public Relations

Society of America. On page 349 in the appendix you'll find a list of professional culinary organizations.

Ask friends who are members of local organizations what they feel they get out of their membership, which organizations they might have dropped out of and why, what they like most about the planned events, and who the other members are. If you can, attend a couple of events as a guest to get a feel for an organization and its members. You might find that the people who belong to a group that sounded appealing on paper have nothing in common with you and/or your career interest—or, more positively, that you loved every second of the meeting or event you attended and met dozens of people whom you cannot wait to see again.

Most national professional organizations plan a conference annually or biannually. Attendance can be costly, but it allows you to meet and mingle with people from around the country, if not the world, which in itself is often worth the investment. The seminars offered at those conferences are also a valuable opportunity to learn new skills or keep up with trends. The IACP (www.iacp.com), for example, hosts a conference that takes place in a different city every year. Pre-conference daylong seminars focus on specific categories of the industry, with section classes and meetings for food writers, educators, marketers, food historians, and cooks, for example. The conference itself offers a wide range of panels, from cooking demonstrations to practical seminars (live pitching and blogging how-to sessions

Ask friends who are members of local organizations what they feel they get out of their membership, which organizations they might have dropped out of and why, what they like most about the planned events, and who the other members are.

are always popular) to discussions on sustainability. The IACP Awards are announced at a reception at the end of the conference. The Club Managers Association of America (www.cmaa.org), the professional association for the managers of membership-oriented clubs (country, yacht, golf, or faculty clubs, for example) has close to seven thousand members and forty-nine chapters. This representative professional organization offers a certification program and a career services department, conducts industry research for its members, and runs an annual world conference.

Organizations also offer exclusive subscriptions to member publications, which are another way not only to expand your skills (these often include educational articles) but also to find out who is doing what and where in your industry.

trade shows

Trade shows are an ideal way to see the latest in professional equipment and specialty foods all in one place. More than that, though, they also offer opportunities to establish connections with professionals from around the country and to expand a particular field of knowledge thanks to their educational seminars. Most of the shows offer a mix of paid sessions, which last a few hours to a full day, and free, shorter ones that last about one hour. For certified professionals, attendance at trade shows and those seminars is a must, since they are a way to maintain these certifications, which often operate on a point system. Many of these shows also offer professionals the opportunity to compete and earn recognition and cash prizes by doing so.

International Hotel/Motel & Restaurant Show (www.ihmrs.com)

The International Hotel/Motel & Restaurant Show takes place every November in New York and is organized by the Hotel Association of New York City, the New York State Hospitality & Tourism Association, and the American Hotel & Lodging Association. Suppliers of the latest developments in food and beverages, equipment, technology, tableware, and more present their products to approximately thirty-five thousand attendees. Local chefs perform in the demonstration kitchen, while educational programs include the daylong Hospitality Leadership Forum and hourlong seminars on industry trends.

International Hospitality Week in Las Vegas features three shows at once: the Nightclub & Bar Convention and Trade Show, the International Restaurant Show—Las Vegas, and the HotelWorld Expo and Conference. More than thirty thousand industry professionals attend this event, which offers educational seminars and other events in addition to the shows themselves.

National Restaurant Association Show (show.restaurant.org)

The National Restaurant Association Show, produced by Reed Exhibitions, takes place in Chicago in May. According to the show's website, 50,100 restaurant, food-service, and lodging professionals (a business card or tax ID number is required to register) attended the show. It offers a wide range of educational programs, with tracks such as Profitability and Entrepreneurship, Jobs and Careers, Food and Healthy Living, Technology, and Sustainability and Social Responsibility as well as demonstrations by well-known chefs. The show allows food-service and hospitality professionals to meet with suppliers of a large range of products, which they can purchase or recommend for their businesses. The show also features the Kitchen Innovation Pavilion, where commercial kitchen equipment manufacturers can unveil their latest wares and compete for awards.

regional restaurant shows

Reed Exhibitions also produces the International Restaurant & Foodservice Show of New York (March; www.international restaurantny.com), the Florida Restaurant & Lodging Show in Orlando (mid-September; www.fraexpo.com), and the Western Foodservice & Hospitality Expo in San Diego (early September; www.western foodexpo.com), which are each sponsored by their respective state restaurant associations. They are restricted to the trade, feature a wide range of suppliers from the geographical region they cover, and offer educational programs through the Ferdinand Metz Foodservice Forum.

World Pastry Forum (www.pastrychampionship.com)

The World Pastry Forum takes place in Phoenix every year in early July (the location changes at times) and is immediately followed by the National or World Pastry Championship (held on alternate years). This is the only program of its kind in this country that is dedicated solely to pastry. The forum offers educational programs that are taught by world-class experts, such as hands-on specialized courses on chocolate and wedding cakes and demonstrations by the likes of Albert Adrià of El Bullì in Spain. The national championships alternate between national qualifiers—with American teams battling one another for the chance to represent the USA in the world competition—and takes place the following year. Those events are open to registrants and are at times broadcast on the Food Network.

Fancy Food Shows (www.specialtyfood.com)

The National Association for the Specialty Food Trade organizes two shows every year: the Winter Fancy Food Show in San

Francisco in January, and the Summer Fancy Food Show in New York in June. These shows offer specialty food and beverage producers large and small the opportunity to present their products and meet with buyers for large supermarkets, gourmet food stores, online retailers, media, and more. Some of the shows' special features include an international pavilion where food producers from around the globe are represented, an area where producers can showcase foods and beverages they make that are typical of their states, and awards for the best products in a variety of categories.

International Home and Housewares Show (housewares.org)

The International Home and Housewares Show also takes place in Chicago, in March. It showcases products "for all areas of the home" divided into four categories, including "dine + design," which includes kitchen accessories, gourmet foods, cookware and bakeware, home décor, and more. Top chefs from around the country typically perform demonstrations and sign their cookbooks throughout the duration of the show.

International Chefs' Congress (starchefs.com)

The International Chefs' Congress, organized by StarChefs in New York every September, is a relative newcomer to the conference scene, having launched in 2005. This three-day event offers hands-on classes, demonstrations, and panels by the world's foremost culinary, pastry, and beverage professionals that follow a given theme ("What Is American Cuisine" was the theme in 2009, for example). Exhibitors present their latest products and technologies in a showcase adjacent to the demonstration and educational area. Restaurant professionals receive a preferential rate, so many working chefs and cooks attend the congress, which is reserved for industry members. Culinary professionals of all kinds, including a large media contingent, are also present.

CaterArts (www.icacater.org)

The International Caterers Association holds its annual conference, CaterArts, every July. There, company owners and catering sales personnel can participate in educational sessions and roundtables, while catering chefs can alternate between those and hands-on continuing education.

having an online presence

There are countless ways to have an online presence, from owning a customized website to tweeting (or twittering, depending on whom you ask). Not all of these media are created equal, but you can use each one smartly to build your profile and network. Social-networking sites also allow you to learn more about your industry by connecting you to chefs, writers and bloggers, food-policy activists, and other sources that post a lot of links. You can also obtain a lot of information quickly by seeing what others post on Facebook or Twitter. The key point to remember, of course, is that if you use these sites for professional purposes, you have to remain professional on them at all times. That includes not posting photos of you partying, for example, or being careful about what you post in your status updates or as links. Don't criticize coworkers or, even worse, employees. The immediacy of on-line communication means that they could hear about it before the workday is over.

Websites

Having a website is essential if you own a business or work as a freelancer or consultant. It allows you to showcase your work easily, clearly, and professionally, giving potential clients the information they need before contacting you. Businesses such as restaurants, food companies, and wineries should have websites that are professionally designed, programmed, and hosted. That's not an expense on which to skimp—think of it as the first impression you'll offer to people who might know nothing about your company or are deciding on whether to eat at your restaurant or the competition's. One way to keep maintenance costs slightly lower once the site is established is to ask your designer to set the site up so that you can update it yourself. Those updates can include menus, changes in hours, media mentions, and staff bios. If you can do that without having to contact your designer for every comma change, your site will also be a more efficient business tool.

A professional-looking site should be the norm regardless of your business. But if you are setting up your own consulting or freelance business, you might not have

the funds right away to build a costly website. You can use services like WordPress, TypePad, and Google to create websites that look polished for free, or for a very low cost if you want more customization. These companies also host the sites, so you do not need to look for a separate hosting provider. All you need to do is buy a domain name, using a company like Go Daddy, for example. Use the templates available to design your site, or customize it if you have the required skills to do so.

It goes without saying that any website should have your contact information displayed prominently. There is nothing worse than having to spend five minutes trying every tab on a site to look for an address or a contact form. On personal sites, post your bio and samples of your work, such as published articles or photographs. Someone looking to contact you for an assignment will know what you do without having to ask you for clips in a separate e-mail and can decide whether or not you have the expertise and style he or she seeks. Link to sites that have published your work, offer recipes, and include other information that complements what you do (gardening tips if you have a fantastic vegetable garden, for example) to maintain your visitor's attention. But you do not need to have ten separate pages on your site. You can also link to your blog, if you have one.

The same type of content is valid for a company or restaurant website. For a restaurant, directions, hours, and reservation information should be accessible within the first seconds spent on your site. Frequently update your menu section; it is a turn-off to read about stews and braises when planning to visit a restaurant in July. Post the bios of the main players of the restaurant or the company, along with media mentions and awards. Keep those current.

Blogs

Everybody has a blog these days, or so it seems. This should not stop you from launching your own, if you have a solid purpose for it. If you want to write, a blog not only provides a great daily or weekly writing practice but also can become a portfolio of your work. However, make sure that your blog contributes something unique to the blogosphere and isn't merely a retelling of what you ate for dinner. Think about the content of your blog before you sit down to type the very first post. What do you want to say? What do you feel is your area of expertise? What are your strengths as a writer and how can you best showcase your voice? Molly Wizenberg (page 285) went through that process when starting her blog, Orangette; it took her some time to figure out what types of posts were best. The *London Times* named Orangette the best blog in the world in 2009, so she must have been right. This does not mean that

you shouldn't start a blog because you know that someone is already writing about cooking with farmers'-market finds in Phoenix, AZ. If you have a voice with character, a unique perspective, and rich content, people will read yours too.

Do not count on obtaining a book contract out of your blog, but blogging can help build your platform by developing a faithful readership. Reading a lot of other blogs and commenting on them helps make that happen, since other bloggers will in turn read and link to your blog. The larger your audience, the more likely you will be able to obtain paid assignments, since it shows that people already like how you write and what you write about. If you decide to take advertisements on your blog, you will also be able to make a little bit of money—not much, but in some cases enough to recoup your Web costs.

You can also use a blog to complement your website if you are a company or a restaurant. Bar Great Harry in Brooklyn, NY, lists its daily beer selection on its blog. Customers know to go to the blog to see the types of beers they'll be able to sample that night. Blog about special wine dinners that you are hosting or unique wine pairings created by your sommelier. As a company, use your blog to talk about new products or unusual ingredients. Offering this type of content helps build brand loyalty and brings return visitors to your site regularly.

Social Networking Sites

LinkedIn, Facebook, and Twitter are the largest social networking sites you'll find, even if countless smaller ones appear

You can also use a blog to complement your website if you are a company or a restaurant. Bar Great Harry in Brooklyn, NY, lists its daily beer selection on its blog.

every day. Each of these sites allows you to search for your contacts through your e-mail address book, for example, so you can instantly connect with colleagues and friends.

LinkedIn (www.linkedin.com) is the most business focused of the three and offers the best opportunity to create an online résumé for strictly professional networking. It allows you to list your current and past positions, education, and professional affiliations, just as you would on a résumé. You can then link to other people you've worked with and join groups of similar interest or the groups of professional organizations to which you might already belong. Those group pages allow you to post topics, such as an announcement that you are hiring, looking for a job, or searching for someone with particular expertise. You can recommend former colleagues and ask them to write you recommendations. The site is most useful for employees and consultants or freelancers.

The primary focus of Facebook (www.facebook.com) is much more social; it allows you to reconnect with old friends, classmates, and colleagues who might now be disseminated around the world. As such, it is easy to find content on Facebook that is less than professional, from old party photos to status updates that reflect slacking off at work. Some people decide to keep their Facebook profile very separate from their professional life and only connect with friends, reserving LinkedIn for business purposes. However, if you use Facebook wisely, it can be a powerful professional networking tool that will allow

you to connect with colleagues and clients and be in more constant contact than if you had to wait to find a reason to e-mail or call them. By following their status updates, and their following yours, you get to know people a lot better than you would by seeing them at functions once or twice a year. It makes it easier to strike up a conversation when you are finally face-to-face.

Posts on Twitter (www.twitter.com) are limited to 140 characters. Its users use a lot of abbreviations and shortened URLs to post links and information. Some users focus strictly on their day-to-day activities, which can become banal, but others offer rich content in the form of links, dish ideas, recipes, flavor combinations, and general inspiration. Chefs, food companies, food writers, and personalities abound on Twitter. You can use the Twitter directory to find people, in addition to letting the site mine your address book to find friends and contacts who are already tweeting. Twitter allows for even more instant interactions than Facebook, and as such also allows you to expand your live network.

The online video site YouTube is another venue that you can use to showcase your work, particularly if you work or seek a position in one of the more creative aspects of the culinary world. It will allow you to send links to your contacts and build your customer base. Cake designer Elisa Strauss (page 163), for example, uploaded a video called "How to Make a Sculpted Dog Cake" in May 2008, which had received more than 1.2 million views as of November 2009. She believed that the video brought her many new customers.

3. OWNERSHIP AND ENTREPRENEURSHIP

For the brave souls who take it on, owning a business is the apogee of their career. Many business owners work years before taking the plunge, while others start their career by forming their own company because they cannot imagine working for anyone else. Knowing when you are ready is entirely personal and cannot be

taught, but a number of elements merit consideration before you launch your own venture. From writing a business plan and ensuring that you have your family's support to raising capital and obtaining permits, the mountain of tasks you must accomplish before you can call yourself an entrepreneur may seem insurmountable. The rewards are numerous, however, and those who go through with it rarely come to regret it, no matter the sacrifices they make along the way.

One key piece of advice that many business owners have mentioned throughout the interviews we conducted is to learn what works and what does not on somebody else's dime. This is not to encourage behaving poorly when working for someone; rather, it means that working in a variety of businesses, both similar to and different from the business you want to own, allows you to garner the experience that you'll need to avoid many mistakes when the time comes to open your own doors. What you can learn working in another business ranges from staff management and inventory needs to software and purveyors. You will see what others do well and what they do poorly, and be able to develop relationships with people who will be useful for your own company. Chefs often find their investors while building a name in a kitchen owned by someone else, for example, until they are able to obtain enough funding to open their own restaurant.

If everything works out, however, the satisfaction of bringing to life a successful business will be worth all the sacrifices you made to get there.

taking the entrepreneurial step

Even the most loyal employees dream of running their own business. Large or small, family-owned or publicly traded—the size of the dream does not matter. What you are really looking for when thinking about opening your own company is the freedom of answering to no one but yourself. That freedom has a price, of course—below we detail the cons of owning a business—which is why ownership often remains nothing but a dream. However, it seems like the food industry is particularly attractive to budding entrepreneurs. For example, do you have a great jam recipe that your friends keep saying you should market? That's an appealing thought, but you must reflect on whether or not you have what it takes to take that great jam to the next level and open a business—or if that even could be the basis for a business.

If you like spending lots of time with your family, having hobbies, and hosting friends at your house on a weekly basis, starting or acquiring a business might not be the right thing for you. You have to be willing to spend every waking hour (upwards of all twenty-four of them at times) on your new business for the early stages of its inception and launch. You can't call in sick or take vacations without your phone or laptop when you are a new business owner. Every penny that you have saved, currently make, or borrow will go toward this new venture. It will cause tension in your existing relationships and

Having the support of your family and close friends is also a vital aspect of starting a business. They might not be able to financially support the venture, but knowing that they think you are doing the right thing at the right time in your life is just as essential.

might prevent you from forming new ones. If everything works out, however, the satisfaction of bringing to life a successful business will be worth all the sacrifices you made to get there. But you have to be aware of them and make it through the difficult times.

Having the support of your family and close friends is also a vital aspect of starting a business. They might not be able to financially support the venture, but knowing that they think you are doing the right thing at the right time in your life is just as essential. You will need people who encourage you when things get tough and you are exhausted, who listen to your gripes when inspections don't go well or your space falls through, who bring you coffee when it's two A.M. and you still have mountains of paperwork to finish before heading to bed. That support team should extend to your professional network. Can you call mentors, colleagues, or former bosses when you have a question or problem to solve or need to find resources? If people around you do not think that launching your own business is a good idea, listen to what they have to say before signing a lease or giving notice. They may have their own agenda for telling you that (perhaps a significant other is not ready to see you working all the time or a colleague does not want competition, for example), which you need to take into consideration. But if the general opinion is negative overall, you might want to wait for a little while and work on areas your support system advises you to improve upon before starting your own company.

You need to understand the importance of getting honest feedback on all aspects of your venture. Too often, budding entrepreneurs seek feedback on a new venture idea only from family and friends. That is a mistake. They will likely tend to tell you what you want to hear, being reluctant to be overly critical of your idea. Seek the advice of a series of unbiased acquaintances, and even strangers. That is who your customers will likely be once you are in business.

When it comes to culinary ventures, all sorts of decisions need to be made based on subjective taste. Recognize that you will need to strike a balance between your vision and business reality. When in doubt, make decisions that raise the probability of your success. For example, in the 1990s, the concept of soup restaurants was tried across the country. Few of those shops are still in business today. Those that offered a broader menu, say soups and salads, were more likely to survive, as they appealed to a larger group of customers year-round.

If you are ready for any and all sacrifices and have the moral support in place, you can start exploring opening the type of business that makes the most sense for your product idea or concept. Start your business plan (more on this on page 65). Is there a market for your product? Where is it? Who are your customers? Who are your competitors? These are not rhetorical questions. You need to invest an enormous amount of time, and often some money too, in finding out the answers. These are components of your business plan, so the initial research will not be wasted. It will also allow you to build the right bases for success. You might discover that your initial idea is already well represented in the marketplace but that a slight tweak will make you unique while still desirable.

Take a look at your résumé. Do you have the right education and background for your intended business? Have you worked for the right companies or people? Imagine an investor reading the bio included in your business plan or a reporter writing a piece about you and your business when you launch. Will your experience, condensed on a page, be enough to convince them and your targeted clientele to trust your expertise and patronize your business? Do you need to work just one more year? Stage at a few restaurants? Travel for a while? Fill the holes now before taking the plunge. But also realize that you can always learn just one more thing, work at one more company, visit one more country. Do not let that paralyze you. At some point you need to dive in, if owning your business is truly what you want to do, and your experience will never be complete. You should always, no matter how long you have been doing something, look for more opportunities to learn.

If you need additional training of any kind to be a performing business owner, take that into consideration as well. What courses are available around you? Can you complete that training while still working for your current employer? Do you need to spend some time in another city for short- or long-term course work? Take advantage of the courses offered by your chamber of commerce, small business bureau office, university extension, community colleges and universities, culinary schools, and panels and seminars organized by local organizations. Factor the cost of that education, if applicable, in the total estimated cost of launching your business.

When launching a business, the old maxim "Know thyself" is important. You must recognize your strengths, weaknesses, areas of wisdom, and blind spots and set your plans accordingly. An all-too-common scenario in the culinary world is for the entrepreneur to be a talented chef or creative type who is not proficient with numbers (as they relate to accounting and business). That can be okay as long as you hire, retain, or include on your team a trustworthy person to manage those issues.

the pros

The ultimate positive aspect is obvious: You are your own boss. No need to answer to anyone anymore; you call the shots, from the color of the walls to the design of your business cards, from the product composi-

tion to the menu—it's all you (in theory at least; see "The Cons" on page 62 for the reality). You choose what your company will focus on, what business philosophy you want to adopt, what your mission is. Instead of following someone else's mission statement, you write your own and get to share your vision with partners, staff, and media. In due time you will delegate many of these decisions because you will need to focus on the bigger picture of your business, but in the early days, it's all you, and nothing takes place if you have not approved it. You are the creative force behind your company as well as its leader, publicist, receptionist, and general contractor.

If it all works out, owning your own business can be very profitable. If it is, you (and your partners/investors) get to decide what to do with those profits. When you work for someone else, you do not get to make that decision. The likelihood of financial success and the scale of profits are inevitably linked to the size and margins of the business. A restaurant generating $800,000 in revenue with a 6 percent profit margin will give you $48,000 in profit. It is thus better to own a restaurant

In some cases, the largest profit that your business can provide comes when you sell it. The chance that your business will be worth a considerable amount to someone else increases if you have built a strong brand name, reputation, and operating systems.

doing $2,500,000 in revenue with a 4.5 percent profit margin, which would give you $112,500 in profit.

Another positive aspect of starting or buying your own business is the challenge it provides. You might be at a point in your professional life where things at work are just not that exciting anymore. You've risen as high as you will; you've worked for the best; you've accomplished the goals you set when you started your career. Starting a restaurant or a company will take care of any boredom that you have been feeling. The rush, the adrenaline, the pressure—all those will bring back the burning desire you felt in your stomach in the early days. For many entrepreneurs, there is no option other than opening a business; you have to do it, because every inch of your body and your mind craves it. That might happen even at an early stage in your career. You might decide to start a company while you are still getting your education or after a few short years of work. In that case, you might not have had time to become bored with a career path but will feel

the thrill of entrepreneurship just the same. Nothing (save perhaps the birth of a child, to be fair) can substitute for the feeling you'll get the first time you flip the "open" sign on your front door or accept your first order.

A family business can also be a legacy for your children. While this is not usually the primary goal of an entrepreneur, launching a sustainable business that will last is. Unless you are only interested in a quick turnaround (in which case the food industry might not be ideal for you), creating a business that will grow year after year and support generations of your family is likely something that you are thinking about when putting together your business plan. You cannot offer such a legacy as an employee, but as a business owner you will be able to offer everything from summer jobs, to valuable lessons, to a full career through the years. Keep in mind that even if your children are not interested in taking over the business, you will have instilled in them an entrepreneurial spirit and taught them essential business-related values that they will carry through their own careers.

You might be at a point in your professional life where things at work are not exciting anymore. You've risen as high as you will; you've worked for the best; you've accomplished the goals you set when you started your career. Starting a restaurant or a company will take care of any boredom.

the cons

In reality, you are never really truly on your own and will need to work with others while you build your business. You'll need to rely on your family and friends, seeking their support and help to paint walls or perform other duties, often on a volunteer basis, as you become established. Your business partners will also be constant presences, though they'll likely be more difficult to deal with. You will be discussing finances with them and will be accountable to them as your business grows and hopefully succeeds. You will be turning in profit and loss sheets to your business partners, and they will expect a certain return on their investment. Depending on your agreement with them, they may have a say in the creative process of your business, not just on the financial side, which might prove a challenge as you develop your vision.

The time you will invest in your business is another factor that might make you think twice before launching a company. You can probably forget days off and vacations for the first couple of years of the life of your business. Even if you manage to get away, you will need, and want, to be reachable at all times. You can be the world's best delegator—it does not matter. That's just the reality of being a business owner. Early on, you might not even have anyone to delegate anything to, as you may be running a company from your living room. That can create tension among your family and friends, who will want to spend time with you and will only be understanding to a certain point. If you like to leave work at five P.M. and devote time to hobbies, keep working for someone else, because it will take many years as an entrepreneur before you are able to enjoy that type of leisure time again.

The risks involved in running a business create an enormous source of stress

If you like to leave work at five P.M. and devote time to hobbies, keep working for someone else, because it will take many years as an entrepreneur before you are able to enjoy that type of leisure time again.

for most entrepreneurs. Even if your business is doing well, you will worry about cash flow, growth, taxes, employees, payroll, regulations, inspections, customer service, and more. All those things and more can go wrong and result in the failure of your company. There is no shame in your business not succeeding—that's a chance you are taking. Ultimately, even if you don't succeed at the level at which you hoped, you will have learned invaluable lessons that will make your next company better.

acquiring an existing business

Those with dreams of owning their own business should consider getting there by buying someone else's. The advantages of this route are that your business will already have customers, cash flow, and a track record. On the other hand, you will also be acquiring that business's issues and problems, if there are any. You may need to immediately manage, discipline, or motivate employees who were not hired by you. In an ideal scenario, you will like and admire the owner you are buying from and encourage him or her to remain part of the business for a little while, perhaps part-time, to help you ease into it.

A myriad of financing models are available for buying existing businesses. Many involve the buyer paying a down payment and then continuing with debt or royalty payments for months (or years). These types of plans allow you to get in the owner's seat without having to come up with all of the purchase price at the outset. If you are taking over an existing business that has seen declining sales, you should clearly come armed with ideas—and the ability—to change that trend. In a restaurant, falling sales might be the result of an outdated menu, a decline in customer service, or a tired-looking dining room. The issues can be changed, but it will take resources ranging from creativity to additional investment capital to succeed.

finding resources

You don't need to enroll in a full-time educational program in order to start your own business or develop a business plan;

The SBA also offers sample business plans that you can review for free, including ten examples for bars and nightclubs, nine for bed-and-breakfasts and hotels, twenty for farm and food production, and forty-three for restaurants, cafés, and bakeries.

countless resources exist for both self- and guided study, from free classes to books and websites. The U.S. Small Business Administration (www.sba.gov) has offices in every state which provide numerous free classes and events as well as general support for all stages of your business, whether you are just starting up, buying a franchise, or have a long-standing company. SBA also offers free online training, such as Small Business Primer: Guide to Starting a Business and How to Prepare a Business Plan. While they are not food-industry-specific programs, the basics of writing a business plan; obtaining financing; securing space; obeying local, state, and federal regulations; and obtaining financial assistance if you qualify are universal enough that you will benefit from spending time on both the national and your local SBA websites.

If you plan on opening a restaurant, the National Restaurant Association (www.restaurant.org) also offers online resources, mostly in the form of extensive lists of websites and books where you will find information to help you start or run your business. The NRA also has a how-to series that is particularly useful once you have opened your restaurant, with articles on how to deal with employee issues (including immigration laws and termination), reporting tips, attracting publicity, and reducing no-shows, for example. Joining your state's chapter of the association is another good way to obtain resources, such as opportunities to network at events with people who can assist you, review your plan, and introduce you to other vital players in your area, or educational seminars and certification courses (such as ServSafe and FoodHandlers) organized by the chapter.

The USDA's Cooperative Extension System (www.csrees.usda.gov/Extension) has a mission to help the public with agriculture-related questions. These services are provided by cooperative extensions located throughout each state. They can help you solve problems related to any crop you might be growing to make food products, general agriculture issues, gardening, recycling, specialized training, food safety, family issues, health and nutrition, and more. Each office has at least one person on staff who answers questions from the public, and often the state offices' websites provide extensive educational material, including booklets and videos. All the services that they offer will be a priceless source of information should your business involve working with the land or its products.

Most cities provide resource centers for small business owners, which are funded by the local government itself. Their services usually include some restaurant-specific information, whether courses or online material, since restaurants are such a vital part of any city's life. In New York, NYC Small Business Services (www.nyc.gov/html/sbs) offers several classes for would-be and established restaurant owners. Restaurant Boot Camp gives attendees a complete rundown of all the steps required to open a restaurant, while the course series No More Kitchen Drama includes classes such as Manage Your Restaurant's Health Inspection and Recruit and Retain Talents for Your Restaurant.

The City of San Francisco's Office of Small Business (www.sfgov.org/site/osb) provides a checklist for restaurateurs looking to buy or start a restaurant as well as a list called "Top Ten Tips to Open a Restaurant in San Francisco."

While all of the above institutional resources are available to aid you in reaching your goal, you will probably find that your best resource will be a helpful professional who is already in the business. That is true whether your interest is in restaurants, cake decorating, catering, specialty food shops, or bars and nightclubs. Find an experienced professional who does not see you as a competitor and listen to their "war stories" of what can go right and what can go wrong. With his or her help, you will be better able to anticipate potential obstacles. At the end of the day, however, your most important resource is you: You need to assess if you have the experience and tools to be an entrepreneur.

preparing your business plan

Resources to help you write a business plan abound. Start with the Small Business Administration, which offers an outline, sample business plans, and workshops on its website. Other free online resources are at the tips of your fingers, thanks to Google, but they vary in quality, so you will have to spend some time deciding which sources are most helpful. Bookstores and your local public library will also have books that cover business plan writing.

Business Plan Outline for a Restaurant or Related Food Business

This outline is based on the one used in ICE's seven-month culinary management diploma program.

Cover Sheet
Who, What, When, Where

Executive Summary

Concept Description
Menu overview
"Mind's-eye tour" from the front door
Drawings, diagrams, or pictures
Service style—uniforms, table settings
Other revenue sources— catering, takeout, etc.

Location
Neighborhood/attractions
Lease
Access—traffic, parking, etc.

Marketing Plan
Target customer profile
Marketing and promotion plans

Competition and Concept Viability
Locally—similar concepts

Elsewhere—similar concepts
Locally—other competition
Why is your concept special?

Management
Your background and experience
Managers' background and experience
Chef's experience

Staffing
Staff plan and budget
Provision for benefits
Market conditions/availability of staff

Facility Construction and Improvement
Required scope of work
Projected work plan and timing

Operations
MIS/technology requirements
Licensing issues, such as liquor, sanitation, etc.
Utility requirements (gas, electric, water)

Financial Information
Proposed company structure
Capital budget
Pre-opening "soft" cost budget
Profit and loss statements with three-year projections
Sources and uses/cash flow statement
Balance sheet with three-year projections
Explanations of assumptions
Exit/Expansion Strategy
Best case
Worst case
Return-on-investment comments

Extras
Menus and recipes
Logo and marketing materials
Résumés
Photos
Job descriptions
Demographic and other maps
Copies of letters of intent from suppliers

Culinary schools and other educational facilities offer various classes that are worthwhile investments of time and money; you will receive feedback from an instructor and be able to ask questions, rather than trying to figure out everything on your own. At a culinary school, you will also be able to learn the specifics of a plan that is geared toward a food business, with an instructor who has written and/or read his share of plans.

Your plan will need to include much more than your creative concept, marketing plan, and competition analysis. These should be the easiest parts to write, because they are part of what prompted the decision to open your own business in the first place. Financial projections, budgets, loans, tax information, and other such information will be more challenging to create or gather. You will need to establish how much it will cost to lease space and buy equipment when applicable, establish your operating costs, determine revenue projections for the next two to five years, and think about the growth and long-term health of the business in as much detail as possible. The more thorough your business plan is, the more likely you are to secure financing.

Take time to write your business plan, and enlist help. Someone you know and trust has likely written one before. Have that friend review your plan and provide you with feedback. Other friends might not have prepared such a document but might be great writers or editors who can help you write and proofread it before you send it out to potential investors. Someone else might be a great designer and could help you lay out your plan in a manner that is both clear and attractive. You might be afraid to share your ideas with too many people before your company is a reality. That should not be too much of a concern—even if someone was tempted to steal your concept, they would not be able to re-create exactly the idea that you have, since you and all the elements and resources that you bring are not part of it. Moreover, a business plan is only a starting point; much more goes into the actual development of the business. Nonetheless, if you are concerned, only share your plan with people close to you, whom you really trust.

Ask them to be as brutally honest as they can; it will serve you well.

raising capital

You can have the best idea for a business in the world, but if you don't have the capital to get it started, it will stay just that—an idea. Having a well-crafted and polished business plan will help you raise capital as you approach those around you with requests for funding. The first step, of course, is to look at how much money you can bring to the project yourself. Investors might be more likely to support your business if they feel that you have something personally invested in it too (aside from your blood, sweat, and tears). How much savings can you put into your company? Do you have anything of value, such as real estate or stocks (depending on the shape of the market, value might be a relative term), that you can sell? Can you, and should you, take a second mortgage on your house? Can you downsize, by moving to a smaller apartment for example, and put your savings in rent toward your capital?

You can be your business's primary investor if you have enough savings, or be a partner among a group of other investors to minimize risk. These individuals can include family members, friends, colleagues, customers, and banks. Family and friends can have various motivations to help you. People might see it as an investment (most likely) or might simply be happy to help you realize your dreams (too

Ten Things to Consider when Building a Partnership

1. Determine how much capital you will need to launch your business. You might be able to start with very limited funds if you rent a kitchen during off hours to prepare your food product and then sell it directly or at farmers' markets, for example, raising enough seed money to be the principal investor in your own business when the time comes to look for partners to take it to the next level.

2. Decide how many partners you want to have. Do you know one investor capable of providing your entire capital, or will you be working with a pool of smaller investors? There are pros and cons to each approach.

3. How will you break down the return percentage for each investor?

4. Do you have a business plan, or at least a proposal, ready to show prospective investors who will ask for it? If not, how long will it take you to create one?

5. If you are on the creative or culinary side, look for partners with business acumen and management experience (front-of-the-house experience for a restaurant).

6. If you have business and management experience but limited creativity or culinary knowledge, look for a partner who has a solid culinary résumé with stints at some of the top places in your area or around the country.

7. Preferably, have at least one partner who has invested in a similar business before and who can provide guidance.

8. Have a lawyer draw up contracts, even with your family members and friends. There is no place for handshake deals in partnerships; if anything goes wrong later on, you want to make sure that your options are spelled out in a contract.

9. Decide if you want partners who are involved in the day-to-day operations or are silent partners happy to receive their return statements once a year.

10. If your partners do not like the location you have chosen for your business or disagree with your logo design, who makes the final decision? In your contract, establish who has the final say on what.

ideal a scenario to happen often). Regardless of your closeness with these types of investors, treat them as you would strangers, and put everything in writing. Decide on what rate of return each one of your investors will receive, how often you will pay those returns, and what will happen if the business does not make it. Spell everything out in contracts that both your lawyer and theirs will review. Do not, under any circumstances, skip this step, regardless of how well everything is going early on in

the process. If problems arise at any point in the life of the business, you want to be protected, and so should your investors.

creative ways to get started

Launching your own business does not mean that you need to buy space right away or raise several million dollars. You can—and often should—start small. As stated in *Becoming a Chef,* Mario Batali opened his first restaurant, Po, in May 1993 for $41,000. These days, you can even start a restaurant out of your apartment, as "secret" dining clubs are proliferating throughout the country. Some young professional cooks and skilled home cooks run such operations on their days off, using vacant retail spaces, lofts, and apartments, all the while developing both experience and a following in the process. Other creative approaches to entrepreneurship that we encountered include a husband-and-wife chef team who take over a local motel kitchen and dining room at night for dinner service (the motel runs the kitchen during the day) and a country club sous chef who has arranged to use the club's kitchen during downtime to launch his own catering business. Before building a kitchen from the ground up, using a commissary kitchen to develop and produce your food product or start your catering company is a good idea—and one that will save you a lot of money.

Think about the desired size of your business. If you are starting a product or media company, for example, you might be able to operate from space in your home, by yourself, before having to lease out space and hire employees. Depending on what your company sells, you might need to at least get warehousing space, but that's usually less expensive than having to set up an entire office or warehouse. If you want to open a restaurant, you might decide on a twenty-to-thirty-seat operation to get some experience under your belt before thinking about something larger. You can

Food products are a viable way to enter the small business world. Before setting up a large-scale production and distribution system, test the waters by selling your homemade products at local grocery stores and farmers' markets.

start an independent PR firm with nothing more than a computer, phone, and well-cultivated contact list. In many cases, you can begin developing your business idea on the side while still working for a steady paycheck. Freelancing does not apply just to writing; you can be a freelance caterer, stylist, winemaker, and much more, as long as your schedule allows it and you are willing to work two full-time jobs.

While large success is elusive, food products are a viable way to enter the small business world. Before setting up a large-scale production and distribution system, test the waters by selling your homemade products at local grocery stores and farmers' markets. Just make sure to have proper insurance at the very least, since you will be operating out of unlicensed kitchens, which is against state and federal regulations. However, it is not unusual for many small business owners to start that way. The smart way to do it, if you plan on selling a food product or a beverage, is to rent space in a commissary kitchen or use a restaurant or culinary school kitchen when they are closed. Commissary kitchens are licensed spaces ready for commercial production. By renting space in one until you can afford your own kitchen, you will at

Lessons Learned

Dan Hoffman works in finance and spent twenty-two years at Bear Stearns after earning a bachelor's degree in economics and an MBA. He was an investor in Jovia, a short-lived New York restaurant that then became Zoë Townhouse. His path to becoming an investor began with his being a diner, since his business involves a lot of client entertaining. The principal at Zoë, a SoHo restaurant, approached several of his regulars with the idea of opening a midtown restaurant, which he'd manage. Hoffman knew that restaurants are risky businesses but decided to take a chance nonetheless.

"As a customer of the restaurant, I knew it was very risky," Hoffman said. "But I thought that the experience would be good and that it would be fun. You must walk in with your eyes wide open, though, knowing that you won't get a great return on your investment. You need to have real expectations." While saying that this is a labor of love, Hoffman confessed to not being interested in investing in restaurants again in a difficult economic climate. Investments can start at $25,000, he said, but most prospective business owners look for minimums that range between $50,000 and $100,000.

"The most important thing is to have a partner running the restaurant in whom you have a great deal of trust, which I had," he said. "I learned how important location is and how to brand a restaurant for the audience that you want. You have to decide if you are a destination or a neighborhood restaurant. There's also much more to dealing with chef personalities than I initially thought. The chef as artist is very different than the chef as businessman. The chef on the project might not be right for a particular area. If you are a destination restaurant, you need the chef, but you need to see eye to eye with the chef to make sure that the restaurant is successful. Monitoring your costs is very important."

least be operating completely legally. Many companies also exist to help you scale up your product, break down its nutritional and caloric values for the label, produce it, and distribute it. Some specialize in organic, allergen-free, or all-natural products, for example, if that is important to your product. Investigating and interviewing such companies is an essential part of the research you have to do before going on the market with a product, since the costs they'll charge you need to be factored into the price you'll charge for your product.

permits, licenses, and certifications

Obtaining the necessary permits and licenses to open your company is among the most tedious tasks you will have to perform to make your dream come true. It is, however, essential, and trying to take shortcuts will always backfire. The city will put a stop order on your construction site if you or your contractor did not secure the right permits. You will not pass inspection if things are not up to code. You will take a big chance if you choose to operate your catering or food-production business out of an unlicensed kitchen. In many states, if you want to open a cooking school, you'll need to get approval from the state's Department of Education.

The first step to obtaining the right authorization is to work with a licensed contractor for any work that is required in your selected location. It goes without saying, but if you are working with a tight budget you might be tempted to save a few dollars here and there. A reputable contractor (ask around for recommendations) will go a very long way toward making your business happen. The contractor might know if there are zoning issues where you want to open your business that would require you to get a special permit.

A city's office of small business—which can have a different name depending on where you live—will be helpful in navigating the local system and helping you figure exactly what permits and licenses you need to acquire. Take the time to meet with someone in person if you can, to establish a relationship that will be useful as you start running your company—and hopefully expand it. But spending time on the office's website will already give you a great deal of information as you get started.

If you prepare food products, you will need to do so in a licensed facility. Everything in the kitchen will need to be built according to the codes of your city. You will also need to pass an inspection before you can start selling food made there.

Certain types of businesses also require that services be performed by certified employees. ServSafe (www.servsafe.com) is the most commonly required certification in restaurants. It offers food safety and alcohol safety certifications.

expanding your business

Once your company is successful and making money, you can start thinking about expanding it. You first need to establish how much capital you have for this. Even when your business is very successful, you will likely still be paying off your investors, who get a share of the profits before you receive any money, based on the agreement that you originally drew up when launching your company (see "Investing in Restaurants," page 72, for a breakdown of a typical payoff plan). You might not be receiving enough money to be the sole investor in your new company. Your investors might be interested in providing you with more funding, however, particularly since you are successful.

There are many ways of expanding, depending on what type of business you run. If you are a fast-casual restaurant, for example, franchising might make the most sense (see Vaughan Lazar, page 196), since others can cook your recipes without compromising the creative effort that goes into them. If you own a high-end restaurant, opening a more casual one in the same town will be a feasible option, since you can build on your existing name

Investing in Restaurants

Attorney Mark Seelig, directly or through one of his clients, has invested in more than twenty restaurants, in New York and elsewhere in the country. He currently is a direct investor with an interest in three restaurants in New York, NY.

What is a typical range of investment? I've been in restaurant deals where the financial raise is as little as $200,000 and others where it is $10 million. The total amount to open the doors of a small restaurant is typically between $250,000 and $750,000. For a larger type, 150 seats or more, raises can be $2 to $3 million. The problem in New York is that people spend too much money on their build-out and then can't pay rent. They end up with a huge revenue number and a very small profit, because all they do is make their rent. If you have to spend $500,000 to $1 million building a restaurant, you're already in such a big hole that your restaurant, in my view, is doomed to failure. A smart option is to renovate a decent existing space. Start with a moderate restaurant. Don't start with too much debt. The reason that most restaurants fail is that they can't afford to pay their debt.

What makes restaurants a good investment idea? It depends. We're not talking fast food or anything like that. I think that restaurants are a good idea if one goes into it with great operators, a solid operation, and a good concept for a good location. There are restaurants that do phenomenally well. A few do extremely well and are very profitable for their investors. But the vast majority are not very successful for their investors. Restaurants are notoriously not good investments, but they are fun investments.

What do you look for in a new project? I want to hear some of the factors, such as the location, type of food, and price range. I want to understand the location and the type of restaurant planned so I can make a general decision as to whether or not it's going to work. Number two, I want to understand what the rent is. It's the single most important factor in determining if the restaurant is going to die. It's a key factor. Then I want to know who is running the kitchen and who is running the business. If all that works, I would consider an investment. I think that most investors are not as sophisticated about the business. They do it because their friends are involved, they know the chef, it's near their house. So they kick in money. I don't think they ever go beyond those basics to really understand the business. They just write a check for $50,000 or $100,000.

What return should an investor expect? I don't think investors should really ever expect a return on restaurants. I've been doing it for twenty years, for reasons not tied to making money on my investment. They're probably the worst type of venture to invest in. I have dozens of clients who've invested in restaurants, and I think only one has made money. Normally, when restaurant deals are set up, promoters promise the investors that they'll make a 10 to 15 percent return before profits are split. If somebody is seeking investors for $1 million, I'd put together a term sheet that'd say investors should invest $1 million. Then money would be distributed as follows: Investors get a 15 percent return on their money before I get anything. Then we split the profit 90 percent to the investors, 10 percent to me, until they've gotten back 20 percent of their money, then 80-20 until 50 percent, then 50-50, then once they've recouped all of their money they get 25 percent and I get 75. Once the money is recouped the person who put the deal together gets more money. For the most part, though, either the restaurant fails or the investors never recoup all of their money.

recognition and keep an eye on both businesses at once. This is the model that Kelly Liken (page 119) chose. Or growing your business might mean cutting one type of clientele and going only after another, as Lee Jones and his company the Chefs' Garden did (page 231); they decided to sell their specialty produce directly to chefs only, no longer at farmers' markets, in order to avoid being stretched too thin and to focus on doing one thing well. Using a distributor rather than handling sales yourself, as Will Goldfarb elected to do (page 260), is another way to grow—the time you are not spending shipping boxes can be spent marketing your products.

You might also, however, decide not to grow your business beyond a certain capacity. Yes, dreams of national branches of your company are wonderful when everything goes well and you have a profitable year and high demand. But that might not always be the case. The demand might only be there because you carry an exclusive product that is not yet available everywhere at a cheap price, for example. Your restaurant might have a long waiting list

Owning and running a food business is not easy. But as hard as it is, opportunities in the culinary universe are more viable than in other areas. Starting an airline, insurance company, or football team comes with extremely high barriers of entry. Opening a butcher shop, restaurant, or food store is much more doable.

every night, which will make you want to double your number of seats. But will that demand remain once it is easier to get in or in troubled economic times, when customers cut down their dining-out budget? Sometimes it is best to keep your business the way it is—a place where you enjoy going every day that gives you a sense of pride and enough profit for the lifestyle that you want. Or you might decide to expand, but only at the local level, as Ari Weinzweig decided to do with his company Zingerman's Community of Businesses in Ann Arbor, MI (see page 100).

4. LESSONS FROM THE STRATOSPHERE

At a time when more and more food industry professionals have reached superstar status, it becomes tempting for aspiring cooks, writers, and entrepreneurs to aim for careers that will similarly transform their lives. Students in culinary schools sometimes want to see themselves on television or writing bestselling cookbooks more than they want to spend years working their way up the line of a hot restaurant kitchen. The point of this chapter is not to tell you how to land a show on the Food Network or get a book published. Rather, it is to inspire you and give you additional tools to become a better professional by learning from people who have made it to the top of their field. We asked them about their work routine, what they like and dislike about the industry, what lessons they learned throughout their career, and more to give you thoughts to consider as you carve your own niche, whatever it may be.

What do we call the stratosphere? The very small slice of the food industry that offers national, if not international, recognition to those who breathe its rarefied air. Some people who belong to the stratosphere may have aspired to get there, while others found themselves gaining recognition without doing anything more than what they consider their job. Some are on television, others are not. Some are strong advocates for a cause and have gained name recognition that way—Dan Barber (page 90), for example. Others have become known worldwide for their culinary innovation, such as Ferran Adrià or Thomas Keller (page 76). They are recognized for their talent not only by the public but, and perhaps more important, by their peers. They have won countless awards. Their restaurants are the ones that other chefs seek out when they travel. Their articles and books are those that others cite as inspiration and favorite reads. Their hotels are reputed for outstanding service and discreet luxury. Their products have national distribution. They have lasted in this industry—ten, twenty, or thirty years—which is not an easy feat. They constantly receive requests from other food professionals at all levels of their career to come and spend time in their kitchen or business, for free, just to learn. The media contact them on a daily basis for interviews, recipes, tips, and more. They have expanded their businesses without compromising the quality of what they do or their reputation. They are leaders—when they speak, others stop to listen—but they are also willing to admit making mistakes and learn from them. They are mentors: A new generation of culinary professionals wants to emulate them.

One of the key points to remember about the stratosphere, as is made clear by the people interviewed here, is that no one reaches it without years of hard work. Sure, you might think of a food television celebrity or two who became instantly famous without perhaps even working in a restaurant kitchen. Shows like *The Next Food Network Star* propagate that idea. But for the one or two personalities who achieve true success on television, how many do not? And how many are flashes in the pan who will be gone after one short season? The

> "I've taken many risks. The way I go about things is that I believe in what I do and am willing to gamble everything on it. Each new restaurant can potentially bring everything down if we don't run it properly."
> —JOHN BESH

people at the top, such as those in this chapter, have all carefully managed their brand and their growth.

Another point that our interviewees make over and over is to work for and with the best people you can early in your career before setting out on your own, if that's what you wish to do. They advise making whatever sacrifices you can, from sleep to money, in order to work with people who will teach you everything you can learn and become lifelong mentors.

So read these interviews and draw lessons from what these talented, admired professionals have done throughout their career to obtain the success that they have. Emulate them—not because you want to be famous, but because you want to be the best that you can at what you do.

THOMAS KELLER

Thomas Keller is the chef-owner of the French Laundry (Yountville, CA), per se (New York, NY), Bouchon (Yountville and Las Vegas, NV), Bouchon Bakery (Yountville, Las Vegas, and New York), and ad hoc (Yountville). He is also the author of *The French Laundry Cookbook*, *Bouchon*, *Under Pressure*, and *Ad Hoc at Home* and the winemaker for Modicum.

SELECTED AWARDS: Outstanding Restaurateur, Outstanding Restaurant—The French Laundry, Best New Restaurant—per se, Outstanding Service, Outstanding Chef, Best Chef—California, and Who's Who of Food & Beverage in America, James Beard Foundation; America's Best Chef, *Time*; honorary doctor of culinary arts, Johnson & Wales; Chef of the Year, Culinary Institute of America; Cooking for Solutions Conservation Leadership Award, Monterey Bay Aquarium.

What made you decide to become a chef?

There's not one reason but many. When I started to cook, it was the excitement of working with a team, a bunch of guys in a very high-energy kitchen; that was very exciting to me. It wasn't necessarily about the quality of food but about the quality of energy, of the team. The first motivation was my mother getting me involved in being a chef where she worked, then the experience with a team. Then really the pivotal point was in 1977, when I went to work with Roland Henin. He made the emotional connection about nurturing, cooking for people, and that really resonated with me. Also, when I was younger, the ritual of repetition, doing the same thing over and over until you get really good at it, pushing yourself to do it better every day, was really appealing.

To what factors do you attribute your success?

Enjoying rituals and repetitions is one of them, because the way you become good at

things is through practice. Many times in our society, we want to become famous right away, but it happens over time. You have to work at something as artisanal as cooking, whether you are a professional or home cook. To make really good potato gnocchi is not to do it once but to make it time and time again. Another thing is appreciation for teamwork and the effort of the team. Running a restaurant is a big commitment that demands a huge amount of resources. Another thing is evolution—to allow the staff, the team, front and back, to have an impact. Listening, not having to be in control all the time, and having confidence in people is not only liberating but also establishes a process that continues to breed success.

How did you decide to expand your business?

It's all about opportunity. I have to analyze if it's the best opportunity for me. In today's market, with the notoriety of chefs, there's a strong desire to have chefs do projects in different parts of the country.

But to me, it goes back to the team philosophy: I see who on my team has the ability to grow and become ready to help me open a new restaurant. It's giving them a chance to move forward.

What do you like most about what you do?

That repetition, that comfort in doing things over and over again. Now what I enjoy most is giving people opportunities, realizing where they are, embracing them, and making it happen, whether it's cookbooks or opening restaurants. That's very exciting to me.

What do you like least about it?

Disappointing people. Ultimately, as much as we do and as hard as we try, there are people who will be disappointed, whether on the team or guests in the restaurants.

What qualities do you look for in a new hire?

That they have a strong desire to do what you ask them to do. It's not about passion or qualifications. Those things are important too, but it's about having a burning desire in your stomach every day. I love passion too, but it has to be more than passion that will last six months or a year. Desire intensifies that.

What words of advice would you offer someone considering a similar career?

Patience is very important—being patient with who you are and what you are trying to achieve. Persistence is great; so are determination and vision. There are so many pieces of advice to give somebody. As a young cook, you have to realize the many directions in which you can go and be patient with that and learn. The foundations that you are establishing for yourself today are what you build your future on. It's hard to tell somebody how to do that because everybody has their own path. We're all different. You have to be very patient and establish the skill sets that you'll need.

"For me it's an extraordinarily gratifying industry. We can't forget that we are in the hospitality industry. It's all about nurturing people, your staff, your guests. And don't forget to nurture yourself."

DANIEL BOULUD

Daniel Boulud is the chef-owner of Restaurant Daniel, Bar Boulud, DBGB Kitchen & Bar, and Feast & Fêtes Catering (New York, NY); Café Boulud (New York and Palm Beach, FL); DB Bistro Moderne (New York and Vancouver, BC); Daniel Boulud Brasserie (Las Vegas, NV); Maison Boulud (Beijing, China); and Lumière (Vancouver) as well as the author of *Braise: A Journey Through International Cuisine, Daniel's Dish: Entertaining at Home with a Four-Star Chef, Letters to a Young Chef, Chef Daniel Boulud Cooking in New York City, Daniel Boulud's Café Boulud Cookbook, Cooking with Daniel Boulud,* and the bimonthly column "Daniel's Dish" in *Elle Décor.* He is also the host of the web series *After Hours with Daniel.*

SELECTED AWARDS: Outstanding Restaurateur, Outstanding Service, Outstanding Chef, Best Chef—New York City, and Who's Who of Food & Beverage in America, James Beard Foundation; Chevalier de la Légion d'Honneur, France; Culinary Humanitarian Award, Citymeals-on-Wheels.

Why did you become a chef?

Because I like the idea of this sort of artisanal, kind of communal sharing of the making of food. I'm still fascinated by how much we do all day and how much we love what we do. That has never changed. From the beginning, I always enjoyed cooking.

Had you set out to open your own restaurant when you became a chef?

Yes. I thought that I was capable of doing it. Not only was I a good cook and a good chef, but I had a good sense of management and marketing, good relationships with guests and personnel, and I worked very hard. So I'd say I had most of the assets necessary to at least believe it could be a good business model. After that, you need a team. It's not all about you. You need to build a team, and you need to drive everybody into your own destiny, in a way. Some of them fall off the ship on the way and some of them stay. You reinvent yourself all the time. Even for us at Daniel, after ten years, I didn't want to feel that I was running on my reputation.

So we closed the place. We redid everything. We refreshed the entire kitchen. We wanted to change style a little bit, also, and at the same time keep evolving. But the business model was fantastic.

What is your creative process like when you're thinking about new dishes?

It comes from many different things. Usually sitting down with a chef, unless I come up with an idea and I bring it to them. And, of course, the menu is seasonal because we are very market driven. That's always been my life, where we follow the market as much as possible. We sit down before a season and talk about new ideas. We always have a series of specials in each station every day. We taste; we discuss; we talk about the supply, the technique, the taste, what the ingredient is going to go well in and all that, and which station might be able to do it. A dish is one thing, but, for example, I cannot just go to all my restaurants and hand the chef a piece of paper with the recipe made if I'm going to tell the chef to be responsible for his food costs, payroll, menus and everything. We work together. I guide them; I listen; I taste.

What risks have you taken to get where you are?

Investing many millions of dollars, more than ten million, to do Restaurant Daniel. Ten years ago, ten million dollars, that was a big check to sign. My partner trusts me. The most important thing in this business is trust. You need to be surrounded by people you can trust, and you need to be supported by people who trust you also.

At what point did you decide to expand beyond one restaurant?

Right away. I opened Daniel; six months later, I opened the catering company, Feast & Fêtes. Two years later, we opened Payard, which we then sold back to François. Then we opened Café Boulud.

To what factors do you attribute your success?

A great deal of my success is in the following I've built with my clients, which developed based on trust and value for what I was offering. Having four restaurants in New York, and a fifth one soon, many of my customers go from one restaurant to the other with the same support and the same trust and confidence they have in us. But we don't take it for granted either. If anything is going wrong, we are very proactive in fixing the issue. I also attribute my success to the team who works with me; we manage our business very closely, very carefully.

What's important is to never be undercapitalized, because you never know where the business can go. With proper capital, you can maintain your staff and your suppliers. There's nothing worse than when a business cannot pay suppliers. That's the beginning of the end. That's one thing I always insisted on, that the supplier has to be paid on time. We cannot afford not to pay the suppliers. There are too many restaurants that play that game. It's terrible.

In very challenging times, I think that success also comes from being very responsible. We make all our staff responsible for their food costs, their payroll—their success, basically. Every chef, every manager, is responsible for the success of the restaurant. And if he's not interested in making it a success, he's not our chef. It's not all on me. It has a lot to do with the team we build.

What do you like most about what you do?

Cooking and being in the dining room with a guest and watching my service. I'm basically watching the action and also getting involved in it with the chefs, tasting the food of all the team, and evaluating every day. Creating new dishes with the chefs, of course, and discovering new things is exciting. I love talking about food—it's the most interesting thing. Finding beautiful ingredients. I don't think there's a chef who doesn't get emotional when he finds beautiful things. That's where the emotion is for us in the kitchen; what we buy, what we prepare, what we finish will give us the most satisfaction.

What do you like least about it?

When the staff is not up to par, or when you don't feel like you have the full power of what you want to get out of them. That can happen. The most important thing in this business is consistency. That's the most challenging aspect, to have the cook repeat the same dish every day, every minute of the day, all the time, perfectly. If you have a very good cook with a cook who is new at a station, the entire organization will be affected, because one's a little slow in what he does, compared to the other. That's why at Daniel we have junior sous chefs who go around and basically rescue every cook. That's the luxury of a big restaurant.

How do you train your staff?

The chef de cuisine is mostly in charge of coaching his sous chef and his cooks. We keep track of the performance of our cooks. We make sure that they master one thing well before we start to move them around. So if they hope to see every station in the restaurant, they'd better be very good at the first one. Otherwise they're going to get stuck there for a little longer. But that's normal. We want to create a pattern of consistency, trust, and ability, where they have to go through the test of the station, going from the station with the least pressure and that is the least difficult to manage to the station where it is the most difficult. It usually takes a few years to get there, unless the cooks already come in at a certain level.

How many cooks do you have in total?

At Daniel we have about 45. In the group, about 160 cooks.

What do you look for in a new hire?

It all depends. Coming out of culinary school, I'd say it's attitude, it's passion, it's dedication, it's discipline, of course. We want people to be smart but to understand a job. The ability to coordinate quickly under pressure is important. Everybody can play with food, but when there's a business behind it, then you're dealing with cost and you're dealing with payroll and you're dealing with managing a business; it's not a fantasy anymore. Whoever chooses such a job should know that nothing is going to come easily unless they are smart enough to make it work.

What words of advice would you offer someone considering a similar career?

Keep your head down and listen to your chef. You should also want to invest yourself. The groundwork, the base of a chef, is developed when he's a cook, and those first few years are the most important, the ones when the young chef has to invest the most of himself. Also, you want to be able to be challenged and succeed in your challenge. That's how you become a better chef. It might be just to cook for the staff meal: we give you five pounds of ground meat and you make a beautiful dish out of it. If you're a cook and you're paid $20,000 a year and you don't even know how to make a good meat sauce or a curry out of it, if you cannot be spontaneous and creative and make something really good out of it, you haven't studied cooking hard enough. Because, for me, all those cooks who dream of becoming great chefs should really know what the basics are about.

RICK BAYLESS

Rick Bayless is the chef-owner of Topolobampo, Frontera Grill, and XOCO (Chicago, IL); the author of *Mexican Everyday, Rick & Lanie's Excellent Kitchen Adventures, Mexico: One Plate at a Time, Salsas That Cook, Rick Bayless's Mexican Kitchen,* and *Authentic Mexican: Regional Cooking from the Heart of Mexico;* the host of *Mexico: One Plate at a Time* (PBS); and the creator of Frontera Foods.

SELECTED AWARDS: Outstanding Restaurant—Frontera Grill, Humanitarian of the Year, Outstanding Chef, Best Chef—Midwest, and Who's Who of Food & Beverage in America, James Beard Foundation; Cooking Teacher of the Year, *Bon Appétit;* Chef of the Year, International Association of Culinary Professionals; Best New Chef, *Food & Wine.*

What made you decide to become a chef?

I grew up in the restaurant business and tried to get away from it, but it was just in my blood. I was finding myself thinking about cooking more than about anything else I was doing. For the most part, being a chef is very much like being an artist: You don't choose to do it; it chooses you.

What factors have contributed to your success?

It's not something I take lightly. Every single thing I've done in my life has contributed. I studied the culture, the language, and lived in Mexico for years. Then I created my own curriculum of studies, since there was no cooking school that I could attend, and it took me five years to complete it. Then I wrote a book about Mexican cooking. Then I decided that I didn't want to just write, so I opened a restaurant for the real food of Mexico. My whole family was entrepreneurial; nobody worked for anyone else. I used my background in theater and public relations to explain to people what I was doing, why it was important, essential.

Success is also in how you manage people. We are still a family-style enterprise. I have 110 employees right now; those same people are part of my family. We don't have a hierarchy. It creates a very direct relationship between all the people and me. I also chose to open only five days a week, which allows us to maintain the same staff, because the extra days give them time with their family.

What risks do you feel you have taken to get where you are?

The biggest one is that I chose to do a cuisine that no one said could translate to fine dining. And not just fine dining, but the highest level of fine dining, to the point that we've won all the awards that you could win, pretty much. We've proved them wrong.

How often are you still in the kitchen?

I learned a long time ago that I am not a businessman. I run my business tightly, but I don't spend a lot of time on it. I'd rather be in the kitchen. But I don't just do the restaurant—I do cookbooks, television shows, and a product line. Everything is right here, though. From my office, I can be in the restaurant in two minutes.

What qualities do you look for in a new hire?

They have to be able to do the job. But sometimes that's not the most important set of skills. If it's a manual skill and they don't quite have it, but they have something else—a passion for what we do, for working with local products—I will often give them a chance to come into our kitchen and learn the manual skills. Then I have a person on my staff who is really perfect for us. Passion is something you can't train.

What do you like most about what you do?

I like eating. That's what I like to do the most, and it's always been my inspiration for what I do. There are chefs who do beautiful food all night and then go and have a double cheeseburger and a light beer. I couldn't do that for love or money. I want everyone on my staff to eat our food. I would never want them to feel like they are doing great food and then go and have peanut butter and jelly after service.

What do you like least about it?

Virtually nothing. I love my job; I really love my job. Sometimes, like right now, because I am involved in so many different things, my schedule gets jammed up because I have to do so many things at one time, or things are due all at the same time. Sometimes it will all come crashing down on me at the same moment. I'm really dedicated to my family, and I get mad if work gets in the way of doing something with my family.

What is your process like when creating a new dish?

It can start from many places. I may have eaten something in another restaurant that I really liked. I wouldn't do the same thing, but I start with what captured me in that dish. That's what I call a translation process. If I were to translate that in the vernacular of my kitchen, what would it look like? A dish is not an independent thing. It's a communication device. For most of us, food is not art that stands alone; it's art that communicates directly between the chef and the diner. What impact will it have on the people? When I send the dish down, how are they going to immediately react to it? Which part of the dish will they first put their fork in? A large part of our dishes is the sauce—what will the sauce do for them? We think about this in the kitchen when we are developing the menu.

What words of advice would you offer someone considering a similar career?

I don't think it's really wise for somebody to go straight from high school to culinary school. They haven't developed enough. Go to college, at least for a couple of years. Study something unrelated but preferably in the arts. The more sophisticated you are at evaluating art, the better you will be as a chef. Then, on top of that, I can't emphasize enough working as a cook in other countries. That will give you the perspective that you need. That will broaden your vision. It's almost impossible to do that working in a restaurant.

JOHN BESH

John Besh is the chef-owner of Restaurant August, Besh Steak, La Provence, Lüke, and Domenica (New Orleans, LA) and the author of *My New Orleans: The Cookbook,* and *The New Orleans Program.*

SELECTED AWARDS: Best Chef—Southeast, James Beard Foundation; Best Chef, *New Orleans*; Best New Chef, *Food & Wine.*

What made you decide to become a chef?

My upbringing was focused on family, hunting, fishing, and cooking; they all go together perfectly. I love making people happy, and growing up in a house with great cooks, I realized early on that great food makes people happy. I started cooking when I was quite young—just nine or ten—and was encouraged by my family to pursue this passion.

To what factors do you attribute your success?

Throughout my career, I've had the opportunity to learn from so many people. Starting out, it was my family. Later, I was fortunate to learn classical techniques in the mountains of the Black Forest in Germany and in southern France, and I developed a real appreciation for local ingredients. I also found mentors there, and also throughout my career, who have helped me to develop my skills in the kitchen, as a manager, and as a restaurateur. I've learned a lot about how to take care of not just my staff and my customers but also my community.

How did you decide on expanding your business?

After restaurant number one, which was August, it took me exactly four years to the date to open restaurant number two. It was just across the street, in partnership with Harrah's Entertainment—it was a safe way for me to segue into multiple operations. It was a great learning experience. When expanding, you need to learn how to divide your time, organize yourself, and move to thinking like an executive chef and restaurateur as opposed to a chef just going through each day. It's about hiring the right people, the type of person to whom hospitality comes naturally. If we are all on the same wavelength as to how hospitality works, how to make people happy, the rest comes easily. Over the years, after having enough of those people move through the ranks, there comes a time when they are ready to do something on their own. About the time we were looking at opening restaurant number three, Hurricane Katrina happened. It changed everything and gave me a new perspective on life. I paid off my investors; I was really out there all by my lonesome. The staff bailed me out. For a time, we all lived in the restaurant; it became the cornerstone of the neighborhood. Ultimately, I made a deal with all these guys and gals who kept us in business, saying I'd invest in them, support what they needed when they were ready to open their own business. The chefs at my restaurants have been with me through the best of times and the worst of times. In this day and age when things are so credit despondent, most young chefs can't get financial support, so we can help them open a restaurant. Each one of our chefs has a percentage of the restaurant, which is large enough to keep them there. We've amassed a great team over the years.

How much further do you want to expand your business?

We've already exhausted our growth strategy; we're there. We have this beautiful incubator of great restaurants that are attracting young men and women who are very talented. I'm at the point where I don't want to fool people into thinking that I am in every restaurant all the time. I am attached to August: When not trying to sell a book or doing a TV show, I am in that kitchen. I want to really make an impact on not just the restaurant community but the community as a whole in New Orleans. I'm achieving some of that. I have no huge plan of massive expansion. But I've also voted against gambling once in my life, so I'll never say never.

What do you like most about what you do?

Making people happy. That's the greatest thing in the world. We all have different gifts, different talents. My talent is cook-

ing food and making people happy. That I get to do that brings me the most joy.

What do you like least?

Being pulled away from what I love the most. Things that make you famous at the same time pull you away from what you really like doing. I have a great passion for just being in the kitchen. I have to go in really early in the morning, turn off my cell phone, and remove myself from the world to practice cooking.

What qualities do you look for in a new hire?

I look first and foremost for somebody with a hospitable nature. Somebody who is at ease looking at you and talking to you. Somebody who is poised about life, about food, about restaurants, about people. If you are not a people person, you're probably not going to do very well in our organization. You need to love being around people. Do you love having people over? Do you pour them a drink when they arrive to your house? Do you pull a chair for a lady? I ask if that person will fit into the culture we are trying to grow.

What risks have you taken throughout your career?

I've taken many risks. The way I go about things is that I believe in what I do and am willing to gamble everything on it. Each new restaurant can potentially bring everything down if we don't run it properly. I don't have financial investors; it's just me and the little bank down the street. We are committed to the business. We are in the business of making people happy and we gamble everything on that.

What made you decide to not have investors and do it all on your own?

I felt really vulnerable after Hurricane Katrina. There's the perception that everything material can be lost at any time. So it made me realize that I need to be as independent as I can, to run my business as I wish. The big deterrent is that having all your eggs in one basket in one city runs huge risks. But at the end of the day, I have only myself to blame and myself to thank. I can run a business the way I think it can be run. That is worthwhile to me. Being as independent as possible is then a blessing, because I managed to get myself relatively out of debt. With each restaurant, we pay our debt off before any profit sharing. Paying debt off is a huge weight lifted off your shoulders. I'm not overextended; I'm really careful about what I do and how I do it. I have a loan from a bank that I can pay back. They know where I am and what I do. I am part of the city and committed to the city. They have the same approach to what I do.

What words of advice would you offer someone considering a similar career?

It's important to set time aside to truly dedicate yourself to cooking, perfecting your craft, and developing your understanding of the business of being a chef. Work for several chefs that you'd like to emulate one day, without regard to pay.

LIDIA BASTIANICH

Lidia Bastianich is the chef-owner of Felidia, Becco, Esca, and Del Posto (New York, NY) and Lidia's (Pittsburgh, PA, and Kansas City, MO); the founder and president of Tavola Productions; the co-owner of Bastianich Vineyards and La Mozza Vineyards in Italy; and the co-owner of a travel company. She's also the host of the cooking shows *Lidia's Italy*, *Lidia's Italian-American Kitchen*, and *Lidia's Family Table* on PBS and the author of *La Cucina di Lidia*, *Lidia's Italian Table*, *Lidia's Italian-American Kitchen*, *Lidia's Family Table*, and *Lidia's Italy*.

SELECTED AWARDS: Best Chef in New York and Outstanding Chef, James Beard Foundation; Wine Spectator's Grand Award; one of the 100 Most Influential Businesswomen in New York, *Crain's Business*.

What made you decide to become a chef?

My love for food and being able to communicate with food. I express myself with food, I give pleasure and affection with food. It started with my family. I received love through food with my mom and my grandmother; I am just perpetuating it.

What prompted you to open your own business?

The challenge of doing something that you love for somebody, for the direction of somebody, is all good, but at some point you want to take your own direction. Owning a restaurant gave me that freedom.

And later, to expand your business to the number of restaurants you have today?

It was to respond to a genuine need for our products. If you are genuinely very busy, when your product could reach more people who long for it, you analyze that opportunity and then respond to it. You need to have business savvy and the mind to execute it. You need to give it a lot of thought, when you go from having one restaurant

where you are the chef and are present all the time to dividing it and having another. My strength was also my family, who knew the philosophy of my business and were involved; that was also part of the thrust to move it forward.

How did your TV show come to be?

I was told I was a great communicator and teacher. I love to communicate, as you can tell. My first experience was with Julia Child; I did two half-hour episodes of *Master Chefs*. After working with the camera, I realized at the end that I could do it. I knew that I could reach more people by being on television. Julia Child's producer came to me and said, "You are really good. Do you want to have your own show?" I said yes, but that I would want it to be on PBS, because of the integrity and reality of passing on information it would afford me.

What did being on TV do to your career?

It's been tremendous. America is based on marketing, advertising, and so on. Being on TV constantly gives me new opportunities. It allows me to extend my knowledge and my passion to the viewing audience. That's a pretty big reward and feeling when you know that someone in Indianapolis has cooked the soup that Lidia taught. I become part of their home.

To what factors do you attribute your success?

I attribute it to lots of hard work done with passion, much commitment, a great deal of research—and humbly.

What do you like most about what you do?

I'm having a grand time. It's been thirty-seven years and I still love it. I'm still challenged by it. I love to give pleasure to people. I just think it's grand. It might even be a maternal instinct. I'm nurturing America with my food.

What risks have you taken, from a business perspective, to get where you are?

The first one was opening the little restaurant. I was twenty-four, not a professional chef but I loved cooking. I borrowed money from my mother. It was just me and my husband. We enlarged, opened another restaurant. At the end of ten years, in 1981, I really became a professional chef—I had been the sous chef. We wanted to open a restaurant where I'd be a chef, so we bought the building that houses Felidia. We sold the two restaurants we had, leveraged everything into Felidia, and found out about everything that needed to be fixed. We almost didn't make it. That came out of a bit of inexperience. Once Felidia took off, I was more cautious.

What lessons have you learned along the way?

Good planning is important. You have to do diligent market research. Put competent people on your team. Be respectful of your employees, who should be as enthusiastic about the project as you are.

What qualities do you look for in a new hire?

I look for somebody who is enthusiastic and passionate. I would say that the overall qualities someone should have are passion, enthusiasm, and a good amount of experience. I want to see their eagerness, that they believe in the same philosophy of food that I believe in—seasonality, simplicity. I can teach, but I need their excitement and their energy.

What words of advice would you offer someone considering a similar career?

You need to know if this is something you want to dedicate your life to. There is no question in my mind that I gave it my all because I'm passionate. Then you have to be able to sacrifice whatever it takes. Along the way, you should look for rewards—accolades or financial—because you need to feed yourself periodically. You need to hold the course. You need to surround yourself with competent and smart people. You need great editors to be at your side. I wasn't a great writer, and I write pretty well thanks to my editors now. You need to continuously be ahead of the curve, research, and anticipate. It's never finished, it's always evolving. And be a leader.

DAVID CHANG

David Chang is the chef-owner of Momofuku Noodle Bar, Momofuku Ssäm Bar, Momofuku Ko, Momofuku Milk Bar, and Má Pêche (New York, NY). He is also the author of *Momofuku,* which was published in 2009.

SELECTED AWARDS: Best New Chef, *Food & Wine*; Chef of the Year, *Bon Appétit*; Chef of the Year, *GQ*; Best New Restaurant for Ssäm Bar, *New York Times*; Rising Star Chef, Best Chef—New York City, Best New Restaurant—Ko, James Beard Foundation; three stars for Ko, *New York Times*; two stars for Ko, *Michelin Guide*.

Why did you become a chef?

I chose this career because cooking is honest work. Even though now, with television shows, it's totally different. Cooking is one of the few things you can learn with your hands. You learn this craft that can be traced back to a few hundred years ago; you could trace a dish you're cooking today to the Troisgros brothers. That makes me very excited. The consistency of food, the creation of food, makes me very excited. I didn't plan on being the chef that I am today. Cooking was honest when I first came to it. There was a level of integrity and purity to it, at the time when I got into it, 1999, that I haven't really seen since.

What made you decide to open your own restaurant?

I didn't think I was good enough to be a three-star or four-star chef. The goal has always been to serve the best food possible that's both affordable and tasty. I can just tell you that nothing was ever really planned. You don't go out and open up the restaurant that we did—in the way that we did—thinking that anything would happen. It's an anomaly.

To what factors do you attribute your success?

It was a progression of accidents. All we ever admit to is that we try very hard, we work very hard, and we try to learn from our mistakes. We make lots of mistakes. It's a very organic process. And it's turning into kind of a joke. It's been strange. Being in the right place at the right time—that's pretty much it. We've had a lot of luck, a lot of good people involved. Being in New York certainly helps, and that's where I worked the most. I had a network of friends and chefs who were very supportive. Cooking has gotten better in other cities, but this is the only place with such a high level of scrutiny. It's a team effort. That's the one misconception about the whole chef bullshit. It's not me; it's a whole team of people. I'm just a mouthpiece for it.

What do you look for in a new hire?

We just hope that they have the right skill sets. We can teach them the kitchen skills, but do they have the integrity, the tenacity, the moral compass, the ability to take on problems? Can they get back at it when they fail? We have over 150 staff members.

What are your long-term goals?

I think open in other places. Right now we're dealing with growth, and that's very hard in general. We would we like to open a location in another city, surely, but we're not doing it if it sucks. It has all happened very fast to me. I'll be thirty-two in August and will have spent five years on these projects. We'll take it as far as we can go. The more successful we become, the more we just want to maintain consistency. The role of a chef is very different than it once was. It's not just confined to the kitchen. I wouldn't just want to be in the kitchen because I'd go crazy. That's why I want to do this. In a lot of ways, having restaurants is like having children. You have to take care of them; they are living, breathing organisms; sometimes you get angry at them and sometimes they make you so happy. Sometimes you can be frustrated to all hell. It's all the good and the bad, all wrapped up in one. It's the hardest, most difficult industry that you can enter.

What do you like most about what you do?

I don't know if I enjoy it. That's the straight-up truth. The only thing that makes me happy is when I am able to provide something to other people that will better their lives. When you're working, it's not just about amassing gobs of money, it's about doing something good with it and making your job worthwhile. It's not just this faceless company.

I'm trying to work less and less, because these restaurants have affected my health quite a bit, and that's always a big concern. I don't work the line anymore; I don't work the pass. It's less physical and more mental.

Describe your creative process.

Creating a new dish usually happens through a series of mistakes. You take a raw idea and continue to shape and inform it to see what happens.

What words of advice would you offer someone considering a similar career?

Just be reckless. What happened to us was just by chance; it truly was. It just happened. A lot of it was deemed just lucky. Know the odds; know that you are going to fail, that the percentages, the odds, are against you. We were not going to let any of that be an excuse for failure. Failure was not an option. Be willing to sacrifice anything. That's the thing that matters the most. You have to be willing to sacrifice everything.

"Why try to be mediocre? I guess I just want to be the best at what I do. The intent was just to open one restaurant. Everything else is just gravy."

DAN BARBER

Dan Barber is the executive chef and co-owner of Blue Hill (New York, NY) and Blue Hill at Stone Barns (Pocantico Hills, NY).

SELECTED AWARDS: Outstanding Chef, Best Chef—New York City, and Who's Who of Food & Beverage in America, James Beard Foundation; Best New Chef, *Food & Wine.*

What made you decide to become a chef?

I wanted to write a novel. I ended up taking a bread-baking job so I could write during the day and bake bread at night. I never thought about when I would sleep. Then I realized I wanted to work more during the day. Working at night was okay too, but not in the middle of the night. I became more serious about cooking. I love the physicality of it.

To what factors do you attribute your success?

I attribute the success of Blue Hill to the awakening and consciousness of America, of the general public, of eaters wanting to know where their food comes from. What Blue Hill has done successfully is talk about these issues in a way that is inviting and inspiring and makes food ultimately more delicious than if you are not thinking about that. We owe a great debt to people in the media, to people who became leaders in talking about agriculture and put this topic on the center of people's plates. This is what makes what we're doing appear more valuable than it otherwise would be in a different era. I really believe that. It's not false modesty. If I had started Blue Hill fifteen years ago, it would have been much less successful.

How do you know when you are ready to be a chef-owner?

That's such a hard question. I don't know that I felt ready to do it on my own. There are so many factors that go into play, in terms of timing in your own life. If the feeling is "I'm going to wait until I know I'm ready," you're never going to be ready. A sign of maturity or nodding to maturity, the sign of a good chef, is that the chef never feels ready. He always wants to work a little bit more with one other chef, wants to know a little bit more about one other culture. It's a sign of humbleness and ambition. If you are 100 percent sure, you probably aren't ready. The more chefs you work for, the more you realize you don't know. That's the reality, the cruelness of the learning experience. You're always pushing that rock up the hill, it's going to roll down, and you're going to push it back up again.

What do you like most about what you do?

The people who have been there since the beginning.

What do you like least about it?

The transience of the business. Cooks, waiters move around a lot. I like the core team that we have and that stays with us for a long time. That's my biggest pleasure, working with people who were with us when we started. But with much of the staff—like the cooks who come for a year or two and then move on—there's a feeling of always starting over, and that can be very frustrating. I find it particularly painful because I get very attached to people.

What lessons have you learned along the way?

I feel like I tend to hit people on the head with the theme of sustainable agriculture, and what I learned is that there are many points of entry. People can learn about food by being in a specific environment; it can be unconscious learning, in a way. I tend to be impatient or very blunt with the message. I've been successful, so I'm happy, but I could probably have handled what we do at times with a little bit of a softer hand.

What qualities do you look for in a new hire?

Hunger. How hungry are you? Have you been really successful before? If you have, I'm not really interested. I'm more interested in the person who's hungry. I think my job is to provide the tools and the access to get that success. Our kitchen is egoless and includes a lot of things that people, including me, have to be modest about. Ego and cockiness don't result in better food; they result in a less spirited environment.

Describe your creative process.

I find that my creative process is at its most productive when I'm most restricted, when I have very little to work with—in the winter, or at different times during the year when there is a slower harvest or there's been bad weather. I never figure out why that is. It's often frustrating to have less choice, but that frustration just as much becomes a creative dish. We create 90 percent of the dishes in the middle of service. We're reacting to pressure. I'm not the kind of guy who thrives on pressure, but I would argue that cooks cook best under pressure. When I expedite, I tend to yell; I want to make sure that there is a good clip in the kitchen. The times when you have tension in your work are the times when you do your best. I don't know why this tension leads to better-tasting dishes, better food, but that's an ironclad rule to me.

What words of advice would you offer someone considering a similar career?

Get obsessed with becoming a craftsman. A craftsman knows not just how to put together a piece of wood, but he knows the right wood, the weather conditions, the right tool, a particular arrangement of the wood, all this stuff. It's knowing these details that are crucial in any craft. I keep saying "craft" because people keep saying "art" and I really disagree with that. I see the emotion in that, but I keep considering it more of a craft. Craft is something you have to know and become proficient in, something that raises you above the common denominator and makes you successful.

"To be an expert, to be very proficient, is often a low commodity."

GALE GAND

Gale Gand is the executive pastry chef and a partner at Tru as well as a partner in Nacional 27 and a consultant for Tramonto's Steak and Seafood, RT Lounge, and more, all in Chicago, IL. She's also currently the host of *The Answered Chef* (answerstv.com) and *The Heirloom Recipe Project* (a recently completed pilot for PBS) and hosted *Sweet Dreams* on the Food Network from 2000 to 2008. Gale Gand is the author of *American Brasserie; Butter, Sugar, Flour, Eggs; Gale Gand's Just a Bite; Gale Gand's Short and Sweet; Chocolate and Vanilla;* and *Gale Gand's Brunch.*

SELECTED AWARDS: Outstanding Pastry Chef, James Beard Foundation; Pastry Chef of the Year, *Bon Appétit*; Best New Chef, *Food & Wine.*

What made you decide to become a chef?

I was a classic starving art student. I decided to waitress for the free family meal. One day a line cook didn't show up. I knew the whole menu from describing it in detail to the customers, so they threw an apron at me and said, "Get in the kitchen." I was nineteen at the time. I was terrified. I had no dreams of being a chef; it was the 1970s, and it was perceived as blue-collar work. Wolfgang Puck hadn't legitimized it yet. My mother was a feminist, so it almost was a disgrace to my family to be in the kitchen. I went in the kitchen with ambivalence for about five seconds. At about second six, I felt this sense of calm come over me. It was as if I was coming home to a place I didn't know was my home. It was almost like a calling. I continued painting for another eight years. As a gift to myself for my twenty-seventh birthday, I gave myself permission to cook full-time.

To what factors do you attribute your success?

I return all my phone calls, I answer all my e-mails, and I always say thank you. Some of it is etiquette; some of it is getting back to people who want something from you, like a recipe. I was always very conscientious about getting things to people when they needed it. They say 51 percent of it is showing up—I'm the one who shows up and gets back to people. I was also at the right place at the right time; I was a female in the industry when it became interesting and acceptable. It also helped that I am not in New York, because often media want people from outside of New York. And I think because I'm still happy in my work and I love it so much, I'm still good at it.

How did your TV show come to be?

It was a big deal that they wanted to have a show completely dedicated to pastry on the Food Network. They struggled with whom to have as host. A lot of pastry chefs were French with strong accents. I was lucky that I fit their criteria. Nowadays, people have this goal to have a TV show, and it's just not possible. In 2000, when I did it, the Food Network just approached me. I didn't have to send in any tapes. They wanted someone who could teach, cook well, and be comfortable on camera. I had been on Sara Moulton's show, on *Chef du Jour*, and on *Ready Set Cook*. I used to call Food Network when I was going to be in New York for something else and ask if I could be on Sara's show. I realized they always said yes, so I started calling even if I had nothing else going on in New York. Then once they said no: "We don't have any spots for you on Sara's show. We want to offer you your own show."

What did being on TV do to your career?

It does something that nothing else can do. It completely changed the angle of the trajectory of my career. It legitimized me in a way that nothing else did. I will never be able to thank them enough.

Is that why you want to get back on TV?

I like being on television because it's a great way to teach. I teach cooking classes and I reach a couple of hundred people, but I can touch a lot of people on television. At my restaurant I reach a hundred people a night versus thirty thousand every day whom I can teach how to make a cobbler.

What do you like most about what you do?

I like how it connects people. I love how it connects me with people in an emotional, almost intimate way—a communion of sorts. I like seeing textures and temperatures contrasting; I like the creative part. It's so multidimensional. The craft, the art, the chemistry, the physics, the entertainment, the social aspect—it's got everything. Then I just like the eating part.

What do you like least about it?

The isolation from your family. I tell people, when they first get in the field, to tell their family to not expect them on holidays, that they will be late for normal events. You have to withdraw from society to join the club. I've been lucky to be able to balance the two, but it's taken decades. I think it's generally getting better in the industry, though.

What lessons have you learned along the way?

Make your mistakes on other people's money. If you can do openings with other people's projects, that's great. It always works out in the end. In the face of problems you have to think that you can solve everything.

What words of advice would you offer someone considering a similar career?

I always recommend wearing comfortable shoes. If your feet hurt, you won't look happy, you won't feel happy, and you will forget to say thank you when you should. Also have an attitude of always saying yes. If someone asks you to make croissants and you don't know how, go home that night, learn how to make them, and by the next morning you will know. That way when you get in the next day, you will not be lying. Also know how to help. Ask around in the kitchen: "What can I do for you? What do you need next?" Because of that attitude, I was always welcomed in kitchens in France, for example. Don't be too proud; be willing to do anything in the kitchen, and you will learn everything that way.

FRANÇOIS PAYARD

François Payard is the pastry chef–owner of FP Chocolates, Payard Pâtisserie & Bistro (New York, NY, 1997–2009), and Payard (Las Vegas, NV; Shibuya, Ikebukuro, and Yokohama, Japan; Seoul, Korea; and Rio de Janeiro, Brazil), as well as the author of *Chocolate Epiphany, Bite Size,* and *Simply Sensational Desserts.*

SELECTED AWARDS: Outstanding Pastry Chef, James Beard Foundation; Pastry Chef of the Year, *Bon Appétit*; Ordre du Mérite Agricole, France; Award of Excellence, *Wine Spectator*; Best Pastry Chef, Relais Desserts.

What made you decide to become a chef?

I think it was to follow a family tradition. I grew up in a pastry shop. I saw my grandparents do it, worked in their pastry shop one summer for fun, and I'm still here. My parents didn't want me to become a pastry chef at the beginning because to be a pastry chef, to have your own business, you become a slave to it. It takes a lot of work to be successful. It takes a lot out of you and it takes a lot out of your family. You have to be there all the time. It is best to realize that the easiest part of it is the cooking; the most difficult part is dealing with all the everyday problems.

To what factors do you attribute your success?

Every day you have to put yourself on the line and try to improve. I never take my success for granted. I still work six days a week. New York City is the most challenging place in the world. One day you can be on top, but staying on top, keeping up, is a challenge you face every single day. People come to see you perform, and you have to make sure you're on point every day for them.

What risks do you feel you have taken to get where you are?

When opening a place, even if you think you know your market, your neighborhood, it's always a challenge because you have to wait for the response of the clients. They are the ones judging you every day. With a restaurant, it also depends where you are. Location, location, location, and the clients' response determines the success of your concept. You have to adapt your concept to your neighborhood. When I opened InTent [a Mediterranean restaurant in SoHo], I thought it would work, but for that area it was too much; we should have done something much simpler. We all make mistakes.

What lessons have you learned along the way?

You have to be open-minded and listen to the response of the clients, what their needs are, rather than trying to impose things onto them. Even if you know what you want, the neighborhood itself has its own needs. At the beginning you have to be a little bit flexible.

What do you like most about what you do?

I love when I have a chance to spend the whole day in the kitchen and not think about the headaches of the business. I was just making desserts for a party we have tonight, for example. Another good part is when you have a chance to travel with many people from the food industry and learn about new ingredients that you don't get in New York. I like traveling to Thailand with local chefs and critics and learning a great deal, or traveling to Las Vegas and seeing who has new ideas and new concepts.

What do you like least about it?

The everyday headaches of the business. If I only had to think about making cakes, it'd be easy. The most difficult thing is to deal with people fighting and other personnel conflicts.

What qualities do you look for in a new hire?

I look for people who are very, very dedicated. It doesn't matter if they have little experience, as long as they care about my work, about the place, and want to prove something to me. That's better than people who think they know everything and have nothing to learn from me. I'd rather train someone.

What words of advice would you offer someone considering a similar career?

You have to find your voice, follow your path, and discover what you want to do. You have to try to be more creative than others. But doing things that are less complicated, more rustic, can be easier and give you fewer headaches.

> "It takes a lot of work to be successful. It takes a lot out of you and it takes a lot out of your family. You have to be there all the time. It is best to realize that the easiest part of it is the cooking; the most difficult part is dealing with all the everyday problems."

RUTH REICHL

Ruth Reichl was the editor in chief of *Gourmet* magazine and is the author of *Not Becoming My Mother, Garlic and Sapphires, Comfort Me with Apples,* and *Tender at the Bone.* She is also the editor of the Modern Library Food Series and several *Gourmet* books, the executive producer of *Gourmet's Diary of a Foodie* (PBS), and the host of *Gourmet's Adventures with Ruth* (PBS).

SELECTED AWARDS: Television Show (twice), Newspaper Restaurant Review or Critique (twice), Newspaper Feature Reporting, and Who's Who of Food & Beverage in America, James Beard Foundation; Elizabeth Cutter Morrow Award, YWCA; Editor of the Year, *Adweek;* Missouri Honor Medal for Distinguished Service in Journalism, Missouri School of Journalism; Matrix Award for Magazines, New York Women in Communications Inc.; and numerous awards from the Association of American Food Journalists.

What made you decide to become a writer?

I kind of fell into it. I got out of graduate school and I couldn't find a job that I liked. I was living on the Lower East Side in a loft, and all my friends came over to eat all the time. One said, "You're such a good cook, you ought to write a cookbook," and I did. This was before the big cookbook revolution, so when I went to a publisher and said I had this idea, they said yes and published it. Then when it came out, people said I was a food writer. It'd be impossible today. It was 1971 and I was twenty-two years old. They thought that a cookbook by a young person might be successful. They gave me a $10,000 advance, which was enough for me to live on for a year.

To what factors do you attribute your success?

One, I was just lucky. I was interested in food at a time when many people weren't. I specialized in food at just the right time. Two, I really, really loved what I was doing. Three, I had imagination. My first restaurant reviews were like short stories with reviews sort of woven into them. They developed a cult following, so when the *Los Angeles Times* looked for a reviewer, I was the person they came to. I've also always been a very hard worker. I am constantly working. I like to work. I feel that working is a privilege. I love what I do. I've never worked for money. Everything I've done is because I want to do it, not because somebody's paid me to do it. No job has ever felt like a job to me. I'm sort of always pushing the boundary, wondering how much better we can do what we do, how we can change it.

What are some of the things that define you as a writer?

Because of my background, I have been describing flavors to myself for a long time, since I was a little kid. I think that I have a great ability to make people taste what I'm tasting, without using words like "delicious" to describe food. I also have a good sensory imagination. And I think I'm honest, in a way. I'm not embarrassed about putting myself out there. You have to earn the right to put yourself out there. I started with these kind of short stories, which were very fanciful. When I went to the *Los Angeles Times,* I had been writing these fictional things, and suddenly I realized that I had to produce journalism, that I couldn't make things up. So I had to find a new way to do that. That's when I started writing very personal reviews.

What did you like most about working at *Gourmet*?

I loved almost everything about my job. There is nothing more collaborative than running a magazine; it's a real group effort. I liked the process of all of us getting together and thinking about making it as good as it possibly could be. It's really exciting to be in the creative process with talented people whom you truly respect.

What did you like least about it?

Management. I had fiftysomething people who worked for me. Management is really hard, especially if you always want people to be happy. With so many people, there was always someone who was not.

What risks have you taken to get where you are?

I don't think you can run a good magazine without being willing to take many risks. I was very clear when I became the editor of *Gourmet* that the magazine was not going to be a magazine for only a few wealthy people. We were going to expand the boundaries and explore different issues in food. The first piece we ran about Thomas Keller, he talked about killing rabbits and how badly he did it the first time. That story was amazing because he was talking about how this experience that was so horrible for him made him a cook, made him understand that food is life itself. I thought it was a really important part of that piece, but it terrified me to put it in there. My sense is that I've printed a lot of stories that have scared me and it's always those that are the ones most worth doing.

What words of advice would you offer someone considering a similar career?

First of all, be sure that you are doing what you want to be doing. When you are young, you have the choice of what you want to do, and it's really important to follow your passion. You should aim to work toward something that will give you pleasure. Work hard and think of creative ways to do the job that you do. How can you stand out from the pack? What can you do that's different from what other people are doing? Think about what you can do that is needed and isn't there.

> "I took this job because I didn't have the faintest idea how to do it and thought, 'This is really going to be fun.' That's the great joy and the challenge. If you think that you are ready to do something you probably aren't."

MICHAEL RUHLMAN

Michael Ruhlman is the author of *Ratio, The Elements of Cooking, The Reach of a Chef, The Soul of a Chef* (which won the International Association of Culinary Professionals Literary Food Award), *The Making of a Chef, House, Walk on Water, Wooden Boats,* and *Boys Themselves,* and the coauthor of *Michael Simon's Live to Cook, Ad Hoc at Home, Under Pressure, Charcuterie, Bouchon, A Return to Cooking,* and *The French Laundry Cookbook.*

SELECTED AWARDS: Magazine Feature Without Recipes, James Beard Foundation; Bert Greene Journalism Award, International Association of Culinary Professionals.

What made you decide to become a writer?

I set my sights on it when I was in fifth grade. I always liked the process of writing; it felt comfortable. My body is sort of designed to do it. I think that anybody can want to write and can do it well if they can sit still for hours every day, six days a week. It's a craft, just like cooking. Some people learn the craft well, and others don't because they don't spend enough time doing it. I like both the act of writing and having written. I enjoy the process of generating stories. It feeds me. You need to train your body and your mind to deliver the goods every day at the same time. I found that I get depressed if I don't do that. I try to sit down at my desk at seven thirty A.M., write from eight thirty to eleven thirty, then again from three P.M. to six. This is my schedule when I'm unimpaired by children, travel, or reporting.

To what factors do you attribute your success?

Luck. The inability to do anything else, and the fear of failure, of poverty. But luck in a number of ways. I happened to write at the right time, when this country began to awake to food. Luck in that I had a sense and a knack for writing about food and translating that into other passions that people could relate to. Luck for the fact that I live in Cleveland. If not for that, I wouldn't have been able to write *The French Laundry Cookbook.* I bumped into Susie Heller, who lived in Cleveland at the time and ran a restaurant, and went to introduce myself. She was testing recipes for the book, and they were looking for a writer.

What risks do you feel you have taken to get where you are?

Fairly substantial ones. The biggest one was renting our house in Cleveland and moving my wife and infant daughter to Hyde Park before the Culinary Institute of America had agreed to let me do anything. The reason I wrote that book that quickly was because we were going to run out of money. I asked my wife how long we could last, she said four months, so I wrote the book in four months. It changed everything.

What lessons have you learned along the way?

That you can accomplish a hell of a lot more than you ever thought possible, and that you can do it better and faster than you thought possible. That's the biggest lesson. I learned this from cooking. When you learn to cook well, you come away with many lessons that translate to life. That's why I wish that all of America would go to culinary school before they do anything else.

What do you like most about what you do?

What's not to like? I get to work with some of the best chefs in the country. I get to eat in the best restaurants; I get to work from home; I get to work with my wife. I'm so lucky in so many ways.

What do you like least about it?

Writing proposals for publishers. I hate the proposal process. You have to write a really convincing proposal for a publisher to take you on.

Describe your creative process.

The creative process really just demands that you be open, ask questions, and pay attention to things outside yourself. You allow your unconscious to generate material by writing at the same time every day. That's a big part of my creative process—routine. Routine is critical to making the writing work.

What words of advice would you offer someone considering a similar career?

Learn how to write, and follow your passion. You have to generate a certain amount of words until you figure out how to write. Learn how to write a compelling sentence, then a sensible paragraph through that. Learn to write a compelling story that will interest strangers. What stranger cares enough to read what you think? You always have to ask yourself that.

ARI WEINZWEIG

Ari Weinzweig is a founding partner of Zingerman's Community of Businesses (Zingerman's Delicatessen, Zingerman's Bakehouse, ZingTrain, Zingerman's Catering & Events, Zingerman's Mail Order, Zingerman's Creamery, Zingerman's Road House, Zingerman's Coffee Company) in Ann Arbor, MI, and the author of *Zingerman's Guide to Good Olive Oil, Zingerman's Guide to Good Vinegar, Zingerman's Guide to Good Parmigiano-Reggiano, Zingerman's Guide to Giving Great Service,* and *Zingerman's Guide to Good Eating.*

SELECTED AWARDS: Who's Who of Food & Beverage in America, James Beard Foundation; Lifetime Achievement Award, *Bon Appétit.*

What made you decide to open your own business?

I really just stumbled into it. I studied Russian history at the University of Michigan. When I graduated, I knew I didn't want to move back home. One of my roommates was waiting tables at a restaurant, so I went in for a job. The only one available was washing dishes, and I took it. I had no interest in the restaurant industry, but I worked up the line. The more I learned about food, the more I realized that what I wanted wasn't compatible with what the place where I worked was doing. I gave a couple months' notice and didn't know what I was going to do. Paul Saginaw had been the manager when I started as a dishwasher. He had opened a fish market about two years earlier. We had talked several times about opening our own business. He called me to say the building across the street was open, and we opened four months later. That was twenty-seven years ago.

What made you want to expand?

In the early 1990s, we had reached a point that I would equate with organizational midlife. We had fulfilled the vision we had when we started. We knew we wanted one deli, not a chain, offering food in a very service-oriented setting, being very bound to the community. We had already expanded twice and had no more room. We wrote a fifteen-year plan, the 2009 Zingerman's plan, for the Zingerman's Community of Businesses. Each would have its own identity and operate as one organization with the same values and same vision for the long term. We would use that to create more opportunities for people in the industry. Three years ago, we started writing the 2020 vision, for twelve to eighteen businesses, all in the Ann Arbor area.

Is a community of businesses like yours only possible in Ann Arbor?

I don't know, I'm only here. You can do whatever you want depending on wherever you are. I think what's important is to do something that corresponds to the terroir of the place. Some grapes will do better in the soil where you plant them. If you respect that and enhance it, you end up with very interesting businesses.

To what factors do you attribute your success?

Hopefully, we are successful because our food is great and our service is good. We've never assumed that we had anything coming to us; we still don't today, other than that we'll always have the chance to do better. We work very hard to make it a great place to work and a great experience for customers. We put in a lot of hard work, extreme attention to details, great recovery from failure, which happens every few hours. And I would add that we do a good job envisioning—starting with the end in mind—and writing down what success looks like. But every day we make changes and adapt the business.

What risks do you feel you have taken to get where you are?

Every day is risky. We could go broke, we could lose money, we could serve bad food, we could provide a bad work environment. It's all risky all the time. There's no point at which it's not risky.

What lessons have you learned along the way?

I learned that it's never done; it's really hard, and it gets harder, not easier. If you want to do something special, it takes an enormous amount of work. I've also learned that people are capable of really great things if you provide them with good leadership, good training, and good structure. You can provide a great work environment for people in your community.

What do you like most about what you do?

I'm very fortunate because it's really a vocation for me. I really like the work; I love the food; I really like working with the people; I really like that we've been able to create something that is very intellectually

and emotionally engaging with something very tangible. We tell customers where the food comes from, how it's made, what its history is, while also teaching open-book finance and leadership.

What do you like least about what you do?

I can't say I love when the health inspector comes. I don't really like filling out the paperwork for governmental regulations.

What qualities do you look for in a new hire?

We look for people who share our values. We are looking for people who are proactive thinkers, who want to make a positive difference. We certainly look for people who like to learn. We look for people who can think and manage complex situations. And then, depending on what the job is, we might look for previous experience. The hiring process is like a date. If the first date is good, you're going to have a second date, but it doesn't mean that you'll get married. And if you get married, that doesn't even mean you'll stay together forever.

What words of advice would you offer someone considering a similar career?

It depends on what they do now. If they already work in the industry, they are off to a good start. If not, I suggest they take a job at the bottom and see if they like it. It's mostly picking up papers, retesting recipes forty times, talking to customers over and over again; it's not glamorous. Very clearly, I would suggest that they write a vision for themselves. Pick a point, five or ten years down the road, and head for that.

JENNIFER BAUM

Jennifer Baum is the president and founder of Bullfrog and Baum, an award-winning hospitality, lifestyle, and consumer-product public relations and marketing firm with offices in New York, NY, and Los Angeles, CA. The firm, which was founded in 2000 and employs about thirty people, represents thirty hospitality clients (including Bobby Flay, Wolfgang Puck, Laurent Tourondel, and Stephen Starr), four wine and spirits clients, seven lifestyle clients, seven consumer-goods clients, and five media clients.

What made you decide to work in restaurant public relations?

My first job out of college was in public relations in the beauty industry. I always wanted a job where I would make something seem appealing to someone. I love a job where everything is a bit different every day, where you use creativity and professionalism. I also like that I work in a position where success and results are often based on relationship building. I had worked in the restaurant industry for many years, in front of house, as a waiter and manager of operations, and loved the industry—I always say that you don't choose the restaurant industry, it chooses you. I went to work in-house for a chef as director of marketing and business development and point person for his PR firm. I got a firsthand look at what PR in the restaurant industry could be. The crux is that I really thought I could do this type of PR differently than I had seen it being done before.

What prompted you to open your own business?

At the end of the day, I was not created to work for someone else. I'm not cut from that cloth, so in a way I didn't have a choice. I got a tiny little office in a very nonfancy suite of offices. It was just me, but I went to an office every single day. I started with one very bad client. Then I got Sara Moulton. I cold-called her. I had seen her on TV and left her a voice mail. She didn't call me back, but I followed up. We ended up having lunch. I was very up-front with her, because we had first spoken when I was freelancing at another firm, but she wanted to work with me.

To what factors do you attribute your success?

Number one, we do all of our work with integrity. I really think that it makes a difference. I'm always looking at the long term, not the short term. I keep in mind the importance of possibly missing out on an opportunity in the short term. It's so much more important to pay attention to the long run. We are very good at building relationships with both clients and press. And also we "show up." If someone asks us to do something, we do it wholeheartedly; we do nothing half-assed.

What do you like most about what you do?

I love that it is different every day. I love the people I work with—my staff and my clients. I love working with most of the media. Once you figure out someone who might be considered difficult, it's easy. I love when you nail that thing that you've been working on for so long, or get that placement that you've been waiting for, or get a marketing plan that works for everyone involved. The work is so hard that the successes are that much sweeter.

What do you like least about it?

Managing expectations. In my industry, everybody thinks that they should be on the cover of every magazine. That's hard to manage. I also don't like when my clients negatively believe their own press and start coasting. Some of them don't know how to handle their own success—it's a hard thing to do. When that happens, I sit down and talk it out with them.

What risks have you taken, from a business perspective, to get where you are?

I think that one risk in this particular industry is that I have always looked to the long run. Most people have their noses buried in the day-to-day. We've expanded outside of restaurants—we have a whole lifestyle division. That was a risk.

What qualities do you look for in a new hire?

You can't teach integrity; you cannot teach people to show up. Danny Meyer said years ago, "I look for nice smart people—I can teach them to be good waiters." I look for someone who is nice, who is smart, who has a service mentality, and who has integrity. I want people who want to work for me. Back in April I posted a job listing for two positions. I must have gotten six hundred résumés on the first day and a thousand résumés in all.

How can someone stand out in such a large pool?

Read the instructions—if I say don't attach your résumé, don't attach it. Pay real attention to typos. I don't like anyone who refers to themselves as a "foodie." The first two sentences should grab my attention. And use the name of my company in your e-mail; don't send me an e-mail that says "your company this" or "your company that," because it doesn't show me that you want to work for me specifically.

What do you look for in a client?

I look for a client with whom we share a similar vision. It has to be a client I believe in. It doesn't have to be that it's the biggest client—not at all. We have to have goods to work with. The clients need to understand they will be part of the process. I can't have a client who comes to me and says, "Make me a star" and when I reach out to them they say, "No, you do it." They have to understand PR and marketing.

What words of advice would you offer someone considering a similar career?

I do think that somebody who wants to do this should spend a little bit of time in a corporate environment. You get a good base for public relations if you do that. Then, to start your own business, start slowly. Choose your clients carefully because they make as much of a statement about your company as you do. Some PR firms will take anything that comes along, just for the money. We've turned down clients when we can't do anything for them.

SUSAN SPUNGEN

Susan Spungen is a cook, food stylist, recipe developer, and food consultant. She is the author of *Recipes: A Collection for the Modern Cook* and coauthor of *Martha Stewart's Hors d'Oeuvres Handbook.* She was the food editor of *Martha Stewart Living* for twelve years. She has worked as a culinary consultant and food stylist on the movies *Julie & Julia, It's Compicated,* and *Eat, Pray, Love.*

What made you decide to become a food stylist?

Throughout college, food was my fallback thing. Over time, I realized that it was what I wanted, and liked, to do. Then I realized that I didn't want to be punching a clock forever—I wanted to be rewarded for my creativity more. It hadn't really occurred to me that there was a whole industry behind the photos and food seen in magazines until I read an article in the *New York Times* in November 1990 about food stylists. I thought that it sounded great. I had met Susan Magrino, who is still Martha Stewart's publicist today, and started picking her brain. She remembered me a year later and called to say that Martha Stewart was starting a magazine and asked if I wanted to meet her. In the meantime, I had taken a job as pastry chef of Coco Pazzo, which was really top at the time, so I had a little bit of buzz going on for that. I had no experience as a stylist, but neither had Martha. It was a very natural, intuitive thing for her, as it was for me. It was okay to do it your way; you didn't have to follow the rules. When I quit in 2003, I wrote my cookbook and went back to freelancing as a food stylist because it's my best way to make money in a day. It's not a lifelong dream—it's just what I do.

What other things do you do?

I'm working on another book project with Artisan, *What's a Hostess to Do?* It's an entertaining handbook that is part of a series. For *Julie & Julia* I trained Amy Adams at ICE for two days. I showed her some of the things she would do on camera. I worked with Nora Ephron to come up with things, such as what would be the best thing for a character to cook in a scene. Throughout the film I did things like fixing the way they were holding a knife. I contribute recipes to a lot of magazines, such as *O, the Oprah Magazine* and *More.* For those, I come up with the concept of the piece, develop the recipes, and do the styling. The visual part of it is part of the concept when I create the recipes.

To what factors do you attribute your success?

To being flexible and being easy to work with. A lot of times people underestimate how important that is, no matter what your work is. Being creative is how I approach problems and challenges. Being willing to do anything—early in my career I would never look at what the downside of a project would be.

What do you like most about what you do?

I feel lucky that I get to do what I love, which is to work with food. I enjoy the environment of a photo shoot. Even though

I came from a high-power job, I like the life of a freelancer: I can work when I want to and not work when I don't want to. I feel like I have more job security as a freelancer. I love being on a photo shoot and collaborating with a team, the photographer, the prop stylist. We all come together to make a beautiful picture. I enjoy the teamwork. I don't really like working at home by myself with no one to eat the food that I cook. Cooking isn't something that is meant to be solitary.

What do you like least about it?

The schlepping [carrying equipment and ingredients]. It reminds me of the old catering days. Luckily I have great assistants who always want to do it for me. They have to be willing to schlep or do dishes, but I always do what needs to be done, too. Martha is the same way. I wouldn't have gone this far in my career if I hadn't had the right attitude and been happy to do anything.

Describe your creative process.

I sort of work backward. I think about what I want to achieve with a recipe. Being someone who really enjoys eating, who enjoys food, I have a concept of what I want the dish to taste like, to feel like in your mouth and look like. Then I experiment.

What risks have you taken to get where you are?

The biggest risk for me was when I left my job in 2003. I am still trying to carve out a lucrative, long-term niche for myself. I make pretty good money but not as good as when I had a full-time job. So I am working toward a place where I don't have to worry or hustle so much. But I never regret it, because money isn't everything. If you don't put yourself in a position where you are available, you miss out on opportunities. I wanted to make myself more available for things that might come up.

What lessons have you learned along the way?

One thing, which might sound funny, is that I never planned too far ahead. I never looked further than the next step. I just wanted to be a food stylist; I was not thinking that I wanted to be the food editor at a big magazine. I always looked at my own path as a road, literally. I know people who have their five-year plan; for me it's just about the next little stretch of road.

What word of advice would you offer someone considering a similar career?

Find someone you admire and assist him or her, even if that means working for free at the beginning. Study photographs and see what you like and don't like about ways to style food. Figure out what you think is beautiful, identify stylists, and approach them to work for them. Stylists are usually freelance and have a list of people they contact to work as their assistants. People who have a first assistant will someday be looking for a new one because assistants move on. Try to work with stylists once and be as helpful as possible so that they call you back. Anticipate their needs. That starts with shopping and goes right through the set, where you should always be thinking one step ahead. Be as prepared as possible.

5. COOKING

Hands-on cooking is what people most immediately associate with the food industry, particularly with the rise in popularity of chefs over the last decade. The countless television shows and print-media features that offer behind-the-scenes looks into the life of a professional kitchen have glamorized the work that takes place there

and driven aspiring culinary professionals to enroll in culinary schools in droves. This is ultimately beneficial for the industry as it raises the status of the cook's work and makes it a valid career choice. Parents, friends, or significant others are much more likely to support your decision to obtain a culinary education and go work in a kitchen than they were twenty years ago, when such jobs were still largely marginalized and not considered career tracks.

Even if your ultimate goal is not to work in a restaurant, spending a couple of years on the line will give you skills—from technical abilities to efficiency and creativity—that will be of use for the rest of your life in this industry. Many alternative occupations, such as certain media positions, teaching, and consulting, also look for professional cooking experience. Working in a restaurant will also be an asset on your résumé and provide you with experience that can be a source of income for the rest of your life (you might travel and find your-

self with opportunities to cook professionally if you run short of money, for example). As you advance in your restaurant career, you will need increasingly strong creative and management skills. You will need to come up with dishes and recipes and will be in charge of a team. The high points of working in a professional kitchen include the adrenaline rush you'll feel during service, the teamwork that takes place and builds camaraderie, and a sense of accomplishment at the end of a good night. The downsides are that for many years, you will work long hours for low pay.

If you want to work in a kitchen, you'll need thick skin—both figuratively and literally. Burns and scars are the marks you'll earn for the hours spent opening and closing ovens; chopping vegetables as accurately, consistently, and rapidly as you can; cooking sugar; deep-frying all types of preparations both savory and sweet; grilling meats; and baking. They are the marks of an experienced cook or baker, but they can also be the marks of someone who doesn't pay enough attention in the kitchen or someone who does things too quickly and not well enough. If you need to be coddled after the smallest amount of pain, take that into consideration when you decide whether or not a restaurant kitchen is the place for you.

Thick skin is useful beyond the ability to work past the pain. Kitchens are places where teasing and ribbing take place, even if the days of kitchens as hellish work environments are long gone. Some of it is funny and humorous; some of it might be downright nasty. Many of the cooks who tease in the kitchen do so expecting a reaction from the object of their joke. If you are sensitive and tend to react to everything that is said to you, you might find yourself subjected to even more teasing. But if you can look past that type of attention, not care about the silly nickname you might acquire, and remain focused on your work, those who tease you will tire of it. You may find yourself joining in on the fun of joking about others. This is a form of release in the tense environment of a professional kitchen and one way to build a camaraderie

that will be useful in the middle of service. Think of the teasing as a form of team building, and it will become much more bearable. That type of work environment will initially require adjustment if you come from a corporate job, for example, which usually has very strict boundaries of what is acceptable or not and what is legal or not.

Being a chef requires more than cooking knowledge. Leadership and teaching skills are essential if you want to make it up the line all the way to the pass. These are skills required for any position as the head of a team, of course. But in the close quarters of a kitchen, weak leadership skills and the inability to teach someone how to replicate what you do are both more noticeable and more costly. If you cannot train a line cook to make a dish you just put on the menu or the sous chef who takes over on your night off to plate the dish as perfectly as you do, you will be trapped having to do everyone's job without delegating and will burn out. Being a leader and a good teacher will also earn you the respect of your team, who will trust you during the rush of service, will want to earn your respect by doing their jobs well, and will take as much pride in cooking your food as you do. As a novice in the kitchen, you will not be expected to demonstrate those skills right off the bat, of course. What you will need to show is that you can listen, focus, and do your job well, hour after hour, shift after shift, week after week. That's what your chef will require of you. But once the chef sees that you are capable of that, he or she will move

The U.S. Department of Labor's Bureau of Statistics indicates that in 2006, the last year for which such numbers are available, "chefs, cooks, and food preparation workers held 3.1 million jobs"—a number that is expected to grow by 11 percent by 2016 to reach more than 3.4 million.

you to the next station, and throw more challenging tasks your way.

When working in a restaurant, you have to remember that you have two audiences: the staff and your customers. Regardless of your position, the way you do your job, the way you show others how to do theirs, and the way you collaborate and lead will reflect in the diner's experience. And through your food, your wine selection, and your service, you get to teach diners about taste and hospitality. This means that your teaching skills need to extend beyond the people who speak the same language you do. To be an effective culinary professional, you need to be able to translate your craft into words that are not jargon, that are not just for other professionals, and make it easy for everyone to have access to your knowledge.

the kitchen

The hierarchy of the kitchen is less strict than it used to be (see the organization that Graham Elliott Bowles has chosen for his restaurant Graham Elliott, for example, on page 116) but is still very much in place. As it is in any industry, you do not get a job out of college as CEO, unless of course you launched your own company. This organization ensures that everyone knows exactly what he or she has to do and that dishes arrive on diners' tables in a timely fashion. A kitchen functions like any system; every component needs to be in its place for everything to run smoothly.

While all kitchens might not have all of these positions, because of their size or style of cuisine, the general organization of a kitchen brigade—a French term, which here refers to the crew—is as follows (the pastry kitchen is covered in its own chapter, page 144):

Commis/apprentice/prep cook
Garde-manger
Entremetier
(Line) Cook
Chef tournant
Chef de partie
Sous chef
Executive sous chef
Chef de cuisine
Chef/executive chef

A more Americanized list might go as follows:

cold apps/hot apps cook
fry cook
grill or pasta cook
sauté cook
roundsman
sous chef
executive chef

The rapidity with which you will be promoted from one position to another depends a great deal on the attitude you display. If you appear eager to learn; do your work without attitude, well, and fast; and ask your chef for additional tasks when you are done so that you can help and learn more, you will progress at a steady pace. Do not be in a rush either; soak in all the

Be prepared to work with people
of varying education levels,
ethnic identities, life experiences,
and work ethics.

knowledge that you can, even if you are ready for a change in title. If you don't get promoted, it is likely that you are not quite ready for it. Of course, some exceptions apply, and it is possible that your boss is not noticing all your efforts. In that case, it is time to move to another restaurant.

A commis or prep cook spends time preparing the ingredients that the cooks will need throughout the day. This position involves a lot of grunt work, as you spend much of your time on tasks such as peeling vegetables. However, with the right skills and attitude, you will not stay there for long. You might start at that level even with a culinary school education. Use it as an opportunity to hone your skills and show your chef what you can do.

A garde-manger takes care of dishes like salads and other cold appetizers. That position typically does not handle hot foods, which are prepared by a line cook or on stations that are in charge of the dish's primary component, such as meat or fish.

An entremetier, or the "hot app" station, will often take care of warm appetizers and vegetable dishes.

Line cooks do just that—cook on the line. Depending on the size of the restaurant, they might be in charge of a particular station—such as grilling, sautéing, pasta cooking, or frying—or assist the cook who handles it. As a line cook, you will likely work every station in the kitchen before being assigned or promoted to one. If you work as a line cook in a seafood res-

taurant, you might not get much experience cooking meat, however, so you might consider spending some time in a restaurant with a more extensive carnivorous menu to round out your skills at this stage of your career or one just above.

A chef tournant ("tournant" is the French word for "revolving") has experience with all the different stations and can jump in wherever he or she is needed during service. The same is true for a roundsman.

In larger restaurants with multiple cooks per station, chef de partie is typically in charge of a specific station, which might be the grill, sauté, meats, sauces, or fish and seafood. The saucier, who handles sauces and most often the cooking of the meats they garnish, is one of the highest positions to attain on the line because of the finesse and skill it requires. Certain cuisines require stations for specific items and might have additional or substitute stations. An Italian restaurant might have a pasta station, for example.

A sous chef is in charge of all the line cooks and chefs de partie, and as such takes on some managerial duties while still cooking every day. In this position, you will be in charge of the kitchen when the chef or chef de cuisine is not there and will work very closely with the chef at the creative level, helping to come up with new dishes. You might also expedite dishes (finish them right before they are handed off to a server). Some larger operations also have executive sous chef positions for people who are not quite ready to be chefs de cuisine but have long proven their worth in the kitchen.

Are You Too Old?

This is a blunt question but one that you have probably asked yourself if you are over thirty. Are you too old for a kitchen job? Kitchens are notoriously young places: According to the National Restaurant Association's 2009 "Restaurant Industry Forecast," "about half of today's restaurant employees are under age 25." Why are young people more prevalent in kitchens? One reason is that restaurants often attract transient workers who are trying to figure out what to do as a career. Another is because the work is so rigorous and demanding. You will be on your feet twelve to eighteen hours a day, five or six days a week, depending on where you work. And all this for very low wages. If you are used to working at a desk, being able to take sick days when you don't feel well, and browsing the Internet when there isn't much to do, the rigorousness of a kitchen will be challenging. That has nothing to do with age but more to do with attitude, of course. But if you've spent fifteen years in an office position, it is harder to make the switch than if you started working in a kitchen at eighteen and have never known anything else. When you are younger, it is also easier to accept these grueling schedules and tasks because it is unlikely that you have some of the other responsibilities and time commitments that come with age.

A chef de cuisine is second in command to the chef or executive chef and in certain kitchens might even be the most highly ranked person. He or she handles many of the day-to-day managerial duties of the kitchen, including training, hiring and firing, ordering, and other administrative tasks. He or she may not cook on the line on a daily basis but is there every day. He or she has a strong hand in the creative conceptualization of the restaurant, and the name of the chef de cuisine might appear on the menu.

The chef or executive chef (the top title varies) drives the creative vision of a restaurant and is the person who will represent it to the public. Some chefs still cook daily, if only for a few hours, but more often than not they spend more time in their office dealing with paperwork pertaining to their employees, answering media queries, designing and costing menus, and poring over financial statements to make sure that their operation is profitable. The chef might be the owner of the restaurant or might answer to a larger executive team as part of a restaurant group. When not an owner, the chef is typically at the same level as the restaurant's general manager, and the two collaborate on large-scale decisions that ensure that the business runs smoothly.

You might take a step back at one point in your career, moving back from sous chef

Being a Woman in the Kitchen

One of the topics of discussion that often comes up in the media is the role of the woman chef in the kitchen. Many pieces that address this take on a sensationalistic tone, looking for evidence of poor treatment and inequality. The women chefs themselves often don't care to discuss the subject because for them, the job is the same regardless of gender.

It is certain that men and women work alongside each other in the kitchen; but then, they do in most work environments. You will hear women cooks and chefs talk about not having a separate locker room to change into and out of their work clothes. Once in those clothes and on the line, they might have to prove themselves to colleagues who might not be willing to admit that women can do the job just as well as them. They may be subject to wisecracks, verbal abuse, grabbing, or general hazing. Ignoring those attitudes is a way to deal with them, focusing instead on work, according to the women who have been subjected to it. Having a brash attitude and a big mouth, becoming one of the guys, is another strategy preferred by some women. Confronting the teaser or abuser or talking to one's chef or manager about it is yet another way to handle the problem.

Generally, all this is changing, and such behavior toward women and minorities is no longer prevalent or tolerated. The professionalization of cooking and the proliferation of women cooks have a lot to do with this change in attitude. Sexism is much less tolerated than it used to be, just like screaming and throwing things are no longer common practice. The kitchen is becoming a much more civilized place, and women—as well as men—are benefiting from these new standards.

to chef de partie, in order to learn different skills or join a larger or more prestigious operation than the one where you are at the time of your move. Do not be afraid to make such a change; it will pay off in the long run as you build your résumé. Similarly, do not be tempted if someone offers you an executive chef position too early in your career, before you feel ready for such a task. You might be better off continuing to move between restaurants in order to learn from others rather than taking that step too soon.

Some larger operations might have a separate staff for events, which will carry its own hierarchy and titles. A hotel might have a banquet chef and a banquet sous chef, for example, while a restaurant might have a private events or special events chef. Small operations might only have a couple of cooks on the line, and in those cases titles become irrelevant since each person does everything.

Cooks, unless they work in a restaurant located within a hotel or in institutional dining, are rarely unionized. If you work in Las Vegas, however, or in a handful of New York restaurants, you will join a union. Union representatives will negotiate on your behalf in case of conflict with your supervisor, for example. Union wages are also at times higher than nonunion ones. However, the free-spirited mentality of the kitchen means that many resent the strict rules that unions impose and prefer not to operate within their constraints.

Because life on the line takes its toll on cooks and chefs after many years spent cooking day in, day out, and working nights, weekends, and holidays, many of them turn to jobs where cooking is still the main task but that are not as taxing as feeding hundreds of people over the course of an evening. Such options include research and development, teaching, working in a test kitchen, corporate food service management, club management, and many of the jobs that are profiled in other chapters.

Chefs with years of experience in the industry also turn to consultancy when they no longer want to be in the kitchen full-time. As a consultant, you will work with restaurants and companies to develop menus and dishes. You will need a high level of creativity and a broad culinary knowledge in order to be able to work in all types of kitchens, and you will also need to have a strong command of food costs, since that will be one of your responsibilities as you create a menu or a product. You might be in charge of staffing a kitchen and training the staff to replicate your creations. Once the project is over, you move on to something else but might come back seasonally to develop new dishes as the need arises.

salaries

An entry-level cook will make between $8 and $10 an hour, while a line cook can expect to make around $12 an hour. According to the 2008 StarChefs salary survey, national average salaries are $44,205 for a sous chef, $56,367 for a chef de cuisine, $74,869 for an executive chef, and $85,179 for a chef-owner. An executive chef for one of the country's top restaurants, a large restaurant group, or in certain research and development positions will make about six figures. In bigger cities, salaries tend to be higher but so is the cost of living. In a chain restaurant, the kitchen manager or chef will receive a median salary of about $51,000, with potential for a bonus, according to HVS Executive Search's 2008 "Chain Restaurant Corporate Annual Report," with a minimum listed at about $22,000 and maximum at around $372,000. A 2006 American Hotel and Lodging Association survey lists a hotel sous chef's median salary as $36,000 and that of an executive chef as $65,300. Ultimately, the way to gain operational and financial leverage is to own several restaurants.

GRAHAM ELLIOT BOWLES

After establishing his name at Avenues, Graham Elliot Bowles opened what he called a "bistronomic" restaurant, serving fine-dining contemporary American cuisine in a casual setting six nights a week. The restaurant seats 120 people in the dining room and 40 in its lounge.

CURRENT POSITION: Chef-owner, Graham Elliot, Chicago, IL, since 2008, www.grahamelliot .com. ★ **EDUCATION:** Culinary arts degree, Johnson & Wales University, Norfolk, VA. ★ **CAREER PATH:** Star Canyon and the Mansion on Turtle Creek, Dallas, TX; Jackson House, Woodstock, VT; in Chicago: Tru, Charlie Trotter's, and chef de cuisine at Avenues. ★ **AWARDS AND RECOGNITION:** Best New Chef, *Food & Wine* (2004); StarChefs Rising Star Chicago (2005); nominee for Rising Star Chef (2006) and Best Chef—Great Lakes (2008), James Beard Foundation; 40 Under 40, *Crain's Chicago Business* (2008); four stars for Avenues, *Chicago Sun-Times* (2006).

Salary notes:

I think that the average yearly salary of cooks in Chicago is around $30,000, and chefs are around double that.

Words of advice for people considering a similar career:

Get in a kitchen as soon as possible and make sure that you work for good people. I don't think that culinary school is a must. You need to know what your end goal is and how you can sell your résumé and background to get that. I knew that I wanted to do that, so I worked at Charlie Trotter's.

Describe a typical day.

We start here at about nine A.M., with bringing in deliveries. We deal with production, storage, roasting bones, and things like that. The cooks will be in around eleven or twelve and take care of the *mise en place* for their own stations. By four thirty or five P.M., we have a preshift meeting. The doors open at five. We're pretty busy from then on until about ten, then from ten to eleven thirty or twelve we clean and get organized. Although it's not a show kitchen, people come in the back to see it. We get out by one A.M.

How many hours a week do you typically work?

I'm probably in the restaurant seventy hours a week, between ten and twelve hours a day, six days a week. But when I go home and wake up in the morning, I'm constantly checking e-mails, calling, and doing things; I live for the restaurant. That's also something to instill in the team, that it's not just work. It's a way of life; it's a journey.

What are your specific responsibilities?

I'm very good at delegating to people and holding them accountable. My overriding focus is driving the bus and establishing the direction that I think we should be taking, while also listening to input and taking it into account. I see that someone is really good at A and B, so I use that to have them oversee what they are best at. People came with me from Avenues and have grown into different roles. In the next five years, we want ten restaurants, so we need to work backward to get to that. This is my core crew to take that goal to fruition. My role is shifting toward stepping back and looking at the bigger picture.

What do you like most about what you do?

My biggest reward is watching people grow. When I started at Charlie Trotter's I was twenty, and I was always watching Charlie. He was always thinking five steps ahead, looking at moving people to other stations. I only wanted to have him show me how to butcher this or cook that. Then in my next role, I saw how important it is to step back and create chefs. You watch people evolve from simply being a cook to becoming a thinker, someone who will think about how to make the restaurant better. They will carry that with them and see things differently.

What do you like least about it?

I think that what probably causes me the most pain is constantly fielding people's criticisms and critiques through blogs, reviews, and things like that. At Avenues, I did nothing but try to achieve as many great reviews as possible. I did that, but it didn't make me happier. We decided with Graham Elliot to not worry about critics and just do what we do. But you still hear opinions. And to me this is not just what I do, it's who I am. There's no way that you can be a genuinely passionate person and wear your heart on your sleeve and not be affected by that.

What skills are most important for you to do your job well?

Communication is probably the biggest. That includes being able to read people, seeing their strengths and weaknesses, knowing that someone over there needs to be motivated by fear and the person over there has more of a liberal arts background and needs to be complimented before you suggest a change. You need them all to make a kitchen run properly. But I try to tell my leaders in the kitchen that the same way you put ingredients together to create a harmonious dish, you need to do it in the kitchen with the staff. You have to be able to inspire people by staying positive.

What prompted you to open your own business?

It's something that I've always wanted to do. Whether it's something in the culinary field or designer, architect, you always want to live your own dream instead of working for somebody else's dream. I knew from early on that my goal was to have my own establishment and work for myself. I told myself that if I didn't have my place by the time I turned thirty, I would change fields.

How large is your operation?

We have just around forty staff, front and back of the house.

How and when do you decide to introduce new dishes?

Many chefs like to use local ingredients and cook with the season, and we do that. But one thing we like to do is to change our dishes to keep the staff motivated. My goal is to train chefs who will go on to open their own restaurants. The kitchen is laid out according to the five different categories on our menu. The chef of each of these stations is responsible for ordering, cooking, plating, and cleaning up for his station. Each dish that comes out of that is reflective of that person's artistry. We have one person who will actually make the phone calls to the vendors, but each chef is responsible for saying, "I want four bass brought tomorrow." Instead of being a cook who's told what to do, they start to think like chefs. There's a lot more freedom and room for people to grow and contribute to the team. It's encouraged.

What keeps you challenged?

I think that's probably my toughest obstacle. I get bored extremely quickly, so whether it's changing dishes or moving people around, I need to have something to focus on all the time. I'm trying to write a book, a behind-the-scenes look at the first year of a restaurant. I want to put out a CD of my own music.

Describe your creative process.

It's funny, I will get inspired by anything and everything, a tree and leaves, a red stop sign, what's in season right now that's red, music, anything. It's about being able to be open to your surroundings and collaborating with different people. I have four hundred different ideas listed in my phone. It's more of a curse than anything else. I don't have much self-discipline. I see Grant Achatz or some of these guys with notepads, looking at how to plate things. We never really plate things twice the same way. I see the benefit of what each one does. I wish I was a bit more disciplined, but I guess that's part of my creative process.

Looking back, what surprises you about the path your career has taken?

I think the most surprising thing is that I worked for all these James Beard Award–winning chefs, did all these tasting menus, but when the time came to open my own place, I went the other direction. I didn't want formal, I wanted fun, not something small, but something large and loud. We don't need linens, we don't need twenty different kinds of plates, of glasses. We don't do bread, we do popcorn instead, because who says that bread is what you have to do? So many restaurants are so formulaic. You can close your eyes and know you will be greeted like this, that service will go like that. That's not us.

"Instead of being a cook who's told what to do, they start to think like chefs. There's a lot more freedom and room for people to grow and contribute to the team. It's encouraged."

KELLY LIKEN

Kelly Liken owns two restaurants, Kelly Liken and Rick and Kelly's American Bistro, in Vail, CO, with her husband, Rick Colomitz, who is the dining room manager at the bistro. The Kelly Liken restaurant has received local and national attention as one of the best fine-dining establishments in Vail for its seasonal American cuisine.

CURRENT POSITION: Chef-owner of Kelly Liken and Rick and Kelly's American Bistro in Vail, CO, since 2004, www.kellyliken.com. ★ **EDUCATION:** Course work in physics, University of Colorado–Boulder; Culinary Institute of America. ★ **CAREER PATH:** Before culinary school, Monterey Bay Fish Grotto, Pittsburgh, PA (five years); Cheesecake Factory, Boulder, CO; the Mediterranean, Boulder; extern at the Inn at Little Washington, VA, and Splendido at the Chateau, Beaver Creek, CO. ★ **AWARDS AND RECOGNITION:** Three awards upon graduation from culinary school: the Catherine Angel Scholastic Award, the Culinary Award (no. 1 culinarian in the class), and scholarship from Chaîne des Rôtisseurs (Young Professional Award of Merit); Emerging Business of the Year, Vail Chamber of Commerce (2005); one of the Top Female Chefs Under 40, *Bon Appétit* (September 2008). ★ **MEMBERSHIPS:** Women Chefs and Restaurateurs; James Beard Foundation; Colorado Restaurant Association; local business organizations.

Salary notes:

It's difficult to say. I probably pay myself half of what I'd make as executive chef of a major hotel. But if this works, in the end, it will pay off. But starting your own business to get rich quick or make $100,000 a year is not realistic. My first year, I budgeted $34,000 for my salary, because that's what I needed to pay my bills, and every year it's gotten better.

Describe a typical day.

I have two restaurants; the second one is brand new, having opened in July 2008. I start my work day at nine A.M., typically at home. I check e-mail, voice mail, paperwork, bank accounts—the not-so-fun but necessary stuff. Part of the day is spent on marketing our business, arranging for local advertising, arranging interviews, writing recipes for publications that have requested them. My time and my husband's time are better spent going after press than on big advertising campaigns. I leave the house around ten thirty or eleven and drop my husband off at our bistro, which he manages. Then I am in the kitchen at Kelly Liken until about four P.M. I do most of the butchering and I make sauces. I try new things, work on production, but also work closely with the pastry chef, and a couple of days a week I work on making pastries. The waitstaff comes in at three thirty, so I try to be free to spend time with them because the menu changes all the time and I like to discuss it. At four thirty, we have staff meal, for which everyone, front and back of the house, sits together. At five thirty service starts, and I am expediting. It's me plus three to four cooks in the kitchen. I see every plate that goes out. It's very important that every recipe be executed perfectly. I have a fabulous sous chef who has been with me for quite a while and understands my vision. At certain times of the year, I can head home by nine P.M., and at other times by eleven P.M. I hired a fantastic chef for the bistro. I meet with him and his sous chef every day, sometimes for fifteen to twenty minutes, sometimes for an hour, depending on what's going on. I also always stop at the bistro at the end of the day when I go pick up Rick, to check in there. We serve dinner there until eleven P.M., so I'm always there before service is over. In the fall and spring, I might only be in the kitchen five days a week and, when we are in high season, seven days a week.

How many hours a week do you typically work?

Most of the hours in the day. But I love my job; it's very social. I live in this great small town, my friends are here, my family is here. Seventy-five hours a week maybe, but twenty-five are fun hours, when I'm researching marketing, creating recipes, changing my menu. If I didn't change my menu as much I wouldn't have to do as much, but I like to come in early a few days a week and play with things.

What are your specific responsibilities?

My name is on the front door—ultimately, I am responsible for everything. I have a great team to whom I can delegate, but I am responsible for the guidance. I am responsible for the kitchen, the financial operations, and public relations. My husband is in charge of dining, training, and personnel. We do the marketing together.

What do you like most about what you do?

It's different every day. I love that. The thing I like the very most is that I feel I was born to cook and born to be a chef. My hands knew how to do it when I first started cooking. And I am able to build this amazing career where we work for ourselves.

What do you like least about it?

There are definitely times when the hours get to be overwhelming. The winter holidays, specifically, are hard. That's our busiest time of the year, and we are more than twice as busy as the rest of the year. There's no way we're ever going to be able to see our families for the holidays. You learn to make concessions and carve other times to see your family. We'll go see his family before the holidays, and my family is here in Colorado so we'll do something with them after.

What skills are most important for you to do your job well?

As a restaurateur and owning my own business, having the willingness to change and evaluate. It's inevitable that some things will not work at some point. You have to multitask and be okay with having multiple things on your plate at once. Some technical skills, obviously. You have to have a real eagle eye for precision and attention to detail. And really passion, because I think that people can taste when you don't have passion.

What skills would you like to develop to help further your career?

I feel like I am always learning and growing. I've taken on a project for this spring where I'm going to make my first wedding cake, for a friend of mine. I've never done this before, but I have friends who have and are helping me. I would like to know more about finance. I learned some with my two restaurants, but I am not trained in this field. I'd like to hone my skills of business modeling and forecasting.

What prompted you to open your own restaurant?

I absolutely couldn't imagine doing this for anybody else. I wanted to do it my way; I wanted to cook my food, see success on my own. Being a chef is a hard life. It's hard work and many hours. I wanted it to be my own. To be honest, I was twenty-seven years old when I opened Kelly Liken, and I had no idea what I was getting myself into. On one end doing it like that is disastrous; on another it's the best thing ever. If I had

known, I might not have gotten into it. I made a lot of mistakes and learned a lot from them.

What are your long-term goals?

I'd love to have a big glossy cookbook. I am working on television segments with a local channel that is in six or seven markets, Plum TV. I would like to explore TV further; that would be a new challenge. But mostly it is to run these businesses for as long as I can and keep making people happy.

How large is your staff?

At Kelly Liken, we employ thirty people, for sixty-five seats and fifteen seats at the wine bar. That's everyone, including accountant, dishwasher, and waitstaff. At the bistro, which has 150 seats, we have fifty people, a lot of whom are part-time. At Kelly Liken we only hire full-time, only people who are interested in food service as a career.

"I feel I was born to cook and born to be a chef. My hands knew how to do it when I first started cooking."

JOSEPH WREDE

Joseph Wrede is the chef and co-owner of five restaurants in New Mexico and Colorado as a principal in the Taos Restaurant Group. His award-winning flagship, Joseph's Table, is one of the most renowned restaurants in the Southwest, with a focus on locally grown ingredients.

CURRENT POSITION: Chef-owner, Joseph's Table (since 1995), Lambert's of Taos, and Brett House Catering in Taos, NM, and Old Blinking Light, Taos and Denver, CO. ★ **EDUCATION:** Regis University, Denver; culinary arts degree, Institute of Culinary Education, New York, NY (1993). ★ **CAREER PATH:** Dishwasher, neighborhood bars, Ohio (at twelve years old); Carelli's, Boulder, CO; garde manger, Highland's Garden Café, Denver, CO; Aubergine Café, Denver. ★ **AWARDS AND RECOGNITION:** Best New Chef, *Food & Wine* (2000); Best Chef, *Taos News* (2001–2002, 2004–2009); DiRoNA Award of Excellence (2004–2009); Best Restaurant in Taos, Alibi (2004); AAA Four-Diamond Award (2005–2009); Alumni Hall of Achievement, ICE (2005); Best Restaurant—Joseph's Table, *Taos News* (2006); Best Restaurant—Lambert's, *Taos News* (2007–2009); Award of Excellence, *Wine Spectator* (2007–2009); Award of Distinction, *Wine Enthusiast* (2007).

Salary notes:

$150,000 base salary, plus profit sharing.

Describe a typical day.

It's changing now because we formed this restaurant group and have been aggressive about purchasing restaurants. My main establishment is Joseph's Table. I grab coffee, go to the restaurant, and set the agenda for the day. I'm often on the line at any of the restaurants. I like to be engaged; I try to make myself comfortable in any of the kitchens. Each restaurant has a different voice and I try to direct that voice as much as possible. It's like picking up a song that is already being played or not totally familiar to all of the musicians. I try to drive the different restaurants and respond as much as possible, keep everybody on point, and cook. I'm only in Denver one week out of the month, so when there I try to take advantage of the chance to spend time in the kitchen. I'm at Joseph's Table three days a week and the other two one day a week each. I've worked now for two straight weeks, but if possible I try not to work more than five days a week. I run every day in the afternoon, around one thirty, between my morning routine and my afternoon routine. In the kitchen, you walk two steps and you feel like a caged lion. Running beats out all the issues that are going on in your head.

How many hours a week do you typically work?

Sixty. Once I go above seventy, it gets grinding. Outside of this time, I do other activities that are related to work, though, such as talking about food, reading cookbooks, planning a garden, and tasting wine, but not cooking. This is my lifestyle, so the majority of what I do revolves around food.

What do you like most about what you do?

I love combining and developing flavors and putting combinations together. I like the abstractness of plating, working with the contrasts in colors and textures and the design of putting a plate together. How that changes from plate to plate, on some level. I like the self-expression of the restaurant business and of cooking.

What are your longer-term goals?

My short-term goal is to get involved in farming, in growing and harvesting food, and be involved in the process from beginning to end as much as possible. My long-term goal is to be financially successful enough to not be cooking anymore. Maybe to do it from a completely intellectual standpoint, not a physical standpoint, such as writing books.

How large is your staff?

Close to about two hundred people. We have about twenty-five cooks total.

What qualities do you look for in a new hire?

Enthusiasm, patience, energy. It's really nice in the kitchen to have people who don't like to talk a lot. A sense of focus is a nice quality in a cook.

Looking back, what surprises you about the path your career has taken?

How I haven't been able to predict the path at all. I just valued being a chef, a culinary artist. Now I also see how valuable it is to be a businessperson, to have a sense of business and understand the financial parameters of the creative process. When we opened, my thought process was, "Cook good food and everything will fall into place." On one hand it's true, but if you understand the business, you can keep things healthy and productive and get many more people involved in it.

How often do you set goals?

I set really small goals every single night. This company I have formed is growing and I have two other partners, so my immediate goal is to make the kitchens operate efficiently and well. I leave my financial goals to one of those partners. I don't know how to spend a lot of time on my long-term goals. I try to operate well in the situation.

GEORGE McNEILL, CMC

As corporate chef of the Ritz-Carlton Hotel Company, George McNeill is in charge of menu development for the seventy-two hotels that the company has in twenty-four countries around the world.

CURRENT POSITION: Vice president culinary and corporate chef, the Ritz-Carlton Hotel Company, Chevy Chase, MD, since 1999. ★ **EDUCATION:** Apprenticeship, London City and Guilds; certified master chef; honorary doctorate in culinary arts, Baltimore International College (May 2008). ★ **CAREER PATH:** Resorts International, Atlantic City; British embassy, Washington, DC; executive chef, Fairmont Royal York Hotel, Toronto; executive chef, Marriott Marquis, New York City; executive chef, Ritz-Carlton Grand Cayman and then Jamaica; food and beverage task force member, Ritz-Carlton corporate office. ★ **AWARDS AND RECOGNITION:** Captain of the Canadian National Culinary Olympic Team, three gold medals and a bronze medal (1996); Escoffier Society Chef of the Year and ACF Chef of the Year; recipient of ACE Award, Marriott's highest national culinary award for culinary excellence; and more. ★ **MEMBERSHIPS:** Les Toques Blanches; London Association of Chefs de Cuisine; American Culinary Federation; Escoffier Society; Canadian Federation of Chefs de Cuisine; Confrérie de la Chaîne des Rôtisseurs.

Words of advice for people considering a similar career:

If you know intuitively that cooking is your skill set, if that excites you, then you will be successful. If it's not and you don't, find out what is and focus your efforts on that.

Describe a typical day.

It involves traveling somewhere. The corporate chef's job is to establish the direction for food and beverage. We're analyzing current trends and working with the industry to keep ourselves ahead of the curve. We're looking at what impacts people's eating habits, therefore determining our strategy to fulfill those needs. With the current economic climate, there's a decrease in disposable income. However, we're definitely seeing signs that socialization is critical, that people are gathering in bars and lounges. So it's a greater opportunity for us to address small plates, sharing plates, and comfort food (which has always been around but is more focused today). We gather that information, communicate with the field, have conference calls with our national and international properties. I'm also responsible for all the senior culinary people—eighty executive chefs, the executive sous chefs, pastry chefs, etc.

How many hours a week do you typically work?

Sixty hours. The challenge today with everybody in the industry is that the BlackBerry causes the work to be endless. Travel is a weekly occurrence. We visit all our hotels, particularly those where there is opportunity for support. I will be traveling to China next week for the opening of our new hotel there. We have five hotels opening this year, and I'll travel to each one to make sure that everyone is trained properly.

What are your specific responsibilities?

To ensure that we have a healthy pipeline of human capital. I'm in contact with existing chefs and potential chefs for the future. If we have an opening for an executive pastry chef in Moscow, I'm responsible for identifying candidates for this position. I work closely with HR and the property to make sure we have the right talent. I identify that they have the right skill set, review their portfolio. I make sure that we have those people available and develop them, making sure they are ready and able to take on these responsibilities. I work with the industry to set the standards for our kitchen and equipment, to make sure that our equipment is proficient, and to ensure that we provide our talent with the best equipment that we can. I work with products, making sure that we source the right quantity and quality of product, to hopefully get a competitive advantage on the marketplace to attract and retain constant revenue. I make sure that distribution channels are available. I speak at schools, on various panels, and give the prospectus of the Ritz-Carlton.

What do you like most about what you do?

The ability to support a large group of people who are like-minded, that you can bring a perspective they may not have thought about. I like constantly support-ing talented culinary professionals in the development of their skills sets, and developing our position in the marketplace.

What do you like least about it?

I miss the kitchen. I work out of the corporate office in Chevy Chase, Maryland. I miss the hustle and bustle that you feed upon when you are in a restaurant or hotel environment. Also, the travel schedule, which is always a little bit hectic; you're always at the mercy of somebody else when traveling.

What skills are most important for you to do your job well?

The ability to communicate, to listen, to analyze the information, and to be able to ask the right questions to get people to give you a better understanding of the challenges they are facing. Knowledge is extremely important and not to be underestimated. You need to understand what they are going through; you've been there, so you can give guidance from practical experience.

What is the outlook for your type of job?

There's only one corporate chef per company, so there are not many opportunities. I think there are many more opportunities for chefs. Thanks to the Food Network, to media, there's a much greater understanding of the skills and artistry that the chefs bring to the table. Great chefs will find themselves with great opportunities. As a company, we are expanding around the globe, to areas that didn't have luxury hotels. The health of the industry long-term is outstanding.

What qualities do you look for in a new hire?

There's an expectation, when going to the Ritz-Carlton, that you will get the best, so natural talent is extremely important. Management skills, because all the talent in the world will not make you a great leader. I make sure that they are able to communicate effectively with our guests and represent the hotel. We pride ourselves in hiring the top 1 percent of the industry.

How do you identify that 1 percent?

Good people tend to be in good places; they understand that building a career is building on the career of others, on the reputation of places and people they've worked for. We look at their background, their awards. We go through a very extensive interview process. Ultimately, there is a cooking skill test at the property level.

Do you decide on new menu items?

We don't say the menu needs to have this or that. I provide and create a variety of tools for chefs on our website. We establish guidelines, such as how many items to have on the menu, and give direction. We allow our chefs to exercise creativity but also provide information on trends and what our customers are looking for.

Looking back, what surprises you about the path your career has taken?

I don't really see that I had many surprises. The biggest surprise was that I was as good as my chosen path. That I was as good a cook as I turned out to be.

Any suggestions to improve work-life balance?

Understand that everything doesn't have to be done right away. You need time to think about things you want to take on, gather information to make stronger decisions. It's very hard today. I do not have a great work-life balance, because I feel compelled to support as many people as I have reaching out to me, but every so often I need a bit of me time.

"Fundamentally, we are in a skill-based environment. You develop skills through repetition; your ability to actively participate allows you to develop those skills. Education is important; so is natural talent."

JASON ROBINSON

The Inn at Dos Brisas, the smallest Relais & Châteaux property in the country, is a three-hundred-acre ranch with a four-acre organic garden. As the chef, Jason Robinson cooks for the guests of the four rooms and a thirty-seat restaurant that is open from Thursday to Sunday.

CURRENT POSITION: Chef, Inn at Dos Brisas, Washington, TX, since 2005. ★ **EDUCATION:** Junior college. ★ **CAREER PATH:** Sauté chef, Fog City Diner, Las Vegas, NV; helped open Chicago, IL, location for Fog City Diner (one year); meat and vegetable cook to chef de cuisine, Tru (Chicago; five years total); chef, Goodfellows, Minneapolis, MN (one year). ★ **AWARDS AND RECOGNITION:** Grand chef, Relais & Châteaux (2009); five stars locally. ★ **MEMBERSHIPS:** James Beard Foundation.

Salary notes:

The money gets better the higher you climb up the ladder. You should expect to be paid what you're worth. If you're a chef at T.G.I. Friday's and your job consists of ordering off a checklist that someone else created for you, ordering products from your own company, you're not going to make the same as someone who sources everything, cooks things from scratch, and has a wide set of experiences. The salary range comes from the skills and experience that you have.

Words of advice for people considering a similar career:

Make sure you like it, because it's long hours and hard work. Make sure that the water is deep enough where you want to jump in.

Describe a typical day.

I usually come in between nine and ten, cook lunch if we have guests on the property, do cooking classes, prep for dinner service, and cook dinner. I make everything, from the savory items to the desserts.

How many hours a week do you typically work?

Sixty-five hours.

What are your specific responsibilities?

I run the restaurant; I'm responsible for the food side, the kitchen side of the restaurant. I handle ordering, menu development, creating new dishes.

What do you like most about what you do?

I like people enjoying good food. I'm not a doctor, I'm not saving lives, but there's a certain satisfaction that people get when they enjoy a meal. When people go to a nice restaurant, they're not just there to get full; they're there to enjoy fine cuisine and to enjoy the food. I enjoy eating, so that's why I do what I do—giving customers an opportunity to enjoy food as much as I do.

What skills are most important for you to do your job well?

You need to be well rounded. You need people skills to deal with housekeeping, sommeliers, the people in the kitchen. You have to be able to demonstrate to the people around you that you can handle any culinary task. Not many people would want to join a small kitchen if the chef can't clean the vegetables, butcher the meat, fillet the fish. You need good handling of food products, knife skills, charcuterie, good food knowledge. We have four acres of organic gardens; if you don't know what the vegetables are, you won't be able to work with them. We grow many types of one vegetable, so having knowledge of food is definitely important.

How large is your operation?

We are the smallest property in Relais Châteaux: We only have four rooms. The restaurant is open Thursday through Sunday only and sits about thirty people. We are a certified organic farm; with the main garden, greenhouse, and orchard, we have five acres total. Staff-wise, I have one sous chef, one line cook, and a pastry chef coming at the end of the month. We're four or five people maximum, with the dishwasher, and that's about all the kitchen can handle.

What qualities do you look for in a new hire?

Good attitude, willingness to learn and take direction, and the ability to grow within the kitchen. In culinary school, they teach them the basics, but unfortunately nowadays people think that once they graduate they are a chef. There's much more to being a chef than that. They take a weeklong butchering course, whereas I've been butchering for ten years. They come and spend a day or two with us before we hire them. That's the biggest telltale to see if they are qualified and able to handle the pressure of a fine-dining kitchen. Things have to be cut precisely, cleaned exactly.

What skills would you like to develop to help further your career?

I'm always looking to put something on the plate that would make people think they've never thought of broccoli that way, for example. I like taking things and challenging myself to create a dish that people can relate to but had never thought of that way. In the last three years, I've also developed the pastry side of my cooking. When I first took this job, I was the only one in the kitchen here, so I did everything from breads to desserts.

What are your long-term goals?

I'd like to come up with my own line of food products for retail sale. I make a Bloody Mary mix, a barbecue sauce, I smoke some ribs, so things like that. Eventually I'd like to spend more time with my daughter but stay in a culinary position.

Describe your creative process.

I grab my sous chef, and we head for the garden for at least an hour every day. We're looking at what's available, what's at what stage of growing. I start with the vegetables rather than the protein.

Who or what are your sources of inspiration?

I definitely hold my hat to Chef Rick Tramonto and Chef Gale Gand. I worked with them for five years in Chicago at Tru. I started at Fog City Diner in Las Vegas as a prep cook, and we did almost everything from scratch. The fact that there are still restaurants out there that do that, versus buying bags of chopped onions, is inspirational. Inspiration comes from the heart for everyone, as long as you like what you do.

Any suggestions to improve work-life balance?

One of the biggest things for me is that you must not bring your work home. You need to have that separation. By focusing on the positives of each day, you bring home the fact that twenty people enjoyed some great food.

"I like people enjoying good food. I'm not a doctor, I'm not saving lives, but there's a certain satisfaction that people get when they enjoy a meal. When people go to a nice restaurant, they're not just there to get full; they're there to enjoy fine cuisine and to enjoy the food."

KATIE BUTTON

Katie Button turned down entering a PhD program in neuroscience with the National Institutes of Health and the Karolinska Institute in Stockholm, Sweden, to work in the food industry. She worked as a line cook at the Bazaar—celebrity chef José Andrés's newest, two-hundred-seat restaurant in Los Angeles—in winter 2009, and we spoke to her shortly before she left for a position in the pastry kitchen at Ferran Adrià's El Bullì in Spain.

CURRENT POSITION: Line cook, Bazaar by José Andrés at the SLS Hotel in Beverly Hills, Los Angeles, CA, winter 2009; pastry cook, El Bullì, Roses, Spain, 2009–2010 season. ⋆
EDUCATION: BS, chemical and biomolecular engineering, Cornell University, Ithaca, NY; specialized master's degree, biomedical engineering, Ecole Centrale, Paris, France (2006). ⋆
CAREER PATH: Server, Café Atlántico/Minibar, Washington, DC (fall 2007–winter 2008); service intern, El Bullì, Roses, Spain (April–June 2008); pastry intern, Jean Georges, New York, NY (fall 2008).

Salary notes:

Learning and working for free to $15.50 an hour.

Words of advice for people considering a similar career:

Be sure to work in a kitchen and decide if this is really the career you want to pursue before deciding to go to culinary school. If you have the work ethic and the drive (and I believe both of these come from simply doing what you love to do), then you will excel, and with some effort and searching, great opportunities will arise. Be proactive with your career.

What made you choose to work where you are now?

Because of my connections to the José Andrés team from my work as a server at Café Atlántico and because of my time at El Bullì, I was interested in being a part of a new restaurant that was bringing some of the techniques from El Bullì to the United States. I was also extremely excited about the concept of the restaurant. It is all about

movement. The restaurant is divided into four sections. The concept is that of a bazaar: You come in, move around, and interact with your meal.

Describe a typical day.

I arrive at work around two P.M. to begin preparations. I and two other line cooks prepare everything for our station for service. Then service opens at six P.M. and I prepare about six different appetizers to order as the tickets come in.

How many hours a week do you typically work?

Forty to forty-five.

What are your specific responsibilities?

I am responsible for making sure that all of the *mise en place* for my station is prepared before every service, preparing the setup for the snacks for the tea service at the restaurant every day by three P.M., preparing six appetizers to order for the restaurant, ordering any items before the end of service so that we have the products that we need at the start of service the next day, writing a prep list for the following day for the *mise en place* for the station.

What do you like most about what you do?

I love the fast pace of working on the line and the necessity for extreme organization. I also love the feeling I get when I put together a dish and everything is perfect, like a steamed bun filled with crème fraîche topped with paddlefish caviar and a lemon air, and the caviar is perfectly balanced on top of the steamed bun and the air is so high on top of the bun that you think it defies gravity and you wonder how it stays like that.

What do you like least about it?

The repetition. I wish I had more time to be creative myself. But if I continue down this career path, I know that eventually I will get to that point.

What skills are most important for you to do your job well?

Organization, cleanliness, an eye for perfection, and speed (being able to prepare perfect dishes one after another as fast as you can).

What skills would you like to develop to help further your career?

Everything. I want to learn as much as I can, and while ultimately I'd like to focus on pastry, I really want to learn as much about savory as I can. I think that in order to be truly great you need to know both, so that you can take influence from both sides

to create truly unique dishes. So I would love to learn how to cook meat to order to the perfect temperature just by sight/touch. I want to improve my knife skills, learn how to make bread. As I said, everything!

What keeps you challenged?

First of all, that I am starting over. I had achieved a certain level of expertise in science and when I realized I wasn't enjoying the work that I was doing and realized I wanted to get into the kitchen and ended everything, I was scared. Yes, I'm only twenty-five years old, but it is still starting over. I haven't been working in restaurants since I was fifteen. I haven't been to culinary school. So the challenge for me is that everything is new. I told the chef at Bazaar, Michael Voltaggio, when I received the job, "You will have to show me how to do everything once—cut a shallot, sharpen my knives, etc.—but I promise you this: you will only have to show me once."

Looking back, what surprises you about the path your career has taken?

I can't believe where I am now. When I was a little girl, I used to cook with my mom, helping her prepare for catering events that she was throwing. But I excelled in school, particularly in math and science. I enjoyed my studies, but I didn't really enjoy the career I initially chose. I always pictured myself as a professor at some prestigious university. I know that I wouldn't have felt fulfilled if I had continued on that path and I am extremely happy that I am where I am now.

CHRIS HENSEL

Chris Hensel is the executive chef of the Children's Medical Center in Dallas, where he and his staff of more than sixty people are in charge of all the food served at the hospital's cafeteria as well as in-room meals for 350 patients plus outpatients.

CURRENT POSITION: Executive chef, Children's Medical Center of Dallas, TX, since 2005. ★
EDUCATION: Seattle Culinary Academy, Seattle Central Community College; Culinary Institute of America for extra credits; apprenticeship at Sun Valley Corporation, Ohio, for about a year. ★ **CAREER PATH:** Cooking jobs at several restaurants, Edmonds, WA; chef, CI Shenanigans, Bellevue, WA; chef, hospital industry, WA (about twenty years ago). ★
AWARDS AND RECOGNITION: Winner of a West Coast seafood competition for chowder; cooking competitions in Dallas. ★ **MEMBERSHIPS:** American Culinary Federation.

Salary notes:

$50,000 to $100,000, depending on your experience and the size of the staff you supervise.

Words of advice for people considering a similar career:

You don't become a chef overnight; it takes a long time. You have to be willing to critique yourself honestly and not let your ego get in the way. As chefs, we tend to sometimes think that our way is the only way. Learn to engage your staff, your clients, to make sure that what you're doing is what they want and what's working.

Describe a typical day.

It's turning into budgeting and managing people. A typical day is opening the facility and making sure that everything is going well. We feed about 350 patients in-house, plus those coming through the ER, and we also have retail outlets and a catering operation. I make sure that all the food and staff are here and that the events and parties are on track. Then I turn to the management side, budget, costing things out, writing new menus, revamping catering menus. I have meetings during the day. I start around five thirty A.M. and finish around two thirty P.M.

How many hours a week do you typically work?

Forty to fifty hours.

What are your specific responsibilities?

My responsibilities are the food, sanitation, safety, management, budget, menu writing. We change the cafeteria's menu weekly. There are staple items that are consistent, but we change the entrées. I have to stay on top of our pricing daily and weekly to make sure that we are not losing money. A lot of the time, it's a matter of showing that we're breaking even or making sure that we're showing the right number. We continue to grow, which is unusual, because the administration sees the cafeteria as a benefit for employees.

What do you like most about what you do?

I came from Seattle three and a half years ago. The people, the culture, are very diverse in the South. I love the different customs and foods. I have learned a whole new type of food for my job. It's fun to fuse pan-Asian with southern food. I also enjoy working with the patients. We have a program called Direct-a-Chef, where a patient who has been here forty-five days or longer can request a meal from me, anything they want, for them and their family.

What do you like least about it?

The kitchen is more than forty-five years old, so we're pushed far beyond its limits. I really wish that we could redesign this place, because I'm worried about someone getting hurt. We could be much more efficient.

What skills are most important for you to do your job well?

Definitely those psychology classes they wanted you to take in culinary school! Mentoring, the ability to write schedules, to write million-dollar budgets. You need to be confident. You need to engage your customers and treat them right. In my field, a culinary degree definitely helps. You're not just a steakhouse; you're serving an international cuisine. You have to be open to diverse people. Culture is a big driving thing in the kitchen, where multiple languages are spoken. We have twenty-four different nationalities in the kitchen. Politics, football—I have to be aware of all of that and how it impacts my staff.

What skills would you like to develop to help further your career?

I enjoy where I am now; it's good for my family and for me. I have no desire anymore to open my own place. So to become a corporate chef, a director, perhaps having more business-type skills, better project management, handling bigger budgets, would be helpful.

What are your long-term goals?

I've always operated with the mind-set that if I am challenged in a place, compensated fairly, treated with respect, I don't go anywhere.

What is the outlook for your type of job?

Up in Seattle I was hired about twenty years ago as the first chef for a hospital. At that time, every hospital had chefs. About ten years ago, all the chefs were let go to cut costs. Then when I was leaving, chefs started to come back. Down here in the South, all hospitals have chefs. So I don't see chefs going away. In Texas, the worth of a chef seems higher than it was in the Northwest.

How large is your staff?

More than sixty people.

What do you look for in a new hire?

You have to pass an extensive background check to work for a hospital. I've had to turn down a lot of people. I would love to get good people in here, and we're definitely willing to train. I'm very proactive in promoting my staff onward and upward.

What is your proudest accomplishment?

To grow from a dishwasher to an executive chef of a multimillion-dollar operation. Everybody can be a cook, but to be a chef you have to be able to manage a lot of people, to put in the time, to come up with new and innovative things, to keep your customer base growing and happy. I love this atmosphere. It's very rewarding.

Looking back, what surprises you about the path your career has taken?

When I went to culinary school, I wanted my own restaurant, to be big and famous. Through growing, learning, seeing what the business is, I ended up in hospitals. It's worked out well for me. A lot of chefs who work in restaurants wouldn't like hospitals at all. You have to be more of a business manager.

PILAR TAYLOR

As the chef of a yacht, Pilar Taylor is responsible for feeding the owners of the boat, their guests, and the crew while out at sea and the crew when the boat is at the marina. This requires menu planning and grocery shopping that can stretch across several countries.

CURRENT POSITION: Chef on a 111-foot expedition-style private yacht, Ft. Lauderdale, FL, since 2006. ★ **EDUCATION:** Culinary arts degree, Art Institute of Seattle (2003). ★ **CAREER PATH:** Cook, Daniel's Broiler, Bellevue, WA (one and a half years, while in school); cook, a couple of restaurants in the Seattle area after graduating; cook, the Ruins (fine-dining private club), Seattle (one and a half years); cook on a charter boat in Alaska (summer 2005); ran Delicious Planet, Seattle (one year). ★ **MEMBERSHIPS:** Greenpeace.

Salary notes:

It's based on the size of the boat. I haven't worked on a vessel larger than 120 feet, where it's typically $4,000 and $6,000 a month. On this boat, since it is private, I am making $6,000 a month, but I'm not getting tips since it doesn't charter. On a charter, you might make $5,000 but get $3,000 extra in tips.

Words of advice for people considering a similar career:

Do your homework. Talk to yacht chefs and different crews. There's a lot to learn about it, and you can't just jump on any boats. You have to make sure you're going to like that boat, that crew, that captain, because you live with them, you work with them. You want to make sure that there's no drama. On bigger boats, you'll have eighteen or so crew members, which leaves more room for politics and drama. Know the different facts about different boats, private and charters, to decide what you're really looking for.

What prompted you to be a private chef on a boat?

I like the traveling part of it. I was sick of the same grind, living from paycheck to paycheck, waking up, going to work, working until midnight, going home. It got a little too mundane for me. This sounded like something I would fit right into. At the end of October every year is the Ft. Lauderdale Boat Show. That's the time to come down, network, and get a job in yachting. In October 2006, I packed everything I owned, got rid of my apartment, and bought a one-way ticket to Ft. Lauderdale. That's where I've been ever since.

Working on a yacht is much different than restaurant cheffing. If somebody wants caviar in St. Lucia, you have to find caviar in St. Lucia. You have to be prepared and know what you're going to find in every place. All the crew lives on the boat; we're nomads, we don't have homes. You can make the same salary as the executive chef of a downtown New York restaurant. There are a lot of sacrifices with this type of career; relationships are hard. If you're on a charter boat for the winter in the Caribbean, you're gone for seven months without coming back to the U.S.

Describe a typical day.

When we have guests, I am up at five thirty and on deck by six, getting breakfast ready. I'll make a baked item, like a scone; a breakfast special (pancakes, eggs Benedict, waffles); a fruit item; eggs to order; bacon, sausage, or ham; toast. They might want a cheese platter or lox and bagels. The guests will send us a prep sheet before they come to tell us if there are things that they can't live without. That gives us a little bit of a heads-up. The stewards will clean up the area. I start making lunch. I make a sweet treat for after lunch, like a cookie or sorbet. At six or seven we do hors d'oeuvres and cocktails if they are into that. Then dinner: first course, entrée, dessert. In Europe, it can stretch out to five or six courses. Then coffee, cheeses if they are interested. Then I clean up and go to bed. I finish by ten or eleven, and try to be in bed by eleven, midnight at the latest.

How many hours a week do you typically work?

Right now, when we don't have guests, Monday through Friday, eight A.M. to five P.M., and Saturday half days. About forty-five hours. When we have guests on board, fifteen to eighteen hours a day.

What are your specific responsibilities?

I go grocery shopping and get all the food for crew and guests. The storage space on this boat is limited. If we go someplace where it's hard to find produce, I do all the provisioning, get seafood, produce, meats, etc. It's already portioned and packaged for me and I can just freeze it. I prepare all the meals for the crew and guests. I do lunch and dinner for the crew but they're on their own for breakfast. I take care of the cleanliness and organization of the galley. This boat was a new build, so I had to go shopping and get all the equipment, baking ware, food processor, KitchenAid—not to mention the things that will secure the equipment to the counters when we're sailing.

What do you like most about what you do?

I really like being in a new place. Playing with a local ingredient that guests have never tried—it's really nice when they really enjoy it and have a good memory of that food item.

What do you like least about it?

I really don't like the fact that I live out of a storage unit. I'm at the mercy of the boat and the owners, and that's something I'm starting to not like about it. I don't get to see my boyfriend whenever I want. We have to plan when to meet.

What skills are most important for you to do your job well?

Organization, for sure. Really knowing what kind of products you're working with, how long it's going to last, what's the best way to make it stay fresh and usable for the longest possible time. And you have to remember where you put it.

How large is your staff?

I'm the only one in the galleys. Stews make coffee and drinks, take the orders, and put them out. Certain boats have a stewardess pantry, but this boat only has one kitchen. Even the captain comes in and does dishes at the end of the night. We all chip in. It's not like that on every board.

How do you decide on your menu?

It depends on the preference sheet that guests send me. Unfortunately, it can be filled out by one person in the party, and they'll speak for eight people. The preference sheet is not very descriptive, so they don't tell you exactly what they like. You have to know where to shop when you get to a place. Among yacht chefs, we call each other and ask where we can find fresh raspberries, a certain kind of wine, etc. You have to order in and wait a couple of days to get the best stuff. It probably takes a couple of seasons to figure it out, to know where the best places are.

If you could open your own business, what would it be?

It would be something very similar to what I was doing at Delicious Planet, where I could tie in food and nutrition. But on a different scale probably. I am interested in teaching people about proper nutrition, what foods to eat and what it does to the body. I won't be cooking for the rest of my life. It's really stressful at times.

"Working on a yacht is much different than restaurant cheffing. If somebody wants caviar in St. Lucia, you have to find caviar in St. Lucia. You have to be prepared and know what you're going to find in every place. All the crew lives on the boat; we're nomads, we don't have homes."

EINAV GEFEN

At Unilever, Einav Gefen has a unique position that sees her supporting several brands by offering them her perspective on food as a chef. She participates in all aspects of product development, from ideas to development to packaging, working with all teams involved. As an internal educational resource, she also conducts cooking demonstrations and invites other chefs to do so to teach her colleagues about a new food trend, a technique, or a cuisine.

CURRENT POSITION: North America corporate chef for retail, Unilever, Englewood Cliffs, NJ, since August 2008. ★ **EDUCATION:** BA, social behavior, Israel; culinary arts degree, Institute of Culinary Education, New York, NY. ★ **CAREER PATH:** Garde-manger up to sous chef, Mul Yam, one of Israel's best restaurants. In New York: extern, Restaurant Daniel; executive chef, Danal; kitchen director, Amsterdam Avenue Jewish Community Center; chef-instructor, ICE. ★ **MEMBERSHIPS:** Women Chefs & Restaurateurs; James Beard Foundation; Experimental Cuisine Collective.

Salary notes:

From $80,000 to $120,000.

Words of advice for people considering a similar career:

Keep learning, and keep in touch with as many sources of knowledge as you can. Don't let a routine drown you. A day that goes by without me feeling that I learned at least one new thing is a wasted day.

Describe a typical day.

It depends on what projects I'm working on. I work on projects with several brands. If we are preparing for a showing, for which I cook, I make four or five tastings, different variations, for consumers, insiders, the research and development team, to see what works and what doesn't. Those days I'm in the kitchen. On other days, we might be in a meeting for several hours for one product. I participate in tastings for different brands, ongoing tastings on certain products, like salad dressings, where I might not be working fully on the product but they need my palate. I also work on packaging, so I can spend half a day scouting, going to supermarkets and looking at products. I always did that before, but now it's with a purpose.

How many hours a week do you typically work?

Definitely more than forty. I like to come in earlier because it's calmer, to get things ready. Some days I work ten hours, some days I work less, depending on what's going on.

What are your specific responsibilities?

To be in touch with the outside world, to keep my finger on the pulse of trends at all times, to know what restaurant trends will be in home kitchens. I have to be the quality checkpoint at the level of restaurants because we aim very high. My job is to try and keep on pushing the envelope in the sense of quality and of new things. Our marketing and brand people are sometimes not as in touch with what's out there, so I open the door for them. The definition is kind of vague and is really what you make it to be. You can make it bigger, make it important. You have to push yourself. I don't have a boss who says, "You'll do this for the next three months, then this." You do that yourself. You create your own structure.

What do you like most about what you do?

I feel like a kid in a toy store. I have access to anything I want, I can go spend the day in the lab with our food scientists to see how a product is developed, I can learn, learn, learn. I love the mentality; it's an awesome company. You're allowed to not have e-mail access on your day off. The mentality is "Don't burn yourself out, we need you fresh." Every idea is welcome. They want us stimulated at all times. An environment with so much knowledge and so many opportunities is amazing.

What skills are most important for you to do your job well?

People skills. Cooking skills for sure, but there are other people here who have those too. You are walking a thin line between different departments at all times, so you have to know how to explain things in a delicate way when you say that what they hope will work out won't. Although I have a big mouth and will say what I think, I will do it in a constructive way. That's one thing that comes out of the time I spent teaching—you have to do that.

What skills would you like to develop to help further your career?

Probably more marketing knowledge. I'd like to learn the American consumer a little better. Being foreign can help in many ways to see with different eyes, but on the other end, you are removed from the American way of consumption. Nothing is too hard for you to make at home, all from scratch, but that's not the case for our customers. A lot of people don't know how to make a tomato sauce from scratch.

What are your long-term goals?

Theoretically, I'm here for three years, until Richard, the chef who left to work at the global level in Germany, comes back. But who knows. Things can change within three years. If Richard comes back, they'll probably find me another position within the company. If he doesn't, I'd love to hold on to my position, because I think that three years are hardly enough to develop the position. If it were up to me, I would love to stay; if not, I would love to find a similar position in another company because I love the job. I love the chemistry of cooking, but this job allows you to have a family.

Describe your creative process.

Much of it comes from the advantages of being a foreigner and being a parent. I have to make boxed lunches for three young kids; I face the same challenges that everyone must face. The creativity starts there, because I discover niches of grocery stores that are not being tapped into. Then I am being challenged here by marketing and consumer people, because every time you have an idea you are being challenged as to why we should or shouldn't go ahead. I have to answer why a certain product isn't on the market yet—maybe someone already tried it and discovered that the idea didn't work. Then I narrow down the options to flavors and tastes, and cook them. I cook as I would in a restaurant; I don't have to be concerned about how we can obtain a certain ingredient—that's somebody else's concern down the road. But I have to be practical; I can put in truffles and it's tasty, but down the road that won't work out in a consumer product.

Looking back, what surprises you about the path your career has taken?

The path itself. When I had to give up restaurants after having my first kid, I had a very hard time. I had many fights with my husband, saying that I had given up more, made more compromises. I had set out to be a restaurant chef. I liked teaching at the Jewish Community Center, but I didn't like running the culinary program. When I went to ICE I didn't know I'd like teaching, but I really did. What keeps me going is that I have no fear of starting out, of looking for new things. This job brought me back to the kitchen. I'm surprised I got this job; I was up against some really experienced and qualified people.

How often do you set goals?

Every day. I used to work on a five-year plan. That was my way of living, asking myself where I saw myself five years from now and working backward from there, but that changed with a husband and kids, because your goals are not everyone else's. I have a three-page list of goals from when I first got to Unilever for what I want to accomplish here.

JASON GRONLUND

In his role in research and development with Tabasco, Jason Gronlund develops dishes and products that make use of Tabasco products for restaurant chains and food companies in the United States and around the world.

CURRENT POSITION: Executive chef, director of culinary and ingredient sales, McIlhenny Company Tabasco brand products, Orlando, FL, since 1998. ★ **EDUCATION:** Culinary arts degree, West Bay Vocational School (1982); U.S. Army Cooking School (1982); BA, culinary arts and food service management, Johnson & Wales University (1987). ★ **CAREER PATH:** Night baker, U.S. Army; Lincoln Cookware; regional corporate chef, Pace Food Picante Sauce/Salsa (1995–1998); culinary director, Creative Food Solutions (1998–2000); chef-partner in several restaurants concurrent with research positions. ★ **AWARDS AND RECOGNITION:** In culinary school, Most Elaborate and Closest to Art Design in Edible Art Contest; in college, American Culinary Federation gold, silver, and bronze medals in hot kitchen and cold salon in the student and professional categories; Humanitarian Award, National Salvation Army; President Award, Research Chefs' Association (2008). ★ **MEMBERSHIPS:** Institute of Food Technologists; Research Chefs Association; Board of West Bay Vocational School; director of Saving from the Heart, a program to feed the homeless in shelters; president of Chef Relief, which provides food when needed during disasters.

Salary notes:

Beginning positions start around $40,000 and it goes up to $200,000 for executive positions.

Words of advice for people considering a similar career:

Learn as much as you can. You're not going to get out of school and get in this business. If you graduate at twenty-one, spend the time until you're thirty learning about everything cooking oriented. School will teach you things, how to use books, but when you get to the kitchen you will really learn the reality of the processes. Today, it's pretty important to go to culinary school for this type of job. If you work with Thomas Keller, maybe not, but those opportunities are few. You need a good toolbox of different cuisines, the knowledge of how to blend flavors. You need to know how to balance your palate with fats and acids; having somebody teaching you that in class is a good thing.

How did you decide to create food products?

By accident. When I started working at Lincoln, they had five restaurants. A food broker came in and showed me a food product. I asked him what the burn temperature was, and he had no clue. I thought I could do this job and know how to answer the questions because I'd be talking to other chefs. I went to work for a food broker and stayed there five months, then I started working for Pace Picante Sauce.

Describe a typical day.

It depends on what project I'm working on. I do all my development work at home and travel wherever the project takes me. It's easier to travel from here than from southern Louisiana, where Tabasco is located. I have all the equipment I need here, and it's a quieter work environment. I work with the top one hundred food manufacturers in the world, trying to see how Tabasco can fit in there as a flavoring. We work through food products, we go through national association shows, multiservice operators, on-site catering. Leads are generated from anywhere. I have a whole series of questions that I ask each operator, which includes what they have in the kitchen, what flavors they have tried in the past, what ingredients they want to use or not. I work a great deal on paper before I start working on the product itself. Then I develop the product in my kitchen. Depending on manufacturers, I develop it as a gram formula, so that if they want to do a hundred-pound batch, they know to use 22 percent Tabasco, for example. A couple of times a week, I report what I do to Tabasco.

How many hours a week do you typically work?

Forty to fifty hours is a normal week. When I'm doing food-service seminars around Asia, I might work eighty to a hundred hours a week and then entertain customers. During overseas trips, the schedule gets pretty exhausting. I can fly as much as two hundred thousand miles a year, and I spend a hundred nights on the road domestically.

What are your specific responsibilities?

I belong to the sales side of the company. Cooking always comes down to the bottom line, whether you're doing a cookbook or having a restaurant. I have to aim for whatever project I'm working on to be profitable to the company. I sell the brand, but I make retailers and food-service companies understand the capabilities of our brand. I always think of myself as a very creative person, and in the kitchen I'm always solving problems. There's an intellectual side as well as a cooking side to this job.

What do you like most about what you do?

The diversity. Yes, I travel all the time, and there are headaches, but if you work as an executive chef somewhere, you have lots of headaches all the time anyway. I have more weekends at home, and the salary ranges are better in this area. I have a company car (a new one every two years), other perks like that.

What do you like least about it?

On the ingredient side, when working with food manufacturers, the biggest dilemma is our cost. We're not a cheap product. What you deliver has to be dead spot-on. But once you get there, there isn't much competition. Also, you spend so much time developing products and end up being 2 percent of the final result.

What is the outlook for your type of job?

As the momentum grew behind research chefs, too many people got into the field. As companies try to pull back and save money, they look to the suppliers to do the research and development that used to take place internally. So we get called more and more to do what they used to do in-house.

How many new products do you work on a year?

For our core products, not really any. I just play around. For our customers, I can write hundreds of recipes a year. It depends on what project comes in.

Describe your creative process.

I accumulate all the information available on the company I'm working with, to understand what they are looking for. That's the beginning of the creative process. Then I sit down with the company that wants a Tabasco product and ask tons of questions. Then I work a paper and decide which direction to take for the product that they need by narrowing it down to the feasible options.

How often do you set goals?

Every September we sit down and set goals. When working on accounts with food manufacturers or restaurants, it sometimes takes one and a half to two years to see the final product. So you need to continuously have something in the works. You always want to set a timeline for completion of a project.

6. PASTRY AND BAKING

Career opportunities for pastry chefs are constantly expanding. Few pastry chefs opened stand-alone operations or restaurants until a few years ago; today, most large cities have dessert-centric restaurants opened by former restaurant pastry chefs. Mindy Segal (page 148) opened HotChocolate in Chicago and Elizabeth Falkner

has Citizen Cake and Orson (a non–dessert-centric restaurant) in San Francisco. Will Goldfarb (page 260) had a dessert restaurant, Room 4 Dessert, in New York for a couple of years, followed now by Picnick, a sandwich kiosk, and equipment and product businesses. As more restaurants offer prix fixe and tasting menus in which dessert is included, they have pastry chefs on staff, list their names on the menu, and promote them as much as they do their executive chefs. When working as a restaurant pastry chef, you will likely spend a lot of time in a cramped kitchen but can look toward countless possibilities for entrepreneurship. Bread bakers are also seeing a renewed interest in good breads, including whole-grain and artisanal products. As such, owning a bakery or working in a local but high-volume operation are two career options for those interested in breads.

Making plated desserts is a creative outlet for many pastry chefs with an artistic background. Pastry and baking work is typically more exacting and more precise than savory cooking. It requires more chemistry and finesse and can be less physical. The focus of the work is often on daily production: a set number of desserts, pastries, and breads might be made, with fewer possibilities for last-minute changes. In restaurants and most independent shops, pastry cooks and chefs usually are trained in many aspects of the work, such as cakes, plated desserts, frozen desserts, and breads, rather than specializing in just one category.

education

As with cooking (see chapter 5, and chapter 1, for all educational options), you can start your career as a pastry chef or baker by working in a restaurant or bakery or obtaining formal training in a school. Most pastry arts programs will teach you all aspects of the business instead of focusing specifically on cake decorating or bread baking. If you have a particular interest in specialty skills, look for additional training at schools like the Institute of Culinary Education in New York, the French Pastry School in Chicago, or the San Francisco Baking Institute.

Most schools teach classic European pastry techniques—mostly French, with some German and Italian techniques. If you are interested in learning Asian desserts, for example, look for continuing-education or recreational courses, which often offer such specialties. The classic foundations form the bases of most desserts, however, so enjoy the time that you spend learning them and perfect these techniques before you start using ingredients like hydrocolloids. Some schools have also started offering classes using specialty ingredients, often at a level reserved for career students and industry professionals, which ensures that everyone in the classroom possesses basic knowledge and can learn these techniques in a way that will allow them to apply them in their own work.

in the kitchen

The majority of restaurant kitchens will have one pastry chef and one pastry assistant at the most. Some do not even have a full-time pastry chef and rely on their garde-manger or another cook to plate desserts that might have been made by a consultant or a part-time pastry chef, or bought elsewhere. Hotel restaurants tend to have larger staff, and some of the country's bigger and high-ranked restaurants have a pastry staff of several people. Here are the potential titles you might encounter in the largest pastry kitchens or pastry shops:

Pastry commis/prep cook/assistant
Pastry cook
Pastry sous chef
Pastry chef/executive pastry chef
Baker

The commis preps the ingredients that are needed for the composition of desserts and breads and typically does not bake anything. The pastry assistant might start mixing and doing other simple baking tasks, in addition to all the prep, particularly if the staff is small.

The pastry cook bakes and prepares desserts under the supervision of the pastry sous chef or chef. He or she will also do some prep work. In a larger pastry kitchen or operation, a pastry cook might be in charge of a station, such as preparing cakes for the display case of a pastry shop.

The pastry sous chef will supervise other staff members in the kitchen and take over expediting and managing duties when the pastry chef is not there. This person may or may not have creative input on the menu and works closely with the pastry chef. Depending on the size of the kitchen again, he or she might perform many tasks that would be assigned to a pastry cook.

The pastry chef or executive pastry chef heads the pastry side of the kitchen. In addition to creating desserts; hiring, firing, and training staff; controlling costs and budgets; and representing the business at events and in the media, the pastry chef also works closely with the executive chef on the savory side of the kitchen and with the establishment's general manager.

A few restaurants will have a dedicated bread baker who will prepare fresh bread for service and as needed in dishes. Most bread bakers work in bakeries, however, whether one-unit neighborhood bakeries or large-volume commercial operations. Restaurants often buy breads directly from the latter. If you are not yet familiar with those types of businesses in your area, start asking your server about the provenance of the bread that you are served when you go out for dinner. You will quickly see which names come up over and over again and can contact them for an interview.

The pastry staff typically arrives earlier in the kitchen than its savory counterpart. Pastry cooks and chefs might leave earlier as well if they work in a restaurant where they do not handle dessert plating, for example. Often, the plating is delegated to the junior staff. Bakers usually start their workday in the middle of the night so that fresh bread and baked goods are ready in the bakery's cases by morning.

While the professional kitchen is no longer a male bastion, the pastry kitchen can have more female chefs than the savory one does. Enrollment in ICE's professional pastry program tends to be 80

percent women and 20 percent men, while it is closer to 50-50 in the culinary arts program.

The restaurant kitchen is not the only place where you will find pastry chefs and bakers. Pastry shops and bakeries, as mentioned above, are seeing a boom in popularity around the country, and as such, more opportunities exist in these work environments. These establishments might look for more specialized workers than restaurants, depending on their size—having, for example, one person responsible for cakes and another for individually sized pastries.

specializations

Chocolates, confections, cake decorating, sugar work, and sugar and chocolate showpieces are all areas of specialization for people with pastry training or experience. Hotel pastry chefs, such as Lucy Martin (page 152), have more opportunities to work on high-end cakes and showpieces because of the large banquets that they usually have to plan, while the pastry chef of a restaurant might just make a couple of wedding cakes a year as a favor to customers or friends. Sugar work refers to pulling and blowing sugar, usually for showpieces or as a decorating item on a cake or dessert. Cake decorators (also called cake designers) tend to work on their own and rarely have a retail operation. Rather, visitors come to their studio or kitchen space to look at their portfolio and discuss what type of cake they want. People specializing in chocolate work might make pralines and bonbons in a restaurant that will give them out to customers or in a shop that will sell them. They can also specialize in large-scale pieces, work that is often tied to competition work.

All these specializations take years to develop. The learning opportunities include taking classes and workshops with top industry experts, staging and working with such experts, and spending years honing your skills through practice, practice, and more practice.

consulting

Because some restaurants cannot afford to employ full-time pastry chefs, and because pastry chefs or their staff are unfortunately often the first to be cut when times get tough in a restaurant, this industry employs many consultants, such as David Guas (page 166). As a consultant, you might be hired on a retainer basis to design a new dessert menu three or four times a year, for example, and teach it to the staff. Or you might have to produce the desserts or baked goods that you created, going in every day or a few times a week to make what's needed. You might go into a bakery to help them evaluate their operation and reduce their costs. Or you might work as a freelancer and provide banquet sites with cakes and showpieces as they need them. As with all consultant positions, it is best to wait until you have acquired enough

experience to confidently command such projects before going off on your own. A solid résumé with several well-known and reputed places on it will also raise the rates that you can charge. Those can be hourly or per-project fees.

salaries

Pastry salaries tend to be lower than cooking ones. Based on its 2008 salary survey, StarChefs reports the national average for pastry chef or executive pastry chef to be $46,228. That's just $2,000 more than a sous chef. The people profiled here cite similar numbers. Expect to make between $8 and $10 per hour at the beginning, when you will be paid on an hourly basis. Corporate pastry chefs or executive pastry chefs in large hotels or high-end restaurants will make closer to $75,000 to $100,000, usually after close to two decades spent in the industry. Consulting pastry chefs will make about $50,000 a year.

> I've always wanted to open up my own restaurant. I wanted to do food from the eye of the pastry chef. They work, or should work, closely with chefs in planning menus, so I think that smart pastry chefs learn how to cook while doing that, which I did.
>
> —MINDY SEGAL,
> chef-owner, HotChocolate

MINDY SEGAL

Mindy Segal's HotChocolate was one of the first dessert-centric restaurants when it opened in 2005. The artisanal restaurant is open for dinner six nights a week, lunch three days, and brunch on weekends, and places a strong emphasis on the use of local ingredients.

CURRENT POSITION: Owner, Mindy's HotChocolate Restaurant and Dessert Bar, Chicago, IL, since 2005, www.hotchocolatechicago.com. ★ **EDUCATION:** AOS in culinary arts, Kendall College, Chicago. ★ **CAREER PATH:** Ambria, Spago, Gordon, Charlie Trotter's, Marché, mk, and others, all in Chicago. ★ **AWARDS AND RECOGNITION:** Jean Banchet Award for Best Celebrity Pastry Chef in Chicago; Chicago's Pastry Chef of the Year; nominated for Outstanding Pastry Chef (2007, 2008, 2009), James Beard Foundation. ★ **MEMBERSHIPS:** Chefs Collaborative; Slow Food.

Salary notes:

I make no money; I always take care of my staff before I take care of me. I have an obligation to my investors to pay them back. I haven't had a raise in five years, and I took a pay cut to open my own place.

Words of advice for people considering a similar career:

Whenever I meet somebody who is a young professional or culinary student who says they want to get into the business for themselves, I always encourage them to go to business school. You can be a great chef, but if you don't know how to run your business and your dining room, you won't be successful. I've been really fortunate to work with chefs who've taught me how to run their businesses. At mk, I was able to ready profit and loss statements, cost recipes, etc. It helped round out my career.

What prompted you to start your own business?

I always wanted to open up my own restaurant. I went into this career wanting to learn how to be a chef. I did my externship in a hotel and became interested in pastry there.

Describe a typical day.

I oversee the restaurant. A typical day is to come in the morning and ensure that production is going well, all orders are in, answer questions that the manager and office manager have for me, and address any problems at the restaurant. The rest of the time is service.

How many hours a week do you typically work?

Eighty to one hundred hours a week. I'm a very hard worker.

What are your specific responsibilities?

I have the ultimate responsibility: that my restaurant is successful. Even though I have a staff, I am ultimately responsible for everything because I am the chef and owner of the restaurant. I'm responsible for the employees and their well-being, for making sure that they are working in a safe environment. I also need to make sure that guests' expectations are met from the beginning.

How many employees do you have?

Thirty-five.

What qualities do you look for in a new hire?

First and foremost, I look for the ability to think and to listen. I'm also looking for desire and the will to work hard toward a goal. I like people who are interested in being part of a team. I always tell my staff when they start, "I'm going to teach you how to think before I teach you how to make pastry." Once they know how to think, then they can use deductive reasoning to teach themselves something. It's one of the hardest things to teach somebody. They come with some experience, and they have to be retrained. Most chefs teach their staff to do the work they want them to do, not to think. I do the opposite, so that they can think outside their box.

What is most challenging as a business owner?

The most difficult thing to do in my restaurant is to get the thirty-five people who are employed by me to think and to put forth my philosophy about food, pastry, and service. That's the hardest thing I've ever done. It's a constant work in progress. You have to make people buy into the things that you believe in so that they are inspired to work hard for your vision. If you can get people to do that and think every day, you can be successful. That's the only way.

What are your long-term goals?

My first and foremost long-term goal is that I will pay my investors back. I have some ideas for other businesses that I'd like to open—more like fantasies. I'd like to open a wood-burning-oven bakery, where when we've sold out of everything, we're done for the day. I've gotten more into bread over the last year. We make 90 percent of our bread.

What keeps you challenged?

Everything. The most challenging thing is making sure that my staff and my guests are happy, that the food goes out and is good, that the bills are paid, that things are going well. If it were not a challenge, I wouldn't strive to be excellent each day. I love what I do; I love motivating my staff. I have a young chef who is twenty-seven and has been working with me for three years. When he started, he didn't know how to boil water. He said, "Let me be your sous chef, I won't go to culinary school, I want you to teach me." His growth, how he's come into his own, what I see in front of my eyes, gets me choked up. There's nothing more important than helping the people around me to be successful.

Have you made creative sacrifices because of your audience?

Absolutely. I make desserts for my guests; I make desserts that will sell. I don't have an ego *because* I have a restaurant. People criticize you, good and bad. It's all about opinion. You can think it's great, but guests have to think it's great. I try to motivate the front-of-house staff by telling them that they are in control of making the guest feel taken care of. They have to anticipate what guests need and take care of the guests before the guests know they need to be taken care of.

ERIN McKENNA

Erin McKenna's bakery, BabyCakes, uses only all-natural and organic products. All her products are free of refined sugar, gluten, wheat, soy, casein, and eggs and are vegan and kosher. Her first cookbook, *BabyCakes,* came out in summer 2009. She has been featured in many magazines and on food talk shows.

CURRENT POSITION: Founder and owner, BabyCakes, New York, NY, since 2005; opening another location in Los Angeles, CA. ★ **EDUCATION:** BA, communications, St. Mary's College of California, Moraga, CA. ★ **CAREER PATH:** In New York: style assistant, various magazines; waitstaff, Lupa; waitstaff, Mermaid Inn. ★ **AWARDS AND RECOGNITIONS:** Best Cupcakes, *New York,* seven months after opening; one of the Trendsetters of the Year, *Modern Bride* (2007); countless media mentions.

Salary notes:

$40,000 to $50,000

Words of advice for people considering a similar career:

The most important thing is to be absolutely infatuated with what you are doing because that will be what carries you through the hard times—when things get rough financially and I ask myself if I want to close. I would never do that. I'd find some way to stay open.

What prompted you to open your own business?

I never wanted to own my own business, but this type of bakery was something that wasn't done anywhere, and I knew exactly how I would do it. So I was inspired to make it happen.

Describe a typical day.

We have a night baker. So I come in and make sure that everything was done perfectly. I cut all the items so that they are ready for retail. I help the main baker with the list for the day. Then I go into the office

and deal with whatever issue we're dealing with that week. I spend about six hours a day in the office and the rest of the time baking.

How many hours a week do you typically work?

At this point not as much, probably about fifty. For the first nine months, I worked about twelve hours a day, seven days a week.

What are your specific responsibilities?

I would describe it as overseeing quality, developing the brand, strategizing growth. When an opportunity for growth happens, raising money and attracting investors. I supervise all decisions, such as those with customers, if people are complaining or asking for donations. Also, developing recipes and staying current with new products that are coming out in the health world.

What do you like most about what you do?

I really love that the business is alive. I love being able to be creative every day and having a following of people who appreciate what we do. That's very rewarding.

What do you like least about it?

Sometimes what I like least is that I don't get to bake as much anymore. I got into it for the baking, and now I'm more a supervising figure, working on more administrative tasks.

What skills are most important for you to do your job well?

Being in tune with your intuition. Not ignoring hunches. Being energetic and positive. Being organized is very important. I struggle with that. Being very aware of what's going on in the food industry. Being a people person, because I have to deal with people all day.

What skills would you like to develop to help further your career?

I think that I would like to know more about anything to do with finance. I'd like to know how to run things more cost-efficiently. And I need to be a little tougher with employees. I let things slide that I shouldn't.

What is the outlook for your type of business?

I think there are going to be more bakeries like BabyCakes. I was the first bakery to open that specialized in products that are vegan, and most are gluten free. We do across-the-board allergy-friendly products, and I have seen more bakeries like that trying to open.

How large is your staff?

Twenty employees. It's mainly people working the counters and 20 percent bakers.

What qualities do you look for in a new hire?

People who are intelligent, open, easy to talk to, enthusiastic about the product, warm, authentic.

What is your proudest accomplishment?

The frosting was my biggest accomplishment, because there was nothing like that on the market. One pastry chef said it was impossible to make frosting without dairy, sugar, and soy. But I figured it out anyway.

Looking back, what surprises you about the path your career has taken?

For my particular bakery, it surprises me how many people who don't have food allergies are die-hard fans. I really wasn't expecting that at all. Also the amount of press that comes through the door. I knew there would be a little of that at the beginning, but the story is still very intriguing for people.

LUCY MARTIN

Lucy Martin is the executive pastry chef of the largest Marriott in the world, which has seven food outlets, two thousand rooms, and 450,000 square feet of catering space. Some of the parties held at the hotel might require her to create desserts for fifteen thousand people.

CURRENT POSITION: Executive pastry chef, Marriott Orlando World Resort, Orlando, FL, since 2005. ★ **EDUCATION:** Associate's degree, theater arts, Florida State University; pastry arts degree, Institute of Culinary Education, New York, NY; classes at the Notter School of Pastry Arts; seminars at World Pastry Forum and at Istituto Europeo. ★ **CAREER PATH:** Pastry assistant, New York Marriott Marquis, New York, NY (1991–1995); extern, Colette's Cakes, New York (1995); pastry chef, Arthur's Catering, Orlando, FL (1995–1996); assistant pastry chef (1996–2001) and pastry chef (2001–2005), Marriott Orlando World Resort, FL. ★ **AWARDS AND RECOGNITION:** Silver medal and first place, Chocolate Showpiece (2005), bronze medal and first place, Chocolate Showpiece (2005), silver medal and second place, Team Super Challenge, and bronze medal, Chocolate Showpiece (2007), American Culinary Federation, Central Florida Chapter; ICE Alumni Hall of Fame (2005).

Salary notes:

All the regions are going to be different. The Southeast will be different than the Northeast. An entry-level pastry cook will earn $8 to $10 an hour. A pastry chef at a smaller country club might be $40,000, and at a much larger place, $70,000 and up.

Words of advice for people considering a similar career:

Go to the type of operation where you think you want to work and get some experience before going to spend $40,000 to $50,000 on school. I take externs, and one out of fifteen, I would say, will do something worthwhile in this industry. I think the expectations are unrealistic. You will not get to play with chocolate and sugar all the time. Go get a job as a pastry cook somewhere, not at a mom-and-pop shop but a restaurant or large hotel. Then find a chef you want to work under and learn from him

or her. I don't think that this is a career for all personalities.

Describe a typical day.

Depending on how busy we are and what projects we are working on, I start between five and seven A.M. I open e-mails to see if there are changes in banquets and what VIPs I need to be aware of. Then I go to the pastry shop and bakery to see how the staff is doing—I communicate with them, I look at charts, I see what everyone is working on. I do rounds to check the product quality of what was produced the night before. Then it depends. If we are really busy, I like to be hands-on and jump in to produce. If I don't have that luxury, I start answering e-mails and working on the projects I have on hand, like developing an item, a formula, or menus for restaurants or banquets. At about one or one thirty P.M., we have a daily meeting with the representatives of each department. We talk about functions, menus, etc. Based on that, I schedule all the production for the staff for the next day. During the course of the day I deal with other issues, like administrative things, hiring, and interviewing. I'm usually out at five, but it can be later, like nine sometimes. Right now I have two good assistants, so I don't have too many nine P.M. nights. I had a pastry chef until about two weeks ago, but I had to cut that position because of the cost. We have seven outlets total, and I'm in charge of all the pastry and bread production for all of them. We do numbers in the thousands. We have a new catering room that can fit fifteen thousand and have filled it a few times. We have other rooms that can fit two thousand. It's the largest Marriott in the world, currently, with 450,000 square feet of catering space and two thousand rooms.

How many hours a week do you typically work?

A minimum of fifty.

What specific training does your position require?

To manage a property like this, you have to be very organized. You have to be able to have backup plans constantly. With such high volume, lots of people are touching your product, so things could go wrong anytime. You have to be creative and know how to get out of a puddle if you get into one. You need good people skills, not just for working with the staff but also with catering managers. I have some guest contact; I do my own ordering with purveyors.

You have to have stamina too and roll with the punches. And enjoy what you do.

What do you like most about what you do?

To me it's fun. I don't do the same thing every single day, and there's plenty of room for creativity. I love developing products and the chemistry behind it. I also love the organization involved and seeing a project all come together. You spend hours at the computer organizing and then everything comes together. The adrenaline is great.

What do you like least about it?

Sometimes the personnel issues. Managing people and personalities can be more challenging than making the products. I can manage products a bit more easily and more quickly than a staff member who doesn't know the industry well or doesn't get along with other staff.

What skills are most important for you to do your job well?

Organization. You must have a very good baking background. People skills, patience, understanding. You have to be self-motivated and be able to motivate others. I don't think you need a pastry degree, but you have to have a very extensive knowledge of the entire field. You have to be very well rounded, not just know how to do cakes and French pastries.

What are your long-term goals?

To stay here. I enjoy what I do. If I had to make another choice, I would probably work at a test kitchen.

What qualities do you look for in a new hire?

Someone who is hungry to learn and passionate about the industry. If they have no energy about them when they come in, that's an instant turnoff. I would rather take someone with little experience but who is eager to learn than someone who has ten years' experience but isn't interested in learning. Communication, kitchen skills, and self-motivation are important. Previous experience in volume production definitely helps.

What keeps you challenged?

Pulling off the volume that we do and having it all go out okay, particularly on days when we have lots of groups. We have two or three ovens and twelve people working on those products. Coming up with new items that work for large banquets is always a challenge. Developing menus that are up-to-date with what's going on in the industry. Showcasing the talent of your team. Coming up with new products.

"To manage a property like this, you have to be very organized. You have to be able to have backup plans constantly. With such high volume, lots of people are touching your product, so things could go wrong anytime. You have to be creative and know how to get out of a puddle if you get into one."

CHRIS HANMER

Chris Hanmer is the executive pastry chef of the Ritz-Carlton in Lake Las Vegas, a 348-room property located seventeen miles from the Vegas Strip. He was the youngest American to win the World Pastry Team Championship as part of the American team in 2004.

CURRENT POSITION: Executive pastry chef, Ritz-Carlton Lake Las Vegas, since 2005. **EDUCATION:** Culinary arts certificate, Orange Coast College, Costa Mesa, CA; some courses at l'Ecole du Grand Chocolat, France; classes with Ewald Notter. ★ **CAREER PATH:** Commis, Candlewood Country Club, Whittier, CA, at fifteen; first pastry cook, Ritz-Carlton Laguna Niguel, CA; assistant corporate pastry chef, Albert Uster Imports, Gaithersburg, MD; assistant pastry chef for Ewald Notter; assistant pastry chef, Bellagio, Las Vegas, NV. ★ **AWARDS AND RECOGNITION:** As a culinary student, competed in three different competitions and won a silver medal as a team for hot food and a silver medal individually for cold food; coached a team in school that won gold; member of the National Pastry Championship team, third place (2003); member of the team that won Best Tasting and won overall at World Pastry Team Championship (2004).

Salary notes:

$80,000 to $100,000

Words of advice for people considering a similar career:

Spend the early part of your career building your résumé. I see so many young culinarians take a job that is undervalued just because of the title. Your résumé is what's going to get you the money later—work your way through it. Take your time. I see people who graduate with two- and four-year degrees and go straight to being a chef. That denigrates the industry. You can make $40,000 at that job, but if you wait a few years you can get to $60,000. It comes through hard work and working for the right people. Guard your résumé and work for the right establishments. When you are ready for that big job, they will say, "Wow, you worked with the best."

Describe a typical day.

I have a team member who comes in at five A.M. I come between seven and eight, depending on what there is to do. A huge part of my job is being up-to-date on my e-mails and communications. I spend the first part of my day on my e-mails. Then I transition to the team and daily operations. I confirm production and banquet schedules. I talk to people and see how things are going. Throughout that time there are fires to put out. After my morning, I do the lunches and transition to studying production schedules for the week and looking at the banquets. I do a lineup of what's coming up for the night to see what we'll need. While doing all of that, I'll also deal with e-mails, phone calls, menus. I wrap up between six and ten P.M., depending on what we have going on. If we have a banquet, depending on the needs, I might stay. If I come in early, by seven A.M.,

I will not stay until ten P.M., but ten-to-twelve-hour days are pretty common.

How many hours a week do you typically work?

Fifty to sixty hours.

What are your specific responsibilities?

That's kind of a moving target. What we create is the last word that the guests get. We are the "wow" of their dinner, of their function. My role is to bring the elegant and unexpected to life. Research, menus, e-mails, and constant evolution as a chef are all part of achieving that. You're only as good as your last creation. We're coming up with something new almost on a daily basis.

What do you like most about what you do?

Instant gratification is one of the best things about being a pastry chef. That's very rare to find. Oftentimes, in your profession, you have to wait for results. With pastry, right away you are able to use your hands and make something that you can be proud of. And you know immediately if it's great or if it's not.

What do you like least about it?

The hours, but even that's not that bad. It's my passion. If I have to say that the hours are the worst part of something you do, that's pretty good. I go home feeling good about what I did.

What skills are most important for you to do your job well?

Flexibility. Your job, your environment, and what's expected of you will all change. If you can't adapt, you will have a difficult time moving forward. Flexibility will also allow you to be creative.

What are your long-term goals?

Until recently I would have said to continue on this path, but now I think I'd like to open something for myself, a small shop. I also really enjoy teaching, so perhaps having my own school.

What is the outlook for your type of job?

I think that it's still good. We're going to need people for the upper-level, high-end hotels. The executive pastry chef level is something that you can't imitate. You will never be able to replace the flair and execution and streamlining that the executive pastry chef has, to motivate the team and impress the guests.

How large is your staff?

Five. At its highest, it was twelve, but we reduced because of the economic downturn. We supply four outlets and all the banquets.

What qualities do you look for in a new hire?

The biggest thing that I look for is attitude. I can train you technically, but I can't train attitude. It can be your first job or your tenth job; what matters is that you have a great attitude, you are willing to learn, and you are buying into the goals of the team you are joining. A culinary degree is a good benchmark, but once I see what they can do, on a scale of importance of one to ten, it's perhaps a two. I must see how they work, how they work with the team, and how they learn.

Any suggestions to improve work-life balance?

Training your staff and trusting them will help you let go of your daily life. Think of the expression, "I'd rather have one person working with me than ten working for me." Be a leader, train them, and trust that it will be done to your standards. As chefs, we need to have these standards. If you can't have the right people around you, that balance will always be skewed in the wrong direction.

"What we create is the last word that the guests get. We are the 'wow' of their dinner, of their function."

MICHAEL LAISKONIS

Michael Laiskonis is the executive pastry chef of Le Bernardin, Eric Ripert and Maguy Le Coze's four-star New York restaurant. He also creates pastry programs for the clients of Ripert Consulting.

CURRENT POSITION: Executive pastry chef, Le Bernardin, since 2004. ★ **EDUCATION:** Course work in visual arts, Wayne State University, Detroit, MI; no formal culinary training. ★ **CAREER PATH:** Cook, sous chef, then pastry chef, Emily's, Northville, MI (1995–1999); cook, then pastry chef, Tribute, Farmington Hills, MI (1999–2004). ★ **AWARDS AND RECOGNITION:** Ten Best Pastry Chefs in America, *Pastry Art & Design* (2002 and 2003); Pastry Chef of the Year, *Bon Appétit* (2004); StarChefs Rising Star (2006); Outstanding Pastry Chef, James Beard Foundation (2007). ★ **MEMBERSHIPS:** James Beard Foundation; Jean-Louis Palladin Foundation.

Salary notes:

Depending on the location and the size of the operation, between $50,000 and $100,000.

What made you decide to work where you are now?

Finding my way to Le Bernardin was the result of equal parts aspiration, hard work, and luck. Ultimately it was being in the right place at the right time and having the confidence to jump in headfirst. And of course, having Eric Ripert as a fan of my work didn't hurt! Working at this level in New York was always my end goal; it certainly happened earlier than I expected.

Describe a typical day.

A day that follows any familiar, predictable pattern is more the exception than the rule. There is never a dull day at Le Bernardin, for sure. There are, of course, constants; for me, that means I can be found at the pass for both lunch and dinner services. But the hours in between are devoted to a large number of wide-ranging projects we take on, from research and development to

PR. Thus, no two days are exactly alike.

How many hours a week do you typically work?

This answer depends on how one defines "work"! In the kitchen proper, my weeks consistently approach seventy hours. Above and beyond that, I take an ample amount of work home with me. In realistic terms, I don't see what I do as a job that I go to for a prescribed period of time each day; it's more of a lifestyle, a frame of mind that you just can't turn off.

Describe your creative process.

When you start out cooking, it's often a matter of seeing a dish—in a book, in another restaurant—and trying to replicate it. But once the process becomes personal, it becomes harder to describe. As chefs mature, a large part of creativity is instinctive, yet informed by an ever-growing foundation of experience and knowledge. For me, I'm increasingly applying something along the lines of a scientific method: Almost every dish begins with a "why" or "what if" question. From there, every step in the process hopefully ensures that I stumble upon some sort of "truth" or refinement.

What skills are most important for you to do your job well?

We are, ultimately, in the hospitality business. A big part of that is purging the word "no" from your vocabulary. And although I'm in the back of house, where I don't interact all that much with the clients, people skills are essential. Your own staff is your most valuable asset. Being a great chef is so much more than simply being a good cook.

What are your specific responsibilities?

I oversee all pastry production for Le Bernardin from conception to execution. In addition, I am responsible for dessert menus for three ongoing consulting projects as well as a significant amount of PR work for the restaurant brand.

If you were to open your own business, what would it be?

I would love to eventually have a multifaceted, multipurpose space that focused on research and teaching yet would also be able to feed the public. It's a tough business model, but what can I say, it's a dream!

How large is your staff?

In addition to myself, we have six full-time pastry cooks, plus additional stages and externs.

What do you look for in a new hire?

Generally speaking, I try to focus on the things you can't teach; passion, drive, and personality all carry more weight than the length and location of someone's experience. That said, it certainly does help if candidates have a base of fundamental skills as well as knowledge of what's going on in the world of fine dining. In the end, I look for someone with his or her own goals; while this person might not stay with me forever, I know he or she will make the most of the experience and bring something of themselves to the table.

Looking back, what surprises you about the path your career has taken?

Gastronomy was not part of my vocabulary growing up, so I just sort of fell into the business by accident; of course, looking back, I can't imagine doing anything else! I've come to realize that certain aspects of my personality are perfectly manifested in professional cooking: I like to work with my hands, I like to make people happy (the instant gratification helps, too), and I like to learn new things. Ultimately, I find that both my scientific curiosity and my urge to create are equally satisfied as a pastry chef.

How often do you set goals?

Honestly, in a stressful, fast-paced kitchen, I set goals on an hourly basis! Because time tends to be fleeting, I think it's important to structure goals of all shapes and sizes on a daily, weekly, monthly, and yearly basis. Knowing what you want to do in five years is great, but what can you do in the next five days to achieve that goal?

What do you do to relax?

I cook at home. Really, it's quite a different thing!

KIMBERLY SCHWENKE

Pastry chef Kimberly Schwenke is in charge of dessert creation and production for 312 Chicago, a restaurant that specializes in Italian cuisine and serves breakfast, lunch, and dinner seven days a week except for Saturday lunch.

CURRENT POSITION: Pastry Chef, 312 Chicago, IL, since 2008. ★ **EDUCATION:** Two years of college studying math before leaving to work in restaurants; pastry arts degree, French Culinary Institute, New York, NY. ★ **CAREER PATH:** Nighttime dessert plater, Magnolia Grill, Durham, NC; pastry cook, NoMI, Chicago; pastry cook, fine-dining outlet of the Ritz-Carlton, Chicago; assistant pastry chef, then pastry chef, Carolina Inn, on the campus of the University of North Carolina–Chapel Hill; pastry chef, Sepia, Chicago. ★ **AWARDS AND RECOGNITION:** While at Sepia, nominated for the Jean Blanchet Rising Pastry Chef Award and featured in *Food & Wine* in January 2008.

Salary notes:

$35,000 to $50,000 depending on what you are doing and the type of property.

Words of advice for people considering a similar career:

If you really enjoy food, and really enjoy cooking, it's totally worth it. I had some people with me in culinary school, and I've met people, who decide that they love cooking at their house and go to school and then never set foot in a restaurant or catering company. It's a hard life, and you need to make sure you understand what your day-to-day life will be like before you commit to it. There are other ways to enjoy baking cakes than making it your career. I gave myself a month, and after two weeks I knew. I never looked back. It can hit you like that—you have a great time and you never leave.

Describe a typical day.

I get here around seven thirty A.M., some days later and some earlier. I have a five-year-old, so sometimes it's hard to get her out the door. It also depends on whether other people are working or I'm the only pastry person for that day. I check what was sold the night before, check my e-mail to see if there are any changes to parties, look at reservations, see what happened last night and what will happen today. I look through the inventory, see what's good, what's bad, what needs to be redone. I reset the line for lunch. Then I start working on production for the day, making ice cream and sorbets, dessert components, etc. There's someone at the table baking all the breads for lunch and dinner service too. I have to have a lunch dessert special ready at ten thirty to show the waitstaff. Downstairs is the prep kitchen and upstairs the line in the restaurant. I stay downstairs at lunchtime; occasionally I go up to help plate if needed. Usually, lunch is the best time to get into the ovens and stoves. Some days I leave at five or six P.M.; some days I stay late, if we have parties or things like that. It's such a small open line up in the restaurant, and the desserts come from the pantry line, so there's literally no room to be standing there. I have to trust the pantry person and the sous chef and chef to keep an eye on what's going out.

How many hours a week do you typically work?

About fifty. This pastry chef job that I have now is more of a mom-friendly pastry chef job, which is one of the reasons I'm here. As opposed to things earlier in my career when I worked three P.M. to one thirty A.M., for example.

What are your specific responsibilities?

There are two major parts. The main part is the pastry responsibilities: writing the menu, supervising the production of all the pastry, *mise en place* items, sourcing the ingredients I need. Then I'm also a supervisor in the kitchen, so I have duties that have nothing to do with pastry, such as payroll, scheduling, and food costs. Sometimes I'm the only supervisor in the kitchen, depending on scheduling. Especially now that everyone's budgets are so tight. I have to make family meal today, for example, because we wanted to save hours, and I went through a bunch of invoices because the chef is off today. Seventy percent of what I do is pastry, and 30 percent is supervisory. We—myself, the sous chef, and the chef—know based on our business how much money we can spend, and we write the schedule to reflect that.

What do you like most about what you do?

I like physically creating things. I like that every day is a new day that allows you to make new products. I enjoy making things that make people happy. Desserts make people happy, and I enjoy that very much.

What do you like least about it?

The one thing that I do like least are some of the constraints of the restaurant business (versus when I worked in an office): You are here on Saturdays, on major holidays, at night when I used to work at night. But it's not that much of a sacrifice.

What skills are most important for you to do your job well?

Obviously, a good palate, as well as understanding food and how to work with it. Also understanding what your customers want. Then there's time management and juggling different tasks at once. Because usually you have too many things to do and not enough hours, pots, and pans to do it. All three are vitally important.

What is the outlook for your type of job?

Right now is a really hard time. People are cutting back on their dining dollars, and when they eat out they cut off appetizers, desserts, and wine. I do know many pastry chefs who've lost their jobs, or lost their pastry cooks, or the pastry cooks stayed and the pastry chef was let go. As a pastry chef right now, you have to make yourself useful to the kitchen as a whole. I think this is short-term. Before the economy slumped, the outlook for pastry chefs was actually good. Many restaurants were realizing the need for pastry chefs—for trained pastry chefs—rather than buying their desserts from somewhere. You need not to be your own little island to the side making pastries and find a way to integrate yourself in the kitchen. We are rewriting our breakfast menu right now, so I volunteered to spearhead that. One, because there are things I can do for breakfast that marry well with a pastry chef's skills, but two, because it's a good way to expand my responsibilities and take some of the stress off the chef.

How large is your staff?

Two pastry cooks and one breadmaker, who also does some other prep in the kitchen.

What qualities do you look for in a new hire?

Someone who hopefully can learn quickly; that's hard to tell in an interview. It's fantastic to get a pastry cook who's trained because you don't have to teach them as much, but sometimes it's harder to get someone who's well trained and also open to new ways, new techniques of doing things that are restaurant-specific. I'm sure I was this way too. It's really hard with a pastry cook right out of culinary school. They think they spent all this time and money, learned these things, this is the way you make a *macaron,* ice cream and sorbet, and you come to a place and the chef says, "Yes, ninety percent of that is true, but I like to do things this way." So you want to find someone who is willing to learn, teach themselves, and talk to people about new foods, new techniques.

Describe your creative process.

312 Chicago is an Italian restaurant, so all of my desserts need to have an Italian edge or flavor. I start with an ingredient. I don't say, "I need a new tart or cake or ice cream." I say, "I really want to do something with chestnuts," for example. Then I think about how I want to use it: whole chestnuts, chestnut flour? I landed on a chestnut cake with candied chestnuts on the side, then moved from there to things that would go with it. I start with the largest flavor I want to get across and move out from there. Sometimes it's a flavor combination.

ELISA STRAUSS

Elisa Strauss works as a cake designer out of her own studio, Confetti Cakes. She began her career while still employed in the fashion industry, creating and decorating cakes part-time. She is the author of two cookbooks, *The Confetti Cakes Cookbook* and *Confetti Cakes for Kids*.

CURRENT POSITION: Head designer and owner, Confetti Cakes, New York, NY, since 1998, www.confetticakes.com. ★ **EDUCATION:** BA, studio arts, Vassar College; one semester at the Art Institute of Chicago; one course at the Fashion Institute of Technology in New York; pastry arts degree, Institute of Culinary Education, New York, NY (2001). ★ **CAREER PATH:** In New York: textile designer, Ralph Lauren (two years); handbag and accessories designer, Frederic Fekkai (one year); freelance designer, Ralph Lauren. ★ **AWARDS AND RECOGNITION:** Best Food Presentation, BizBash (2005); 25 Trendsetters award, *Modern Bride* (2006); Food Network Extreme Cake Challenge winner (2007); Ten Best Pastry Chefs, *Pastry Art & Design* (2008); appearances on *The Apprentice,* the *Today* show, and other Food Network Challenges. ★ **MEMBERSHIPS:** Board of Baker's Dozen; donates to countless charities.

Salary notes:

I don't pay myself anything. When I first started, I would only pay myself when I had to in order to pay the bills. The secret of a small business owner is to keep money in the business. People who work for me get between $10 and $20 an hour—$10 for three months, then up from there. Twenty dollars is more than I make. You don't get into this business to make money.

Words of advice for people considering a similar career:

Intern for an establishment that is similar to what you are looking to create for yourself. That way, you will have a real-life frame of reference when it comes to running your own business.

Describe a typical day.

There is no typical day. You make a list, and by the time you get to the first item on the list, there are already five more things to do before you even get to the list. I don't think of myself as entrepreneur, but that's what people usually refer to me as. I have the entrepreneurial feeling of always looking toward the next thing. I don't stop to think about it. Bobby Flay said once that if you are not nervous doing something, it's not worth doing. I lose five pounds before each Food Network Challenge. I meet with clients, handle press queries, teach, and make a cake. A lot of people come through here; it's hard to retain employees. It's a stressful business; it's time and temperature sensitive. It's so rewarding when I see my past interns and employees say they completely understand now.

How many hours a week do you typically work?

At the beginning, I felt like I worked all the time. Now on most days, I work nine to five here in the office. But I wake up early and check my e-mail; I take calls on weekends, work on evenings. You can't call in sick when people ordered the cake a year ago.

How does the process with your clients work?

They come here to the office for tastings and to look through my portfolio. We talk about details and flavors they want. People come to us either because they have seen our cakes or because they have a unique design for us. Usually they come with an idea but then we design the cake. It's very rare that they tell us exactly what they want to do. It's kind of like leaving yourself in the hands of the chef. It's just as important that they tell me what they don't like as what they do like. Our minimum order is a cake for fifty people. Whether it's for ten or for a hundred, it will take us the same amount of time. We have to educate people as to how long it takes to design our cakes. We used to do mini cakes, cupcakes, cookies. I love to do that stuff, but I don't do it anymore because it doesn't make sense financially.

How many cakes a week do you do?

I do three or four cakes a week. I teach too, and I do photo shoots. It's really hard because we don't do the same cakes twice; that's one of the hardest aspects of the business.

How large is your staff?

I have five employees. For many years, it was just three people. I'm trying to grow.

What do you like most about what you do?

When I talk to the client on Monday. Or when I e-mail them pictures and follow up and hear what people thought of the cake. I assume that's why we keep doing what we do. Our cakes are dessert but also decoration. They make people's events. One of the things I'm most proud of is that our cakes are from scratch and that they taste good. Everything I do tends to be high-end, so it can be hard to diversify. That's why I love teaching and writing books, because people can have a little piece of Confetti Cakes. That's something I always struggle with for the business: how to make it available to everyone.

What do you like least about it?

It's all-consuming. I'm always just doing the same thing, like a hamster on the wheel. It's very difficult to change anything because I've been doing it for ten years. It's a tough business. The thing I dislike the most is pricing because I still don't feel like I know how to do it. It's like a guessing game.

What skills are most important for you to do your job well?

Multitasking is the number one skill. But without talent for the work you can't do it. Maybe some people have less talent but are great at multitasking. Some people are very talented but are stuck because they don't know how to run the business. Cake decorating is like architecture. You can be the best baker and not be able to run a business.

What is the outlook for your type of job?

It's a very difficult business. I hope there will be traditional cake designers, but I wouldn't be surprised if cake designers will use more technology. You can use a scanner to repeat a pattern or put a logo on a cake. We do it by hand. Franchising seems to be the only way that bakeries can stay in business, in the U.S. at least. I wouldn't be willing to dumb down our cakes and have them mass-produced.

"There is no typical day. You make a list, and by the time you get to the first item on the list, there are already five more things to do before you even get to the list."

DAVID GUAS

As a consulting pastry chef, David Guas works for several restaurants and pastry shops around Washington, DC, to establish and/or produce their dessert and pastry programs. His first cookbook, *Damgoodsweet,* came out in fall 2009. He is also opening a pastry shop.

CURRENT POSITION: Chef-owner, Damgoodsweet Consulting Group, McLean, VA, since September 2007, www.damgoodsweet.com. ★ **EDUCATION:** Two years at Colorado Mountain College, Glenwood Springs, CO; culinary arts degree, Sclafani Cooking School, New Orleans, LA. ★ **CAREER PATH:** Executive pastry chef, Acadiana, Ceiba, DC Coast, and TenPenh, Washington, DC (about ten years total). ★ **AWARDS AND RECOGNITION:** Washington, DC, Pastry Chef of the year, American Culinary Federation, 2003; one of the Top 8 Pastry Chefs in the Country, with his dessert featured on the cover, *Bon Appétit* (2003); Pastry Chef of the Year, Washington Restaurant Association (2004); numerous TV appearances. ★ **MEMBERSHIPS:** Slow Food; Southern Foodways Alliance.

Salary notes:

I left a group where I was making about $80,000 to $85,000, and now make about $50,000. But I am my own boss, and that's part of the deal. For chefs in general who aren't owners of their establishments, the range is $45,000 to $70,000 or $75,000. A pastry chef is a bit lower—it can be $35,000.

Words of advice for people considering a similar career:

Do not get into this business unless you absolutely love food. It's a hard business; it's not for the weak. It has to be everything for you. You have to be able to take criticism. You can't be overly sensitive as you grow in your career.

Describe a typical day.

These days, I'm juggling a couple of clients whose openings overlapped. I get up at three thirty A.M. to drive to the Virginia suburbs. I have keys to the client's kitchen and I do all the production out there for a 250-seat restaurant. I get out by eight or nine A.M. to drive to DC to another client, a cupcake shop, to do the training, supervise production, and make sure that operations are smooth. Every day they get better, so every day gets easier. Another client, a Middle Eastern restaurant group, has over fifteen different restaurants, and I am working on a second proposal for them. Then I race back to my area to pick up my two kids at five P.M., drive them to tae kwon do, then I go home and make dinner and a bath and put them to sleep by eight thirty. Then I do another hour of work in my home office, billing, pitching clients. I try to get to bed by ten or ten thirty P.M. That's been my schedule of the last six weeks. Once one of my contracts ends, I'll be able to get to my suburban client by six A.M. and spend more time in my home office.

How long do your contracts last?

I try to get yearly contracts where I am on retainer and maintain menus. I have one in Bethesda, MD, where I go in every three months and train the sous chef, and I am available by phone for consultation to make things smaller or bigger. That's ideal. I create a menu, send it to the owner for approval, he approves it, I order products, train the sous chef, monitor production, tweak what's needed, get feedback, and leave. They have a very capable staff; they just don't have the time or energy to create recipes or execute.

How many hours a week do you typically work?

Fifty to seventy.

What do you like most about what you do?

The flexibility, the freedom that I feel. I don't have to call a boss to ask if I can leave town for two days or take the weekend off. I know my responsibilities to my clients and I can manage accordingly.

What do you like least about it?

I am my own boss. I have to think about where my next paycheck is coming from.

What skills are most important for you to do your job well?

Being organized and having good time management. You need to have a general overview of all your responsibilities and be in touch with your clients. And then you need people skills, social skills, to talk with clients and check in with them and express my interest in their operations. It's a very social industry.

What skills would you like to develop to help further your career?

Money management, definitely. The innards of running a business. I'd like to strengthen my skills for the daily routine of running a business, balancing checkbooks, invoicing clients, staying on top of receivables and payables. I need to get to the point where it is automatic to me—I'm almost there. I have an accountant and someone who comes in once a month to make sure I did it right.

What are your long-term goals?

To open my own bakery, then to have multiple bakeries. I'm not greedy, but I know that I would need more than one to afford a good lifestyle where I am secure and can put my kids through college. The first thing would be to have a bakery where I can sell retail, because that's sometimes confusing for people who liked a dessert I made for an event and would like to know where they can get it.

DAN GRIFFIN

Pearl Bakery, which opened in 1997 in Portland, OR, uses local, organic, and small-batch ingredients in its breads and baked goods. As production manager, Dan Griffin is in charge of all the items sold in the bakery and at the farmers' market, and in charge of the production staff who bakes them.

CURRENT POSITION: Production manager, Pearl Bakery, Portland, OR, since 2006. ★
EDUCATION: Chemistry major, UC Santa Cruz; pastry arts degree, California Culinary Academy, San Francisco; individual training with people throughout career. ★ **CAREER PATH:** Intern, San Francisco Baking Institute; Artisan Bakers, San Francisco (1997–2006) with Craig Ponsford, head of Bread Baker's Guild; during that time, left to be head baker at Bouchon Bakery, Yountville, CA, for six months. ★ **MEMBERSHIPS:** Bread Baker's Guild.

Salary notes:

Between $9 and $14 an hour. People making $14 have a lot of responsibilities, including ordering. I have complete confidence in them to change formulas and update files. As far as managers, it's different between here and California. I'm getting $40,000 to $45,000 a year, while a colleague in California in a slightly larger bakery makes $75,000.

Words of advice for people considering a similar career:

Know what you're getting yourself into. The baking field itself is a labor field, like cooking, but the hours are much different. Being a chef and being a baker probably carry the same stress, the same physical activity, but the hours are completely different and will eat at you slowly. There's a huge time range for working shifts. I have people working eleven P.M. to six A.M., others two P.M. to eleven P.M. We run twenty-four hours a day. And nobody wants to stay on the same shift forever. In order to open your own bakery, you'll have to work all the shifts and change constantly.

It can be very lonely. The higher you go, the lonelier it gets. When you are a manager, you get calls at all hours of the night, and your schedule is never the same. It can turn you into an insomniac and make you hate your job. I've seen that happen time and time again. You need to be able to take naps and regulate your sleep.

Describe a typical day.

In my job, there's not really a typical day. I come in any time from eleven P.M. to five A.M., or I sometimes work all night. In a perfect world, I'd come in around three or four A.M., work for about ten hours, do administrative work during that time too, deal with personnel issues, adjust the formulas because of the many different flours that we use. I do hands-on work; I force myself to get back there and get my hands in the dough. The job I have doesn't really allow for that, but I feel it's important because if I can't teach my staff, I'm not really worth it. All product development is done through me or by me. Nothing goes out unless it goes through me. We taste it, change formulas. Another part of my job is teaching my bakers. We haven't had much turnover over the last two to five years, so I have guys who've learned a lot from me. Now, over the last six months, they have been able to develop their own formulas.

How many hours a week do you typically work?

It depends on the season. From January through February, seven to eight hours a day, five days a week. In the summer and November through December, twelve to fifteen hours a day, six to seven days a week.

What are your specific responsibilities?

Production, personnel, changing formulas, keeping everything on track. With the staff, it's answering their questions, sitting with them to talk about production and people issues.

What do you like most about what you do?

I love to see the end products. I switched from becoming a chemist to the culinary field because of the immediate gratification. I love producing something over a two-to-three-day period and seeing what the result is, what my hand can produce. We deal with very basic ingredients—flour, yeast, and salt—but the sky is the limit with what you can do.

What do you like least about it?

The personnel issues. Every month, I learn to deal with people much better. People don't always get along with other people.

I've always been able to go and talk to someone I had an issue with and solve it. Here I am more of a mediator, and it's not the most fun thing that I have to deal with. Especially when employees don't see eye to eye and I can't make them, or I can't fix the problem.

What skills are most important for you to do your job well?

Patience is a big one, for both personnel and production matters. We deal with a lot of hurry-up-and-wait. It's very fast and furious. We mix the doughs and then we have to wait. It takes patience and timing, to wait for the right moment to shape the bread. And obviously patience with people. You also have to constantly challenge yourself, to learn and not be complacent with the skill set that you have. I've learned with the best people in the country. My teachers are awesome. But even having said that, there's always more to learn.

How large is your staff?

We have forty employees in total. Other than ten to twenty retail employees, everyone reports to me, so about twenty-five to thirty people.

What do you look for in a new hire?

I look for dedication to the craft, mainly. Many people dream of working in bakeries because it's a romantic idea, but half the people I interview are kind of lackadaisical about working in a bakery. So I look for a passion for bread, dedication, and willingness to learn. I can teach a lot. I can teach them to make bread, but I can't teach them if they think they know everything.

The biggest indicator on whether or not I hire somebody is my crew. I value their input quite a bit, because they've been with me such a long time. You have to be able to work as a team and get your hands dirty.

What keeps you challenged?

Coming up with new ideas. The procedures are all kind of the same. I like the challenge of coming up with something new that people are going to like, implementing that into production, and making sure that everything fits together. Sometimes, putting it all together is more difficult than coming up with new products.

"I do hands-on work; I force myself to get back there and get my hands in the dough. The job I have doesn't really allow for that, but I feel it's important because if I can't teach my staff, I'm not really worth it."

7. CATERING, EVENTS, PERSONAL AND PRIVATE CHEF WORK

Catering, events, and personal and private chef work involve superior organizational skills, in addition to the actual ability to cook food. Each category has its own set of requirements, challenges, and rewards, but all of these roles are clear alternatives to restaurant work. Personal chef work offers the most flexible schedule of all, while catering and event-planning professionals are subject to long hours and weekend work—even if you are part of the planning staff rather than the hands-on cooking team. Having restaurant cooking experience will be useful when looking for catering and private or personal chef positions. It is not necessary on the event-planning side, but a certain knowledge of what's going on in a professional kitchen will go a long way toward making your job easier because you will be able to communicate more clearly with the kitchen staff.

catering and events

Caterers and event planners work hand in hand on most projects. The event planner of a venue will work with clients on all aspects of their events, while the catering department will focus on the food component. Many restaurants offer catering and special-events options and have a separate department to handle such work. In smaller operations, a chef's assistant might handle special-event requests, but as soon as the volume is sufficient a separate person is generally hired who will then also take on business development. Possible employers for event-planning positions include restaurants, hotels and resorts, corporations, independent companies, nonprofit organizations, and institutions. Working on the planning side of events requires a significant degree of organization. If you cannot stand Excel spreadsheets, you might not want to begin a career in this field. You also need to be very diplomatic and patient since you will be dealing with people planning important work and life events, such as business conferences and weddings. You might deal with your clients directly or instead work with a wedding planner or someone in an event-planning department at the client company. In the latter case, it means that they in turn have to please their boss or client. This adds to their stress level, and that stress can then be passed on to you.

The work you do in catering and events ranges from not involving cooking at all if you are on the planning and sales side of the company, to doing some cooking if you own a small company and need to work alongside your cooking staff in addition to handling sales and managerial duties, to cooking 100 percent of the time if you are a cook or chef. Having a cooking background might help you with catering sales and event planning, since you might be more able to explain what can be done food-wise based on the size and scope of your client's desired event. The work also varies depending on the size of the operation; caterers can be very small—a one-person operation—or deal with $20 million in sales at a large event company or resort.

As an event planner, your tasks will include contract negotiations as well as handling all the details leading to the event, including equipment rental and being the in-house point person for all vendors. You will mostly work Monday through Friday but might have to be present during weekend and evening events. Your schedule might thus be Tuesday through Saturday, or you might start later in the morning in order to be available in the early evening when your event starts.

When you work on the cooking side of catering, you might be in a restaurant, in a catering facility, in a hotel, in an event space, or on your own. You might do it part-time, keeping a desk job during the week, for example. A restaurant might see a slightly smaller volume of business than if you work in a hotel that does events for thousands of people at a time. An event space might not be booked every day of the week, which gives you more flexibility in your schedule. When you work on your own, you might specialize in small events, since you may not have access to facilities and staff. It is tempting to launch a catering business out of your home since it's a relatively easy way to make additional income while working elsewhere, for example. However, to operate legally, you will need to prepare your food in a certified kitchen and carry liability insurance.

One of the cooking challenges of catering is that you might work in different kitchens all the time—at least to finish the food just before service. You might also have to set up your serving stations outdoors, which will require special equipment. On the other end, an outdoor setting will allow you to interact with your clients and their guests and get instant feedback on the food you prepared. Other than your core staff, you might also work with different servers and cooks all the time, since the number of people you'll have at your disposal will depend on the size and budget of the event and will thus vary.

Many caterers who are able to grow their company develop a niche, such as Scott Wagner (page 182), or sign exclusivity contracts with some venues, like Jim Horan (page 175), which can include managing a café or restaurant for a museum or stadium, for example. You can start your business small and grow it first by hiring additional people or renting space as you need it, until you can buy or build your own larger space.

personal and private chefs

Personal chefs work for multiple clients, usually preparing a few meals at a time in the client's kitchen or in a commercial kitchen and freezing them for the rest of the week. If you cook in their kitchen, expect to bring all your equipment with you, including reusable plastic containers and resealable plastic bags to store the food. You will typically spend just a few hours a week at one client's kitchen, leaving you the opportunity to work for many at once. This freedom means that you can decide how many days a week you want to work and what income you want to have. The more clients you have, the more money you'll make.

The American Personal & Private Chef Association reports that close to nine thousand personal chefs are in business, serving about seventy-two thousand consumers (the organization itself has about forty-five hundred members). The organization offers its members the opportunity to list their business on its website, which is an important source of client recruiting for personal chefs. Your own website and ads in local newspapers or on community websites are also ways through which you will find clients. Some of it takes place through word of mouth—your happy clients will recommend you to their friends. Keep in mind that expenses for advertising and publicity, organizational memberships, groceries, and travel are all part of the costs you will incur while running your business. As such, it is important that you factor them into the price that you charge your client.

As a personal chef, you might deal with people who have dietary restrictions and find it too tedious to cook themselves. As such, knowing how to cook for people with food allergies will help develop your client base. You can acquire this knowledge through classes but mostly through plenty of reading. Because feeding people with such needs can be challenging, do not do it unless you are absolutely sure that you are up to the task. Other clients might be families that require you to cook different meals for each person, based on food preferences. You will usually submit menus to your clients, who will then pick what they want you to cook that week.

A private chef, in contrast, works for

one family at a time, five or six days a week, and might even live with their clients. Their duties might go beyond cooking, from administrative work to dog walking. Mutual trust is an essential component of the relationship between chef and client since you are in their home all day, sometimes alone with their children, for example. You will be responsible for all grocery shopping, including staying within the budget decided upon with your client. The rewards, particularly financial (private chef salaries can go over six figures), are high: You will likely work in a beautiful, well-equipped kitchen, will have access to good ingredients, and might even travel with the family. Some of the challenges of the position are the fact that you cook for the same people all the time. While you get to know their palates, it also means that you need to keep them excited by your food. You have to create a new menu every day. You also need to remember that you are an employee. Some employers will make that clear to you, but others might become close to you and blur that line. However, if things suddenly don't go well, they have the power to let you go. Finally, some people might find this type of work isolating, compared to either commercial kitchens or offices.

Many private chef positions are listed through staffing agencies, which often require that you have prior experience in domestic service. Some families are willing to give a chance to a chef who hasn't worked in this field; this is particularly true if you have worked in top restaurants, since your employer can then mention that when inviting friends and business associates over for parties. Private parties can range in scope from an intimate dinner for eight to a sit-down feast for fifty, so you need to be comfortable with volume cooking for when those needs arise.

salaries

Event and catering sales staff receive a commission on top of a base salary. At the beginning of your career, expect base salaries between $35,000 and $45,000; those can go up past $100,000 when you are the director of a large operation. The American Hotel & Lodging Association stated in a 2006 survey that the median salary for a catering sales manager in a hotel was $65,000.

Cooking positions or catering pay ranges from an hourly wage between $10 and $15 to salaries around $50,000 in mid-career, which go higher if you work in a high-volume establishment. Often, clients will also tip the staff, so you might get additional cash at the end of an event.

The American Personal & Private Chef Association states that its members make between $200 and $500 a day. Several times a year, ICE's career services department gets job listings for private-chef positions that pay more than $100,000.

JIM HORAN

Jim Horan is the founder and CEO of Blue Plate, one of the largest catering companies in Chicago, with sales that near $40 million, more than five hundred employees, and a thirteen-thousand-square-foot facility. It has preferred caterer status at more than eighty-five venues and owns and operates three restaurants: Rhapsody at the Symphony Center, Park Grill in Millennium Park, and Bluprint at the Merchandise Mart.

CURRENT POSITION: CEO of Blue Plate and managing partner at Park Grill, Chicago, IL, since 1983, blueplatechicago.com. ★ **EDUCATION:** BA, psychology, St. Mary's University, MN; master's degree, clinical social work, University of Illinois, Chicago. ★ **CAREER PATH:** In or around Chicago: program social worker, various programs, Maryville Academy (1972–1979); program director, ECHO Family Services and Central Baptist Family Services (1979–1981); program social work, Special Education Special Service, Maine Township (1981–1983). ★ **AWARDS AND RECOGNITION:** Various over time. Some include Top 50 Event Companies, *Special Events* (2005–2007); Caterer of the Year, *Catering Magazine* (2006); Best of Citysearch winner (2006 and 2007); one of Inc. 5000's Fastest Growing Companies, *Inc.* (2007); Best Caterer, *Illinois Meetings and Events* (2007); the Knot Best of Weddings pick (2007 and 2008). ★ **MEMBERSHIPS:** Illinois Restaurant Association; *Catering Magazine* advisory board; Catholic Charities; West Loop Gates Association; Grant Park Conservancy; Chicago Convention and Tourism Bureau; and more.

Words of advice for people considering a similar career:

I always encourage people to get some experience first, to make sure they are truly interested in the work at hand. The food-service industry is a really seductive industry. It seems we all have this dormant restaurant or food-service dream—we go out to eat; it seems like fun; we dream about having our own place. As with any career, it's best to pursue that which is a true passion, but you better first fully understand what it entails. It's not all glamorous. It's really hard work. I would imagine that it's like a marriage, in some ways. You better date a little before you get married. That will increase your chance of success. Too often people run into things too quickly. Also, I would really advise that people place value on relationships. Any success I've had has been to some extent because of the relationships I've had, because you never know where you'll meet people again.

How did you start your business?

As a hobby. One summer, I took some time off from working in the school district to just tinker with catering. I had every intention of going back to school in the fall. But the business just blossomed. I started with $50, three chafing dishes, and a van, and today sales are close to $40 million. I had an interest in food and enjoyed bringing groups together. It's really about entertaining groups, pulling them together, and throwing a party. I was doing it for some friends. Then I realized that I had a knack for handling logistics and planning to cook in volume. Fortunately for me, I grew up in a big family and we all learned to handle big groups of people. My mom unwittingly taught me how to do it, just through the family routine.

I think we might be the largest catering company in Chicago but am not sure. I like to say that we haven't changed through the years. I like to know my employees and know them very well. If I could personally cook for every client I would. I also like to say that we were built by our customers. We have healthy revenues, and we are professionally managed. We have MBAs, CPAs, world-trained chefs, top-level HR people, high-level IT people. We've grown in a very dynamic way. I am very sensitive to the issue of size, because we provide a very personal product.

Describe a typical day.

I'm a lucky guy. I used to have more of a routine when we were smaller and I was directly responsible for production. These days, one day I might be dealing with employees, the next I might be on-site at one of the restaurants, visiting clients, meeting with prospective clients, researching opportunities and new projects, or sitting with staff. In this economic climate, we're actually reinventing ourselves. We're thinking about what's going on around us. We're researching opportunities and looking at other business models out there. We're developing our wine program within all our companies; that's a very important part of what we do. This year, that calls for making our own wines. Earlier this year, I was in California to decide which grapes to buy. Because of our

growth, we need new facilities, so I am also looking at that. I am working with international artists to build a program for them to come to Chicago. There's no typical day. I might have to go say hello to a VIP visiting a restaurant. We do work on weekends and in evenings. Some days I come home around four or five P.M. and change into a suit to visit restaurants in the evening. It's important that our customers and our clients see that I am involved. On weekends we're open, I'll stop in and say hello to the chefs and see what they're making. The job is a great deal of public relations, internal and external. I don't have to be doing this. I have great people working for me. There are certain events that I have to go to but others where if I get sidetracked because I ran into somebody, it's not a big deal because I know that some people are covering the work. I'm not involved with the production.

Do you miss the production?

Absolutely. What I do now is that on Sunday, I'll make a few gallons of soup. On Tuesday I take it to the office and pass it around. Whenever I have a chance to go out to dinner at one of our restaurants, I'll help out as much as I can. My favorite years were working the grill at Wrigley Field. I miss the hands-on stuff, I really do. It's a dilemma. I'm fortunate because I can delegate, but I love doing that stuff.

How many hours a week do you typically work?

People tease me all the time because of the hours when they get e-mails from me—

typically the only time frame in which they don't get e-mails is between twelve A.M. and three A.M. I'd say I work seventy to eighty hours a week, but I don't really count. When I go and meet people in my restaurants, is it really work? I like what I do to the point that I don't consider much of what I do work. Once every four to five days I'll need eight hours of sleep. But otherwise I'll get up at three or four A.M., do some work, and work out. We're all doing work in the back of cabs and at lunch, thanks to technology. The work environment has become virtual.

What do you like most about what you do?

Working with people. I like making things; it's no longer making the dish but figuring out new models for the business and seeing how we can grow. I get to meet so many great people. The common denominator among everyone is food. We all eat every day. The biggest source of satisfaction that I have is probably helping our employees realize their own dreams, their goals, and I hope that they are happy. I really get a kick out of the fact that the company is helping to provide, helping people to be happy.

What do you like least about it?

I don't like public speaking; I get bored with financial analysis; I don't like being the bearer of bad news. I hate losing in an area where we're competing with other companies. I like doing my job. I don't like distractions from it. I am a very private person. I'd just as soon not have people know who I am. I'm just a lucky guy. I go to

work every day and work really hard. Everything is the result of a team effort.

What skills are most important for you to do your job well?

Probably the most important skill is listening. Not just with your ears, but understanding and hearing what message someone is sending your way. With employees, you have to feel what they are experiencing. With clients, you have to understand what they need from you. With a business, you have to understand what else they are trying to do. They are trying to look good in front of their clients, but also their bosses and constituency. With a project, you have to know what is the problem to be solved. When listening you have to accept the fact that people look at things differently than you. Set your biases aside. Don't superimpose your own needs over theirs. That's so important. You have to understand when there are legitimate opportunities and where there aren't. It's important to be as selfless as possible. You have to have a little trust and faith that your needs are going to be met if you're helping other people meet theirs.

What qualities do you look for in a new hire?

Personality and skills. Character is number one, meaning the ability to care, integrity, honesty, trustworthiness. In interviews I will find out where people are from, about their family, how they grew up, what's valuable to them, if they've been able to hold on to relationships for a long time, if they are humble, proud. What are they proud of? That they have things or that they have good relationships? And then personality is also important. Are they quiet people? Are they the type who is good in very small groups, the type who's good at making friendships? In accounting I need someone very finicky, very detailed; I don't need a salesperson. In sales, I need someone who can confidently walk up to a stranger. Skills are important, of course. You can teach that; you can train people to do things. The skills have to fit with the tasks at hand, but if you don't have a good character, you can't do it.

"It seems we all have this dormant restaurant or food-service dream—we go out to eat; it seems like fun; we dream about having our own place. As with any career, it's best to pursue that which is a true passion, but you better first fully understand what it entails. It's not all glamorous. It's really hard work."

MARK KLEIN

Mark Klein is the director of conferences and catering at the Broadmoor, a AAA Five-Diamond and *Mobil Travel Guide* five-star resort in Colorado Springs. He is in charge of all the events that take place at the property, which has seven hundred rooms and forty-four cottage bedrooms, 185,000 square feet of event and meeting space, and eighteen restaurants, cafés, and lounges.

CURRENT POSITION: Director of conferences and catering, the Broadmoor, Colorado Springs, CO, since 1992. ★ **EDUCATION:** Associate's degree, hotel and restaurant management, SUNY-Cobleskill, NY. ★ **CAREER PATH:** Interstate Hotels (at the time, the largest franchiser of Marriott hotels) for eight years; catering in Albany, NY; worked in a restaurant and lounge in Cincinnati, OH, then back to catering; catering in Minneapolis, MN, and Colorado Springs. ★ **AWARDS AND RECOGNITION:** Manager of the Quarter, the Broadmoor; Convention Services Management of the Year nominee.

Salary notes:

It's a wide range, depending on experience. And each hotel has a different concept of how it gives incentives to its team. It goes from $50,000 with a couple of years of experience up to $150,000, with incentive plans in almost all hotels.

Words of advice for people considering a similar career:

Get as much hotel experience as you can get. Understand the value of great relationships, hard work, and great plans. Understand that it's hard and you have to rely on a lot of people but that when you do your job well, you feel good and you sleep well at night.

Describe a typical day.

Our team is made up of seven conference managers, who handle large conventions and meetings, and five executive meeting managers, who are a one-stop shop for smaller groups. These people sell it and do all the logistics and details. Four catering managers handle events that come to the hotel without sleeping-room bookings. My job is to pave the way, clear the hurdles, communicate with departments, set policies and procedures, and facilitate the needs of the team members. We handle approximately fifteen hundred to sixteen hundred groups a year, for thirty-five thousand to forty thousand events, from coffee breaks to golf tournaments. I handle some accounts, such as things that are sponsored by the Broadmoor. My role is also to go out and see the clients when they are here, to make sure that they have everything they need. We have two to three interdepartmental meetings a week, to review where we are and what's coming. I have to be on top of new trends and food items. I work very closely with the food and banquet department.

How many hours a week do you typically work?

Fifty-five to seventy-five hours. I'm here six days a week and sometimes seven.

What are your specific responsibilities?

To oversee. We have to meet the goals of two customers: the paying customers who are coming in and using the facility to reach their goals, whatever these might be, and the goals of the hotel, such as food costs and labor costs, which our team is entrusted with protecting. The banquet department, culinary team, golf team, etc., each have goals. Our goal is to create a plan together that accomplishes the goals of both the client and the hotel, both financially and service-wise. My role is to ensure that our team and facility have the proper tools, knowledge, experience, and expertise to be able to accomplish that for both parties.

What do you like most about what you do?

The relationships that we build with customers; meeting new people; building lifelong friendships with people that you just met. I like the end of the day, when everything has gone as expected and people are just thrilled. You get accolades when things have gone well. Once a group is set and confirmed with the sales team, they turn it over to my team. Then we are pretty much the only contact that the clients have with hotel staff, from start to finish. We are very close to these customers and these planners. We become friends and develop a lot of trust. I think that's a cool thing to have.

What do you like least about it?

I don't like to make the same mistake twice. There are people in this business who can be a little transient. Not so much here, because people really use this place to build a career. The tenure of my staff is probably ten years plus, but there's waitstaff, setup crew, etc., who are more transient, so you have to repeat things and mistakes can happen again. This is really a race with no finish line, you just continue, and if somebody makes a mistake, you address it and teach the staff how to better handle it next time, and next thing you know there's a new guy.

What skills are most important for you to do your job well?

You have to be outgoing, knowledgeable, and able to learn from your mistakes. You have to be unselfish with your personal time, because you work many hours. You have to be in several places really quickly, be able to multitask, and have many irons in the fire at a time. You have to be a planner; our success is only based on how good a plan we have in place before a group arrives. That can't take place once seven hundred people are here. You have to be able to force yourself to plan ahead so that everybody has their information a couple of weeks in advance.

What qualities do you look for in a new hire?

I look for people who are passionate about service and guests. We have to have a bit of a servant mentality, because that's what we are here for, to accomplish the needs of our customers. You check your ego at the door. I look for people who are passionate about taking care of people, service minded, unselfish with their own time. Being knowledgeable about food and beverage is always helpful, but we can always teach some of those. College is important but not something that I hang my hat on. It's a great indicator because it shows commitment from people—that they can see a goal and accomplish it—but that's not all I look for. I look for people on my team whom I can promote.

Describe your creative process.

We get together as a team and look at what the client wants to achieve while here. Then we put on our creative hat and interact with the many different departments and see what we can accomplish with different groups. We try to come up with something a little more unique, since our groups have usually been in many other hotels. We look at how we can put new twists and new angles into an event. Can we do a new location outside? Everybody is always trying to outdo their last event.

What keeps you challenged?

Financial responsibilities right now. The economy is tough. When things are great economically, you're trying to outdo the next event. When times are tough we're looking for business and are making sure that every client who gets in understands what a great place this is and wants to come back. Every time a group comes here we have the opportunity to blow them away.

SCOTT WAGNER

Scott Wagner's ChileCo Catering is a high-end organic and sustainable catering company that serves San Diego, Orange, and Los Angeles counties in California. It handles small sit-down dinners as well as large events for thousands of people.

CURRENT POSITION: Executive chef–owner, ChileCo Catering, San Diego, CA, since 2004, and Chi Cuisine, a line of organic food products, since 2008, www.chilecocatering.com. ★
EDUCATION: Culinary arts degree, California Culinary Academy, San Francisco, CA. ★
CAREER PATH: Pastry assistant, then sous chef, Mecca, San Francisco, under Michael Fennelly and Hugh Acheson. ★ **AWARDS AND RECOGNITION:** Named among Powers to Be (upcoming civic leaders) for food, *San Diego* Magazine (December 2008); Best Caterer, *San Diego Magazine* (June 2009); praise in local and national media, including an appearance as a guest chef on Bravo's *Queer Eye for the Straight Girl;* frequent guest on San Diego's top-rated cable news station KUSI; regular contributor to charity events throughout San Diego. ★
MEMBERSHIPS: Board member, Slow Food San Diego; environmental organizations; Organic Consumer Association.

Words of advice for people considering a similar career:

Follow your passion, whatever that may be.

Describe a typical day.

First thing in the morning, I meet with my director of operations. We review menus, see what needs to happen for the day, and he delegates tasks. Then I generally leave the office to go to my purveyors. I buy fish daily and swing by a couple of farmers' markets. Then I go to the kitchen, taste the food, see how the cooks are doing. We're into customizing food, so the dishes are constantly changing. I usually produce a couple of things myself. If we have an event that evening, I work it, or I might have appointments lined up for proposals or with vendors. I work fourteen to sixteen hours a day. Doing the production is by choice. I'm kind of a perfectionist. I usually help when we are behind. I always taste and tweak what my chefs have prepared.

How many hours a week do you typically work?

About eighty-five.

What are your specific responsibilities?

Leadership and helping organize and delegate tasks. It's definitely a stressful industry. Being all organic and fresh and customizing each menu makes things a little more challenging for my employees. While it means it's not boring, it also makes it more complicated. I'm kind of a jack-of-all-trades. I supervise front of the house and back of the house. I'm too much of a perfectionist to let go of any of it much. But I'm getting a little better; I've had to with this organic product line. There's only so much one person can do.

What do you like most about what you do?

The creativity. I feel very honored and blessed that I am able to do what I love for a living. It's not work; it's a God-given talent.

I have a very unique style, and to be able to do that unrestricted while making a living out of it is awesome.

What do you like least about it?

Doing the dishes. We make every aspect of every dish. When you don't purchase anything, you end up with a lot of dishes. When I started out of my apartment, I was doing all the dishes myself. Now I have a full-time dishwasher—but I still despise cleaning the dishes. When I do a tasting, I do the dishes myself.

What skills are most important for you to do your job well?

Patience, which I probably don't have. It's such a stressful industry that to stay in it, to keep your heart and passion in it, you need a sense of humor. You definitely need an eye for details. Catering is both production and service. Attention to details on the highest level is important.

What skills would you like to develop to help further your career?

Money management. I definitely place artistry before economics, and that has probably weighed down some of the success, as far as the numbers of the company. Any true leader needs to constantly evolve and grow. I'm constantly learning better ways to communicate, to find ways to fine-tune menus.

What are your long-term goals?

They supersede anything to do with food. I was born on Earth Day; I started a recycling program in high school. Chi Cuisine is designed to get me in touch with cus-

tomers, and ChileCo, as a high-end organic company in California, is designed to get more exposure and access to celebrities. The goal is to develop an environmental and humanitarian lobbying firm. That's my ideal at least. Chi Cuisine is phase two, and a nonprofit company, EtreTerra, is phase three. Part of the profits of Chi Cuisine will go to EtreTerra.

How large is your staff?

I have seven full-time and forty-two part-time employees. I run my company from top to bottom. Every employee has a salary. Everyone makes their own hours. I don't schedule anyone; we just do what needs to get done. It's a bit unconventional. All my full-time employees can work from home if they don't want to come in, as long as the job gets done.

What qualities do you look for in a new hire?

I start with the personality—a little shine in the eye, confidence, charisma. What I look for the least is experience. You can't train someone to have charisma and personality, but you can train them and give them experience. The kitchen is such a stressful environment. The front-of-the-house staff is where I need people with personality, because these people are the ones selling your business. They are the ones handing out the business cards.

JONATHAN BODNAR

As a caterer in Napa, CA, Jonathan Bodnar works mainly with wineries, cooking for their special events and wine dinners. He is a one-man operation and hires staff as needed for the events that he runs.

CURRENT POSITION: Caterer/owner, Very Tall Chef, Napa, CA, since 2004. ★ **EDUCATION:** BA, hotel management, University of Massachusetts–Amherst; culinary arts degree, Cambridge School of Culinary Arts; three certificates from CIA-Greystone, including Food and Wine Pairing for Chefs. ★ **CAREER PATH:** Manager, corporate dining rooms in office buildings (six years, before cooking school); various sous chef positions, including at Clio, Boston, MA (about ten years); chef, seasonal restaurant, Martha's Vineyard, MA (2001 and 2002 summer seasons).

Salary notes:

In my situation, it depends on how much work you actually do. I don't have the same paycheck every week. One month I can have a $20,000 week in revenue. I have to pay the waitstaff and kitchen staff, but it's okay if I don't have an event the following week. I don't have my own commercial kitchen. I have to use the winery's kitchen, so I do smaller events, usually under fifty people.

Words of advice for people considering a similar career:

Try it out first. If you want to be a chef, go work in the best restaurants, offer your time, work for free if you have to—but make sure that it's what you really want to do. That's why I bounced around a lot, I think. I should have committed to one year after culinary school. If you know the direction you want to take, find out who does it and go work for them.

What is your business model?

I work with very few clients—mainly Stags' Leap Wine Cellars and a few other wineries—and I do high-end wine dinners. I do either private dinners for owners or corporate events. It really is catering, but as a private caterer. I have an on-call staff. For a while, I had a sous chef who worked with me at every event, and depending on the size of the event I would call in a prep cook, dishwasher, and front-of-the-house staff. Some of the side work that I do is also for wineries, but more on the private side, such as if they have guests staying over. I present clients with a menu to look at, and 90 percent of the time they approve of what I present to them. It's much more of a captive audience. When my clients are going to spend a lot of money, $350 to $400 a person for dinner, they feel more comfortable putting it all in the chef's hands. The meals are specifically for wineries to showcase their wines and promote future wine sales. So each meal starts with the wine.

How many hours a week do you typically work?

August to November is peak season. Last year I worked every single day in September and October. In February, it's possible that I don't work for a whole week because there aren't any events. I have to budget, since there are flush times and drier times, which can be challenging.

What do you like most about what you do?

For the most part, I like the whole idea that it's a party. That everything I do—from writing a menu to going to the farmers' market to going to a purveyor for local eggs—results in a dinner party. People are eating and drinking and enjoying themselves. It's very rewarding when the whole dinner comes together well. It's always a challenge; I try to always make it a little bit different, reinvent the menu, try a little bit of molecular gastronomy. When I pull it off, it's very rewarding.

What do you like least about it?

The office work that is involved. I have to file everything, receipts, invoices. It takes a lot of organization, planning, prep lists. You really have to be on top of it. And I have a different staff for almost every event. It's hard to delegate to someone who hasn't worked with you before. Sometimes it's hard to express the vision that you have to the two or three people you work with when you try to get an event done, hard to

find a server, pacify an owner, an event coordinator. I would prefer to just be in the kitchen cooking, without having to deal with the other dynamics of putting an event together.

What skills would you like to develop to help further your career?

I would love to make wine. A chef friend of mine is a garage winemaker; I helped him and got bit by the bug. I also would like to be a better gardener. I grow about eighteen kinds of peppers for sauces and spice rubs. I would love to be an expert in every aspect of the food that I work with. I would love to make cheese, be a cattle rancher and a butcher, to know every aspect of my profession that I'm passionate about.

What are your long-term goals?

If I don't open a restaurant, I would like to have a bigger, more exclusive catering business and get into food-and-wine-pairing education.

What is the outlook for your type of job?

As long as the economy turns around, I think there's a very bright future. I think a lot of wineries are leaning toward having their own chefs, because "wine and food pairing" is such a catchphrase.

CHRISTINA LANDRUM

Christina Landrum is the director of catering at OC in Houston, where she handles events in the restaurant's dining room, bar, and rooftop. Those events range from staff luncheons to weddings and mixers for singles that can attract up to four hundred people.

CURRENT POSITION: Director of catering, OC (Open City) Restaurant and Bar, Houston, TX, since January 2009. ★ **EDUCATION:** Course work in marketing, University of Houston; certificate in culinary arts and hospitality management, Art Institute of Houston. ★ **CAREER PATH:** In Houston: server and waitstaff supervisor (while in college); catering sales manager, Canyon Café (four years). ★ **MEMBERSHIPS:** Les Dames d'Escoffier International (new membership chair of the Houston chapter).

Salary notes:

In Houston it's all across the board, from $30,000 to $65,000, depending on experience. Before accepting this position, I had an offer with a catering company that was looking to pay $30,000, and in a hotel where I was briefly, the director made about $65,000. And everybody is on commission. Right now I make a 12 percent commission, with $35,000 as my base.

Words of advice for people considering a similar career:

Culinary school is not necessarily the best route to take to work in events. Get the right experience by doing internships with various event companies, and build a portfolio in order to obtain the job that you want.

Describe a typical day.

I get in around eleven A.M., since we open late. I meet with prospective clients to look at the space. I handle sales calls and outside calls, and I go to marketing seminars and networking groups. I do a lot of sales and all the in-house event coordinating. Next month, we are launching our off-premise catering, which I'll also be in charge of. Tomorrow is my first big event here: Three hundred and fifty people RSVP'd, plus seventy-five from Facebook, for a mixer that we are having,

How many hours a week do you typically work?

Forty to forty-five hours.

What are your specific responsibilities?

I handle all aspects of private events, including staffing, working with the chef to create menus, working with the clients to prepare the contracts, sending out proposals, finding new business, and the sales side.

What do you like most about what you do?

Working with clients. I do a lot of social business. Brides can be very emotional, but I get so much pleasure out of wedding events. You get to be creative. You give people exactly what they want. Especially with weddings; that's a day they'll always remember.

What do you like least about it?

Cold-calling. Sales is a big part of my job. I love going to networking mixers and bringing in people that way, but cold-calling is not my favorite. Cold-calling brides is not that bad, but cold-calling businesses without any leads can be hard.

What skills are most important for you to do your job well?

Attention to details. You have to be very organized; you can't mix details for various events. Creativity. You have to be able to visualize what the other people want so that you can make it happen.

What skills would you like to develop to help further your career?

I would love to develop my sales skills. I eventually want to open my own event-planning firm—that's in the five-year plan—and I think I need to get a little more experience under my belt and hone my sales skills.

What is the outlook for your type of job?

Right now there are a lot of event-planning companies in Houston. Catering is big here, but the job market is not fantastic. Anybody thinks that they can do it, but many don't have any experience. People are still planning events here; they're just doing it a little cheaper.

How large is your staff?

I have two assistants, and then the service staff for each event, bartenders and servers, report to me.

What keeps you challenged?

A tiny budget. When the client wants it all but doesn't have the budget, it's a challenge to give them everything—the décor, the food—and still have the ambiance and the service in the budget. That's a lot of what I'm going through right now.

Did you originally want to cook when going to school?

Yes, my original thought was to work in the kitchen. Then I realized I was not suited for it. My husband is a chef and he works sixty hours a week. I loved events and found my niche here. I still get to do menu planning and creating.

SHERRI BEAUCHAMP

Through her company the Seasonal Kitchen, Sherri Beauchamp offers personal chef services to the Charlotte, NC, metro region and areas surrounding Fort Mill and Lake Wylie, SC. She specializes in customized meals, meals for people with dietary restrictions, dinner parties, food and wine tastings, corporate lunches, and cooking lessons.

CURRENT POSITION: Personal chef, the Seasonal Kitchen, Charlotte, NC, since 2004 (in Michigan until 2007), www.theseasonalkitchen.com. ★ **EDUCATION:** Cook Street School of Fine Cooking in Denver, CO; chef of wine arts; certified wine sommelier; certification from the Chef de Cuisine Association of Colorado. ★ **CAREER PATH:** Operated a water-treatment system, then sold the business and went to culinary school. ★ **MEMBERSHIPS:** American Personal Chef Association; United States Personal Chef Association.

Salary notes:

With eight clients, around $50,000, minus what you spend on groceries or the expenses to run the business, such as marketing, gas, groceries, phone bills, and organizational memberships.

Words of advice for people considering a similar career:

Contact other personal chefs, interview them, and join the local chapters of personal chef organizations, so that you have others to help mentor you and assist you when you are in over your head. Personal chefs seem to be—especially within an organization's chapter—very eager to help each other. We pass business to each other; we provide help if someone needs assistance with a job; we pass along recipes; we bounce ideas and questions off each other.

How did you decide to become a personal chef?

I started directly after culinary school. I didn't want to work in or open a restaurant. The personal chef industry has very flexible hours. I found my first clients by having a website. After culinary school, I lived in Michigan, from 2004 to 2007. Now I'm regrowing the business in North Carolina. The first client in Michigan who called me was a dietary-restricted client, which was not what I had focused on in school. I had a background in French and Italian cooking, with lots of butter and olive oil. She was looking for a chef to cook meals at their home, and the whole family would eat the same food. She was very happy and I stayed there until I moved to North Carolina. Other clients came through word of mouth, my website, advertising online through chefs' associations, and postcards for certain subdivisions, which I sent out based on the dollar value of the homes.

Describe a typical day.

I go shopping around nine A.M., then I am at a client's house around ten. I'm there three to four hours, cooking, packaging all the food, labeling everything, and cleaning before I leave. Many of my clients leave me a key or have a nanny at home who lets me in. It helps if you are referred, since there needs to be trust in the relationship. Most of my clients aren't home, which is the whole point of me doing the cooking.

They want healthy, convenient meals for their family. I mainly cook entrées, a side starch, and a vegetable. Most times, I'll end up making a little sweet treat as a gift. I like to have around eight clients. It ranges from weekly and biweekly clients to once-a-month clients. Eighty percent is repeat business, where I cook once a week in their house. Then I do a little bit of catering.

How many hours a week do you typically work?

Under thirty.

What are your specific responsibilities?

When the client contacts me, it's narrowing in on my client's assessment form, establishing what type of cuisine they might like, what dietary concerns they might have, if they are on medications and I need to avoid certain foods. I have them fill out a whole form with types of vegetables and proteins that they like. Then I make menu recommendations by e-mail for what they want the following week. If I'm cooking five entrées, I send a choice of ten, and the clients e-mail me back with their five choices.

What do you like most about what you do?

I love being creative. I love when I have a client who says, "I love everything, make me anything," and there are no restrictions. And I like the opposite end, when the clients enjoy a meal they didn't think they could have because of their dietary restrictions. It's great to teach them how to cook with the restrictions. I like being my own business owner. I'm always cooking three days a week, with the hours I am cooking for my clients. If I needed to move my Thursday client to Monday, I could. It's really flexible. I can double up one day.

What do you like least about it?

Getting into a client's kitchen that is set up really poorly, where there's a giant island in the middle of the kitchen, the stove in one corner and the sink in the other corner. Kitchen size doesn't matter, it's more about how it's laid out. Most kitchens I've worked in have been fine. Having worked in so many kitchens, I now have a high level of comfort when I walk into a house to set up for a dinner party. I don't like cooking on an electric stove (even though I have one myself).

What skills are most important for you to do your job well?

The ability to go with plan B, if you forget an item, for example, or get to the house with an item that is bad and you have to change the menu. You have to be creative on the spot.

What is the outlook for your type of job?

Over the past four years, the growth has been astronomical. It's really taken off. Of course, now the economy is putting a big damper on things. What I'm seeing is that clients are eager to do parties and catering, but they don't have as much ability to sign up for repeat business. I'm hoping this isn't the trend, that it's just growing a new business.

KIERAN O'MAHONY

Kieran O'Mahony left a career in fine dining to become a private chef for a high-net-worth family with four children. He started working for the family in London and followed them to New York in 2005. He now also functions as estate administrator for his employer, which requires more administrative duties.

CURRENT POSITION: Private chef/estate administrator, New York, NY, since 2004. ★
EDUCATION: Institute of Technology, Dublin, Ireland (two years); BS, international culinary arts, Thames Valley University, London, England. ★ **CAREER PATH:** In London, England: commis, chef de partie, and sous chef, the Meridien Hotel, Greenhouse Restaurant, and Royal Automobile Club; corporate chef, Zurich Insurance. ★ **AWARDS AND RECOGNITION:** Student of the Year twice, at Trinity and at Thames Valley; bronze medal, British Open Salon Culinaire, for lamb dish; gold medal in Breadmaking and Plated Main Course and numerous silver medals, Director's Table. ★ **MEMBERSHIPS:** The Panel of Chefs of Ireland; local group of private chefs.

Salary notes:

Between $70,000 and $120,000, depending on experience. I started at $80,000 and was reviewed after six months, because it was my first position. It depends on the client, but the person who can afford a private chef can afford to pay the right amount.

Words of advice for people considering a similar career:

Give it 100 percent. Always remember that you're only as good as your last meal. You have to be inventive—remember that you are cooking for the same people every day. It's not an easy living. I used to think that it would be, but it's not. The other thing is to remember that you are still an employee, even if a lot of times you might not feel like you are.

Describe a typical day.

I work Monday through Friday, predominantly. In the summer I work weekends, because the family goes to Nantucket. I start at nine A.M. and finish between seven P.M. and midnight, depending on what's going on. If they don't go out, they sit for dinner by seven thirty and are done by nine thirty or ten P.M. When there is a dinner party, it can be midnight or later. When I started, I would have muffins or things like that ready for breakfast. I'd prepare lunch and set the table, because they don't have a butler. I make sure that there are flowers on the table if guests are present. Then I tidy up and go shopping straight after lunch, for one to two hours. I prepare snacks for the kids when they get back from school. Then I start preparing dinner. That was the original workday. Now I do all the paperwork first and open all the mail. I am kind of my boss's assistant, so there are certain things that she needs me to do, like manage her calendar and a calendar for the house and liaise with the driver and other staff to make sure that they do what they are supposed to do. I liaise with her husband's secretary. Then I will start cooking lunch around eleven A.M.

if that's needed. Around two P.M. I leave the paperwork behind to concentrate on cooking. I go shopping; I top up my staples in the fridge. I usually cook two or three courses for a typical family dinner, at the very least a starter and main, but not dessert every night. I'm back on the computer before I leave.

How many hours a week do you typically work?

An average of fifty. I generally don't work weekends. But most private chefs I know would work Tuesday through Saturday. Sometimes I travel with them. They have a place in Idaho where I usually go with them. It's pretty average for private chefs to have six weeks' vacation. I have somewhat more.

What do you like most about what you do?

I like working in close contact with the family because I get to know them and what they like. The challenge is to influence them to change. I'll say, "Let's do this," and my boss says, "Uh-uh"; I tell her to trust me. She likes it, and I'm happy to have shown her something new.

What do you like least about it?

I miss the pressure of cooking for sixty to eighty people in two hours. I do get an adrenaline rush when I do a dinner for fifty, but that's four or five times a year, whereas I used to get that rush twice a day. It's more level now and less a roller coaster of pressure. I think that's where my running for exercise comes in; it helps relieve that a bit. I ran three marathons in 2008. I also don't meet as many people. In the restaurant business, people come and go and you make many friends. Now I don't get that anymore. I miss that bit.

What skills are most important for you to do your job well?

For the initial interview, you have to be very personable. Obviously you have to be able to cook. But you also have to be adaptable. In a restaurant, if people don't like what you're cooking, they won't order it. In a home, you have to do it day after day. The kitchen is not just the chef; people come and go. It's their kitchen. That takes adaptation. You need a wider variety of food knowledge, because you might have Indian one night, sushi the next, and Mexican the following night. Sometimes I even decorate the room. It's challenging in a good way, because I try to do food I haven't done before and that they haven't had before.

What skills would you like to develop to help further your career?

One of my fears is that I'll lose my restaurant skills. I would like to be more well-rounded in other cuisines, like Asian cooking. From the budgeting point of view, I'd like to work more on purchasing, like I did in fine dining. In one job I did all of the costing for each dish on the menu. I also like to know the science behind the cooking.

What is the average length of time private chefs spend with one employer?

The average is five years. I'm probably at my maximum.

What is the outlook for your type of job?

A year ago I would have said there'll be more private chefs in ten years. But now, it's different. Private chefs depend on wealthy people who can cut back and eat out a couple of nights a week to save money. As long as people are wealthy enough, there will be private chefs, but it might not pay as much. At a certain level, they will always have private chefs. At a level below they might not—those people whose wealth fluctuates might get rid of their chefs when they are a bit lower. At the moment I know four private chefs who are out of work and can't find anything.

What keeps you challenged?

I like to try to challenge myself with regard to dishes that I haven't done and my boss hasn't tried. I joke that I have to keep some stuff back in case she wants to fire me. On rare occasions, my boss might go grocery shopping and bring back things, like a mystery basket. Or I have to make do with just what's in the fridge. That's one of the main things that keep me challenged. Insecurity keeps me challenged, the idea that it's a job and that I can get fired anytime. You're only as good as your last meal; that keeps the pressure on.

Describe your creative process.

I usually sit down with my boss and decide on something. Sometimes it's something I've done before, sometimes I go through cookbooks with her. The menu is decided day to day, but for parties I'll sit down well in advance. I read cookbooks; I eat out; my boss challenges me with something. Every once in a while I'm alone in the kitchen and can come up with something completely unique.

8. MANAGEMENT

Food-service managers are the ones in charge of the "front of the house"—the dining room of a restaurant or hotel—and the business operation of the entreprise. They generally do not cook (unless it is a small operation, perhaps even their own, and they need to pitch in because of an emergency) but might have acquired culinary training and even professional experience before switching to the managing side.

Managers function as the liaison between the dining room and the kitchen, and as the liaison between customers and the restaurant itself. While they work with numbers and flowcharts, they mostly deal with people. To do your job well as a manager, it is thus essential to have strong communication and people skills. You will need to listen patiently to recriminations, whether they come from your staff or from a diner, and work to resolve the issue at hand. You need to be friendly and approachable but also display leadership abilities that will earn you the respect of your staff. Without that respect, you will not be able to lead. Knowledge of point-of-sale systems and finance or payroll systems are also essential.

Chapter 1 introduced a range of management programs that are offered in schools around the country. Many managers start their career as a server, even if they possess a management or other college degree. This experience will prove crucial as you move up through the ranks, since you will often be assisting your service team to ensure that all your customers have a perfect experience. The typical management career track looks like this:

Server/waitstaff
Captain/floor manager
Maître d'
Assistant manager
Assistant general manager
General manager

A captain manages the waitstaff and is also on the floor, ready to help when needs arise. He or she might be the one called first when a service issue arises, unless it seems like it requires the intervention of the highest-ranked person there.

The maître d' tends to manage the entrance of the restaurant with the hosting staff and will supervise reservations and the flow of the tables on any given night, relaying vital information to the general manager. While the image of the stiff maître d' (the word is short for "maître d'hôtel"—French for "master of the hotel," which in this case refers to a hospitality establishment) is no longer accurate, it tends to be a somewhat formal position.

Assistant managers work closely with the upper management team to make sure that their decisions are applied during service. They might spend time assisting a server who needs it during service. They might be assigned a morning shift to take care of small details long before service starts.

The assistant general manager takes over when the general manager is not on duty and performs many of the same tasks, albeit without final say. The shift might differ from that of the general manager and might be the night shift in a hotel, for example. The assistant GM will help the GM with staffing, training, budgeting, and ordering, and functions as the direct supervisor of the staff.

The general manager is the ultimate voice on service and nonkitchen-related matters in an establishment. The owner of a restaurant might function as GM if he or she so desires. The GM is in charge of scheduling, staffing, hiring and firing, training, and budgeting the operations of their establishment. They decide how many shifts are needed for each service and how many employees will be needed at that time. The GM will work with the sommelier or the wine team on ordering wines and other beverages. Some operations, particularly larger ones, will have a sepa-rate food and beverage director, who will handle ordering for the establishment. That position is also part of the executive management team. The GM goes over each day's numbers and makes sure that everything totals up, pays bills or makes sure that they are getting paid, and works closely with the financial team of an operation, even if it is just one bookkeeper. Needless to say, if you would like to open your own restaurant, it would be invaluable to have prior experience as a GM. Where the GM's work ends and someone else's begins is highly variable. In some cases, the GM might be in charge of facility repairs and procuring business insurance. In others, such tasks will be somebody else's job.

Another path to management goes through the kitchen. Chefs and sous chefs are in management positions thanks to the number of people who answer to them and the nature of their responsibilities. They might thus move up through the management ranks of an organization and make the transition to a front-of-the-house managerial position.

A management career track does not just occur in a restaurant kitchen. Hotels, private clubs, cruise ships, and chain restaurants are among the many places where one can become a manager. Chain restaurants in particular provide solid management training programs to their employees, along with complex systems and processes that would be useful to apply, even at a smaller scale, when opening one's own restaurant later on. The management track in those establishments also begins with service.

Other positions that pertain to the financial and operational aspects of the business are considered management, such as food and beverage director, purchasing director, and sommelier. The first two positions listed here are not floor positions and will likely require shorter hours and no weekend work. These people take care of needs, such as ordering, receiving, and presenting the chef with new ingredients, while keeping the department within budget. These positions tend to exist in larger operations, such as hotels and clubs, rather than in small independent restaurants.

Obtaining a degree in culinary or hospitality management will prove helpful as you move forward with your career, as will a range of other business and supervision courses. If you seek to work for a large restaurant or hotel group or one of the top restaurants in the country, your formal education could become an asset in gaining upper-management positions or handling several establishments. A degree will also allow you to teach in a community college or vocational school should you decide to leave the restaurant world behind.

Most operations conduct daily managers' meetings, which include the chef de cuisine and/or executive chef as well as a sommelier and/or food and beverage director, to address any issue related to the smooth running of the business, special needs to be addressed during service that night, the presence of VIPs, etc. The general manager and the executive chef generally sit on equal footing, but at times the GM will supervise the chef. In such cases, a GM's knowledge of food and prior experience in a kitchen will be helpful, since it will prevent many potential conflicts.

Most managerial positions will require you to work during service, which means spending long hours on your feet on the floor. You might come in after the kitchen crew but will leave after them, since they can start breaking down their stations and cleaning the kitchen while customers are still lingering in the dining room. That's a luxury that you do not have.

salaries

A waiter will typically make minimum wage plus tips. According to the U.S. Department of Labor's Bureau of Labor Statistics, the median salary for a food-service manager is $46,320, going from a low end of $29,450 to a high end of $76,940. Hotels and fine-dining restaurants or larger operations will pay more than these averages, with salaries for general managers reaching six figures. A recent American Hotel and Lodging Association survey gave the median salary of food and beverage director as $73,000. The general manager of a high-end private club might make as much as $300,000, with a midrange salary between $100,000 and $160,000. HVS Executive Search's 2008 "Chain Restaurant Corporate Annual Report" indicates that in chain restaurants, an assistant general manager will make $42,039 on average and a general manager $55,702, plus bonuses of about $3,000 for the assistant GM and $8,000 for the GM.

VAUGHAN LAZAR

Vaughan Lazar founded Pizza Fusion with a college friend in Ft. Lauderdale, FL. The environmentally friendly and organic chain of casual restaurants has twenty-three locations in eleven states, where it serves pizzas, pastas, salads, sandwiches, and desserts. Each location is built according to LEED (Leadership in Energy and Environmental Design) standards, and all the food is made from scratch daily.

CURRENT POSITION: President, cofounder, and executive vice president of marketing, Pizza Fusion, Ft. Lauderdale, FL, since 2006, www.pizzafusion.com; owner of Stellar Concepts and Design, Ft. Lauderdale. ★ **EDUCATION:** BA, marketing, Florida Atlantic University. ★ **CAREER PATH:** Owner, Stellar Concepts & Design, a large graphic design firm (still in business). ★ **AWARDS AND RECOGNITION:** one of the top ten vegan-friendly restaurants, PETA; one of the top five green restaurants, *Cookie* magazine; Vaughan Lazar and his partner listed among the top eight green business founders, Grist; Emerald Award (for efforts for the sustainable world), Broward County, Florida. ★ **MEMBERSHIPS:** Surfrider Foundation; Co-Op America; Organic Trade Association; World Wildlife Federation; and more.

Salary notes:

On the corporate level, $36,000 to about $150,000 a year. Bigger franchise groups will pay more. At the restaurant level, you can go from earning $8 an hour to owning a successful franchise.

Words of advice for people considering a similar career:

Do your homework, your research. Make sure this is something you will fall in love with and will be able to do for at least ten years. Don't expect instant gratification—that's the worst thing to do, because you let yourself down. Don't go into it thinking you'll make great money immediately. And don't let anyone tell you that you can't do it. I wouldn't be here right now if I had listened to people who said that I couldn't do it. You've got to walk the walk and have integrity. Find a business with which your personal values align.

Describe a typical day.

What I do now is very different than what I did when I was running the restaurant. My title now is president and executive VP of marketing. I work closely with all of our franchises to help them increase sales and support them on the marketing level. I touch base with them daily to see how they are doing, what they are doing to market their stores, how I can help them with that. We have six restaurants in South Florida, and I visit almost all of them on a weekly basis. In the office, I work with the communication and marketing departments to come up with material for marketing the stores, material for franchises. And I'm always coming up with new ways to market the business, new viral strategies, social networking sites. It's becoming essential to be on social networking sites. Now that we are more public, we have to be more careful with those. I want the company to have a soul, so I keep a lot of my personal activities. I like snowboarding, being outdoors, working with charitable organizations—I like to show that part, show what we do and the meat and potatoes behind us, that we're people.

How many hours a week do you typically work?

I work all the hours that are in a week. I get to the office around eight thirty A.M. and stay until at least seven P.M. I also do a lot of things on weekends. About seventy hours a week.

What are your specific responsibilities?

Marketing. I am the environmental steward here. I focus on many of our green efforts. I'm always looking at new products, new organic products for our stores. Our core mission is to have as low an impact as possible on the environment, so I work for that.

What do you like most about what you do?

I absolutely love the people I work with. We've attracted such an amazing staff. Starbucks has created a real community around coffee and Whole Foods has done the same. We saw that, when we started the company, and wanted to create a place where people fall in love with what they do. It's exciting. It's also exciting to see change happen. It's really humbling. A couple of years ago we only had a couple of restaurants; now we have created 250 jobs in eight states.

What do you like least about it?

Franchising can be a challenge. It's absolutely wonderful, as each franchise is a member of our extended family. But when you have to make suggestions to a franchisee, it's not as easy as if you owned all the stores. So what I like least is not being able to act on decisions right away but having to consult everyone. We have a marketing fund committee, a franchising committee. There's a little more red tape, a little more bureaucracy. Being an outdoorsman who's also an entrepreneur, there's a lot of politics for my taste, but I love coming to work every day.

What skills are most important for you to do your job well?

First and foremost, you have to understand the marketplace, how people are spending their money and on what. Understanding demographics, predicting the market, and being able to react are important. When the economy got really bad really fast, being what some people would consider a more high-end-ticket item, we would have been in a lot of trouble if we hadn't made changes to the menu. I have two sets of customers: the customers and the franchisees. I have to be a great people person and be willing to listen. I have to have patience and know how to deal with many different personalities. You have to put yourself in their shoes and understand where they are coming from. And we do, because we started that way. We lived and died in the restaurant when we first opened.

What are your long-term goals?

I want to grow Pizza Fusion to where it is a household name, as a company that has made a difference in the world. I want to continue to be at the forefront of the sustainability side of the restaurant industry and lead in that. I want people to look at us as a model of sustainability.

What prompted you to start your own business?

My partner and I went to college together. We maintained that friendship after college. We started talking about how we were not necessarily satisfied with the legacy we were leaving and wondering what we could do that would make us feel good about what we're doing. We are both very committed to the environment and fond of the outdoors. I was eating organically at the time. We had both worked in restaurants before, like Chili's and others, everything from bartending to waiting on tables, but we were never at the operation level that would lead us to open a restaurant. I couldn't find a place to eat organic food other than home or Whole Foods, and Whole Foods is not convenient if you don't live or work near one. We thought pizza would be easy. Extending from the simple aspect of organic food, we decided that we needed to deliver in hybrid cars, make sure that our ingredients were grown without pesticides or hormones. That started the whole concept. Not having experience opening restaurants allowed us to open this with our eyes wide shut. We were able to make choices like bamboo or reclaimed wood without thinking about the bottom line. We give employees health benefits, too.

How large is your staff?

About five hundred employees, including fifteen to eighteen at the corporate level. We have about thirty per store.

What qualities do you look for in a new hire?

That's changed. When we first started, not coming from the restaurant industry, we just thought, "Hey, cool, they want to work in something environment related." We just wanted good people. Now we still want good people, but we are realizing that some people invest their retirement or refinance their house to get a franchise, so we have a lot more responsibilities. We now look for people who are experts in their field. We also look for a real commitment to sustainability.

What is your proudest accomplishment?

Going from an 850-square-foot restaurant to being featured in magazines and in books; it's the most humbling experience. Having seventeen restaurants with more opening and really making a difference. The biggest accomplishment is that we are really making a difference.

DEREK NOTTINGHAM

Derek Nottingham is the general manager of a secure government facility—whose name he cannot disclose—that handles ten thousand covers a day. He is employed by Sodexo Government Services, which manages the facility.

CURRENT POSITION: General manager, Sodexo Government Services, secure facility, Fort Meade, MD, since June 2007. ★ **EDUCATION:** Culinary arts degree, Institute of Culinary Education, New York, NY. ★ **CAREER PATH:** Sous chef, Jacob's Pillow Resort, Becket, MA (two summer seasons, 1991 and 1992); sous chef, executive dining room, Macmillan, New York, NY (1992–1994); sous chef, Exxon executive dining room, Sodexo Marriott Services, Irving, TX (1994–1998); executive chef, Food Glorious Food, Dallas, TX (1998–2001); executive sous chef, National Gallery of Art, Restaurant Associates/Compass Group, Washington, DC (2001–2004); chef de cuisine, International Monetary Fund, Guckenheimer Enterprises, Washington, DC (2004–2005); group executive chef, Sodexo Government Services, McLean, VA (2005–2007). ★ **AWARDS AND RECOGNITION:** Alumni Hall of Achievement, Institute of Culinary Education (2005). ★ **MEMBERSHIPS:** National Registry of Food Safety Professionals; American Culinary Federation.

Salary notes:

You're paid based on how much business your operation does. If you're managing a small operation, you're paid less. The greater the risk, the greater the reward. In small law firms, a chef-manager might make $40,000 a year. I've seen positions within this company for $200,000 a year.

Words of advice for people considering a similar career:

Learn how to take care of a team. I've reached the decision that no matter how good you are, you're only one person. If you can't make ten, twenty, fifty people work together efficiently, you can't succeed. It doesn't matter how good you are alone.

Describe a typical day.

Working in contract food service is always a different challenge, because you don't have to worry about reservations or the menu. You're selling a brand. Usually the biggest challenge is the staff—who decided to come to work and who decided not to come to work, because regardless, you have to serve lunch. We have a couple of snow days, but otherwise people come in to eat. We serve breakfast and lunch; we cater for dignitaries and politicians. I'm always in the customer's presence during service. The rest of the day is spent planning and improving everything. We have big projects, and then there's all the little things to take care of during the day, like an employee getting hurt on the job or someone who has something going on at home. I meet with clients for special events. We had the president and vice president of the United States come in recently. Such visits always happen on short notice, so we have clients' needs to meet immediately and everything has to change.

How large is your staff?

As GM, I supervise about sixty people.

How many hours a week do you typically work?

Fifty.

What are your specific responsibilities?

To ensure the quality food services that we've promised the clients of Sodexo. After that, I have a financial responsibility to the company. I scratch my head and figure out how the price increase of one product affects overall pricing. I have to stop myself at times and say this is why I have an executive chef. There are times I drive my guy nuts, when I'm too tempted to be in the kitchen. There are times when my team is glad that I have twenty-eight years of experience in the kitchen, those days when I jump in and make 160 gallons of soup in two hours. They can ask for help and get it.

What do you like most about what you do?

Watching the young culinary talent come in and figure out how to work.

What do you like least about it?

Customers who have no idea how to cook telling my staff or me how to cook. They're telling us how to cook scrambled eggs when we cook 160 pounds every morning. They're missing the bigger picture of cooking for food service; it's not cooking at home.

How many covers a day do you do?

A little over ten thousand; slightly over sixty-four transactions per labor hour. We operate with 30 percent food cost and about 43 percent labor cost. My goal is one cent of profit per $1 rung in the register.

What skills are most important for you to do your job well?

Time management is crucial. There are never enough hours in the day. After that, it's being able to work with all types of personalities. Anyone who tells me that they were a psychology major or that they left psychology for food service is among the most efficient leaders I've ever seen. Balancing everyone's personalities is essential; dealing with everyone is the key to survival in this business. We have to meet a deadline every day; there's not an option. You can't push lunch back an hour. It's like Broadway: when the curtain goes up it's showtime. You have to orchestrate everything to be successful.

What skills would you like to develop to help further your career?

I'm always working on learning new things. Right now, it's business-specific things, like sales, client retention. Where I am now, knowing how things happen in the kitchen is one thing, but dealing with clients is another.

What qualities do you look for in a new hire?

First, I look at their résumé to see what they've done and what work cycle they've had. I really believe in young culinarians changing jobs every two years. I like to see that they've had varied experiences. Someone with a month here, a month there doesn't have enough commitment. Then, I look at attitude. If they seem too uptight or not able to manage pressure or stress, they can't survive. There's always a lot of stress.

Describe your creative process.

I always start with what the customer is looking for, whether it's a new process, a new operation, resolving a problem, or getting more money in the door, for example. I find out why they want to make a change. I figure out what our competitors do. Am I losing money because competitors are doing value meals? If I can't do a value meal, can I do a healthier meal or find green products?

"Learn how to take care of a team. I've reached the decision that no matter how good you are, you're only one person. If you can't make ten, twenty, fifty people work together efficiently, you can't succeed. It doesn't matter how good you are alone."

HEATHER LAISKONIS

Heather Laiskonis is the general manager of Aldea, a restaurant in New York, NY, that features cuisine inspired by the Iberian Peninsula and the Portuguese heritage of the chef, George Mendes. The restaurant is open for dinner six nights a week.

CURRENT POSITION: General manager, Aldea, New York, NY. ★ **EDUCATION:** Ten college credits. ★ **CAREER PATH:** Chopstick Inn, Riverview, MI (at fourteen); nightclub, Dearborn, MI (four years); several bartending and table-waiting jobs, Detroit, MI; manager, restaurant, Detroit suburbs; manager, Silverdome, for all of the Detroit Lions' home games; other careers in between jobs, most notably building computers in Silicon Valley, CA, and selling carpets in Cappadocia, Turkey; back waiter, Tribute, Farmington Hills, MI.

Salary notes:

$60,000 to $80,000

Words of advice for people considering a similar career:

It's very rewarding but not for many. If your dreams include days off, being able to attend weddings and other family events— or even *having* a family—it's not for you.

Describe a typical day.

Right now, my days are atypical, as the restaurant is still a construction site. Typically, however, they begin with me arriving at work around noon, then leaving around midnight to one A.M.

How many hours a week do you typically work?

Seventy-ish.

What are your specific responsibilities in the preopening process and once the restaurant is open?

Preopening: I am currently the only employee, so I'm doing everything. I am working on preopening budgets and projections. Slowly building a wine list. Interviewing for some key positions, writing the employee handbooks, choosing uniforms, meeting with purveyors, and compiling opening silver, glass, and china orders.

Once open: If you work for a restaurant group or in fine dining, the roles are more defined. You have a general manager who does just numbers; you have a sommelier who does just wine, and the maître d', who only does service. In the smaller restaurants (the ones I prefer), I will have all of these responsibilities and then some. That is why it is crucial that I hire an amazing support team.

What do you like most about what you do?

I find restaurant work to be the most honest work there is. It is instant gratification. While I respect the work, I could never imagine being an architect! Waiting up to ten years to see all of your work come to fruition! I open the doors, say hello, and feed you. I ask how your day was and treat you with respect. If you like me, my team, and what we do, you come back and let me feed you again. If not, you don't.

What do you like least about it?

I haven't been to bed before two A.M. since I was fourteen.

What skills are most important for you to do your job well?

Is sleep a skill? I think you need to be a lot more than polite. You have to actually care about the people who come through your doors. Everyone can spot someone fake or someone who is just going through the motions. Caring for the people who come through your doors is the most important skill.

What skills would you like to develop to help further your career?

I would love to have the skill of not having something spilled on me throughout the night! Or the ability to have my business card on me at the right time. I know those industry professionals who are always immaculate. Never a hair out of place. I'm in awe of them and would love to know how they do it.

What challenges does someone in your position specifically face during a restaurant's opening process?

The biggest challenge has been construction; it's never anyone's fault (or always the other guy's fault). They recently built our bathrooms, only to find that the ADA bathroom [handicapped-accessible bathroom] was built one foot shy of code. That meant that it took two weeks to build a bathroom that should have taken three days. Once open, I fear the bloggers—the people who come two days after your opening and expose the fact that I forgot to put a wine list down at a table.

What do you look for when deciding where you'll work?

Chef-owned and/or -operated. I have never cared for "concept" restaurants. I prefer to work for a chef who has vision and talent. Chefs who own their own place have so much more to lose than a corporate chef. They give you intensity and passion that raises the bar for everyone else around them.

Any suggestions to improve work-life balance?

I think it's taken me a long time to get to know myself. The best thing that I ever learned was the ability to say no. If you know that you are not very good at working fourteen hours a day on four hours of sleep, it means you have to say no to someone. Restaurant people, by nature, are pleasers. We want to make everyone happy. It's hard for us to say no.

LIZ QUILL

Liz Quill is the general manager of Persephone, a Boston restaurant that uses only locally grown and raised ingredients and practices sustainability in all aspects of its operations. With the adjacent designer clothing and lifestyle items boutique, Achilles, it forms the Achilles Project.

CURRENT POSITION: General manager, Persephone, Boston, MA, since 2009. ★
EDUCATION: BA, arts and interior design, Framingham State College, Framingham, MA. ★
CAREER PATH: In Boston: interior designer as a residential, hospital, and corporate designer (seventeen years); hostess, Spier (now called KO Prime) (about one year); private events manager, Number 9 Park (three years); events manager at another restaurant (about six months). ★ **AWARDS AND RECOGNITION:** When I was at Spier, there were lots of management changes, and they handed me the keys about a month into my employment there. I won an Over the Top Award for stepping up into other positions and making sure that the restaurant kept running smoothly.

Salary notes:

Between $50,000 and $100,000, depending on the type of restaurant.

Words of advice for people considering a similar career:

Be ready for anything. People come to restaurants with certain expectations. You have to be ready to give your guests the best you can possibly give.

How many hours a week do you typically work?

About sixty-five hours. We're open five days a week.

Describe a typical day.

One day we could be holding an event for a hundred people, another day hosting a VIP or a TV personality, the next day it's perfectly normal. That's what I love about this industry the most: It's constantly changing. If I am opening, I'm in at nine thirty A.M.; if I'm closing, I come in at about two P.M. I work in the office doing financial stuff, human resources, payroll. I also manage the large private events if we have a buyout, for example. I do the scheduling. And I work the floor and make sure there's always a manager.

What are your specific responsibilities?

I manage the payroll, front-of-the-house staff; I handle hiring, training, scheduling, posting positions. I maintain the schedules of the service staff, bartender, manager, host, and motivate them all. I make sure that workers' comp is done, I maintain and order uniforms, open and close, maintain the employee handbook. I am the liaison with the accountant and accounts payable; I book private events; I make sure that guests are satisfied on a nightly basis; I maintain the website, updating the menu and menu descriptions.

What do you like most about what you do?

That every day is different. That with the staff, we create a special day for our guests. It's like throwing a dinner party every night.

What do you like least about it?

On the rare occasion when a guest isn't happy and you can't turn them around, it's disappointing.

What skills are most important for you to do your job well?

Patience, kindness, and humility. Those are more traits than skills, but they are the most important things you can have in this industry. There are so many things you can be taught, like how to use a computer and the food terminology, but you need to have this innate sense of caring for people that can't be trained.

What skills would you like to develop to help further your career?

I'm always looking to educate myself. My wine knowledge could be stronger, and that's what I'm continuing to develop. Our wine director educates us daily here, so I get in-house training.

What are your long-term goals?

I want to be part of a team that receives local and national attention for our food and service.

How large is your staff?

I have twenty people in the front of the house who answer to me.

What is the outlook for your type of job?

You definitely hope for more. Boston has really come into its own. People have a desire to dine out and appreciate what chefs are doing, so there's a need for people in my position.

What qualities do you look for in a new hire?

I look for happy people who have an innate love of serving people and are passionate about food and wine. I want people with restaurant experience. It doesn't have to be fine dining, but it shows a passion for food and wine.

What is your proudest accomplishment?

My proudest accomplishment is starting as a hostess at thirty-nine years old and five years later being a general manager. But having had to manage projects before gave me a sense of how to control things and what to do.

What keeps you challenged?

Essentially, everyone around me. But mostly working on the Achilles Project. We have several different concepts under one roof, so maintaining the direction that the owners want to go in. The energy that the owners have is challenging to keep up with, for sure.

MATT DIX

Matt Dix is the assistant general manager of the New York branch of the Ace Hotel, a boutique hotel chain that started in Seattle, WA, and also has locations in Portland, OR, and Palm Springs, CA. The hotel also hosts a gastropub, a coffee shop, and an event hall. He left a career in music to join the hospitality industry after realizing that post-performance meals were what he liked best about playing professionally.

CURRENT POSITION: Assistant general manager, Ace Hotel, New York, NY, since July 2008. ★ **EDUCATION:** Tufts University for two years, Boston, MA; BM, violin performance, Eastman School of Music, Rochester, NY; culinary arts and management degrees, Institute of Culinary Education, New York, NY. ★ **CAREER PATH:** In New York: garde-manger to poissonier, Aureole; helped open Pier 116, Brooklyn; cook, Superfine; cook, Top of the Week (*Newsweek*'s executive dining room); Savoy; 5 Ninth; food and beverage manager, Soho Grand Hotel; assistant general manager, 202 Café at Nicole Farhi. ★ **AWARDS AND RECOGNITION:** Two stars at Pier 116. ★ **MEMBERSHIPS:** Streets International; string orchestra in Brooklyn.

Salary notes:

It can really vary, but for what I'm doing, slightly below $100,000 to several hundred thousand. It depends on the size of the property, the amount of responsibilities, and if you have a vested interest.

Words of advice for people considering a similar career:

Be focused but flexible. There are several paths to the same destination. There's a lot to be said for being sturdy and resilient, also, particularly in New York. The business can really beat some people up. Let your mission be known to the people who matter.

Describe a typical day.

Right now we're still in the opening stage. I get in to work at eight thirty or nine A.M., I check my schedule, check in with all the department heads (housekeeping and engineering, front office, sales and marketing) to coordinate with them and un-

derstand how far along they are with their projects. I meet with all of them to understand where they stand and relay much of that to the general manager. I handle the organization of preopening events, contact vendors, send out invitations, include guests. I'm at work until seven thirty P.M. at least. Once we open, I will be working in the evening, from four P.M. to one or two A.M.

How many hours a week do you typically work?

Sixty to seventy hours a week.

What are your specific responsibilities?

Once we open, I'll be responsible for everyone having what they need when I am there, and if they don't, making sure that they can get it. I'll also be wrapping everything up, to make sure that the people who come in the morning know everything that happened the evening prior. I'll handle client relationships, checking in with clients having events, with the catering staff running the events, and with the people responsible for the engineering of the building.

What do you like most about what you do?

I really appreciate the excitement of the job and the fact that I'm not just focused on one task. I like the idea of being responsible for various aspects of the operation. I came from a music background, where I basically did one thing, playing the violin, and could devote all my time to it. I realized that I have the type of personality where I can easily split my time and attention. I like that every day is different.

What do you like least about it?

It could be the same answer. The same thing that excites me and keeps me interested can also be what requires the most energy. You can get too wrapped up in it. I've learned to step back and look at the whole situation to see what piece needs to be moved where in order to make the best of the situation.

What are your long-term goals?

The next step is to be general manager of a hotel. Beyond that, developing properties. Opening my own hotel would be amazing. I don't know if I want to be on the creative or development or financial side, but I know that I definitely want to develop my own properties.

What is the outlook for your type of job?

Right now it's a little gloomy, but I think that you weather a short storm and the long term is great. The outlook for my job is great. There's always someone who wants to travel, and there's always a creative way to target who's going where.

How large is your staff?

When I first started there were five of us; now there are twenty-five to thirty. It's going to grow to upwards of a hundred staff working here, in everything from engineering to concierge. Each one of the departments has its own direct boss, and what I am here for is to make sure that the brand is being represented properly by everyone.

What qualities do you look for in a new hire?

That changes from company to company, whoever the directors may be, from the top down. But for me personally, I appreciate someone who has a great work ethic and who seems naturally happy. People who are very respectful—somebody who wants to work hard and naturally has respect for others. The rest you can train; how to perform tasks on daily basis is very trainable.

TOM DOWLING

After spending twenty years as executive chef of the award-winning restaurant of the Rancho Bernardo Inn Golf Resort & Spa, Tom Dowling became the purchasing director for the 287-room AAA four-diamond and Mobil four-star hotel.

CURRENT POSITION: Purchasing director, Rancho Bernardo Inn Golf Resort & Spa, San Diego, CA, since 2006. ★ **EDUCATION:** Associate's degree in culinary arts, Culinary Institute of America, Hyde Park, NY (1980). ★ **CAREER PATH:** Intern, Hyatt Resort on Hilton Head Island, SC. In New York: sous chef, Helmsley Palace; sous chef, Gotham Bar and Grill. Executive chef, Le Plumet Royal at the Peacock Inn, Princeton, NJ; sous chef, then executive chef, El Bizcocho, Rancho Bernardo Inn, San Diego, CA (about twenty years). ★ **AWARDS AND RECOGNITION:** Rising Star Chef, James Beard Foundation; three stars from the *New York Times* while at Le Plumet Royal; Best Hotel Restaurant, Zagat (1991–1993); AAA Four Diamond.

Salary notes:

A purchasing director's salary will be in direct correlation with the volume that the hotel or the restaurant does. Entry-level purchasing people make anywhere between $35,000 and $65,000. But some people definitely make $150,000.

Words of advice for people considering a similar career:

Get an accounting background, and know how to use Excel. You absolutely want to make sure that you have the product knowledge of what it is you are buying and selling, wherever you can get that exposure: through classes, seminars, events, the Internet.

Describe a typical day.

My job is to ensure that anything we need in the hotel is here. It starts with me working ahead, looking for things I'm going to need in the coming days, whether it's one ingredient or something we use in bulk. I establish an average of that product that I want to have on hand, based on our use of it and when I can get deliveries. I make sure that things are ordered, received, and appropriately delivered. I handle shipping and receiving. In any guest-driven business, the goal is getting what the guest needs. We have to always remember that. Then I place orders, check prices, negotiate for deals, check the quality of the products, make sure that everything is up to code from a storage standpoint. I attend many different meetings for the food and beverage department; I go to food shows; I host people who come in and show me new products, to see what works for our company. I'm involved in buying food, wine and liqueurs, and paper products.

How many hours a week do you typically work?

I'm on salary, so I'd be more inclined to say I work when I need to work. We might have a delivery of a hundred boxes coming in for a group that is doing an event at the hotel, so I'll come in on a Sunday to ensure that their boxes are received and that they go where they need to go. Maybe fifty hours a week. If I only need to put in forty, I'll put in forty, but if I need to put in sixty, I'll put in sixty. I'll do whatever is needed. What is nice is that we can really work around business hours.

What are your specific responsibilities?

Sourcing, negotiating, receiving, storing, delivering the products. I don't prepare the product. There's a specific cycle in this industry of where food production starts and where it ends, and my involvement is much more at the beginning than at the end. I've done my job when I've given the product to the chef.

What do you like least about what you do?

I guess what I don't like to a degree is that people are becoming harder to deal with. They are becoming more picky about things. They want caffeine-free Dr Pepper on all breaks because that's what the CEO drinks. This whole menu has to be garlic free. You can have the nicest people, who say, "Just do this for me." And then you have very demanding people who enjoy the fact that they are running you ragged, and they barely say thank you. It's a service industry, but sometimes it's hard to provide service to people who treat you poorly. But we also thrive on making things happen.

What skills are most important for you to do your job well?

My particular job right now is very much an organization job; it's almost like an accounting job. I work hand in hand with the accounting department as much as I do with the food and beverage department.

How large is your staff?

Three people.

What qualities do you look for in a new hire?

It's a physical job; there's a lot of lifting. I'm looking for someone who has the work ethic, can physically do the job, and is organized. You have to follow rules and regulations here. It's about troubleshooting and prioritizing. If we get a bunch of products at the same time, you put away the perishables first, then what needs to go in the kitchen, what can stay out. I need someone who can multitask and prioritize.

Do you need to have prior hands-on cooking experience to work in purchasing?

Not necessarily. You need to have knowledge of the product to be a good purchaser. You may have come in as an assistant. I have some guys working for me who are just doing deliveries, and they're here every day and learning about the products. You learn, you go to the market, you do research, etc. You have to be a good negotiator. You want the best products at the best price. You work with perishable products. You have to design your operations around your facility. If you have tons of French fries on the menu but no fryer, you will get buried. Same thing, if you have room to store things, you can buy in quantity. As a buyer, you have to know what you are buying. Some places only deliver once a week. What has really changed this industry is that you can get things sent via FedEx overnight from anywhere in the world.

9. WINE AND BEVERAGES

Wine and beverage careers offer the opportunity to work in close relation to the restaurant world without having to deal with strenuous kitchen work. Many of those jobs also offer slightly higher salaries than those of the food side of the culinary industry. Additionally, in difficult economic times, wine and liquor sales tend

to go up. People might not go out to dinner as much, but they will go out for a drink or buy a bottle of wine (albeit usually a cheaper one than they might have previously) to enjoy at home with friends. More and more, food service operators see beverages other than alcohol as a source of both profit and differentiation. Whether you work as a sommelier in a restaurant or sell spirits as an independent distributor, it is crucial to understand and appreciate the beverages that you market and sell so that you can communicate that passion to your customers and encourage them to trust you with their purchasing decisions. In the restaurant and hotel world, the top beverage position would be either sommelier or wine and beverage manager or director. Working in a wine shop or for a wine distributor is another path that can lead to a sommelier position in a restaurant.

restaurant work

While many restaurants do not employ a designated sommelier, some wine knowledge will make you a better server, if that is your position, and can eventually lead to working as a sommelier somewhere else. A typical career track in wine service might be as follows:

Server or bartender
Assistant sommelier
Sommelier
Beverage or wine director

Starting as a server is often the first position that many sommeliers held. After being a server (at some places you might even be required to start as a busboy or server assistant), you may continue on the path to assistant sommelier, then sommelier, and then beverage or wine director. Some people rise up quickly through the ranks, as did Nelson Daquip (see page 220), and can reach the level of sommelier within a few short years. A smaller establishment might also promote you more quickly, particularly if no one else currently holds the title. Promotions will come not only through the obvious expansion of your knowledge and growth of your general service skills, but also through the sales that you make. If your wine sales go up, you are likely doing something right, and that will attract the attention of your manager.

The career of a sommelier benefits greatly from acquiring certifications, it's almost a requirement. The rigorous exams of programs such as the Wine and Spirit Education Trust (WSET; see page 44) let employers and customers alike know that you are serious about your craft and spend countless hours expanding your knowledge. Because these tests are very demanding and require that you take classes and extensively taste beverages, they demonstrate a commitment to knowledge and point out the fact that you are not doing your job only to pay the bills but truly see yourself building a lifelong wine-related career.

Certain sommeliers, such as Cynthia Gold at the Boston Park Plaza Hotel and Towers, specialize in other types of beverages, like tea or water. These jobs are very rare, and these specialty sommeliers tend to perform their jobs on a part-time basis, with other activities on the side contributing to their income or while holding a management role within the operation. These people have a rare passion for the beverage they present and study even the smallest aspect of its industry in the most minute details. They may have to convince businesses to hire them, although they might be drawn into that position by a manager seeking to add a unique attraction to its facility (offering high tea in the afternoon is a great way to keep a restaurant busy between lunch and dinner services, for example). Because their jobs are rare and are akin to consultancies, it is hard to tell what salaries you should expect. They reflect years of acquired expertise and in-depth knowledge, along with a reputation solidified by much media attention that will contribute to what you can charge.

More and more restaurants serve food at their bar, whether it is the complete menu or a reduced bar menu. As such, diners are getting used to eating at the bar and conversing with the bartender in the process. In such establishments, good wine knowledge will be valuable if you are a bartender, since you will be asked for recommendations and food pairings. It will also be helpful if you know something about food—which is not necessarily the case if you work in a stand-alone bar—since you will need to tell diners about the dishes available to them and will be right in front of them should they have any questions about their meal.

bar work

Working as a bartender is a great way to learn about alcohol or apply previously acquired knowledge, particularly if you work at establishments that have a high-end liquor selection, create interesting cocktails, or have a specialty beer list. At such places, you can be assured that patrons will ask for more than light draft beer and tequila shots, thus challenging you to constantly improve your knowledge.

With the cocktail renaissance that has taken place in the United States over the last few years, more cocktail-focused bars are opening than ever, particularly in large cities like New York and San Francisco. In those, you will be expected to mix drinks using only fresh ingredients and measuring your pours, which makes them more labor and time intensive but also infinitely better. If you prefer to work quickly and make simpler drinks, high-volume establishments offering a smaller selection of widely known mixed drinks might be more appropriate to your aspirations. Coming in with a knowledge of classic cocktails as well as with a few twists of your own, in case you are asked to whip something up on the fly during your interviewing process, is a must to show that you are genuinely interested in working in establishments that require a certain level of expertise. The term "mixologist" has gained popularity as a way to refer to bartenders in specialty cocktail bars, but many are just as happy with the traditional title.

If you prefer to work with wines, wine bars are now common in even the smallest town, it seems, making them a great place to use your knowledge if you prefer not to work in a restaurant. Some wine bars specialize in French, Italian, or other types of wines (such as New York wines in New York City and California wines in California). Having existing knowledge of and interest for that area will be beneficial when you apply for a job.

Breweries and bars focusing on local and artisanal beers are other specialty establishments to explore if beer is what you are most interested in. Many restaurants also offer well-edited beer lists, which lean away from the mass-market American beers and focus on brews that have more complex flavor profiles. If you start working in a bar that does not offer such selections, but you are knowledgeable about certain beers and feel that your clientele will enjoy them, suggest adding them to the list. This will show your employer that you are enterprising. In addition this may increase the bar's revenues, which would be a valuable point to present to potential employers as you move forward with your career.

Regardless of the area of specialization you choose in the bar business, the contacts that you make within the industry will be valuable, especially as you move up the career ladder. Sales representatives for all kinds of beverages will seek your business and present you with all kinds of samples, specials, and discounts. Certain smaller brands, however, do not have enough supply to serve all the locations that would like to offer their products.

Having a good relationship with a sales representative for that small company, or with the executives of that company, will be helpful in acquiring the product. Being the only one in your neighborhood or area to offer a certain wine, spirit, or beer will bring you the clientele who seek it.

sales

Working in sales demands a love for both beverages and commerce. Having passion for the product that you sell will give you credibility as you meet with customers, but ultimately you will need to meet your sales goals. When dealing with restaurants, having some food knowledge will go a long way toward convincing the buyer or chef that you know why such and such wine will go well with the food that they serve. Having prior cooking or service experience will help you obtain your first sales position. Many companies take on interns, so if you are still in school or in a position where you can do so, apply with local distributors in order to learn the business.

As a salesperson, your job is to meet with suppliers and customers in order to first obtain and then sell your product. You will contact and meet with sommeliers, beverage directors, and bartenders—both current and prospective clients—to present your products to them, take their order, and introduce them to new programs you might be offering, such as a promotion on a particular product or something that you are introducing in limited availability.

People skills and patience are thus essential, in addition to good old salesmanship.

Taking classes, gaining certification, and displaying expertise in one country's wines, for example, are all ways in which you can both advance your career and gain additional credibility with your customers. Traveling to wineries, distilleries, and breweries will also help increase your knowledge and give you stories about your product that will become part of your sales pitch. The key is to always be genuine when displaying that knowledge—if you are truly passionate about the products that you sell, you will be able to share them without a shtick, simply by talking about the characteristics of what you represent.

When working in wine sales, the end of the year is particularly important. Steve Kelley of Lauber Imports (page 223) says that 30 to 40 percent of his company's income is made at year's end, thanks to champagne sales, corporate gifts, and parties. If you choose to work in this field, do not expect to take vacations at this time of year.

education

As Americans' love for wines continues to grow, so does the need for qualified wine educators. Wine stores and culinary schools offer ever-expanding wine course offerings, which range from wine 101 to classes that focus on one varietal. There is also a market for wine "edutainment" at corporate retreats, resorts, and country clubs, as well as on cruise ships and at a wide range of other venues.

As with any type of teaching, being charismatic and engaging when you present information will go a long way in building repeat attendance for your classes. Beverages offer fewer opportunities for flashy displays in the classroom than food does, so your personality is even more important. Tasting classes are very interactive because everyone gets to sip the same wine as you and follow what you have to say, but ultimately people sit for a couple of hours and listen to you while looking at glasses filled with liquids of a similar color.

salaries

Like other service employees, restaurant bartenders and servers make minimum wage, which varies by state, and tips. The range of money you will make will vary widely depending on the number of shifts that you work a week, the volume of the operation, and the price of the food and drink. You will likely make between $25,000 and $40,000 as a midrange. Sommeliers and beverage directors are salaried employees and can expect to earn between $50,000 and $100,000, depending again on experience and the type and volume of the restaurant. The wine direc-

tor of a restaurant group will break the six-figure salary mark.

Bartenders typically earn minimum wage plus tips, like other service workers. Minimum wage will depend on the city or state in which you work, while the amount of tips you make will depend on how busy your bar is. You can expect to make around $40,000 as an average and significantly more if you work in a high-volume establishment in a city like Las Vegas, for example.

Sales salaries are based on commission, so they vary based on the size of the operation for which you work, your tenure there, and the number of products on the list, but you can expect to make close to six figures as a midlevel professional and well into that amount as a seasoned sales manager and above. To an unusual degree, these salaries are affected by state laws on liquor and alcohol sales. For example, in states where the alcohol tax is high, profits on sales are lower and so commissions are lower.

Your salary as an educator will depend on how many classes you want to teach, how many events you might run, and if you take on side projects such as working as a consultant for a wine company. You will be paid per class that you teach, usually in the starting range of a couple hundred dollars as a cooking instructor, and can command more as your reputation and knowledge grow.

BEN WILEY

Ben Wiley owns Bar Great Harry, a neighborhood bar in Brooklyn, with his brother. The focus of their drink list is on local and craft beers; they change the list of beers available on tap every day, using a blog to communicate the day's selection to their customers.

CURRENT POSITION: Owner, Bar Great Harry, Brooklyn, NY, since 2007, www.bargreatharry .com. ★ **EDUCATION:** BA, Japanese, University of Illinois—Urbana-Champaign; master's degree, Inter-University Center for Japanese Language Studies, Stanford University, Yokohama, Japan; pastry arts degree, Institute of Culinary Education (2006). ★ **CAREER PATH:** Bartender and manager, Yokohama, Japan, while a student; governmental translator-interpreter, Fukui, Japan (three years); worked in garbage and recycling business when back in the United States (six months); pastry assistant, Del Posto, New York (one year). ★ **AWARDS AND RECOGNITION:** *Village Voice* Best of NYC (2008): Best Spot for Unsnobby Beer Snobs. ★ **MEMBERSHIPS:** New York State Restaurant Association; New York City Nightlife Association; Slow Food; Westin A. Price Foundation.

Salary notes:

$220,000

Words of advice for people considering a similar career:

Try to have a partner. It's really hard to do on your own. You can do it on your own if you are single. Pick your business partner really well. Become friends with local businesses. I know the owners of every business around our neighborhood. If the ice machine breaks down, I can go to the restaurant next door and get ice from there. One day we had no power and ran power from other businesses. It's friendly because we all think like that. It's important.

Describe a typical day.

We open at two P.M. I come here any time between ten A.M. and twelve P.M. to do the prior day's books and accounting. We have two shifts a day, so two sets of books. I enter them into our spreadsheets, which takes about half an hour. I give bartenders money for the day. All the banking takes about two hours. Then it's about two hours of moving things downstairs, cleaning up the walking box, behind-the-scenes work, all the things you don't see. Then I disappear and come back at eight P.M. every day, when we switch from the day shift to the evening shift. I talk to the bartenders to see how it went. I'm here until nine thirty or ten P.M., then I come back around one thirty or two A.M. to see how things are. I work an average day, between six and nine hours, but it's not broken down like most jobs. Except on Saturdays, when I bartend. I do all the ordering, receiving, moving of kegs downstairs. It's a lot of work but it's fun. I have no boss. That's the most important thing.

How many hours a week do you typically work?

When you own a business, it's hard to count, because you work at home sometimes. I work six days a week. I do fifty to sixty hours of what I would call work, mental time spent dealing with bar stuff. I only bartend one day a week.

What are your specific responsibilities?

Everything. It's just my brother and me. We are an LLC. I'm vice president and he's president, because we flipped a coin in the lawyer's office. We share all responsibilities fifty-fifty. I would not recommend that to somebody; the only reason it works is that we have a very easy relationship. I order everything and take care of the inventory, which is a big thing. We handle personnel issues—which include bartending any time someone doesn't show up. I do the day-to-day bookkeeping. I write the chalkboard, on which we change one beer a day. My brother takes care of the website, for the most part. Every two weeks we have a special event where a brewery sends a representative and we buy the beer and sell it cheap. I handle the listing of those events on the biggest four or five beer websites, like beeradvocate.com. We don't do any advertising—that's free advertising.

What do you like most about what you do?

The single most important thing is the freedom. I can't take two weeks off or be home at six P.M., but I can wake up at eight A.M. one day, ten A.M. the next. I'm very disciplined so I don't really do that, but I could. Having no boss—that's very important. It's the main reason to get into your own business. My brother and I are very good friends. I do it for one reason, for the freedom, the lifestyle, not for the money.

What do you like least about it?

The flip side: the lack of freedom. The fact that it's never off your mind. You can never leave it at work. There are times when I wake up in the middle of the night worrying. I have complete responsibility for everything. It's also hard at the beginning to maintain relationships outside of your business. When we opened, I was here every waking hour. My schedule was wake up, go to the bar. It was all in a blur. The loss of anonymity can be tough to deal with at times. I'll take the F train to Midtown and sit at a café because I won't know anyone there. I know many bar owners and we all deal with that. Everybody knows who you're going out with, when you break up with someone. But that's going to change when we open a second bar.

What skills are most important for you to do your job well?

Being able to judge character. Multitasking, being able to deal with many things at once and to juggle them. We have no general manager. This is going to have to change within the next two to three years. The ability to put on a happy face all the time: When it's your own place, everybody knows you, and our place is a reflection of us. You can't show up in a bad mood. You have to be able to be happy all the time, even if you're pissed off.

What is the outlook for your type of job?

A lot of people like to say that bars are economy-proof. It's a really good business to get into if you have bartending and waitressing experience and/or cooking experience. But what happens is that nine out of ten owners have no experience. They're actors or lawyers; at some point they're forty-five years old and say, "That's what I want to do." All of my experience my entire life has been bartending; I would recommend opening your own bar to anyone who has that experience.

What qualities do you look for in a new hire?

The most important thing you have to do is to pick your employees, I think. First and foremost, I look for friendliness. We have five bartenders, and two of them had never bartended before. People care more about friendly faces. Then I have to establish whether I think I can trust them or not. I call all of their prior employers. I only hire local people who can all walk to my bar. They are more likely to show up, because they are part of the same community; they shop where I shop. There's more accountability, and I can track them down. They can think, "He knows everything about me, so it's harder for me to steal from him." I don't hire strangers—they all know somebody I know. But you don't want to know them too well. You want to keep a certain distance. I like hiring female bartenders; they tend to drink less. I almost always hire ones who are married, so their husbands will often come in to help them close up. It's good to know someone will be there.

How do you pick the beers you serve?

I never serve anything I haven't tasted. So I only serve beers that I drink and think are good. I always talk to the brewers. I go to a beer store and buy beers, or now brewers send us samples. At the beginning, I spent all my money drinking beer.

"I know the owners of every business around our neighborhood. If the ice machine breaks down, I can go to the restaurant next door and get ice from there. One day we had no power and ran power from other businesses. It's friendly because we all think like that. It's important."

ERIC BREHM

As sommelier for Rancho Bernardo Inn Golf Resort & Spa, a 287-room AAA four-diamond and Mobil four-star hotel in San Diego, CA, Eric Brehm handles all beverage-related functions for the hotel's award-winning restaurant, El Bizcocho, its two other venues, and all events. He manages an inventory of more than thirty thousand bottles.

CURRENT POSITION: Sommelier, Rancho Bernardo Inn Golf Resort & Spa, San Diego, CA, since 2006. ★ **EDUCATION:** Associate's degree, business; working toward a BA, business, University of Redlands, CA; Level 1 of the master sommelier course, Court of Master Sommeliers; certified specialist of wine through the Society of Wine Educators. ★ **CAREER PATH:** Headwaiter, Iva Lee's, San Clemente, CA; headwaiter, wine sales, and food service, Bernard'O Restaurant, CA; restaurant manager, the Crosby (private club), Rancho Santa Fe, CA (about four and a half years). ★ **AWARDS AND RECOGNITION:** *Wine Spectator* Best Award of Excellence for wine list. ★ **MEMBERSHIPS:** Court of Master Sommeliers; Society of Wine Educators; private weekly tasting group with fellow sommeliers.

Salary notes:

Around $60,000

Words of advice for people considering a similar career:

Make sure that you enjoy it. Keep up with your knowledge, because wine changes every day. Live today as if you are going to die tomorrow, but learn as if you are going to live forever—a friend told me that.

Describe a typical day.

When I get in, I check in with everybody, answer my e-mails, order all the wines that we need, touch up the wine list, make corrections for wines by the glass or on the wine list. I talk to my assistant about wines that we need to bring up from the cellar, and either he does it or I do it. Then we get all the wines that we want to showcase that night during service ready. We chill the white wines, put the reds on the wine table. Then I have lunch or an early dinner, put on my suit, and hold meetings with the staff. I have at least one office day a week during which I focus on desk work, the wine list, orders—typically from ten A.M. to six P.M. The rest of the four or five days, I get in around three P.M. and leave around eleven thirty P.M.

How many hours a week do you typically work?

Forty-five to fifty hours.

What are your specific responsibilities?

I'm in charge of the wine program for three venues and the catering/events/banquets. Considering that we have an almost $800,000 inventory, it's a pretty high responsibility. I have one assistant.

What do you like most about what you do?

The most fun thing is working with the wines and introducing new wines to guests who haven't had them before. I turn them on to something they would enjoy.

What do you like least about it?

Counting all those bottles on inventory day. That takes me one and a half to two days. We have over thirty thousand bottles and count each and every one of them. I don't mind it, but it's very cumbersome.

What skills are most important for you to do your job well?

You really need to have a thorough knowledge of the wines. You need to know geography, geology (the soil types in which the grapes grow). You have to know different styles of winemaking, if it was a good year or a bad year. Especially if you get to the range where someone wants to spend $2,000 on a bottle of wine. Another important skill is to be a people person, to get diners to trust you to find the best wine for them.

What are your long-term goals?

To work in this for a long enough time to feel that I've mastered it and then work as a consultant in a winery on their wines or making my own wine. Another thing would be to go into supplying and become a distributor.

Who or what are your sources of inspiration?

Some past people that I've worked through and with. Robert Bigelow, master sommelier and food and beverage director at the Bellagio in Las Vegas. He currently has three master sommeliers working under him at that hotel. Master sommelier Sheridan Dowling is a great inspiration. The way he talks about wine is really passionate. Greg Harris at the Crosby country club, my former boss. He helped me spread my wings and introduced me to really cool Italian and Californian wines. He got me started with wines.

What keeps you challenged?

I like trying new wines with foods. The chef occasionally challenges me with his food. Also, being part of the community of sommeliers, staying on top of the game to be among the best, keeps me challenged. I'm very competitive. And the economy right now; you really have to focus on what customers want.

NELSON DAQUIP

Nelson Daquip is the wine director of the award-winning Canlis, a fifty-nine-year-old institution of the Seattle restaurant scene that is widely recognized as one of the top restaurants in the country. He rose from server assistant, to server, to assistant sommelier, to wine director in only four years.

CURRENT POSITION: Wine director, Canlis, Seattle, WA, since 2006. ★ **EDUCATION:** Culinary arts degree, Kapi'olani Community College, University of Hawaii; master sommelier candidate (advanced course for Court of Master Sommeliers). ★ **CAREER PATH:** Small sushi restaurant in Waikiki; Alan Wong (three years, Honolulu); vinternship program at Canlis (2002). ★ **AWARDS AND RECOGNITION:** Profiled in *Food & Wine* feature on national up-and-coming sommeliers (2005); one of *Wine & Spirits'* best new sommeliers (2006); Seattle's Best Sommelier, *Seattle Magazine* (2008); StarChefs' Seattle Rising Star Sommelier (2009), holder of the *Wine Spectator* Grand Award for Canlis since 1997. ★ **MEMBERSHIPS:** International Sommelier Guild (received sommelier diploma); Chaîne des Rôtisseurs.

Salary notes:

In general, when starting off as a wine director, your salary is related to what the program is doing. If the restaurant is doing $3 million on wine sales only, the wine director there should be paid $100,000 minimum. It's usually $50,000 as a starting point.

Words of advice for people considering a similar career:

Get ready. It's fun, exciting, and challenging, but you will be moving lots of cases of wine and working long hours. It's not as glamorous as it seems. Tasting wine all day can be fun, but tasting four hundred wines a day is not. Stay in control, be responsible, and have a high standard for yourself. Be willing to work hard. You'll love the job. If you can move sixty cases of wine from one to four P.M., polish glassware, change your shoes and put on a suit and be ready at five and still be smiling at ten, you're a kick-ass sommelier. It's hard work, but if you can do it until ten at night, it's rewarding.

Describe a typical day.

I get in around eleven or eleven thirty A.M. I start by putting out small fires. I try to return phone calls. All the wine distributors want to taste with you, so I try to say no to fifteen and meet with two. Around one P.M., I meet with key members of the management team. By then the chef has arrived, so I take him a bottle of water and we talk about the previous night, see what's going on. Then I meet with managers and with private dining. Around two P.M., my sommelier team rolls in. We detail our glassware, make sure all the wines are there, and see what's in the cellar. I meet with accounting. Then I look at who's coming in that night. Around four P.M. is one of my favorite times of the day: family meal. This is always the best family meal I've ever had. Our chefs take really good care of us; they know how to manage the food and use the same care for this food as for that which goes to the floor. We all sit around a big table—you can't eat standing up. It's been a huge part of the culture of the restaurant for fifty-nine years. Afterward, I do my last-minute prep for the wine. I get dressed for our four forty-five P.M. managers' meeting, which assembles the chefs, owners, private dining, and managers. At five everybody is dressed, the restaurant is set, and we have a meeting for thirty minutes. We taste wine; we talk about food specials; we talk about food and wine pairings and about who's coming in that night. At five thirty, the curtain goes up. I'm on the floor four or five nights a week. Once the last wine has been sent out, I usually start going back to the office to do paperwork, at around ten thirty or eleven, and I leave around eleven thirty P.M.

How many hours a week do you typically work?

About sixty.

What are your specific responsibilities?

To carry our philosophy of wine service. One of the biggest aspects of our philosophy has always been to serve the right wine to the guests and make sure they get what they want. We always say, "Make it perfect." I lead service on the floor, train servers, and challenge members of the wine team so that they know what they do. That's the service part. The job is also about the management of the wine system. It's reaching your cost percentages and those goals that have been set for you, and finding ways to create a balanced wine list.

What do you like most about what you do?

The flexibility and the creativity that it allows. Every guest will have their own set of rules, of experience they've had before. You have to get information from them in order to help them make the right decision. Tell me about the wine that you like the most, what is it about it. Maybe it's giving them wine they had last time, or pushing the boundaries and giving them something new. You have a whole toy box to play with, a hundred-page wine list. The guests trust you. If I recommend something and they don't like it, I'll take it back every time.

What skills are most important for you to do your job well?

It's a combination of a few things. Regardless of what you do, you have to have passion. You have to want to learn more than you are asked to do. If I'm the wine guy, I have to know about food and be on the page of what the chef is doing when he's writing a menu; I have to keep up with trends. You have to continue to learn. The world is going to change—be the one changing it and bringing knowledge to your team. Be other-centered to make the guests' experience right every night. And whether you're selling a $50 wine or a $17,000 wine, you have to be trustworthy and genuine. Customers have to have the right wine at the right time. That's what builds trust. If you're driven by something else, you're in it for the wrong reason. If you don't feel like you can do that, you're in it with the wrong agenda.

What is the outlook for your type of job?

In the last two years, there's been a change from a restaurant manager or maître d' being the buyer for the restaurant. Wine director is now a very important job: You have to know wine, taste wine, and be a manager. A beverage program now is much bigger than just that. We're at the point where owners realize that wine has to be an entity in itself, with someone who can look over the program and make it profitable. So I think that every restaurant will have a sommelier who'll realize that his job is not just to sell wine but to take care of the guests, clear food, etc. A sommelier has to know how to do it all.

How large is your staff?

We have twenty-two servers and eight runners. I have an assistant wine director, a cellar master, and two sommeliers in training (in what we call the "vinternship").

What qualities do you look for in a new hire?

I have to be able to trust them. That's not something you really get from an interview. I trust my instinct. I always want to be served by them, so I might have a meal where they are working. If I can trust them, we'll get there. I'll entrust everything that I can offer to them. You have to be willing to learn, put in the hard work, be honest, without a hidden agenda of "I'm going to learn everything I can from you and bail."

How and when do you decide to introduce new wines on the list?

Some happen through our allocations, meaning certain times of year when our share of certain wines comes in. We need to make sure that we can take our full allocations, that our cellar will be ready to accept fifteen cases of wine. When I receive them, I won't be buying to replace wines just yet. That's one part. Another part is having to change and adapt to the season, when the new vintages are coming in, switching to heartier reds when we get close to winter. Since our chef is influenced by what's in season, his style will change and the wines will change, too. Maybe the last part has more to do with the historical precedent that has been set. If we've bought a wine several years in a row, we'll continue to do so, and we'll build verticals on the list. When I want to buy something funky for our guests or for our staff, I try it by the glass. If it works, we'll add some to the list.

STEVE KELLEY

As regional manager of Lauber Imports, Steve Kelley manages a portfolio of three hundred producers and fifteen hundred wines from all over the world. With his seven-person sales team, they represent these wines in the New York area, selling them to restaurants and retail stores.

CURRENT POSITION: Regional manager, Lauber Imports, division of Southern Wine & Spirits, New York, NY, since 2005. ★ **EDUCATION:** BA, French, State University of New York–Albany (1985); culinary certificate course, French Culinary Institute, New York (1991); viticulture/vinification certificate, American Sommelier Association (2002); advanced certificate—level 3, Wine & Spirit Education Trust (2008). ★ **CAREER PATH:** Cook, Charlotte's Harborview Restaurant, Sag Harbor, NY (1985); waiter, Brasserie Les Halles, Boston, MA (1987); part-time work, particularly demos, Williams-Sonoma, Boston and New York (1988–1997). In New York: general manager, U.S. Operations, Dalet Digital Media Systems (1994–1997); director of alumni affairs, the French Culinary Institute (1997–1999); director of career services, Institute of Culinary Education (1999–2002); sales representative, Village Wine Imports (2002–2003); sales representative (2003–2004), then sales director (2004–2005), Baron François wines. ★ **MEMBERSHIPS:** Board of directors of the American Institute of Wine and Food for five years; Society of Wine Educators.

Salary notes:

A salesperson at a medium to large company with some pretty cool brands can make $80,000 to $100,000. Veterans can make between $150,000 and $250,000. Two hundred and fifty thousand dollars is rare—probably only one at each company. At Lauber, we have many representatives who make between $100,000 and $150,000—it's pretty off the charts. Low six figures is pretty standard for midmanagement in a wine company.

Words of advice for people considering a similar career:

Get started as soon as you can, and don't give up. I almost gave up six months into it, after a very frustrating week. My wife said, "Maybe sales isn't your thing." I decided I wouldn't let people who said no to me stand in the way of my goal. If you put time into it, you'll prosper. Work hard and work smart.

Describe a typical day.

I wake up and go over the reports and e-mails I got overnight. My job is tracking programs. Certain wines might be more in demand at certain times of year; I track that and the numbers of the sales staff. Then I look at reports and updates to make sure that everyone has what he or she needs for the day. I do that from home. If I don't have to drive to the warehouse to pick up wines, I head for the city. My day is full of meetings with suppliers and accounts. Then I do tastings with sommeliers. I manage the reps, help suppliers get their staff trained, and go to restaurants and stores to present our wines and discuss orders. I attend lots of events and media promotions. Or sometimes a winemaker wants to spend more time with people from the company, so we'll have dinner. I help mostly with events related to our French wines. Otherwise we have an event person. What I do on the side is being the French specialist.

How many hours a week do you typically work?

I work from eight A.M. to five P.M. or eleven P.M., on average, when we have events. So sixty to seventy hours. We often have events on weekends. It's as much a lifestyle as it is a job. Even if your role is to crunch numbers and make goals, you still get to go to events. When I go to a dinner and get home at eleven P.M., I spent my evening with a winemaker and heard the history of great American wines. If you're not out there living the life and making it your lifestyle, you're not going to be successful.

What are your specific responsibilities?

To drive the numbers, to make sure that we reach our goals. It trickles down. Reps have to make their goal. If I don't make my goal, the regional division manager won't make his goal, then the VP of sales won't make his goal. Beyond that, it's supporting my reps in the market, supporting my wines, and supporting my suppliers as well. I won't get a call from a winemaker directly—but will get a call from a supplier who says, "Such and such winemaker is having trouble getting in this place, can you help?" Selling wine, and selling specific wines, is my job. I have a lot of autonomy, which is good and bad. I also train

and hire new people. I go with reps to visit an account, give support to new people, help them build relationships. I pull samples and set up a day of appointments, which is when I walk around with a wine bag and talk about the wines all day.

What do you like most about what you do?

Day to day, it's sharing time and experience with people who love food and wine as much as I do. I'm in sales, and there are some aspects of it that I'm not fond of—when everything turns into a number—but every day I learn something.

What skills are most important for you to do your job well?

The first manager that I worked for when I started in wines said it's people skills. You have to listen to the sommelier and to what he or she is telling you. You might walk into a restaurant that has a very specific food profile or into a neighborhood wine store that needs to make money, and you need to find the right wines for them. You have to think ahead of the game. It's art meeting commerce: You have to have passion and knowledge but also know the numbers behind it so that you can show them how to make money.

What is the outlook for your type of job?

Where I am, it's pretty good. People are drinking more and more wine; it's become much more of an American cultural norm. Right now, people are drinking fewer American wines but not fewer wines.

How large is your staff?

I manage a sales force of seven people, who cover Manhattan and most of Brooklyn. We have about three hundred producers in our portfolio, with fifteen hundred wines from all over the world.

What qualities do you look for in a new hire?

They have to have wine knowledge. I'm not looking for someone with a WSET diploma, but if they do have one it means that they care and know something about it. They have to have people skills and a certain level of organization. They have to be self-motivated. It's a sales job, so they have to learn how to deal with numbers. They should be smart, driven. It's a weird hybrid; it's business, but you also have to have a real passion for it, to love wine and food. It's not a prerequisite, but I would favor someone who's worked in a restaurant or wine store. On the other end, one of my most successful hires was a former corporate attorney.

How often do you set goals?

It's almost constant. We have monthly and quarterly goals. I have daily goals and I tell that to reps too: see where you want to be in a year, and break it down into quarter, month, week, then day. Then you can see if you made your goals today, and if not you can make it tomorrow. I know what my team does; I track it by individual reps every single morning.

"I decided I wouldn't let people who said no to me stand in the way of my goal. If you put time into it, you'll prosper. Work hard and work smart."

LAURIE FORSTER

Through her company, the Wine Coach, Laurie Forster runs wine-focused educational seminars; tastings and dinners; and team-building, corporate, and social events around the country. She also designs wine programs for restaurants that don't have a sommelier on staff. She is the author of *The Sipping Point* and the host of two radio shows.

CURRENT POSITION: Wine educator and owner, the Wine Coach, Easton, MD, since September 2004, thewinecoach.com. ★ **EDUCATION:** BS, business logistics, Pennsylvania State University; American Sommelier Association certificate in viticulture and vinification (2002); working toward master sommelier designation; coach training with Coach U. ★ **CAREER PATH:** Software sales; sales executive (salesperson), Astor Wines, New York, NY (about one year); wine program of a local restaurant, MD (about a year). ★ **AWARDS AND RECOGNITION:** Numerous media features; *The Sipping Point* was featured in the November 2008 issue of *Wine Enthusiast.* ★ **MEMBERSHIPS:** Society of Wine Educators; International Coach Federation; Court of Master Sommelier program.

Salary notes:

The average range for independent wine educators is $50,000 to $75,000, but there is potential to make more, and the range is broad. You have to invest a lot in training and branding your business.

Words of advice for people considering a similar career:

Most of what I've invested in the business is in my education; learning and committing to learning as part of the process is essential to me. Experience wine from the street level, not just from the book level. Starting in retail is a great way to learn the business. Meet other sommeliers, travel to wineries. Use any background you have that can make you effective. I wouldn't be half the wine educator I am today if I didn't have the presentation experience that I have. Presenting at a wine seminar is a piece of cake after having talked to top executives. It's hard work. Any time you have your own business, be prepared.

What do you do as a wine educator?

I do corporate events, education seminars at festivals and large-scale events, radio shows, wine writing for magazines. I wrote a book, *The Sipping Point: A Crash Course in Wine.* My focus is creating events where people can learn about wine in a way that is approachable and fun. I'm here to get them back into the fold, to tell them they don't need to speak six foreign languages or make a million dollars to enjoy a bottle of wine. I call myself the wine coach because I'm a trained life coach as well. That's a person who is both your cheerleader and your enforcer. I create events that are about wine but that are also designed to help people connect and get to know each other.

Describe a typical day.

Mondays and Fridays tend to be marketing, office kind of days. I typically have education stuff I'm working on, studying for the master sommelier program, marketing my business, looking for ways to promote events I have going on. On Tuesday and Wednesday mornings, I have radio shows. Once or twice a month I have magazine deadlines. I prepare for events. I start at seven thirty or eight A.M., and end at different times depending on the day. If I have an event, it might not be over until ten P.M., so I'm home by midnight.

How many hours a week do you typically work?

Fifty to seventy hours a week. It might be more. When you love it, it doesn't feel like work. Because most of my work is corporate, it tends to fall during the week, which is nice.

What do you like most about what you do?

When the lightbulb comes on in people's heads, when they come out really excited, when for the first time they understand a certain aspect of wine appreciation. They have a great time, connect at the table, leave really excited to go home and talk to their spouse about wine, look forward to going to the wine store. I try to feature more unusual wines to get them to try things they might not try otherwise. It's really about the connection, watching people connect with wines.

What do you like least about it?

One of the challenges of having your own business is that often, outside of events, you're working on your own. I'm a huge people person—I love being with people—and there is a certain isolation. You don't have a team to bounce ideas off of. You have

to build your own, find advisers. That can be difficult.

What skills are most important for you to do your job well?

Communication skills are paramount. Obviously, you need to have the education; you can't just run out and say you're the wine expert. You need to invest in some sort of structured program, like master sommelier or WSET. It's important that you be an interactive, entertaining speaker. I have been in the business six or seven years, so there are people who know more than I do, but not everybody can communicate what they know. If you're a genius but you can't share that with a group at a level that they can understand, you won't be as successful. People want to know how to find a wine that they can enjoy; they might not want to understand the science behind it. So you have to find a way to help them understand. It takes dedication, flexibility, and the ability to go with the flow. You have to be able to think on your feet when doing events. You have to read the crowd.

What is the outlook for your type of job?

It's amazing how much interest and demand there is. Wine is becoming so much more of a part of our culture, at all levels of society, not just for white-collar professionals or wealthy people. So I think that the outlook is very promising. There's a lot of market share out there, especially for people who are able to make it accessible. Some people want to make it more elite, but there's a whole marketplace of people who are at grocery stores or have been drinking wine for thirty years but only have bought based on brands, without real knowledge. People drink wine whether the economy is good or bad, but the price of what they drink might change.

Describe your wine-selection process.
I work in conjunction with clients. Once I have the theme or topic of discussion, then I look through wines I've already tasted that might fit the theme. I go out and look for samples. The whole time I'm working with the chefs or caterers who create the meal. Most times, food is in the mix, whether it's hors d'oeuvres or a full meal.

"It's amazing how much interest and demand there is. Wine is becoming so much more of a part of our culture, at all levels of society, not just for white-collar professionals or wealthy people."

10. FOOD ARTISANS

Producing your own food at a commercial level is the dream of many good cooks. Often this dream comes after friends and families constantly compliment a particular dish or homemade product for long enough that the seed they plant starts to germinate. Becoming an artisanal food producer happens when following an

interest and passion for a specific item—cheese in the case of Helen Feete (page 245) and beer for Rob Tod (page 234)—to the point of taking the risk to build a business around it. Focusing on products with unique characteristics and making sure to make them at a very high level of quality helps bring in success, particularly at a time when America is in love with artisanal, sustainable, small-batch, and local producers. Many consumers are willing to pay a premium for a product they feel is made with special care and great ingredients. Tight production standards might make it harder to meet the margins of a large distributor or might require compromises. Those are choices that food producers must make on an almost daily basis. Selling directly to consumers, whether through mail order or a storefront, allows you to keep more control over such things.

You might also find yourself a food producer because your family is already in the business, as was the case for Lee Jones (page 231). As a new generation, however, you might want to make changes, which may include altering distribution strategy, introducing technology, and developing new products to set the stage for survival and growth.

Plunging into the business of artisanal food production is often more complicated than it appears, however, mostly because of the legalities involved with producing food. A licensed kitchen and liability insurance are only two of the hurdles that need to be cleared before you get to see your product on a shelf somewhere. It is essential to contact the local small business association, chamber of commerce, and cooperative extension if needed to make sure that everything is done according to codes and regulations. But the reward of being your own boss and having the satisfaction of creating a quality food product is often worth all the troubles.

As mentioned above, food production is heavily regulated. Alcohol, in particular, is complicated because each state has its own regulations and you need to deal with many different distributors. In states where the government handles liquor sales, you cannot even sell directly and *must* rely on a distributor. You might have noticed before, depending on where you live, that you could not get wine or spirits delivered from another state.

The food products that small entrepreneurs launch tend to emphasize attributes such as local, organic, small batch, artisanal, high quality, or niche. These allow them to stand apart in a crowded marketplace. Keep that in mind as you develop your own food product. What is unique about it? How will you position it? Who is your target audience? If a product is made with local ingredients only, look into getting a booth at the farmers' market. While selling at markets can be time consuming, it allows you to build an audience and demand for your product. Frequently, food artisans find that gaining adequate distribution for their product is a more difficult task than developing the product itself.

' Trade shows are often essential to food artisans and producers. This is where buyers, media, and in some instances, the public come to look for new products to distribute or sell in their stores, profile, and buy. Most shows also give awards for the best products, product designs, and more, which would make an invaluable addition to your press kit. They can be pricey to attend but are usually worth it if you plan ahead, make contacts with retailers, and set up meetings. If you can, attend a couple of shows the year before you launch your own company so that you know what to expect.

You will notice one point that the interviewees who follow make over and over again: Don't do this for the money. As an entrepreneur, it might take years before you make any money out of your business. You might not be able to pay yourself a salary at first and will have to keep another job to pay the bills. Many food producers are able, however, to launch their business without going into much debt, if any at all, because they choose to do everything themselves. That's one thing to take into account as you start sketching out your business plan. Are you able, and willing, to do everything at your company in its early days? Will be you okay spending hours by yourself in a kitchen making your product and then delivering it too? Or do you need to be part of a team at all times?

salaries

It is nearly impossible to estimate what food artisans earn because the size of their operation and of their sales, the nature of their product, their operating costs, their location, and many other factors varies. What is fair to say is that the starting salaries or earnings are low—sometimes as little as $20,000—but will increase as success comes. Some artisans might decide to sell their company if they receive a good offer and might benefit from a great payoff—think about the founders of Ben & Jerry's and Terra Chips. Being a food producer might also be a part-time job, with accordingly reduced earnings.

LEE JONES

The Jones family nearly lost its farm (which Lee Jones's father, Bob, had started and was working with his two sons, Lee and Bobby) in the 1980s when interest rates went up 21 percent and a hailstorm destroyed the crops. Thanks to the advice of Chef Jean-Louis Palladin, who introduced them to Chefs Daniel Boulud, Alain Ducasse, Charlie Trotter, Thomas Keller, and others, they redeveloped it as an organic farm specializing in miniature vegetables, specialty lettuces, herbs, and edible flowers that are sold directly to chefs around the country.

CURRENT POSITION: Co-owner, the Chef's Garden, Huron, OH, since 1983, www.chefsgarden .com. ★ **AWARDS AND RECOGNITION:** Jones says, "That's for the chefs. We are more about creating opportunities for chefs to win awards." ★ **MEMBERSHIPS:** American Culinary Federation; James Beard Foundation; Jean-Louis Palladin Foundation.

Salary notes:

The lowest salary is $10 per hour and ranges up to $75,000 to $100,000 for the CFO or product specialists. There are many different ranges, depending on what people bring to the table.

Words of advice for people considering a similar career:

Identify your demand before your produce. That's a big fallacy that farmers have had over the years, to grow crops and then try to sell them. You have to identify a need before you fulfill it. Many times, people jump into the market too late to make it a profitable thing. That will saturate the market. It's about doing the due diligence and your homework to identify a real need. Do that by working in areas that you would identify as the craft in which you are interested.

Describe a typical day.

We start around four thirty A.M., taking orders. We want to harvest products when it's nice and cool—some of them even before daylight. Our inventory is a growing inventory until it's sold. It's a just-in-time inventory. For food safety and quality, our inventory is only what has been ordered. We pack and ship it somewhere in twenty-four hours. It's so exciting to see that reconnection that is growing between farms and chefs. It's a team effort. I'm primarily in charge of visits with chefs, either here or in their facility. There are times when I do a front-of-the-house presentation for a restaurant. It's one thing to use good ingredients, but it's just as important to let the clientele know about those quality ingredients. We have about six hundred products. What we learned from chefs is that every stage of the plant's life offers something unique to plate. So we developed a sizing chart. Bok choy is available at seven different stages of growth. Each offers a different texture and flavor. It gives the chef more diversity and opens up creativity.

How many hours a week do you typically work?

About eighty. Traveling goes in spurts. In the summer, when we have more visiting chefs, I stay close to home. I travel pretty much all winter.

What are your specific responsibilities?

Working with the chefs, trying to communicate the vision and the needs of a chef to our team. I'm the family member who was selected to represent the farm. It's really about carrying my passion. If it's just about what I can physically get done in a day, it would be limited. So it's really about sharing the culture. One of the biggest compliments we hear from chefs is that they can feel the love and the pride that went into the container of produce they receive. That's a very special compliment to us. We work with 350 to 400 chefs a week. It's just about the relationships, listening to them, and having a better understanding of their needs. Chefs don't like waste and cannot afford not to have enough products. So one of the big differences is that we take orders by count rather than by case. Another big difference is that the product keeps growing until it's sold.

What do you like most about what you do?

Getting to work with the chefs—really trying to understand their needs, responding to things they are looking for. It's been unbelievable to have exposure to the wonderful people in that industry. I go to Raymond Blanc in England, or we have Wolfgang Puck or Charlie Trotter come here. It's a long ways from the farm.

What do you like least about it?

That there are not twenty-six hours in a day, so that I could do more. I can't think of a downside. We're doing what we love. We're so eternally grateful to the chefs, because they allow us to follow our passion of working for the farm.

What skills are most important for you to do your job well?

Your ears. Listening skills are the most important.

Did you have to learn the language of the kitchen?

Yes, I had to learn a certain protocol. There's a process; you have to understand the whole dynamic of how things work and when to get out of the way. It's important not to be afraid to tell a chef no. Lots of times, they'll want a product that's out of season, or the quality is not prime. We always want to please the chefs, but the products have to be quality. There's a trust factor, that what you're doing is really in the best interest of making chefs look good. We think of ourselves as part of their team, helping eliminate some of the pressure. They don't have to worry about the count, the right size, if it's going to arrive on time. Those things are very critical.

What are your long-term goals?

Health and wellness is the future, we think. There's a direct correlation between how we farm and the health of our nation. It's about growing products that can be a benefit for society.

What is the outlook for your type of job?

I don't know if any two farms can be exactly the same. Everything cycles. We're seeing a resurgence in small family farms and more farmers' markets. There's more interest from consumers who are looking to reconnect with producers. We got in trouble in the last fifty years when producers and users lost touch with one another. It's very exciting to see this change here.

How large is your staff?

We have about 112 staff members right now.

What keeps you challenged?

Chefs. They're under so much pressure to compete and perform and are constantly looking for what will differentiate their plate from their competitors'. Also, finding people who have the right attitude and willingness to work. The work is physically hard. I can go in 98 percent of restaurants in the U.S. today and find products that have been grown and harvested by people paid $3 a day. We try to pay our staff a real-life wage. The base pay is $10 an hour. Once you factor in workers' comp and benefits, it's certainly a challenge to provide a competitive product.

ROB TOD

Rob Tod founded Allagash Brewing Company in Portland, ME, after just one year of experience in the business, because he fell in love with beer brewing. He brews a unique variety of traditional and experimental Belgian-style beers for a production of thirteen thousand barrels a year available in eighteen states.

CURRENT POSITION: Founder/brewer, Allagash Brewing Company, Portland, ME, since 1994, www.allagash.com. ★ **EDUCATION:** BS, geology, Middlebury College, VT. ★ **CAREER PATH:** Construction, dishwasher, and skier, CO (two years); keg washer and assistant brewer, Middlebury, VT (one year). ★ **AWARDS AND RECOGNITION:** *Saveur* 100; countless press mentions. ★ **MEMBERSHIPS:** Brewer's Association.

Salary notes:

It varies tremendously. The manager of a brewery at a three- or four-person operation will make between $30,000 and $40,000 a year. At a larger, well-known microbrewery with ten to twenty employees, it could go up to $70,000. The first five years, I paid myself hardly anything. The next five, I paid myself a little bit but not much. I bet I never made over $25,000 even nine years into it. It hasn't been until recently that I've been able to pay myself something reasonable. It took us ten years to make any money, to get the brand established.

Words of advice for people considering a similar career:

Number one, it's essential to have experience in another production brewery. A lot of people who are home brewers are interested in starting a brewery, but the first thing I tell them is to get commercial experience. Try to get experience with as many facets of the beer business as you can, from washing to making boxes, cleaning, sweeping, fixing things. You have to be able to do these things. If a pump breaks, you have to be able to fix it. You'll need electrical and commercial experience. Consistency is essential. No amount of book reading or home brewing or even brewing school can replace practice.

What prompted you to start your own business?

It just kind of happened. I didn't think about it when graduating college. After just a few months in the other brewery, I decided that I wanted to be in the beer business. I thought that the most fun way to do it would be with my own brewery. I had the opportunity to be innovative and do something different. I also liked the challenge of it.

Describe a typical day.

The first ten or eleven years, I was on the floor of the brewery regularly. Until not so long ago I used to still do a fair amount of brewing and bottling and mechanical work. But within the last couple of years, I haven't had time to do that. I spend way more time running the business. I take care of payables, receivables, HR issues, sales, which I love to do. Over the last couple of years, the beer category has exploded. We can't keep up. We have our beer in eighteen states. Our brewmaster has been with us for over ten years. During the expansion we had a system and ingredients that we were very familiar with, so it was good timing for us; we were well positioned for that growth.

How many hours a week do you typically work?

Sixty hours. But my phone is always on. I look at the last thirteen years of my life and don't think of them as work. I love it. I never want to retire. It's extremely rare that I wake up not fired up to get into work.

What do you like most about what you do?

There's a ton of things. I love getting out on the road, doing beer dinners, educating people about the beer, meeting people. I love when things break in the brewery because I get to go and fix them. I like interacting with everyone at the brewery—they are all engaging people. I like working with wholesalers and retailers. I love the creative part of coming up with new beers. We're doing a ton of barrel-aged stuff now; it's very fun.

How large is your staff?

Twelve people. We're very small. We run pretty lean in terms of number of em-

ployees. Everyone there works hard. We consider ourselves a very small artisanal brewery.

What qualities do you look for in a new hire?

Experience is very low on the list. I look for someone who comes in and wants to work for Allagash, who is passionate about beer and what we do. Someone who when he comes into work doesn't just look to punch in, go through the motions, and then leave. I want someone who is engaged, who thinks of ways to make things better, of what cool beer we can come up with, how we can improve things in retail stores, how we can improve the brewing process.

What skills are most important for you to do your job well?

It depends on what part you're involved in. One of the things I really like about this job is that it involves so many different tasks. I'm never doing the same thing day after day. One day I'm traveling to a market, that night I have a beer dinner, then I'm fixing something at the brewery, then I'm formulating a recipe. So a pretty well-rounded experience of the industry is important. It depends on what your role is at the brewery. At a brewery that might have three owners, one is in charge of marketing, one of the financial, one of sales. I do all of those things.

RICHARD CUTLER

Richard Cutler started the Flying Dutchman Winery on the Oregon coast as a way to drum up attention for the restaurant he was managing at the time. The small winery produces about two thousand cases of wine a year, using grapes from local suppliers.

CURRENT POSITION: Winemaker and owner, the Flying Dutchman Winery, Otter Rock, OR, since 1997, full-time since 2001, www.dutchmanwinery.com. ★ **EDUCATION:** BS, mechanical engineering; course work in enology and winemaking, Salem Community College, OR. ★ **CAREER PATH:** Construction, Iowa and Colorado; manager and leaser, the Flying Dutchman (restaurant of the Inn at Otter Crest; 1995–2001). ★ **AWARDS AND RECOGNITION:** Pinot Noir: Bronze Medal, Oregon State Fair, 1997, and more awards since. ★ **MEMBERSHIPS:** Many local organizations; Oregon Wine Board.

Salary notes:

At a fully integrated winery, with a full distribution network, about $40,000. You're not getting in this for the money.

Words of advice for people considering a similar career:

Strictly from the business, not the winemaking standpoint, make sure you have a plan to sell your product. So many people want to be in the business of making wine but don't think ahead about how they will sell their wines. You have to have a sales plan first. Then work on making the best wine possible.

What prompted you to start your own business?

I spent most of my life in the construction business. I came to Oregon to be closer to my three grown children and got into the hospitality business. I came here to manage the Inn at Otter Crest and lease the restaurant. I started the winery in the restaurant as a publicity move: the Flying Dutchman Microwinery and Restaurant. It got to be a lot more fun making wine than running the inn. I broke up my contract with the inn six years later and went full-time into making wine. I moved the winery to a little peninsula that lets out onto the ocean. We make the wine—only enough to sell out of our two tasting rooms—right in front of the ocean. It just happened; we started making wine where our customers were rather than trying to make wine where the grapes are and trying to make customers go to them. Once we got started, I went to community college in Salem and took all the basic courses, including wine chemistry, in the department of enology and winemaking. Most of my knowledge has come from reading and experimentation. The benefit of being so small is that we can experiment. We're small, so we are able to let wines age the proper amounts of time, very much as they do in Europe. We only sell about two thousand cases of wine a year.

How many hours a week do you typically work?

During the height of the crush, seventy to eighty hours, then it slides down to a more normal amount. At larger wineries, the work is more sustained throughout, to sustain the demand of their wholesalers.

Describe a typical day.

In the fall, it starts as soon as it gets light out. I work with the wines, opening up the fermenters and exposing them to air, punching down, testing, and tasting. That takes a couple of hours in the morning. Today, we're rearranging barrels. We move wines to different barrels. We build barrel stacks for the new wines, in new and old oak barrels. During the time that the grapes come in—ten more tons this week—we take the stems out and drop them off in fermenters. In between we do cold soaks, which is when grapes sit in their own juice for a week to ten days. Grapes are basically in fermentation and cold soak for up to a month. Then we press them down, barrel the wine, and age it from one to three years. During the rest of the year, we don't do much as far as winemaking is concerned. We top the barrels off. At certain times, when we consolidate the wines, we blend them and bottle them. But a small winery doesn't require too much attention after the first of December. From December to March, one day every two weeks. It takes a few days to bottle the wine. The only full-time part to making wine is between the first of October through the month of November.

The hard part of the whole business is selling the wine. We have some good help selling it. No matter how good you think your product is, it still has to be sold. Our salespeople do have to work every day.

We're open every day but Christmas. I don't have to be at the winery every day, unless I choose to give tours or join the wine tasting or sales effort. I do that from time to time, but only when the mood strikes me. That's the beauty of being the boss.

What are your specific responsibilities?

Quality control of the wine, from the moment we receive the grapes to the moment it gets in the bottle. Then running a small business, manufacturing, sales. I look at it like a sales organization that is supported by a manufacturing organization. Sales is full-time, year-round. I make sure that our approach to the customers is friendly and polite; I invite them to come back. It's common sense—there's nothing magic in sales.

What do you like most about what you do?

The satisfaction that comes when people like the product, when we win an award and people tell us that we did well. Showing people the barrel room and the winery itself. I think I enjoy taking people through the most. You can brag about what you do. If they enjoy the product, it's even better.

What do you like least about it?

The heavy lifting. We are not a mechanized winery. Now we have younger people helping with that. This year is the first that we have a forklift. Most people my age look forward to taking a cruise, and my geriatric goal was to own a forklift. We all have goals.

How large is your staff?

We have three full-time employees, then seasonal employees, neighbors, friends, and people who enjoy making wine.

What are your long-term goals?

I have purchased land in a little coastal community. Right now, we are on a very tiny piece of land; it's like working in a closet. To bottle the wine, we have to load it up on a trailer and drive seventy-five miles to the facility. I have plans for a gravity-flow winery, old-world style, where everything flows without pumping the wine. I hope to get started with that next year. Our plans for the future include a larger winery but never a big one. Maybe six thousand cases and three tasting rooms.

"Most of my knowledge has come from reading and experimentation. The benefit of being so small is that we can experiment. We're small, so we are able to let wines age the proper amounts of time, very much as they do in Europe."

LISA AVERBUCH

LOFT is the first certified organic liqueur in the United States. Founder Lisa Averbuch was inspired by Italian limoncellos when creating her liqueur, which uses organic produce from local farms and is sweetened with agave nectar. Because of the nature of the ingredients used, some of the flavors of LOFT are only available when the fruits it contains are in season.

CURRENT POSITION: Founder, LOFT Organic Liqueurs, San Francisco, CA, incorporated in 2006 and launched in 2008, www.loftliqueurs.com. ★ **EDUCATION:** BS, hospitality administration, Boston University, MA; Wine and Spirit Education Trust advanced certificate. ★ **CAREER PATH:** Food and beverage controller, Royal Sonesta, Cambridge, MA (eight years); restaurant manager, Mandarin Oriental, Boston; conference concierge, Ritz-Carlton, San Francisco, CA; floor manager and visitor activities manager, Copia, Napa, CA (two years). ★ **AWARDS AND RECOGNITION:** Three bronze medals and one silver medal, 2007 and 2008 San Francisco World Spirits Competitions; three gold medals and one silver medal, Beverage Testing Institute; appearances on the Donny Deutsch show and Martha Stewart Radio and in *Organic Spa Magazine, Edible San Francisco,* and more. ★ **MEMBERSHIPS:** President of Toastmasters Club (international organization to practice public speaking).

Salary notes:

It's been put to me a couple of different ways. One, that I shouldn't be taking any salary until I am profitable, and the other that I should be taking a salary. People starting their own business who can afford to pay themselves a salary should pay themselves what they need to live, but when you're just starting, don't give yourself a huge six-figure salary. Until profitable, take a modest salary.

Words of advice for people considering a similar career:

If you have an idea for a business that you want to pursue, you should (a) pursue it; (b) do as much research beforehand as possible; (c) expect that it will take twice as long and twice as much money as you planned. Take your budget and double it. But if you want to try it, you should do it.

What prompted you to start your own business?

I've always known that I wanted to have my own business, something in food and beverages, but not necessarily in operations. That was always my ultimate goal. I knew that when I found it, I would know it. To an extent, I thought that when I got to Copia, that was it. So when I decided to leave Copia, I started playing around with limoncello recipes and then other recipes. I've always been oddly good at making a decision and saying that's it. I had quit my job, sold my condo, and moved to San Francisco from Massachusetts. I was very naïve and didn't know what I was getting into. I started talking to people and working on my business. I'm heading in the right direction. You always need more money, more time, more people, but here I am.

How large is your staff?

There are two others besides me: my partner, Sabrina Marino-Dolan, who lives in New York City—we are best friends from San Francisco—and someone in Portland who acts as a consultant. Unless you want to hire a huge sales staff, the staff of a liqueur company doesn't need to be too large because you outsource things like marketing and PR. We contracted a distillery in Portland to make the product for us. There are a number of distilleries in San Francisco, but they weren't interested in being organic. We go up to Portland and help out with production. They do the production, bottling, labeling. We picked out the bottles but hired a designer for the label.

Describe a typical day.

It starts with e-mails. I check in with Sabrina in New York and the guy in Oregon to see what's going on. I do some boring paperwork. Three days a week, I need to focus on sales. Even if we had a distributor, I'd still need to do a lot of the sales myself. I decide who I want to talk to and get the info I need for those people and places. We warehouse our product near Napa, so sometimes I have to go there to pick things up. I go on sales calls, deal with more e-mails and calls from people seeking donations. Time just disappears. I always feel bad calling a place where I haven't been yet, so I first get to know the people who will sell my product. All business comes down to people. If I don't know the people, it feels strange. Sometimes it's just having a drink; sometimes it's a formal meeting. Sales is not my forte; the more creative side of it is. I created the product from scratch. Some people will hire a chemist, or the distiller will develop the formula, but I did that myself.

How many hours a week do you typically work?

It's hard to determine, because all my days are basically the same, seven days a week. I don't really distinguish between weekdays and weekends. I work every day, but not always a set number of hours. The benefit of having your own business is that you can take time in the middle of the day to run errands.

What do you like most about what you do?

I love the fact that I created an awesome product. I made something better than those awful appletini mixes that are on the market. And I can share it with people so that they can have a better product—something that tastes like it's supposed to taste. It's great to go out and be able to offer something so good. It's very rewarding.

What do you like least about it?

Having to go out and sell. It's tough, because it is my product and I should be the person out there, and the idea of having someone else out there doesn't necessarily excite me either. Having the weight of the entire operation on your shoulders. I get all the rewards, but I take all the risks and have to deal with the stress of it all.

What skills are most important for you to do your job well?

Sales skills. Time management is a big thing. Computer skills for sure—if I knew a little bit more, I could put out a better newsletter or update the website. Persistence seems required.

What skills would you like to develop to help further your career?

I'm working on my public-speaking skills through the Toastmasters Club. There are more things I could learn about the chemistry of alcohol, but my formula is so basic that it's not essential. Many things that could improve my business involve more outside help, such as experts in finance, marketing, and PR. It would be good for me to be proficient at everything, but people go to school for finance for a reason—so that I don't have to.

What are your long-term goals?

In my head, I would love for my product to be in every bar in America. That's just in my head, though, and isn't realistic because it's a very specialized product. My short-term goal is to pick up more states, hopefully another ten in the next year. We sell lavender, lemongrass, and spicy ginger year-round as well as seasonal flavors. The long-term goal is to continue developing seasonal flavors.

How do you decide in which state to expand your business next?

We look at control states and franchise states, which are probably not high on our list. We look for states with high urban areas with a concentration of our target market.

TED DENNARD

At Savannah Bee Company, founder Ted Dennard offers award-winning rare, artisanal, and varietal honeys, as well as a line of honey-based beauty products. The honeys—some from the company's own hives and some that come from suppliers that abide by the same principles—are extracted directly from the hive's comb and poured into jars without being processed or blended. Launching his company was the culmination of an interest in beekeeping that spanned more than twenty years.

CURRENT POSITION: President and beekeeper, Savannah Bee Company, Savannah, GA, since 2002, www.savannahbee.com. ★ **EDUCATION:** BA, philosophy of religion, University of the South, Sewanee, TN. ★ **CAREER PATH:** Volunteer beekeeping teacher, Peace Corps, Jamaica (two years); co-owner, wilderness adventure company, AZ and CO; odd jobs, Savannah. ★ **AWARDS AND RECOGNITIONS:** Tupelo honey: second place, Georgia Beekeepers' Association (very early on); Outstanding Visual Presentation, Best of Market Temporaries Category, Atlanta International Gift & Home Furnishings Market (2006); Michael Bunn Sr. Memorial and Rising Star Award, Small Business Assistance Administration (2007); Georgia Small Business Person of the Year (2007); Best New Natural/Organic Product, Ex.Tracts—New Discoveries in Beauty and Wellness (2007); first place, Natural/Organic, Flavor of Georgia Food Contest (2007); Georgia Small Business Administration Rising Star (2008); grand prize winner for Outstanding Condiment, Gallo Family Vineyards Gold Medal Awards (2008); Best Natural/Organic Product, Flavor of Georgia Contest (2008); southern region finalist, Entrepreneur of the Year (2008). ★ **MEMBERSHIPS:** National Association for the Specialty Food Trade (NASFT); Georgia Beekeeper Association; Southern Foodways Alliance.

Salary notes:

As a salary, I am making about 2.5 percent of my total sales, so about $50,000 currently. But I have had royalties with other contracts where I've made many times that in a year. There are other compensations aside from salary. In the beginning you will make nothing. Then as it grows you can make some money.

Words of advice for people considering a similar career:

If it's truly what you're most passionate about, what excites you the most, you should follow that passion. If you just think that it's interesting and neat and cool, you probably won't have the staying power to push against all odds. What distinguished me was making honey look high-end and of super high quality; for others it might be making a great recipe. It depends.

What prompted you to open your own company?

An old man taught me about beekeeping when I was little. Then one of my landlords had vineyards and beehives and taught me all kinds of fascinating stuff about honeybees. When I went to the Peace Corps after college, I had four months of formal training in beekeeping, which is where I accumulated the bulk of my knowledge. When I moved to Savannah, I was saddled with debt and worked three or four jobs. I bought a couple of hives, my roommate bought more hives, and we started selling a few jars of honey. I was selling to one store, then another store called, then another store, etc. I sold to about twenty stores in two years, which seemed like a lot back then. Then I decided to do it as more of a job. At the end of 2001, I put all of my efforts in the honey company, to see if it would work for one year. If I was going to fail, I didn't want to keep doing it for longer than that. I incorporated in 2002 and went to my first trade show in January 2002. If I had studied business, I would never have done this. But I was doing it from passion. Putting the honey in a wine bottle from France took it into the gift category. I got tons of press, prestige, and business by having put it in that bottle. I did it because I knew that my honey was better and wanted people to know that by looking at it on the shelf. In 2003, Williams-Sonoma picked us up for national distribution, and then other companies followed.

Describe a typical day.

I wish it was me getting in the truck and driving to the swamps and fields to work on bees. But now I spend most of my time in an office. I drop off my daughter at the bus at seven, then come to the office, check e-mail, prepare for the day—basically do all manners of things to run the company. We're planning a store in Charleston; we just opened a store in Savannah this year. We meet on boosting our Web sales. We taste different honeys to see if we want to bottle that batch. We have a taster when we make a batch, and we test and analyze. If it's not good enough to go into our bottle,

we'll sell it to people who make mead or things like that. It's not that the honey is bad—it's just that we want it to be perfect. Not all companies do that. We want to make 100 percent tupelo honey, which is very expensive for us to do, but we don't want to do a blend. People who make tupelo honey like to sell it to us because they are proud of it and they know that we won't heat it or blend it. A lot of my day is busy work—I hate it. I end up doing a lot of that, but I'm not great at it. I'm better at ideas and trends and designing a new product, marketing and sales, things like that. I have a lot of people helping me, and I am beginning to work smarter.

How many hours a week do you typically work?

Forty-five to fifty-five hours.

What are your specific responsibilities?

I'm supposed to be the leader, the CEO, the president. I lead the group, the direction of the company. I make sure that I have a healthy environment for the company. My responsibility is to build the brand, lead the sales, and do new product development. In the beginning, I did everything, including packing and shipping. I did everything perfectly, the way I wanted to do it. Now that we have over two thousand stores that carry our products, how do you keep the same quality of service—on the phone, packaging, bottling, shipping—with the volume a hundred times what it was? That's a challenge. I have had to hand over the cutting of the honeycomb to someone else. To release some of that control is hard.

What do you like most about what you do?

I love education. The first line of our mission statement is to educate. We're selling the highest-quality honey products while educating people on the wonder of honeybees. I teach in schools; I teach a college class with my president of operations. We have a theater, which is a place for kids to play and learn. We're always hoping to educate people on how beneficial bees are. I also love that I really had a dream for this business and we have been able to carry it through. A company has become successful from this dream and has become beneficial to those who have been in contact with it.

What do you like least about it?

The management of people. Dealing with the volume, the vast amount of paperwork, tax information, insurance—all these things that can just bury you with busy work and take so much time and energy.

What is the outlook for your type of company?

I can tell you that since I've come along, a handful of boutique honey companies have sprung up. There will be more of them. I've been swimming in pretty blue waters, and I see people beginning to move into them now. It's going to be beneficial in educating people.

How large is your staff?

About twenty-two employees.

What qualities do you look for in a new hire?

The ability to fit in with us as a culture. That they bring in a certain talent that is needed. Or that they are very open to learning and moving around to see where they best fit the company. I look for an open-minded and like-minded person. Some experience is useful as well. I've taught people a lot of things, but now I'm more looking for people who are bringing something to the table.

"In the beginning, I did everything, including packing and shipping. I did everything perfectly, the way I wanted to do it. Now that we have over two thousand stores that carry our products, how do you keep the same quality of service with the volume a hundred times what it was? That's a challenge. To release some of that control is hard."

HELEN FEETE

At Meadow Creek Dairy, cheesemaking follows the milking season for the farm's eighty cows, with production beginning in April and ending in November. Cheesemaker and owner Helen Feete makes three types of award-winning seasonal cheeses based on that schedule: Grayson, which is generally available from June through March; Appalachian, which is available from June through April; and Mountaineer, which is available from November through July.

CURRENT POSITION: Owner/cheesemaker, Meadow Creek Dairy, Galax, VA, for twenty years (ten making cheese), www.meadowcreekdairy.com. ★ **EDUCATION:** BA, psychology. ★ **CAREER PATH:** Secretary (one year); raised feeder pigs, hog farm; worked on a dairy farm; bought a small dairy farm with seventeen cows. ★ **AWARDS AND RECOGNITION:** Appalachian cheese: third place, Farmstead Category, ACS (2006). Grayson cheese: third place, Farmstead Category, ACS (2007); first place, Farmstead Category, second overall, American Cheese Society (2008). ★ **MEMBERSHIPS:** American Cheese Society; Slow Food; Raw Milk Cheesemakers' Association.

Salary notes:

The starting salary for our employees is $20,000. But we provide all the meat and produce for their meals and provide or help with housing. We have some housing, which we try to reserve for people from abroad.

Words of advice for people considering a similar career:

You have to really want this. This cannot be just a financial decision or to be able to tell people you do it because it sounds like fun. If you don't have lot of passion and drive, you're going to be miserable. It takes a lot of work and dedication. We used to wonder each year if we were going to do this the next—we're past that now. You have to want your work and your life to be one and the same.

Describe a typical day.

It usually starts around six thirty A.M. Last fall, we went up to working seven days a week, making cheese four or five days. We receive milk from the dairy; the morning milking comes straight to the cheese house. We mix it with the milking from the night before. At eight thirty we start making cheese; it's over by noon. We press and flip the cheeses in the afternoon, and we clean up. If anybody has time, they go help in the cellar to wash up, then we are done by six P.M.

How many hours a week do you typically work?

I try not to count them. Probably fifty to sixty. We have an apartment right above the cheese house, so I can escape every once in a while. It's getting better now that my daughter can make cheese too. It's important to vocalize what you're doing as you do it, to teach it. I have learned to make the process easier to repeat, so that I can teach it and it is not so dependent on me. I went to Italy for ten days, and they made cheese without me the whole time. It's healthier for the business as well.

What are your specific responsibilities?

My primary responsibility is to make cheese. Also to make sure that everything is going smoothly, that we are staying on track, that we do not drift from where we want the cheese to be. I always taste the cheese. The office runs smoothly without me, so I don't do much sales. I handle personnel, having learned management skills that I didn't start with. We moved from being producers, where we did everything, to managing people.

What do you like most about what you do?

Making cheese. I get frustrated when I'm pulled away from it too much. I love to see how you can tweak things just a little bit and make a big change. I love the aging of it. The bacterial balance has to be just right in the cellar; if it's not right, you have to know how to fix it. And I do enjoy teaching interns and getting people excited about cheese.

What skills are most important for you to do your job well?

Attention to details and not allowing them to make you blind to the overall picture. You have to find that balance. You have to be aware of all the little things you might have done differently. It's hard to make farmstead products consistent. We learned

a lot on the fly, by doing things wrong. In 2001 or 2002, we were able to start traveling, so we went to Ireland, New Zealand, Europe, and learned a great deal from visiting cheesemakers abroad. We figured out what worked and how to adapt it here.

What skills would you like to develop to help further your business?

Whether I like it or not, I have to develop some of these management skills. I'm trying to work on that, developing skills in hiring and managing people, and developing procedures in the cellar and in shipping.

How large is your staff?

I keep between six and twelve people working for me. We have people in the field as well as in the office. Dairy itself doesn't use as much labor as cheesemaking. My expenses and labor costs are much higher than the dairy's. We have permanent people, family, and interns every year. My daughter makes cheese with me; my son is our farm manager; my son-in-law does sales. We have a sales team. We use a few distributors, but we mostly sell directly.

What qualities do you look for in a new hire?

I take the right attitude and a willingness to learn over experience any day. When they are open to learning, they will do fine, even if they have never worked with cows before. They should be flexible, willing to go with whatever happens. People set in their ways, who resist change, will have a hard time.

What is your proudest accomplishment?

Getting the Grayson to where it is now, because it's been a long haul. We started with it nine years ago. We put a lot of time, energy, and traveling in to figure out how to make a washed-rind cheese that would do well when aged sixty days or more and that could hold up when in retail too, because sometimes cheese doesn't move fast.

Describe your creative process.

I start with a ton of research. I look at the cheese or the type of problem I'm having with it specifically. I read everything I can, then I try to think about what I need to do to get it where I need it to be. How can I end up with a cheese with the texture and flavor profile that I want?

"You have to be aware of all the little things you might have done differently. It's hard to make farmstead products consistent. We learned a lot on the fly, by doing things wrong."

PETER O'DONOVAN

At Nantucket Wild Gourmet and Smokehouse, Peter O'Donovan and co-owner Marco Protano only smoke wild fish—the only people in the northeastern United States to do so. Their products are smoked for two to three days, after being pressed in kosher organic sea salt from the Pacific Ocean. Because they only smoke fishes that are eighteen pounds and heavier, they can only run two salmon-smoking sessions a week.

CURRENT POSITION: Cofounder with Marco Protano, Nantucket Wild Gourmet & Smokehouse, Chatham, MA, since 2006, nantucketwildgourmet.com. ★ **EDUCATION:** Ballymaloe Cookery School, Shanagarry, Ireland; Tante Marie's Cooking School, San Francisco, CA; Techniques of Fine Cooking 1 and 2, Institute of Culinary Education, New York, NY. ★ **CAREER PATH:** Chef, Ireland; caterer, San Francisco; hotel chef, Ireland; private chef, New York; chef, Woodcock Smokery, Ireland; private chef, Florida. ★ **AWARDS AND RECOGNITION:** Best New Product in New England (2006); Best Gourmet Shop in Cape Cod; featured on the *Today* show, in many articles, and on Oprah's favorite-things list for Christmas 2007. ★ **MEMBERSHIPS:** Slow Food; Chamber of Commerce; Greenpeace.

Salary notes:

Most start-ups are not profitable until their fifth or sixth year. We were profitable in our second year.

Words of advice for people considering a similar career:

Most importantly, create a niche. There's so much production of crap out there. You have to make a difference. Slowly build yourself. You have to control the market.

What prompted you to open your own business?

I was a private chef and an estate manager. I wanted to open a business, maybe a coffee shop, and was trying to find a niche. I wanted something that I hadn't come across in the U.S., something unique. I'd worked in Ireland with Sally Barnes of Woodcock Smokery, who is well recognized in the slow food movement. I looked at the smoked salmon found here and didn't

think that it was anything really exceptional. So Marco and I spent about one year doing research. We only smoke wild fish. We're the only ones in the Northeast making this product. Other things that set us apart are kosher organic sea salt, from the Pacific, and we smoke with a pesticide-free wood from Canada. We do two types of salting: dry salting and brining. Brining is most typical in the U.S. Dry salting is a more complex process.

Describe a typical day.

I'm in the store by eight. I check my voice mail and the faxes. I make bread, check all the temperatures of all refrigerators and freezers, check my stock, check the orders that are going out. I talk to my employees. Then I go downstairs and put on my white coat, my white boots, and my hairnet and work five or six hours in the smokehouse. I take a break, have lunch, slice fish, train someone new, record all the processes. It takes a lot of time: You have to record each batch of fish. I watch the vacuum-packing to make sure we do it quickly. I put more fish to salt overnight or brine some fish. The smoker is going most days. We do a big cleanup—it's basically like a surgery room, as close as possible to sterile. I see what's happening upstairs in the store, return some phone calls and faxes, see what's happening the next day. We have lots of events. Around eight thirty P.M. or so, I come home, shower, and go to bed.

How many hours a week do you typically work?

Many hours. I've been working seven days a week since last May. Twelve hours a day minimum, but I'm not always standing on my feet. I do paperwork, salt and slice fish, do two or three hours of recording. We are profitable, and that's always rewarding.

What do you like most about what you do?

I love what I do. I love our end product. I'm very challenge-driven. It's very challenging to get it right. In the Pacific, there are five kinds of salmon, which are different at different times of year, so they absorb smoke and salt differently. We have children who don't eat fish come to our store, eat our product, and then they eat fish. Our product is a treat. It's a special, expensive product.

What do you like least about it?

I don't like filleting tuna. Albacore tuna are not easy to fillet. That's probably what I dislike most. When it's your business, there's no point in disliking anything, because you have to do it.

What skills are most important for you to do your job well?

Some people have a knack with food. Some people can bake using their hand as a measure. What I do, especially with the salmon, I have a feel for it. I've seen amazing chefs not being able to fillet salmon. I've been to their restaurants and had amazing food, but they don't have a feel and knack for fish. You have to be passionate about it too. It will be a constant struggle trying to succeed without that. It took a lot of long hours to get our company where it is.

How large is your staff?

We have eight employees in the summer and three in the winter. I am the only one who handles the smoking.

What is the outlook for your type of job?

It's challenging. A lot of businesses struggle and fall by the wayside. A lot of it is educating consumers. Presently, a lot of people have returned to the main street of their village to shop locally. With high oil prices, people think twice about driving. It's challenging for producers. It depends on products. We don't have a very perishable product; it has a longer shelf life. If we were doing smoked mozzarella, it would be different. The slowdown of the economy is killing small producers. People need to spend, go out, support local stores.

What is your proudest accomplishment?

I've cooked for and worked with amazing people. This is a recognized business, and it's really rewarding that people come down from Boston on a drive in the summertime to come to our store. I'm really into food; one of the pinnacles was to get written up by the editor in chief of *Gourmet*. Also, that people pay $10 for a piece of fish and come back the next Saturday.

What keeps you challenged?

Every single day, the fish keeps me challenged. Not one fish is the same, because it's wild fish. Every single fish I smoke takes its own process. That is very challenging. Getting the salt right, depending on the time of year. For example, local bluefish in July and August gets very oily, so I had to develop a process. Developing products with the fish that best feature it.

"Most start-ups are not profitable until their fifth or sixth year. We were profitable in our second year."

11. RETAIL, DISTRIBUTION, SALES

Like food production, retail, sales, and distribution allow much autonomy for those who open a business centered around such services. Gourmet, specialty, and local food products are what American customers—at both the professional and the public level—are looking for, whether it is at farmers' markets, online, or retail stores. Targeting that type of product also allows you to create your own niche market. The key is to offer a product for which there is enough demand but where there isn't yet overcrowding in the market. We cannot stress enough the importance of research before you launch your own retail operation in order to find exactly what is missing on the market in your area, or even at a larger scale for a Web-based retail business.

When you launch a food business centered around retail, you will need to carefully consider who your target audience is. You will see that some of the people profiled here sell almost strictly to chefs, while others sell to the public. Picking a clear target audience means that you can then tailor your marketing message to that audience and ensure that it hears what you have to say.

Starting a retail business does not mean that you have to put all your savings into the process. Being creative and resourceful, and picking a business model adapted to your finances, will increase your chances of success. Food trucks, such as Thomas Odermatt's RoliRoti (page 262) have become enormously popular over the last couple of years, because they require a smaller up-front investment than a restaurant but still allow a cook, chef, or food producer to sell his or her food directly to consumers. A food truck can also be moved; if demand in one area is low, you can drive elsewhere and hope that business picks up for the rest of the day. Food trucks and other mobile food retail units are well served by social media sites such as Twitter, on which they can post their whereabouts.

Because virtual sales—conducted either by phone, e-mail, or an automated online ordering system—are a lot easier to handle logistically now than they were a few years ago, you might not even need a storefront and could conduct your business from your phone and laptop, anywhere you are, as does Thom Furhmann with his coffee company (page 258).

Some of these jobs are ways through which people have been able to remain connected to the restaurant world without dealing with the lifestyle and sacrifices that are inherent in it. The hours might not necessarily be easier, but the work might be different or offer more flexibility. John Duffy (page 265), for example, left a cooking career to become a salesperson for specialty food products. His background in and knowledge of the restaurant industry is invaluable when he makes sales calls.

If you decide on importing food from abroad for distribution purposes, be prepared to file a mountain of paperwork. U.S. Customs does not make it easy for foreign products to land on our shelves. Many food-trade organizations, such as the National Association for the Specialty Food Trade, organize seminars at trade shows and on the Internet so that you can remain informed on the latest regulations. Be sure to carefully study the regulations, potential costs attached to them, and transit duration as part of your business plan so that you don't have any surprises when the time comes to place your first order.

Selecting products to sell in a retail operation or carry as a distributor is one of the fun aspects of the job, since it allows you to travel and taste many great food products (with a few duds along the way undoubtedly). But it's not just about fun—it is perhaps the most crucial aspect of the business. If you pick products that no customer wants, you will quickly go out of business. It is also important to determine how many products to carry. Logistical details such as your storage capacity and the size of your retail display play an important role in determining that aspect of the operation. It also depends on where you are located. In a large city, having a niche and focusing on a very small number of one type of item that is impossible to obtain elsewhere might work. In a rural area with few shopping options, having a larger selection might be better for the viability of the business.

Finance and business knowledge are more than helpful when operating a retail business. It is not essential to have it if you surround yourself with capable people who will handle accounting and accounts payable, for example, but you want to make sure that you know how to read the documents they turn in. Knowledge of and passion for the products you are selling are a must, as is previous experience working with them—as a wine salesperson before opening a wine store, for example, like Jon Smith (page 253).

salaries

The money made in retail, distribution, and sales depends of course on the size of the operation and on the market in which you operate. It might take up to five years for a retail store to become profitable; the salary owners pay themselves in that time period will be low—likely just enough to cover their bills. Salespeople earn a commission on top of a fixed salary, which means that income will be largely dependent on volume sold. Entry-level sales positions within food distribution start in the $30,000 to $40,000 range.

JON SMITH

Jon Smith opened Cork & Bottle Fine Wines, a wine store, in 2002 in New Orleans, LA, but was forced to close when Hurricane Katrina devastated the city three years later. He was able to reopen and has since added a wine bar to his company.

CURRENT POSITION: Founder and owner, Cork & Bottle Fine Wines, since 2002, and Clever Wine Bar, since 2008, New Orleans, LA, www.cbwines.com. ★ **EDUCATION:** BA, city planning, University of New Orleans; master's course work in urban planning at UNO. ★ **CAREER PATH:** In New Orleans: short-order cook at a very casual neighborhood restaurant (when nineteen years old); bartender; casual restaurant job; waiter, fine-dining restaurant (two and a half years); fine-wine division, large wine company; job at a computer company; fine-wine division, wholesaler; sales manager, Robert Mondavi, New Orleans and Atlanta, GA. ★ **AWARDS AND RECOGNITION:** One of *New Orleans Magazine*'s Top People to Watch (2008).

Salary notes:

Generally, entry-level employees get paid hourly, with a median starting range of $10 to $12 an hour. Managers typically make $3,000 to $4,000 a month, with a chance of profit bonus.

Words of advice for people considering a similar career:

Pick up a book, read everything you can about wines, go to tastings, to restaurants holding events. Taste as many things as you can. There are a lot free or cheap tasting events in every city. Absorb as much as you can.

What prompted you to open your own business?

I always had the entrepreneurial spirit in me. I always knew I'd have my own business. I saw that the time was right. I was in my early thirties, and there were a ton of jobs available in the wine industry. So I knew that if I failed, I was still young enough and employable enough to get another job. I did it on a shoestring as a good, calculated risk. I didn't have an income for a year, but because I was married I could fall back on my spouse's. Be ready to do it and know that you won't get an income for one year. Number one, I really wanted to do it, and number two, I knew that I could lose everything and still be okay.

Describe a typical day.

I get up and am usually in the shop a couple of hours before it opens, doing the accounting log, receipts of the day before, taking a look at the books to make sure that they are balanced from the day before, doing all the paperwork, seeing what orders came in and what orders need to be put in. I have a staff of eight, but I still pretty much run it as if I was the only person there, because I have to have my finger on the pulse of the business. Then it's a regular retail day. I meet with sales reps through the day, and they make their presentations to me. By the middle of the afternoon I break off and meet with my bar manager (I started a wine bar in November 2008) and do for the bar all the work I did for the shop in the morning—looking at inventory, purchasing, addition and subtraction. The bar is still a brand-new business, so every day there is something we need to take care of. Then I either stay at the bar or go back to the shop, depending on what needs to be done. There's no magic formula of what I do every day. I work late nights, weekends, holidays, long days—just what I was trying to get away from in the restaurant business. I still work the bar a couple of nights a week, to have my fingers on its pulse.

How many hours a week do you typically work?

Fifty-five to sixty on average. During the holidays I might work eighteen- to-twenty-hour days. It's definitely not easy.

What are your specific responsibilities?

I do everything, from spearheading the creative direction of the store to scrubbing the bathroom. In an owner-proprietor situation, there's no duty you can escape. I let my staff do the retail management of the shop. I do financial management and I handle clients at the high level. We do a great deal of e-communications, which has been our cornerstone, so much of my time is spent planning those communications. I can't worry about that if I'm checking out someone at the cash register.

What do you like most about what you do?

It never stops changing, evolving. You have to stay on your toes to know what's coming out in a new vintage or if there's a new region or a new discovery. There's a real human connection behind the products I work with, a genuineness. I focus on smaller, rarer wines at all price points. I deal with people who are in connection with the land on which the grapes are grown and the wine is made. You're not caught up in a commodity market. It's still a business, but there's almost a romantic side to it; it's very rare to find that.

What do you like least about it?

There's a lot of drudgery. There's a lot more minutiae with paper trails, getting shelf tags on wines—a million little details, probably more than in other industries. One thing that is frustrating is that there is an ocean of wine in the world right now, and there's a crush of salespeople trying to sell the wine. Historically, the sale process has been a very natural, organic one, and now you're seeing big companies fighting over things, almost coming to blows to see who will be at the front of the line. There is a growing and noticeable competitive fierceness in the wine business that never existed before. It exists because of how much product is available. Unless it corrects itself—and I don't know how it will—I think it's going to continue to be pervasive.

What skills are most important for you to do your job well?

In my job and in any food-service-industry job, number one has got to be tenacity. There's no greater skill to have in whole-sale, retail, the bar side, than tenacity. For example, you've been in the middle of dinner service and have been able to keep your cool, understanding that being rushed and people being rude is no reflection on you, it's the job. If you thrive on it, it's a good skill to have. Maybe the pace of it is a little more calm on the wine retail side, but it's there. I've had employees that had amazing palates or an amazing ability to connect with people, but at the end of the day they weren't able to deal with the reality of working retail. Number two is the ability to understand what is at the core of your business. If you are a wholesaler, understand that you are a wholesaler but you also need to understand the business that you are in. Number three is being creative. If you need your hand held and to be told how to go from A to B to C, the wine side might not be the best side for you. You

have to be nimble; there is no template, there is no Wine Business 101 in college. A somewhat entrepreneurial spirit is a trait of paramount importance. Those three things are really three qualities that people should see if they possess before considering a career in the wine business.

What skills would you like to develop to help further your career?

There are skills that I thought that I had when I first started, like organizational skills and wine knowledge, that I still had to work on. I had run one of the largest territories of one of the largest companies in the business, so I thought I knew how to work with spreadsheets. But then I realized that these numbers were never real to me. I had on-the-job training with economics, finance, and accounting, and I have certainly honed my skills on that. But I am always working on understanding finance and accounting functions. If someone has the ability to be educated beyond Econ 101, that's the skill set that really sets people apart.

JENNIFER JANSEN

Jennifer Jansen and her husband opened Milk & Honey Bazaar, an artisanal cheese and specialty food market, in 2004, after both had spent several years working in the hospitality industry. The store is open seven days a week in the summer and fall and six days a week the rest of the year, and it carries more than a hundred types of cheese.

CURRENT POSITION: Owner, Milk & Honey Bazaar, Tiverton, RI, since 2004, www .milkandhoneybazaar.com. ★ **EDUCATION:** BA, hotel restaurant institutional management, Mercy Hearst College, Erie, PA. ★ **CAREER PATH:** Marriott International, Boston, MA (1997–1999); catering sales and event planning, Museum of Fine Arts, Boston (1999–2002). ★ **AWARDS AND RECOGNITION:** Best of Rhode Island for Gourmet Shop (2005); Best of Newport County Editor's Pick (2006); *Boston* magazine's New England Travel and Life Best of New England (2007). ★ **MEMBERSHIPS:** Treasurer, Tiverton Four Corners Merchants Association; chamber of commerce.

Salary notes:

Being an owner, there are many variables. Someone in his or her first year is not going to make the same as later. It starts around $60,000.

Words of advice for people considering a similar career:

Someone told me this when I was in school and I never forgot it: Make mistakes with other people's money first—meaning acquire experience working for others before going off on your own.

Describe a typical day.

It is very much about being on the front line, behind the counter, making sure that everything is cleaned and well stocked. First, I check on orders for the day, any pickups or platters that we might have, making sure that's all set. I keep on top of orders coming up for the next couple of days. Then we open the doors and deal with business as usual. Customers might be looking for a specific cheese. We go through the day, working with the customers. If we are really busy, both of us are behind the counter, but often I'm with our kids in the back room dealing with billing, invoices, and other back room work and my husband is in the front. We deal with a lot of restaurants, so I do that.

How do you source the cheeses that you carry?

We started with sixty to seventy cheeses that we wanted as staples. Since then, we've added many through customer requests—50 percent of the cheeses we carry, I would say. Cheesemakers send us samples, and we have decided to carry some that way.

How many hours a week do you typically work?

Forty to sixty hours physically in the shop, depending on the season. But because my husband and I work and live together, we talk about the business all the time and end up working at home too. Between Memorial and Labor Day and Thanksgiving and Christmas, we are open seven days a week; the rest of the year six days. We also do mail-order.

What are your specific responsibilities?

Everything from dishwasher to CFO. You do everything when you have your own business.

How did you decide on cheese as your sales product?

When working in sales, catering, and restaurants, my husband and I had always been interested in cheese. We wanted something that was kind of like catering but where people could pick up the platter themselves. There also wasn't anything around here that offered that service. There are lots of foodies, lots of great home cooks around here, and people entertain at home. It's nice for them to have a place where they can pick up cheese.

What do you like most about what you do?

The flexibility of working for yourself, making changes as you need to, without needing to clear it with someone else. I also like that we are still learning. There's so much out there to discuss as far as cheese is concerned. Nobody knows how many cheeses are out there. It's exciting, never stale; we are never bored.

What do you like least about it?

This is the case across the board for the hospitality industry: You are busiest on weekends and holidays. When you have a family, it's harder to not have everyone together on weekends and holidays.

What skills are most important for you to do your job well?

You need to be a jack-of-all-trades. You have your hands in everything, from maintenance of equipment to merchandising to sales. Being flexible and having an open mind are very much a part of it. You need to evolve with your business.

What is the outlook for your type of business?

I think that the idea of the specialized shop is coming back. With all the talk of eating more local foods, people are shopping at farmers' markets. So I could see a trend of there being more cheese shops.

How large is your staff?

It's just my husband and myself. Here and there, we have part-time help, in the summer or around the holidays. We sell 140 cheeses, give or take a few.

What qualities do you look for in a new hire?

They have to be very service orientated. It's great if they have cheese or food knowledge, but we are so personable with our customers that it's key for them to be very service orientated.

What keeps you challenged?

My customers. I like to keep up with their evolving taste. I want to keep the store new and fresh (as in "different"). I don't want it to become that people see a platter at a party and say, "Of course, that comes from Milk and Honey." I want them to be surprised. I don't want it to become stale.

THOM FUHRMANN

Thom Fuhrmann is a professional musician who stumbled into the coffee business when he went to California for a media interview and saw an ad in a coffee shop for a position at a coffee company. He's now been working with coffee for twenty-two years. Through his mail-order company, Monkey & Son, he sells coffee that is 100 percent fair trade and organic to 103 coffee shops and restaurants around the country. The twenty-five hundred pounds of coffee he sells a month are roasted in Minnesota. He still tours with his band, Savage Republic.

CURRENT POSITION: Owner, Monkey & Son Coffee Company, Claremont, CA, since 2004, www.monkeyandson.com. ★ **EDUCATION:** BA, special education, University of California–Los Angeles. ★ **CAREER PATH:** Musician, Savage Republic (ongoing); worked for Deeter's Coffee, Peet's Coffee, then two companies in California, Steaming Beans Coffee Co. in Colorado, and European Coffee. ★ **AWARDS AND RECOGNITION:** Three reviews from Jonathan Gold in the *Los Angeles Times*. ★ **MEMBERSHIPS:** Fair Trade; USDA Organic.

Salary notes:

It depends on how hard you want to work. I make between $60,000 and $80,000 a year but could probably make $250,000 if I really wanted to.

Words of advice for people considering a similar career:

Don't be afraid. Don't wait too long. I started this business with no money. I took out a credit card and bought some coffee. If you want something bad enough, you can do it. It sounds cliché but it's absolutely true.

What prompted you to open your own business?

I started on August 20, 2004, on my son's birthday, hence the name. I had been in the coffee business for twenty-two years. Later, I decided to start a mail-order company with a virtual location. It's pretty small—twenty-five hundred pounds a month. The beans are contract-roasted in Minnesota, since I can store more green coffee there. I had worked with the roasting company for ten years beforehand. They do everything. I handle sales and marketing and I design the flavor profiles.

Describe a typical day.

I get up at about four in the morning, get online to see where the coffee price is, go to the gym, then go out and visit my accounts to discuss their orders. I'm a big believer in face-to-face contact.

How many hours a week do you typically work?

Twenty to forty hours; it depends. Since I got back from touring with the band, I'm really focused. I don't really consider it work. I'm going down to Santa Barbara, to the wine country, driving and seeing clients.

What are your specific responsibilities?

I'm everything. I drive the ship. I just placed an order now for 750 pounds of coffee. I speak to customers, develop new flavors of coffee, and it's up to me to sell it. I upgraded the website to add a blog. Networking and word of mouth is everything. Networking is my strong suit. I can go in a restaurant, just as a consumer, and sell them something. I can get an account when I am not even looking for an account. In this economy, you have to think outside of the box. I just talk to people. I always carry samples with me. I come to New York with 200 pounds of coffee.

What do you like least about it?

Dealing with the coffee machines. I give people a better price if they have their own equipment. We have customers all around the country; if they don't pay their bills, I have to go and take the equipment I lease them.

What skills are most important for you to do your job well?

To be able to communicate and do so honestly, to mean what you say and say what you mean.

What skills would you like to develop to help further your career?

I would like to take formal sommelier training. It would enhance my ability to sell and to show product. You can never know enough.

How often do you set goals?

Every month I reevaluate. I want to open one account a week. You lose one every once in a while. I have 103 accounts right now.

WILL GOLDFARB

Will Goldfarb is a multifaceted entrepreneur who uses his background as a pastry chef to tap into unexplored niches. His specialty product company, WillPowder, sells ingredients typically used in a professional kitchen in small quantities, to give people who cannot otherwise obtain such ingredients the opportunity to use them. WillEquipped follows the same model but for equipment. Picnick, his food kiosk in Battery Park in New York, NY, follows sustainable practices.

CURRENT POSITION: Chef-owner, WillPowder (specialty products), since 2005; Picnick (innovative sandwich concept with a strong green and social-welfare component), since 2007; and WillEquipped (specialty equipment), since 2009, New York, NY, www.willpowder .com. ★ **EDUCATION:** BA, history (Duke), 1997; pastry grand diploma, Cordon Bleu, Paris (1998). ★ **CAREER PATH:** While at Cordon Bleu, Bistro Ivan and stagiaire at Gérard Mulot in Paris; private chef in south of France; Cibrèo, Florence, Italy; stagiaire, El Bullì, Rosas, Spain (1999); pastry chef, Ryland Inn, Readington, NJ (1999 and 2001); El Bullì Taller (2000); the Grange, Adelaide, Australia; Tetsuya's, Sydney, Australia; Atlas; opening pastry chef, Papillon, New York, NY (2001); The Castine Inn, Castine, ME (2002); pastry chef, Morimoto, Philadelphia, PA (2002–2004). In New York: pastry chef, Cru (2004–2005); chef-owner, Room 4 Dessert, 2006–2007. ★ **AWARDS AND RECOGNITION:** Ten Best Pastry Chefs in America, *Pastry Art & Design* (2006); StarChefs Rising Star (2006); Best Up-and-Coming Chef, *New York* (2006); nominee, Best Pastry Chef in America, James Beard Foundation (2007); Chopin Vodka's Unconventional Genius Award (2007); presented at Identita Golose in Milan, StarChefs International Chefs Congress, Melbourne Food and Wine, and Montreal Lumière; the New York Future Grant, AIGA; published article and recipe in *Apicius* and *Art Culinaire;* cover profile in the *New Yorker* written by Bill Buford. ★ **MEMBERSHIPS:** Experimental Cuisine Collective (cofounder); AKWA (founder).

Words of advice for people considering a similar career:

Always be a little bit kinder than necessary; always fold your towels neatly; always keep your spoon water clean; never go home.

Describe a typical day.

My workday is dictated by the season or the priority. I set my agenda each day depending on what I need to do for each business. I am at Picnick all day when it is open, so I do my other work before or after, or on weekends. I do a ton of consulting, and at some point I was in three different restaurants in a day. I traditionally work until about two A.M.

How many hours a week do you typically work?

A hundred and ten hours.

What are your specific responsibilities?

Basically, as executive chef and owner of Picnick, I am responsible for every aspect of the operations, from menu design to park compliance, future locations, business development, etc. As owner of Will-

Powder, I am responsible for all the content, recipes, business development, website, partnership and distribution agreements, sales and marketing, sourcing of products. I am responsible for all the direct consumer support; I respond personally to all customers' technical questions. For WillEquipped, as a startup, I'm responsible for all items: compliance, banking, retail, sales tax, certifications, all of the arrangements with all of the manufacturers and publishers, all content of the website, all of the recipes, content, images, inspiration and combination of the products, total product design, in addition to graphics, logo, and associated brand identity. When we launch, I'll be responsible for all of the ordering, invoicing, sales, and customer service.

What do you like most about what you do?

That I am starting to put myself in positions where I am able to choose what I want to do. It's taken me more than twelve years to get there. I'm always at the mercy of the environment and the customers, but I'm focusing more on what I want to do.

What skills are most important for you to do your job well?

Quick, analytical thinking and physical endurance.

What skills would you like to develop to help further your career?

Personal communication skills and the ability to remain above the fray at all times.

What is the outlook for your type of job?

In a down economy, it's the right time to start businesses with small capitalization, because the opportunities for partnership are great. People are desperate to sell things. People are looking for support, so strong partners in bad times are very important. A down economy allows you to focus on not wasting money.

What qualities do you look for in a new hire?

Intelligence and humility.

THOMAS ODERMATT

Thomas Odermatt founded RoliRoti, a rotisserie truck company that uses a European-style rotisserie system to spit-roast meats of all kinds. He and his staff drive the company's three trucks to twenty-seven farmers' markets around the Bay Area in California.

CURRENT POSITION: Owner, RoliRoti, Napa, CA, since 2002, www.roliroti.com. ★
EDUCATION: Farming studies, Swiss Federal Institute of Technology (ETH), Zurich, Switzerland; master's, environmental management with a focus on farming, Switzerland; course work in marketing and management, University of California–Berkeley extension. ★
CAREER PATH: Organic-ingredient and sustainably grown product sourcing, Hiestind (large bakery), Switzerland; "happy rabbit farming" implementer, brother's rabbit farm, Hungary. ★
AWARDS AND RECOGNITION: Many media mentions, including making *USA Today*'s list of the ten best food trucks to visit and being featured in *Food & Wine*. ★ **MEMBERSHIPS:** Farmers' market organization.

Salary notes:

The number of trucks that you have does not matter. If you have one truck, focus on that one, make a very good product, and you could make $80,000 to $150,000 a year. One truck must make $450,000 to $490,000 a year. That's what they need to bring in to justify $80,000-to-$150,000 salaries. Then you can use that money to either grow your business or for your personal use.

Words of advice for people considering a similar career:

Work, work, work, work. You must do what the customer wants. If the customer demands something from you, you have to do it. Another word of advice is speak to your business, work in your business, and don't jump out. When you get successful, don't stop being there. People want to see you—they want to see the operator. If you start regularly oversleeping in the morning, that's the time you need to look into yourself and say you might be doing something wrong and need to change.

What prompted you to open your own business?

I came with the intention to stay here for three months in order to learn English. Then I wanted to go back to Switzerland or Hungary. But I enrolled in an extension course and had to write a business plan, so I decided to create a business about what I know. Until the day I was finishing the business plan, I thought it was a great project but I didn't think about it as a real business. We opened a business, imported a truck from Germany, and started to sell chickens. It was a very bad decision. We should have started at a farmers' market. I was here with a student visa, then an E-2 visa, which is an investor visa. I'm still on that. I don't have the intention to stop any time soon. I'm trying to grow and to diversify myself. I don't have any intention of being a franchise or big corporation. I want to keep it rather small and controllable. I have three trucks, and we do twenty-seven markets in the summer. We installed a system that enables us to turn them over in between markets, similar to the turnover system at Southwest Airlines. The crew that comes in the afternoon is ready with tools. They help sanitize and load the truck and within fifteen minutes are ready to go to the next farmers' market. We also have a little takeout place in Napa and a catering business at night and on weekends with RoliRoti trucks. We deal mostly with wineries in Napa Valley for that.

Describe a typical day.

I go to the office, talk to the production facility, answer e-mails, propose caterings, make sure the quality is okay, that the money is okay when they come back. Those are typical tasks that need to be fulfilled. I go to the Ferry Market Plaza on Saturday morning.

How many hours a week do you typically work?

In the summer, between seventy and eighty. In the winter, between fifty and sixty. When we started, it was ninety to a hundred hours; that's what you have to do.

What are your specific responsibilities?

Ordering, payroll, permitting, making sure that our permits are up-to-date. Making sure that we are in good standing with the health department. We are regularly inspected on-site and have to bring the trucks in once a year. We need to wash the trucks and sanitize them twice a day, then we restock and refill them twice a day. I have someone here who does that at night. I don't want the driver to do that. They're tired and want to go home. At big markets, there are two persons in each truck, and one at the smaller markets.

What do you like most about what you do?

Being around the customers all the time and being at the farmers' market. I can see if I do something right or wrong. Don't step out way too early. Stay connected to your business, visit your customers at the market, be around them. You also build a brand based on personality that way.

What do you like least about it?

Dealing with employee issues. I don't like that. I cannot fire people or be harsh. In Switzerland, people work for the boss. Here people work for themselves. It's a very different work ethic. People who work for me are from all around the world and are people used to working the markets. Many of my employees come from Kenya. They're farmers, ranchers, truck drivers in their home country. They're hard workers. They know that the better the company does, the better they do. We provide them health insurance, bonuses, 401(k). This is a must. This is something that I am very proud of. RoliRoti is able to provide health insurance and a decent livable salary for the Bay Area. What shows me that I'm doing something right and correct is that I have a very low employee turnover.

How large is your staff?

We have thirteen on the payroll, including my wife and me.

What qualities do you look for in a new hire?

I don't look too much at the qualities; it's a gut feeling, a gut decision. If the person has a good appearance, a good smile, is in good health, he's my guy. I definitely can reach out and train him. I don't look much at the paperwork and the books and the résumé.

What is the outlook for your type of business?

I see that during the next recession, you'll see more people getting into my business. The cost of acquiring a truck is lower than acquiring a restaurant. You can move it if it doesn't work in one location. People are seeking new ways to make money, to get into the business world. I appreciate that.

"I don't have the intention to stop any time soon. I'm trying to grow and to diversify myself. I don't have any intention of being a franchise or big corporation. I want to keep it rather small and controllable."

JOHN DUFFY

As a sales manager for Paris Gourmet, a leading specialty food import and distribution company, John Duffy sells 1,250 products to chefs and restaurateurs in New York, New Jersey, and Connecticut. The company also works on a national scale through a network of distributors.

CURRENT POSITION: Sales manager, Paris Gourmet, Carlstadt, NJ, since 1995. ★
EDUCATION: BA, English literature, Boston College, MA; culinary arts degree, Culinary Institute of America, Hyde Park, NY. ★ **CAREER PATH:** Pastry sous chef; sous chef at a variety of places, from T.G.I. Friday's to four-star restaurants, between New York State and Boston (for about fifteen years).

Salary notes:

Starts between $30,000 and $40,000. You can grow within the same position and compensation is based on performance.

Words of advice for people considering a similar career:

There is no school for sales. The only way to learn is to do it. That's one thing that's very different for people who have worked in kitchen. As a manager, when we hired a cook, we'd have them trail for a few days and have a very good sense of their work habits and capabilities in a short amount of time. With what we do it takes much, much longer than that. For us to develop somebody, it takes a lot longer than in the kitchen. It's a psychological process. They have to give themselves time to learn. From a management perspective, we might not know a person's capabilities for about a year. We are not sure how they are going to work out until we give them time and opportunities.

What prompted you to work where you are now?

I'd been working in the food industry, and I was looking for something that allowed me to be in the business and also have a life. Sales seemed like it could give me both. I didn't know for sure if it'd work out or not. It's a good option for people who have put in a number of years in the kitchen. If you don't have enough experience in the kitchen first, you might feel the pull to go back. But if you are done with the line, this is a good next move.

Describe a typical day.

When I started, I was a salesperson, so I was in the field, taking orders. Now I manage the people who do that and provide support for them in a myriad of ways. Also I work more in the product field. I'm part of the group that decides which products to add to our inventory.

How many hours a week do you typically work?

Around sixty hours.

What are your specific responsibilities?

The management of people who directly respond to me. I'm fiscally responsible for certain goals. We work on annual and monthly goals.

What do you like most about what you do?

That balance of being involved in an industry that I love and being able to do it without sacrificing too much.

What skills are most important for you to do your job well?

Patience is a big one. Overall the most important thing is the ability to communicate. I'm the linchpin in many relationships. It's not so much generating the ideas that you are communicating but making them flow in several directions.

What skills would you like to develop to help further your career?

For most people in the industry, when you come from a food background you could always know more about technology and business, which I don't really know about—economics, things like that. The problem is time.

How large is your staff?

About fifty people total. Fourteen answer directly to me.

What qualities do you look for in a new hire?

The number one thing for a salesperson is how other people will react to them. It doesn't have to do with their experience right off the bat. It has to be someone to whom a stranger would feel comfortable talking. Then there are plenty of other things, such as culinary experience, which is not mandatory but is very helpful, to

have just a basic understanding of the world. The salesperson works in the kitchen, so you have to understand what the environment is like. If they don't have that experience but have a love of food, of restaurants, etc., it can almost make up for a lack of hands-on experience.

What is your proudest accomplishment?

Over the years, I've worked with different people and trained them. I've never hired anyone who's done this exact job before. Some of those people have moved on to other places. So I am proud to have trained people who make it a full-blown career.

How many products do you carry?

One thousand two hundred and fifty products. That's a small range—it puts us in the specialty range. A big range would be twenty thousand products. We want to grow, but we don't want to be at that twenty thousand range. It'll be very healthy if we double within five or ten years.

Describe your selection process for new products.

Some of our ideas come from our customers, but that's a minority. The goal of some distributors is to carry what their customers want. We're top down, where we decide what we are going to carry and then go out and sell it. So we will take some risks on products that haven't been sold before or that people might not be familiar with. Everybody who's here likes that approach.

12. MEDIA, MARKETING, PUBLIC RELATIONS

The media sector of the food industry is an ever-evolving one, with opportunities that range from working for magazines and television shows to websites and restaurant organizations. These jobs can either require an artistic sensibility and highly creative abilities, such as when working as a food stylist or photographer, or be ideal for

someone looking for a job in the food industry that requires more time spent at a computer than at a stove. The opportunities in these fields clearly have been expanding but so have the number of people interested in them. Many media positions see very little turnover, so getting a foot in the door as a freelancer is often the best way to obtain these jobs.

television and radio

Many seasoned and aspiring food professionals dream of being on television. During a talk at the Institute of Culinary Education's Center for Food Media, Susan Stockton, vice president of culinary productions for the Food Network, explained that the network receives countless video submissions every week, but that the executive team also mines YouTube and other digital video channels to find talent for their shows. She advised against getting an overly produced, costly pilot, which might showcase a production company rather than a host, since the network is just as willing to review material produced by the submitters themselves. Network executives often have concepts in mind, which they then must pair with the right talent. As such, they are more likely to take on someone with little culinary experience but a sizzling personality than someone whose culinary pedigree is absolutely stellar but who does not resonate on camera.

Besides hosting, which is a career only for a select few, many other opportunities are available in television, including cooking, styling, producing, and web editing. Courtney Knapp (page 272), for example, is a culinary producer for *Martha*. Most shows have their own website, which needs content. Recipe editors also work on television, since the recipes that someone hosting or making a guest appearance on a show provides need to be organized in a script format for the shoot itself and in a print format for associated publications.

Working as a television producer is one of the tracks in media that requires specialized training, or at least prior experience. Thankfully, most production companies are always looking for interns and production assistants, which are great positions through which to get your foot in the door. You often will not need to have taken audiovisual production classes, although they might help. Culinary training might be a requirement for certain production positions, such as culinary producer.

Some food radio shows, such as Lynne Rossetto Kasper's *The Splendid Table,* are mainstays of public radio, while Martha Stewart offers a daily show on Sirius Satellite Radio. However, radio opportunities seem few and far between, as many people who want to do audio interviews and features seem to have turned to podcasting and Web broadcasting instead.

editorial work

We keep hearing that food magazines are struggling, cookbook proposals are not being sold, and newspaper food sections are being cut down. Is it a good time to think about editorial work if you want to write about food? While the people we regularly speak with on this topic express concern as to the state of the industry, they are optimistic. Staff cuts mean more opportunities for freelance writers, for example. Fewer pages in print might mean that a publication will add more online content, for which they will need material.

The editorial side of a magazine is separate from the test kitchen, which develops the recipes that appear in the publication. If you want to write, you will want to work on the features side of the publication. Most publications, from trade to high-end glossy magazines, take on interns and will typically let them write short blurbs for the "front of the book" (the section with short notes on products, ingredients, or places). Such an opportunity will allow you to start building your writing portfolio, which you will need when applying for full-time jobs. A culinary degree is not necessary to work in editorial, but it will be a valuable asset to your résumé nonetheless. You might spend a year or two as an editorial assistant, once you get hired, before being promoted when an opportunity arises. Trade publications offer faster career advancement and the opportunity to write more often but are often perceived as being less glamorous.

Having worked on staff at a few recognizable places will be helpful when you try to establish a freelance career, since you will already have contacts at those publications. That is by no means a requirement for success, however. The key when pitching articles as a freelancer, as does Stacey Brugeman (page 280), is to know the publication very well, to capture its voice in your pitch, to contact the right editor, and to send them an idea that they have not yet covered the way that you have. Making a living strictly out of freelancing for magazines can be tedious, which is why many freelancers take on less creative projects, such as corporate writing, to help pay the bills. Diversifying your source of income is the key to success as a freelancer.

As for cookbooks, while reports from aspiring and established authors alike confirm that advances have lowered significantly, contracts are still being signed. Several blog authors, such as Molly Wizenberg of Orangette (page 285), have published books that are based on their blogs, showing that blogs might not be the flash in the pan some feared after the publication of *Julie & Julia* (which was released as a movie in August 2009). A cookbook editor or an agent specializing in food titles might not have professional culinary training, but again, experience in the field will help you be better at your job, as you will be more able to spot errors in techniques or ingredient measurements. An agent functions as an advocate for the author, presenting book proposals to publishing companies and negotiating contracts with editors. You will learn the business by starting as an assistant, reading manuscripts to decide if agents should consider them. As a cookbook editorial assistant, you will often do a first read through a manuscript, before your editor

goes through it, and handle the administrative aspects of the publishing process. Since there is relatively little movement at the top of the publishing food chain, the way to get promoted from associate editor to editor can be by changing companies.

food styling

Food-styling positions tend to be freelance rather than full-time ones and mostly take place on projects such as television shows, magazine and cookbook photo shoots, satellite media tours, and food product shoots. The work may take place in a corporate test kitchen, in an office park, or on the beach at an exotic vacation destination. Jeannie Chen (page 288) has experience with most of those, since diversifying is key to maintaining a livable income. Because of the freelance factor, it is particularly important to be flexible and reliable so that clients will hire you again for future projects. Television projects are especially likely to work with freelancers. It is a hard sector to crack, but once you get your foot in the door and convince the production team of your skills and friendliness, you will continue to be called back, since shows like to work with people who know how they run. Hands-on experience is often the best training for food styling, but classes are available at most large culinary schools. Before styling completely on your own, you will also spend considerable time working under a senior stylist's supervision.

test kitchens

Both magazines and large food corporations have test kitchens. When working for a magazine, you will usually start with whatever ingredient or idea you have, based on what was discussed at planning meetings. At a food company, you will usually build your testing around a specific product for which you must develop recipes. Magazines, just like companies, know who their audience is, which will play a role in what you can and cannot do. If research shows that the average reader of your publication does not have access to a particular ingredient or does not like to spend more than twenty minutes preparing a dish, it will affect the types of recipes that you will create.

Lauren Dellabella of Unilever (page 291) says that while test kitchen staff members used to come from a home economics background, today it is more likely that they will have a culinary arts or a food science degree. Having a culinary arts degree is also somewhat essential in magazine test kitchens, unless you have years of industry experience behind you. Test kitchens also appreciate staff who have restaurant cooking experience because they bring valuable efficiency, speed, and problem-solving skills to the job.

digital media

Blogs, websites, podcasts, social networks—digital media teem with food content. Not all of this work is lucrative, however, and some websites keep only a limited crew. As a freelancer, you can send in pitches to websites the way you would to a magazine or newspaper. Most websites take on interns and give them plenty to do so they acquire valuable new media skills.

Cooking videos and podcasts are relatively easy to produce on your own with little equipment and easy editing software programs. If you have a blog and want to stand out, adding this type of content will be helpful in getting you noticed.

Social networking sites, like Facebook and Twitter, abound with food writers. Use those sites to follow people whose work you admire, keep up with food news, and promote yourself. If you blog, post links to your new blog posts. If you write, post links to your articles. Do not push the self-promotion too far, however, or it will backfire.

Photography also falls under digital media these days, since most professionals take food photographs with digital cameras. Even relatively inexpensive cameras have become quite nice and will allow you to take photos to illustrate your online presence. To become a professional food photographer, however, you will need to invest in serious equipment as well as some training. Working with an established photographer, such as Ben Fink (page 298), as an unpaid assistant even, will teach you valuable skills not only on the photography side, but also on how to run an independent photography business.

public relations and marketing

Food-specific public relations and marketing opportunities have greatly expanded. You can now do PR for a chef or for an all-natural artisanal product, as both have realized the need for their voice to be heard. Certain chefs will have their assistants handle their PR in-house and hire an outside firm to help them with large-scale placement, special promotions, launches, and more. In addition to handling media queries, chefs also need help coordinating or developing their marketing opportunities, which can be alliances with products, a spokesperson role, or product development, for example. If you wish to work in PR or marketing, you can do so via one of the many agencies that handle such types of accounts, usually starting as an account coordinator or assistant account executive. You will then move up to account executive, senior account executive, and vice president positions as you climb up the ladder.

These positions see much movement, so promotions tend to happen rather rapidly. You can also work for a chef or a restaurant group directly. A small restaurant will not have a separate PR employee, but a chef who is relatively well known in your community and is seeking to establish his or her image more strongly on the national stage might. Restaurant groups typically have someone who handles publicity and marketing.

The market for representing people is, however, a small one. You'll find that there are just as many opportunities in representing trade commissions, agricultural boards, producers associations, and manufacturers. You can also work in book public relations, as does Carrie Bachman (page 294), either in-house at a publishing company or on a freelance basis for authors or companies.

salaries

Because of the wide range of positions and areas covered in this section, refer to specific comments made in the profiles for salary information.

COURTNEY KNAPP

As associate producer for food at *Martha,* Martha Stewart's live lifestyle show, which airs five days a week, Courtney Knapp is part of the team that produces all the food segments that appear on the show.

CURRENT POSITION: Associate producer, food, *The Martha Stewart Show,* New York, NY. ★ **EDUCATION:** BA, sociology, Connecticut College; culinary arts degree, Natural Gourmet Institute, New York; MA, food studies, New York University. ★ **CAREER PATH:** Catering and intern, Millennium, San Francisco, CA. In Chicago, IL: intern, roundsman, Frontera Grill; line cook, Topolobampo; saucier, Frontera Grill and Topolobampo. In New York: sous-chef, Studio del Gusto; freelance caterer; assistant, Clark Wolf Company; associate placement manager, Institute of Culinary Education. Freelance positions: assistant to the producer/writers' assistant, *The Mark Twain Prize* (PBS, 2003–2008); writers' assistant, *The Library of Congress Gershwin Prize for Popular Song* (PBS, 2007); researcher, *A Chef's Story* (PBS, 2007); producer, *Insatiably Curious,* a food podcast (2008); freelance researcher for many books and articles; freelance writer. ★ **MEMBERSHIPS:** New York Women's Culinary Alliance; Slow Food; National Academy of Television Arts & Sciences.

Salary notes:

Associate producer positions range from $45,000 to $60,000, I believe.

Words of advice for people considering a similar career:

Say yes to everything. Create a network of people who can help you with your career and personally.

How did you choose to work where you are today?

It was kind of organic. I worked for an amazing food writer, Peter Kaminsky, who believed in my skills. He believed that the skill set of a cook was very similar to the skill set of a person working in television: the ability to always have your eye on the big picture while maintaining close attention to detail. Cooking on a line, working as a saucier, catering an event—all of those positions required a similar focus. Erika

Lesser from Slow Food recommended me to him; Peter recommended me for another position where I met a coworker who recommended me for my current position. Along the way I had a number of similar situations for freelance projects. I have been very fortunate to have great people in my life.

Describe a typical day.

Our show tapes live at ten A.M., so we start off at seven thirty A.M. with our first production meeting. I'm in the studio for rehearsals, prepping our guests, coordinating with the art department on props and giveaways, checking with the kitchen for any problems or recipe changes. I review cue cards, the counter, and "process" if it's my segment. After the show, I'm back across the street to check voice mails and e-mails. We have a second production meeting. Then I work on coordinating all of the other segment details (research, photos/permission, B-roll/video clips, and other elements), arranging audience give-aways, working with chefs on recipes, coordinating with the field team if it's a tape piece, writing scripts, etc. I put together potential guest pitches for my producer, Greta Anthony. Other research or vetting of potential guests and segment ideas to review with Greta and supervising producers. Back across the street for the afternoon show. Typically, we shoot three days a week. Those other two days are pre-production.

How many hours a week do you typically work?

Around fifty-five, more or less, depending on how many segments we have a week.

What do you like most about what you do?

It's something new every day. It offers a lot of what I loved about being in the kitchen: variety, stress, endurance, creativity, a connection to food.

What do you like least about it?

The stress-to-pay ratio could be better.

What skills are most important for you to do your job well?

Organization, attention to detail, creativity, writing skills, production skills. Culinary experience and knowledge of the food industry—those are so important that they are kind of a given.

What skills would you like to develop to help further your career?

More Final Cut Pro training and experience producing in the field rather than just in the studio.

What are your long-term goals?

Martha is a great place to learn, so I'd like to produce here for as long as we're on the air. I also have a food and travel show rolling around in my head that I'd like to see come to fruition.

What keeps you challenged?

The Martha Stewart Living Omnimedia brand definitely demands perfection, so that keeps me on my toes. You can't really slack. Every segment requires 100 percent; you need to know your material, your recipes, really everything.

GAIL SIMMONS

As special projects editor for *Food & Wine,* Gail Simmons is in charge of organizing the *Food & Wine* Classic (a large event with culinary demonstrations, wine tastings, and panels) that takes place every June in Aspen, CO, as well as other special events for the magazine. She is also one of the judges on Bravo TV's *Top Chef.*

CURRENT POSITION: Special projects editor, *Food & Wine,* since 2005. Judge, Bravo's *Top Chef,* since 2005. ★ **EDUCATION:** BA, humanistic studies (focus on culinary anthropology and Spanish), McGill University, Montreal, Canada (1998); culinary arts degree, Institute of Culinary Education, New York, NY (1999). ★ **CAREER PATH:** Editorial intern, *Toronto Life,* Toronto, Canada (1998); editorial assistant, *National Post,* Canada. In New York: culinary extern, Le Cirque 2000 and Vong (1999); research and recipe assistant to food critic Jeffrey Steingarten, *Vogue* (2000–2001); special events manager, the Dinex Group (2002–2004); merchandising manager, *Food & Wine* (2004–2005). ★ **AWARDS AND RECOGNITION:** Nominated for an Emmy award for *Top Chef* season two. *Top Chef* has been nominated for four Emmys in total, and won for Outstanding Nonfiction Editing. The show was nominated for two James Beard Awards and won for Broadcast Media for Food Special. ★ **MEMBERSHIPS:** James Beard Foundation; Academy of Television Arts & Sciences.

Salary notes:

It's tricky because I have two different roles: the one at the magazine, and then everything I do for *Food & Wine* in relation to *Top Chef.* Most people would do one or the other. At another magazine without the show, my title would be events director, and the salary range would be $75,000 to $150,000.

Words of advice for people considering a similar career:

Have a general plan, but don't get too bogged down in feeling that you need to have a plan. Be open to the doors around you. Those doors often turn into great opportunities if you take the step.

Describe what you do.

I'm the director of the *Food & Wine* Classic in Aspen, which takes place every year in June. That's what I do for my job. If I didn't do television, this would be 70 percent of my job. The other 30 percent would be working on key partnerships at events the magazine works with, like the festivals in South Beach, New York, and Pebble Beach, and working with chefs around the country on different events. At this point it takes more like 40, 45 percent of my time, depending on the time of year. Sometimes it's all I'm doing. But we are a great team, the four of us who work on it all year. All of the marketing department is also involved, in some way or another, and the editor in chief—there's a huge team in Aspen. I'm technically part of the marketing department.

Over the last four years, since I've been with *Food & Wine,* my job has changed a little bit; I've done more and more media work. It's started small, and now it's taken over more of my job, where I represent the magazine as a spokesperson. I started taking on this role before *Top Chef.* The person I replaced was doing quite a bit of TV; they needed a strong media person, because the editor in chief, Dana Cowin, didn't have time to do it all. When I worked at Daniel Boulud, I did a lot of PR, I had contacts, I had been behind the scenes a lot, so I knew the landscape. When I came they asked me if I would take a stab at doing more media and sent me through media training. They put me through a quick TV news segment. About a year later, Bravo came and talked to us about *Top Chef.* I did a screen test and I got the job. There were a few of us up for it. Apparently I struck a chord with the executive producer. They said that part of why I got the job was that I told a story of how I once cried because someone sent me the wrong food at a restaurant.

How many hours a week do you typically work?

About sixty hours. It depends on the time of year. When filming *Top Chef,* fourteen to fifteen hours a day. When we are on the air, I write a blog and do weekend events and TV appearances. I might not be sitting at my desk sixty hours a week, but I'm doing work-related things.

What are your specific responsibilities?

At the classic, I oversee every aspect: all sponsorship, talent, advertisers, venue, exhibitors, volunteers, pass registration, VIP card members, signage, artwork, creating the 150-page program, evening programs, etc. I need to look at all the details

while keeping the event running. *Food & Wine* is a presenting sponsor of the South Beach and New York City Wine & Food Festivals (I use those as examples; we do more). We sometimes bring our own advertisers to help with sponsorships, so we manage that. Sometimes we bring in chefs and talents, so I manage all aspects of that. We have to make sure that the sponsor's presence is acknowledged correctly. I also do a lot of on-site press. I might judge a cooking presentation.

Do you need a culinary degree to work at *Food & Wine*?

I wouldn't say that you need a culinary degree, but in the whole marketing department, there are at least three of us who have gone to culinary school, because you need to speak that language with the chefs we work with, to plan demos, dinners, etc. It also helps you to think about the details. We also do many cooking segments on TV. We have to demonstrate recipes, prep for it, think strategically, break down a recipe, make sure we have extra food for subbing, for the beauty shot. My culinary degree has proved very beneficial. I would never have gotten the job if not for my culinary school training.

What qualities do you look for in a new hire?

They have to be detail oriented, dedicated, and loyal. We want people who understand the brand. *Food & Wine* has been around for thirty years; we have a specific point of view, a specific way in which we see the world. I want someone who is thinking and is a problem solver and with whom there's synergy. We work long hours together; we travel together. We get really great work done and have fun. Our team is in Aspen for two weeks in a condo all together.

What do you like most about what you do?

I love how diverse it is. I don't have a typical day, and I love that. When I left culinary school, I worked in restaurants as a cook. But before that was writing. I always knew I wanted to write. I didn't want to stay in the kitchen, but I knew it would make my skills stronger and help me to be taken seriously. I love cooking but found that I wasn't using my brain the way I wanted to in the kitchen. Especially when you're a young cook right out of school. I was never a chef, just a cook. You have to be a cook for a long time; no one out of culinary school can be a chef. A chef is leader of a team, and you need years of experience to become that. So when you're a cook, it's mostly manual labor, not creative work. I found that I missed the strategic thinking, the intellectualism that I wasn't getting in the kitchen. What I love so much about my job now is that I get both. I get to cook, use my hands, taste food constantly, use my cook-

ing skills, but also use my brain, write a lot, problem-solve. There's a duality to my job; it doesn't have to be one or the other.

What do you like least about it?

The biggest challenge is managing people, being a boss. I love being a boss, having a team of people, working with a team, mentoring them. But it's a hard thing to do well. You don't realize until you become a boss what pressure it is. You want people to do well without micromanaging them, but at the same time you have to give them guidance. I can only hope to be a good boss and a good example, thanks to the good examples I've been given. I've had amazing mentors. A piece of advice I can give to anyone is to find really good mentors to learn from.

What skills are most important for you to do your job well?

Precision, flexibility, adaptability. Being positive, having really good relationships. Being able to have a really great attitude, being comfortable with myself and the people around me, being positive and enthusiastic about what I do. It's very important when managing people.

PAMELA MITCHELL

As executive food editor of *Every Day with Rachael Ray*—one of the fastest growing-magazines in the country, with a circulation of 1,766,692—Pamela Mitchell is responsible for all the food content of the magazine. This job is the most recent in a long line of magazine editorial positions that she has held over the years.

CURRENT POSITION: Executive food editor, *Every Day with Rachael Ray,* since July 2006, five issues into the launch. ★ **EDUCATION:** BA, theater studies, Connecticut College, New London, CT; culinary arts degree, Institute of Culinary Education, New York, NY. ★ **CAREER PATH:** Cofounder and baker, Sweet Satisfaction Catering, Monterey, CA (1982–1983). In New York: advertising sales representative, *Women's Sports and Fitness* (1983–1985); assistant food editor, *House Beautiful* (1985–1986); associate editor, Irena Chalmers Books, Inc. (1986–1988); associate editor (1988–1994) and senior editor (1994–1996), *Food & Wine;* food editor and managing editor, International Masters Publishers, Inc. (1996–1998); managing editor, *Child* (1999–2000); senior editor, *Departures* (2000–2001); senior editor, *Everyday Food* (2001–2002); freelance editor (2003–2004); managing editor, *Saveur* (2004–2005); food editor, *All You* (2005–2006).

Salary notes:

Assistants, such as editorial assistants, get $25,000 to $30,000. An associate food editor should be making around $50,000. A food editor should be making around $70,000. At the executive level, depending on the company, between $90,000 and $120,000.

Words of advice for people considering a similar career:

Keep at it. Stick to it. Be diligent. Before I went to cooking school, I knocked on the door at *Food & Wine;* I had my eye set on it. I knocked on their door four times, and I finally got in because I went to Peter Kump's [ICE]. Someone else would have given up. I'm sure there's an element of fate, of luck, in all of those things, but perseverance pays off in the end. This is not to say put all your eggs in one basket. Always compromise. You need to *not* put all your eggs in one basket.

Describe a typical day.

They are all different. I love my position, because I get to delegate. It's a wonderful role, because I have more than twenty years of food editing experience, and I feel like I have something to offer, something to teach. At least 25 percent of my day is giving advice to junior staff: how to assign an article, how to talk to an author, what recipe should we do, what direction should the piece take. People ask to go over layout issues: Should we add a Web feature, did I edit this right? I devised a recipe routing schedule, and now my assistant runs it. I take care of procedural things and I coordinate schedules. Management is a big part of the job. Then I am the top editor of the department: Any recipes or food-related articles have to pass over my desk, in several stages. For food stories, I see the text and recipes. For lifestyle and entertainment stories, I see the recipes. It's a long process from the start of an idea to the finish. We also have to build in test-kitchen time.

We're always working on three issues at a time. We are working on proofs for February, manuscript for March, development for April. That requires a great deal of management and organization. I'm either editing a manuscript on the computer file or proofs of the actual issue. I read first and final proofs over a one-to-two-week period. There's a lot of upper-management stuff in this position. We just finished our first special-interest publication, for the holidays. A select group was asked to work on that. So on top of our regular job, we were editing this other magazine. I also work with special projects, with the Web— we have a very integrated Web team. Administrative things also come up. We have an initiative called Smart Spending, where we have to watch our budget. I'm on the task team that watches costs. Every month I have a meeting with the marketing and sales team where I debrief them on what food stories are coming up. We have photo meetings once a month, weekly production meetings, monthly brainstorming meetings, various forward-looking and administrative meetings.

A huge part is also testing food. Every day, we test five to ten recipes. The test-kitchen staff has a flexible schedule. They work two days at home and three days in the office. When they are both in the office, we taste about ten recipes, otherwise about five. The associate editor might test too if it's a busy time. I'm in the kitchen every time something is tested—I'm the final palate to say yes or no. But it's a very demo-cratic place. I want it that way. It's very collaborative. We come up with story ideas together, we taste food together. At weekly food-department meetings, I see how their load is and we work out kinks.

I hate doing TV, so I don't do that. But I do PR and publicity demos about five times a year. I review the scripts for our Web videos.

How many hours a week do you typically work?

Nine A.M. to six thirty P.M. is pretty much standard here. During a close, once or twice a month we might be here until nine. It's very decent, and I try to keep it that way.

What skills are most important for you to do your job well?

You have to be good with people. That's the primary one. You need patience, because you are working up, with your own bosses, and down, with your staff. Communication skills—keeping everyone on the same page. I want everyone to know what everyone is working on so that everyone can collaborate. Being open, so that the staff feels comfortable coming and talking to me. Good organization skills—you have to juggle several things at once. Being on top of your scheduling and deadlines. You have to have a good palate. You need to have gone through cooking school to be in this position. All the people in the food department went to cooking school, aside from the editorial assistant, who came through the editorial side. You could make it up, but you would still need to take some classes; you need some sort of formal training.

Training allows you to make a recipe better and more efficient. Being a team player, especially at the executive level—you want to work well with all levels.

What is the outlook for your type of job?

Rachael could burn out—she runs herself ragged. When she started, she just said and made it clear, "Cooking can just be fun; I would rather have you make a simple meal that is doable than go to a fast-food store." She got that message out there and believes it. I feel good that it's part of our message. The magazine is very lively and fun and chatty.

STACEY BRUGEMAN

Stacey Brugeman transitioned from a career in public relations to one in food writing and editing in 2004. After working on staff at *Food & Wine,* she moved to Colorado and turned to freelance full-time. She writes a column for *Denver Magazine* and articles for local and national publications.

CURRENT POSITION: Freelance food, beverage, and travel writer and editor, Denver, CO, since 2008; columnist, *Denver Magazine.* ★ **EDUCATION:** BA, history, University of Virginia, Charlottesville, VA (1997); MA, food studies, New York University, NY (2007); intermediate certificate in wine, International Wine Center, New York; food and wine seminars and classes at the Institute of Culinary Education, New York University, the City University of New York, and the American Society of Magazine Editors, all in New York. ★ **CAREER PATH:** End-user specialist and district sales representative, Black and Decker Inc., Hoboken, NJ (1997–1998). In New York: account executive, account manager, and assistant vice president, Morgen Walke Associates Inc. (1998–2001); account supervisor and vice president, Aronow and Pollock Communications Inc. (2001–2003); editorial assistant, *Saveur* (2004); assistant editor and research editor, *Food & Wine* (2004–2007). ★ **AWARDS AND RECOGNITION:** PR awards; 2006 American Express Publishing Pubby Award for Best New Editorial Platform (team award).

Salary notes:

It depends on so many things. At most magazines, you're paid by the word, but it also depends on your experience and tenure, and on the budget of the title. A city magazine will pay less than a national one. Someone just starting out will get paid much less than someone very famous whom a magazine really wants to have. For city magazines, I've heard as low as thirty cents a word, up to $2 to $3. At a national magazine, from $1 to $4 or $5, to the sky is the limit for famous writers. I'm somewhere in the middle of those ranges.

Words of advice for people considering a similar career:

Be humble in the beginning. It may take that unpaid internship or unpaid article for your alumni magazine to establish a portfolio of published work and get your foot in the door.

Describe a typical day.

I work in my kitchen, with my laptop set up and my Rolodex, files, a huge bookshelf of cookbooks and food books beside me. I spend a lot of time pitching new stories, writing for existing assignments, and writing expense sheets and things like that. Then I'm out and about. I might have a drink with a sommelier at a wine bar at three P.M. because that's when he's available. I might have lunch with a chef for an interview. I've been to Sonoma recently on a press trip to learn about this wine region. I work on the weekends, too. When you write about this topic, you're thinking about it all the time because you eat three times a day. We were entertaining guests last weekend, so we ate at brand-new places so that I could check them out. Those are just examples of the last ten days.

I don't follow a schedule as much as I follow my creative moments. If some great lead for a story comes to me on a Sunday, I won't hesitate to go in and write. If I'm behind, I might work on weekends. But in general I don't really fall behind. I also choose to not overpitch. The work-life balance is superb. But it is not the road to oodles of cash. You can certainly make a living, but a modest living. I do it because I love it. The love of my work has become much more valuable for me than the six figures I was making in public relations.

How many hours a week do you typically work?

I have no idea. It can change from week to week. I don't keep track, but because I cover food and wine, my brain is always on; there's such a great link between my personal interest and the way I explore it professionally. I just get my projects done in however long it takes me.

What do you like least about it?

Working from home is wonderful in most ways, but it can be isolating. It takes a conscious effort to keep in touch with a lot of people, with my sources and my sources of inspiration. I have to go out and meet people for breakfast, lunch, dinner, wine. I would caution anyone who is not self-motivated.

What skills are most important for you to do your job well?

Curiosity, vocabulary, self-motivation. I think you need a surprising amount of business savvy. You have to market yourself, know people, and be connected. When on staff, you're there and everything is handed to you. When you freelance, you

have to sell yourself and get the assignment. I'm grateful for my business experience; I use those skills every day.

How did you establish connections when moving to Denver?

The caliber of the titles I worked for in New York helped. Also, editors here are not as bombarded as they are in New York, so they read their e-mail more thoroughly. Also because of my topic, living in New York gave me a particular expertise. If I wanted to cover rock climbing, I wouldn't have gone far, but eating in New York helped.

Describe your creative process.

I'll see something or hear of something that would make a great story. Then I think of whom it'd make a great story for, which title and which audience. Who at this publication is the right person to pitch? Who do I know, how do I get in there? Then there's that moment where it changes from your original idea to the idea that the magazine has. Sometimes it may be the same; sometimes they may like part of your idea and the rest changes. I research the hell out of a topic. Then the hard part is to take all that knowledge and boil it down to a few hundred words. That's where writing skills come in, to make the story concise and interesting. That's the process. Then I turn in the story—on time, of course. I have some editors who hardly change a thing and run it almost as is. Then there are other editors who can only envision something in their voice or their way, so they change it up and we go back and forth. You get used to that. You have to have a pretty thick skin when it comes to the editing process.

MARCIA GAGLIARDI

Marcia Gagliardi is a freelance writer for many San Francisco–based and national publications, but she is perhaps most known for her weekly column, "The Tablehopper," which includes restaurant reviews, bar news, restaurant gossip, and announcements and goes out via e-mail to ten thousand subscribers.

CURRENT POSITION: Freelance food writer; founder, tablehopper.com, San Francisco, CA. **EDUCATION:** BA, world literature and English, UCLA. ★ **CAREER PATH:** In San Francisco: writer, restaurant and nightlife reviews, Citysearch.com; *Where Magazine*'s "Hot Tips—Dining" columnist (2004); regional managing editor for Northern California, Gayot.com (2006–2008); weekly column, Foodie 411, San Francisco Convention & Visitors Bureau; monthly gossip column, "The Tablehopper"; freelance writing for *Northside San Francisco, Travel + Leisure, Fodor's, San Francisco* magazine, *Travel Weekly, Where* magazine, *Dining Out Magazine, Edible San Francisco,* and *San Francisco Bay Guardian;* contributor, "*BlackBook* List: San Francisco 2006." ★ **AWARDS AND RECOGNITION:** Most Obsessive Restaurant Informant, *7x7* magazine; Best of the Bay Area 2008: Readers' Choice for Best Blog for Getting the Scoop on Food; Best Fresh Scuttlebutt, *San Francisco Bay Guardian.*

Salary notes:

Anywhere from $30,000 to $70,000, depending on how much you hustle. You start on the low end and can command more when you start writing for national magazines. I remember writing thousand-word articles for $100 when starting.

Words of advice for people considering a similar career:

Make sure that you have other ways to make money. I am very grateful that I could do copywriting at the beginning of my career so that I could make money while following my passion. You really only earn scraps at the beginning. You need to make money somehow. Believe that what you can do can be different and relevant. Yes, there are lots of food writers out there, but the really good ones stand out. It's important to find your identity as a writer.

Describe a typical day.

The hardest part is that I get about two hundred e-mails a day, so I'm constantly trying to keep my in-box low. I feel like I'm a conduit for a lot of people, so I get a lot of questions. People want me to connect them with people. I make lots of phone calls to follow up on leads. I'm constantly following up on stories for "Tablehopper." Since I freelance, too, I have deadlines every week in addition to that. My writing happens in the afternoon, once I have gotten a handle on the day. I don't do too many lunches, because I'm out six nights a week, often to several locations a night. I might start at a bar, party, or launch event, then a dinner, then a bar or an after-party. I have at least two destinations each night. I have meetings with people, I tour restaurant spaces, I conduct interviews for stories. I work every day—I don't have a day off. Every week the one thing that is the same is that on Monday I am home writing and fact-checking "Tablehopper." Tuesday is the day I edit "Tablehopper" and that's the day we post it. From nine A.M. to three P.M. I'm super busy, then I leave the house, go for a walk, for yoga. Sometimes during the week I will give myself some time off to go to lunch with someone or go shopping, or go on an overnight trip for research. If you are a media guest, they don't want you there on weekends. I get a lot done on weekends when I write, because people don't e-mail and call as much. I get my groceries and dry cleaning done during the week and then I work on weekends.

How many hours a week do you typically work?

Forty to sixty-five. Even though I'm eating out, it's still work; I'm taking notes, asking questions to the chef, paying attention to everything the whole time. It adds up.

What are your specific responsibilities?

To report on what is happening on the San Francisco restaurant scene. To write about new or established restaurants that are good. I only write up places that I like. Managing all the press releases I get, keeping track of all the events happening. It's a lot of data procurement, scouting, following up, and then writing about it. I read about 150 RSS feeds, most about food, cocktails, restaurants. Every week I read Chowhound and all the food magazines.

What do you like most about what you do?

I cannot believe how many passionate people I get to meet. It's really invigorating. I love the pleasure in this field—chefs like feeding people, making people feel good. I love the creativity in this field, whether in the restaurant design or the food itself. It's a very good community—people are very supportive. I love knowing the city very well, the best places to go and eat and drink and get the best coffee, go on the best date, where to take your parents. That's really a pleasure.

What do you like least about it?

I never turn off. Everything kind of turns into work. Everything I eat, everywhere I go, could become a story. It's hard to go on a date; I'm going to run into someone I know. It's hard to take a day off. The e-mails are getting burdensome. I'd like to not be so scheduled all the time. Eventually it's going to take having an assistant and setting up different e-mail accounts for different things. I have one intern right now, but it's tricky since it's also my personal life.

What skills are most important for you to do your job well?

Definitely organization, because I'm constantly receiving information. I am constantly working on different documents at once. I keep track of all my phone calls. I list in my daily calendar whom I need to call that day. I'm very diligent about deadlines every day, especially writing deadlines. So when I look at my calendar every week I've planned for it, and if I have a deadline I'll be home early the night before. Having a good memory, listening to people. Being available has really helped. My readers send in tips. A lot of people trust me; they know that if they say, "Off the record," it will stay that way. I never gossip until the story can come out. Be a little fearless. Don't be afraid to find your voice.

What skills would you like to develop to help further your career?

I would love to start pursuing my master's in wine. It'd be great to be certified. I would love to go to cooking school. I would love ongoing education and classes. I really would love to work with someone to manage new business development for me. I have so many ideas, but it's hard for me to execute everything because I have to work to make money.

What prompted you to start this e-newsletter?

Total frustration. I was pitching stories to magazines and not hearing back. There was so much happening in San Francisco and no way to write about it all. I didn't want to do a blog because there were so many blogs. I realized there was no weekly e-newsletter about food, which was surprising. So I came up with this idea. I looked at my Rolodex and realized that I knew a lot of people. All my friends have known me as being the restaurant maven, so I thought it was time to share the knowledge.

What are your long-term goals?

One of them is happening right now, because I'm working on a book. That was a big thing. I'd love to have a TV show and a radio show about dining. I also plan on launching "Tablehopper" in different cities. I see "Tablehopper" being a multimedia entity but with different end points.

MOLLY WIZENBERG

Molly Wizenberg started blogging when she quit graduate school because she had always loved writing but wasn't sure she was ready yet to do it full-time. Since then, her blog has been named Best Blog in the World by the *Times* of London (2009), she has made the transition to a successful writing career, and she got married—to a chef who contacted her through her blog. They opened the restaurant Delancey in August 2009.

CURRENT POSITION: Freelancer writer (since 2007); blogger, Orangette (orangette .blogspot.com; since 2004); columnist, *Bon Appétit;* author, *A Homemade Life* (2009), Seattle, WA. ★ **EDUCATION:** BA, human biology, Stanford University; MA, cultural anthropology, University of Washington. **CAREER PATH:** Instructor, English conversation, Saintoux, France; intern, then editorial assistant, University of Washington Press. ★ **AWARDS AND RECOGNITION:** Food Blog Awards: Best Overall Food Blog (2005); Best Food Blog Writing (2006); Best Blog in the World, London *Times* (2009).

Words of advice for people considering a similar career:

You just have to go after it. You have to sit down and write, and write about what moves you. If you write about things you really care about, that energy and enthusiasm is contagious. Don't get fatigued, and do stick your neck out.

Describe a typical day.

I don't have a typical day. I'm not one of those people who sit down at the computer and log in four hours of work. I spend much of the morning attending to e-mail, things related to my business, such as invoicing and responding to readers' questions. If I have a piece of writing to do, I'll work on it in the afternoon and evening. There are many days when I am not writing, I'm just gathering information and testing recipes. I do a lot of photography.

How many hours a week do you typically work?

About twenty hours actually writing. Because my primary medium has been the Internet, I've tended to be fairly available to people. So I spend a huge amount of time, easily thirty hours a week, responding to e-mails, maintaining relationships, invoicing, things like that.

What are your specific responsibilities?

There are two ways of answering this. On the one end I have specific responsibilities, deadlines I've set up for my blog or that magazine editors have set up for me. Second, so much of what I write about is about everyday life—one of my responsibilities is also to gather inspiration. I feel terribly hokey saying that, but I need to make sure that I give myself plenty of time to stare out the window and read books, go to museums, things like that. I never beat myself up for taking time off. I know that's what I need to meet my deadline, so I do work that is less direct. But gathering information is as much part of my work. When I first left the University of Washington Press to focus on writing full-time, I thought that to get anything done I would have to set a strict schedule for myself. I quickly discovered that I don't work well that way. I have to allow myself the time to float around and fill my head with all kinds of ideas.

What do you like most about what you do?

On the most basic level, I feel incredibly lucky to do work that I love and that I feel is meaningful to me. But on another level, I really like being able to do work that makes others happy. Food has a unique effect on people. Especially when you're combining food with memories, family, loss, and love—all these things that we experience every day—it's very powerful. The response I've gotten is that my work makes people happy. I hadn't thought about that until people started telling me. And that's really meaningful to me.

What do you like least about it?

There's a tricky part of what I do. Being on the Internet makes me a somewhat public person. I like exchanging ideas with people and e-mailing them, but it opens me to some nastiness. That's just one of the difficult parts—being available to people in a way that sometimes they say mean things to me.

What skills are most important for you to do your job well?

Self-discipline. That doesn't necessarily mean that I hold myself to a rigid schedule but does mean that at some point I sit down and get the job done. The ability to listen, to listen to other people's stories, to be present with other people. I'm always in-terested in other people's experiences with food; that's a huge part of where I draw my work from. Also, perseverance. Even though I am getting to do work that I love, it's really hard. It's a very cerebral, in-my-head kind of difficult. It requires a lot of perseverance, sometimes, to get the words out of my head and onto paper.

What prompted you to start a blog?

I had just decided to quit graduate school. That had been the culmination of many realizations. I had always loved to write but never gave it a real shot because I think I was afraid to rely on it for a living. I had always loved to cook—making dinner had always been the high point of my day. I realized that I liked writing and cooking more than grad school. I had this dream that maybe one day I would write for a food magazine, but I had nothing to go toward that. A journalist friend said, "You should start a blog; who knows, maybe one day that would be a portfolio to show editors."

How did you decide on its concept?

It kind of chose me. When I first started, I was just ecstatic to have made that decision to leave graduate school. I was just so excited to have this blank space to fill every day with what I did that day. So I just wrote. Then two to three months into it, I wrote something about making sourdough bread. There was something I really liked about that piece; it felt like it had a beginning, a middle, and an end. So I kept trying to tap into whatever had felt so right that time. As I went along I realized that what had felt so right was that it was a story.

Food is a very tangible way to get at things that are intangible. Food is a way to learn about a city that we live in, about the people we love. That's the direction that the blog has taken. At the beginning, I was writing every other day or so; then, because of necessity, I slowed down a bit. I realized that the posts I liked took more time to write. About two years ago, I cut back to one day a week, and that way I could give the post the attention it deserved.

How do writing for the Web and writing for print relate and differ?

I feel that the type of writing I do about food is for both print and the Web. When I write for the blog, my writing is more rooted in my daily life; it's a bit more casual and spontaneous. When writing for print, I want it to feel a little bit more timeless. I try to tell a story that is rooted in perhaps a larger experience. Maybe I write a little bit more formally for magazines or for my book. Online feels like sitting down with a group of friends; it feels very much like a conversation. I have about eight thousand unique visitors a day.

"You just have to go after it. You have to sit down and write, and write about what moves you. If you write about things you really care about, that energy and enthusiasm is contagious. Don't get fatigued, and do stick your neck out.."

JEANNIE CHEN

Jeannie Chen works as a freelance food stylist for television shows and recipe developer and tester for television and print projects. She works on many Food Network projects, in addition to shows filmed by other production companies, and with large food corporations.

CURRENT POSITION: Freelance food stylist and recipe developer and tester, New York, NY, since 2002, www.jeanniechen.com. ★ **EDUCATION:** BFA, fashion design, Parsons School of Design, New York, NY (1994); culinary arts degree and additional classes, Institute of Culinary Education, New York, NY (2002). ★ **CAREER PATH:** In New York: extern, Food Network test kitchens; cake decorator/production manager, Buttercup Bake Shop; production assistant, Sara's Secrets; caterer. Television food styling/production experience: Taylor Public Relations, AOL Productions, Real Simple Productions, DWJ Television, True Entertainment Productions, Food Network, Follow Productions, Stonehouse Productions. Print food styling experience: *Fine Cooking,* Food Network. Recipe development/testing experience: B. Smith, Unilever Best Foods, Food Network, James Peterson, *Food & Wine, Wine Spectator.* ★ **MEMBERSHIPS:** International Association of Culinary Professionals; New York Women's Culinary Alliance.

Salary notes:

Food styling ranges from $175 for ten hours or beyond, with no overtime (because we are not union), to $900 a day for a satellite media tour, because that's really hard and you might work two jobs, props and food. It's lower for print: $500 a day maximum. Recipe development pays $100 to $150 a recipe, then $25 an hour, or $200 to $450 a day.

Words of advice for people considering a similar career:

You want to go into this career because you have a love for it, not because it could get you a show or allow you to meet the talent. Ego is not going to get you anywhere. People will automatically detect that love and desire in you. Volunteer as much as you can, and work hard at it. I would hire back a lot of interns because they did a great job on set; others I wouldn't, because they just sat around. While you can intern, do so. People will take chances with someone who works for free, while you can't do that with an assistant stylist.

Describe a typical day.

It's early call time for TV: six or seven A.M. You always work a day ahead. You prep all the recipes the day before with your team. I read through the script again, I pull out all the dishes prepped the day before. If we're working as a team, each person is in charge of a recipe. I sit down with them and they tell me exactly what they did because I'm the one on set. I put the food in chronological order on the table right outside the set. When the talent is ready, I walk through the script with the talent, talking about how they are going to cook it, about exactly what the recipe is. They need the reminder, unless it's Emeril, who's been doing it for so long. I sit at the ready in case something needs to be adjusted. I will cover whatever problem there is on set. At the end of the segment, we clear off the kitchen, place everything in the kitchen for the next segment, and walk the talent through again. Meanwhile I'm coordinating the team for the following day of shooting. They can only ask me questions during the downtime of the shoot. At the end of the day, after my assistant clears off the set, I spend another hour or two going through everything with my team, to know exactly where everything is for the next day's shoot, what's going on, etc. In the morning, they remind me again. There's no room for mistakes. If we do one show a day, about three segments, I could have only one assistant, up to three. If it's a veteran talent who can do three to four segments a day, I have four to five assistants and extra interns. It is such a different process.

TV and print are like night and day. Once you master television, you can do print. It's harder the other way around, because you need to master the process of the script.

How many hours a week do you typically work?

Before having kids, I worked five to six days a week and lots of weekend work—twelve-hour averages, sometimes up to sixteen. Now I work three to four days, for about ten hours. I try not to do Food Network shows anymore—they are too much work. I focus on recipe development and

cookbook development. That kind of stuff I do from home.

What are your specific responsibilities?

For food styling, to make sure that all the food is ready and that all the ingredients are available, to the talent's specifications. If he or she doesn't like it, I'm screwed. It's my fault. The director and producer don't care. I really have to please the talent. If the recipe doesn't work out at the end, I still have to figure it out, even if it looked like it worked on TV.

What do you like least about it?

The hours. Sometimes the drama, the people. And that's pretty much it. I love creating the food and being challenged by the script. I love the challenge of each different project I have.

What skills are most important for you to do your job well?

Being extremely organized. We're talking different markers, different highlighters.

What skills would you like to develop to help further your career?

There are some techniques I wish I knew a little bit better, to be able to cook them blindly when I get to a shoot. But that's not the case because I don't use them that often. I'm not going to bake bread every day to be able to style bread.

Describe your creative process.

With food styling, it's a little hard sometimes. I usually work with a prop stylist. I have to read the recipe ahead of time to visualize what the dish looks like. If it's a casserole, I go to the prop stylist and she'll give me options, a lot of visualization. If I'm not too sure, I will usually sit down with the talent and ask questions. Then I get an idea and translate to the prop stylist, who will pull out dishes for me. Then the talent will plate it and I will beautify it for the beauty shot. For print, sometimes the person took a photo of the dish without styling it, to give me an idea of what he or she wants, so I'll try to replicate that idea.

For recipe development, Unilever might say, "We want you to make an Asian soup for this product." I will go through my entire Asian book library. If I find something that strikes my fancy, I will use it as inspiration. If it's something close, I might pull it from memory. I write all the ingredients out and what the recipe requires. Then they give me a recipe development sheet, and I fill in the blanks. It's very methodical.

What is the outlook for your type of job?

There's a continuous need for food stylists, because cooking shows have gotten so big. Other networks are catching on, so there are openings for more food stylists. There are also webisodes and websites, so the need might continue to grow but more on the digital side.

LAUREN DELLABELLA

Lauren Dellabella is a test kitchen group manager for Unilever, the international corporation. Her division, Unilever Consumer Kitchens, ensures that the products developed by the company will find their way to consumers' kitchens by assisting food scientists with flavor development, coming up with product ideas, developing recipes that use those products and clear directions for their use, maintaining the consumer website, and presenting product ideas to sales and development teams, among other things.

CURRENT POSITION: Test Kitchen Group Manager, Unilever, Englewood Cliffs, NJ, since 1998. ★ **EDUCATION:** BS, home economics with concentration on foods and nutrition, Montclair University, Montclair, NJ. ★ **CAREER PATH:** Hospital nutritionist; test kitchen, Panasonic; microwave and food appliance department, *Good Housekeeping*; consultant. ★ **MEMBERSHIPS:** International Association of Culinary Professionals; Consumer Trends Forum International; International Microwave Power Institute.

Salary notes:

Someone just starting would make about $50,000 in a corporate test kitchen.

Describe a typical day.

It's more project management. We don't do much cooking—that's more for our consultants. Every day is different. We might do a recipe showing, a food showing. What we do every day is test a lot of food. We taste and give guidelines for recipes. Everything we do is very strategic. We know who our consumer is and approach our work strategically before starting a recipe-development project, deciding how many ingredients the recipe should have, which tools to use based on what we know our customers have at home, if our customers have family at home. We give those guidelines to our consultants, who then develop the recipes, which are entered in an editorial database and released to our website. We're a global company. We may have our management come from Europe, so we'll do a showing of our product innovations from all over the world. We will work with marketing groups and do team-building exercises to get them familiar with brands and recipes. It's different all the time, because we have so many brands. It keeps the job diverse and exciting. Two weeks ago, I went to Los Angeles for the Golden Globes because we were doing gift bags, and I supervised the food there. We wear so many different hats, from the scientific to the creative. One minute you are carefully measuring and keeping temperatures, the next you are coordinating events on- and off-site, the next brainstorming a recipe. We all love our jobs and have an incredible passion for food.

How many hours a week do you typically work?

I have a job-share, so I work three days a week, and sometimes more as needed. I'm supposed to work twenty-four hours a week—that's what I get paid for. But I put in the time as needed.

What are your specific responsibilities?

We have so many brands—we divide them up. We have three teams: consumer, professional, specialist. Together with my job sharer, Annamarie Cesario, we handle all the multibrand events. So if there's something with three of our brands, we handle that. We provide website support for all our brands. Makinglifebetter.com is our corporate brand; we provide content and expert advice for it. We have editorial responsibilities, so we are the editors of all the recipes that our brands have. We coordinate the special events that we have. We are involved in the Keystone Project: Everybody has their own nutritional guidelines, which the industry has realized is confusing for the consumers, so the industry has come together to create a Smart Choice label, which will be an industry-wide standard.

What skills are most important for you to do your job well?

I would say, with us, it's flexibility. You have to be able to put on your scientific and your creative hats and go back and forth between the two. Culinary skills are important. The more you have the better off you'll be. Some basic training is essential. But we have people who work with us who are self-trained, who have a knack and can grow on the job. People should get some sort of hands-on experience. We take many interns.

How large is your team?

We have six people on staff, plus a large bank of consultants—two to eight on a daily basis. We also work with food stylists and food photographers. We probably have over twenty consultants.

What qualities do you look for in a new hire?

It depends on the need at the time. Two positions ago, we were looking for someone with Hispanic expertise, because that market is growing so much. The following time, we were looking for someone with a nutrition background. We look for people who have food and test-kitchen experience. Because there are not many jobs in this area, we get many qualified applicants every time. We find consultants through word of mouth. We can bring them in for a couple of days, and if they don't work out we don't bring them back. We have many consultants who have grown with us. Our company is a nice place to consult because we invest in our consultants. We're very loyal to them and they are very loyal to us.

Describe your creative process.

You always work in teams. If a new product comes out, we look at what's out there in supermarkets and restaurants. For our Bertolli frozen line, we scout restaurants and supermarkets. We have tastings for the brand team to stimulate people into thinking about what the consumers would like. Eating the food stimulates a whole new thinking process. What would you like your new product to look like? What pasta and sauce varieties do we need, what new trends are there? With a food company, you are not trendsetting, because consumers are not ready for that. By the time we come out with them, they are at the mainstream level. Typically you look at white-tablecloth restaurants and see trends start there, then you see them filter down to fast-casual restaurants, then by the time it's in chains you know it's everywhere. We are the voice of the consumers; we're always thinking about what they want.

"Home economics is the older and more traditional route. Now a lot more people are coming to test kitchens out of culinary schools, with short- or long-term degrees."

CARRIE BACHMAN

Carrie Bachman launched her full-service boutique public relations firm specializing in the cookbook and gourmet product industry in 2006. She works with about six clients at a time and has represented more than 350 cookbooks.

CURRENT POSITION: Owner, Carrie Bachman Public Relations, Short Hills, NJ, since 2006, www.carriebachman.com. ★ **EDUCATION:** Bachelor's degree in communications with concentration in public relations, University of Delaware; complete series of technique classes at the Institute of Culinary Education. ★ **CAREER PATH:** In New York: account executive, Hunter Public Relations, working on accounts like Kraft and Tabasco (1992–1996); director of publicity for cookbooks and lifestyle, William Morrow/HarperCollins (1996–2006). ★ **MEMBERSHIPS:** New York Women's Culinary Alliance; local group of freelance publicists.

Salary notes:

More than $100,000, depending on the number and scope of the projects taken on per year.

Words of advice for people considering a similar career:

You get great experience working at a public relations firm; a lot of firms specialize in food products. What's great about those is that they come up with really fun, interesting ideas. Those projects teach you to be really creative and think out of the box and give you a different way to look at food. When making the switch to cookbooks, you work with a lot of the same people. Working on food products gives you an edge because it makes you think creatively. You learn how to be a good publicist at those places before you go out on your own. And it's important to network and really get out there to meet people in the industry.

What prompted you to open your own business?

When I left HarperCollins, they were cutting back on their cookbooks and laid off their two cookbook publicists. But they offered me work on their cookbooks on a freelance basis. Everyone moves around a lot in publishing, so even though I only worked at HarperCollins I knew people at all these other publishing companies. They hired me to work on their cookbooks. Being very honest and being a hard worker, having a strong work ethic, getting along with pretty much any author, you get referred to people. Establishing relationships is very important.

Describe a typical day.

I have meetings in the city two days a week, literally back to back—breakfast, lunch, coffee after lunch, etc. I meet with producers, editors, people I used to work with in the industry, and I network for new business. The other three days, I really need to be sitting at my desk, doing e-mails, pitching. I usually start with an e-mail and follow up by phone. On Wednesdays I read all the big food sections. I try to go to book parties, restaurant openings, events, because those are a great way to see people and network.

How many hours a week do you typically work?

Ten hours a day, so about fifty hours a week. But they are hours that I get to pick. Fall and spring are always busy.

What are your specific responsibilities?

Getting my authors broadcast and print placements in newspapers, magazines, TV, radio. Setting up events, book signings; securing their participation in various events. I also work on spokespeople opportunities for my clients. At the end of the day, a book that sells is what I strive for the most. I'm not necessarily paid to sell the book, I'm paid to get publicity, but going beyond that and having it really sell is what I want.

What do you like most about what you do?

I love meeting new people. But it's also a very small, tight-knit community, and I love reconnecting with authors I haven't worked with for a decade. Traveling and meeting an author, eating at an author's restaurant. Going to festivals and book signings. I like that it's different every day.

What do you like least about it?

Working with authors who have unrealistic expectations. One of the things that's most important on a day-to-day basis is managing expectations. No, you're not getting on *Oprah.*

What skills are most important for you to do your job well?

You have to be disciplined. A lot of people couldn't work from home. I get up, I shower, and I'm in my office all day long. I don't get up. You have to be creative—why should someone write about my cookbook rather than another cookbook? You need to have good writing skills, good pitching skills, and now social media skills.

What are your long-term goals?

I'm very happy working freelance and getting to pick and choose my projects. I have two young children; while they are still in the house, being freelance definitely gives me flexibility. I can take off if they have something at school and work at night. I love being my own boss. I work by myself, but I'm constantly talking on the phone and networking with people so I'm never lonely.

What is the outlook for your type of job?

I'm not really sure. There are about six hundred cookbooks coming out a year. Some people work on cookbooks and other books, some just on cookbooks. There's definitely room for more people, whether it's cookbooks or food products—food PR professionals or newcomers into the field, especially people who have a background in food, because they have a unique way to pitch the product or the client.

RACHEL COLE

Rachel Cole is an account coordinator for Straus Communications, a public relations firm for sustainable agriculture and organic companies, including food-service management groups, food producers, and organizations.

CURRENT POSITION: Account coordinator, Straus Communications, Oakland, CA, since 2008. ★ **EDUCATION:** BA, political science, the College of Wooster, OH (2004); MA, holistic health education, John F. Kennedy University, Pleasant Hill, CA (2008). ★ **CAREER PATH:** Prevention and health education intern, the College of Wooster Student Wellness Center, OH (2004–2005); counter person, the Pasta Shop, Oakland (2005–2006). In Berkeley, CA: founder, Grub (community potlucks; 2006–present); kitchen intern, Three Stone Hearth (2006–2007); wholesale and farmers' market representative, Three Twins Ice Cream (2006–2007); counter person, Café Fanny (2006–2007). Farm apprentice, Fresh Run Farm, Bolinas, CA (2007). In San Francisco, CA: regular contributor, mightyfoods.com (2007–2008); regular contributor and columnist, *Edible San Francisco* (2008–present); education programs intern, the Center for Urban Education About Sustainable Agriculture (2008). ★ **AWARDS AND RECOGNITION:** Fellowship recipient, Taste3 Conference, Napa, CA (2008); educational awards.

Salary notes:

It's a small organization that straddles the line between for- and nonprofit. I also just started. I make about $40,000 a year and I have benefits.

Words of advice for people considering a similar career:

My general advice is to follow your passion and do what makes you happy—and pays your bills, wherever that leads you. It helps that I had parents who really wanted my sister and me to do what made us happy and who fed us in a way such that food became our passion.

Describe a typical day.

Because I am filtering what's going on in the sustainable food world, usually I spend the first two hours of my day reading a lot of trade newsletters, organic newsletters, the British Soil Association, blogs like Grist or ChewWise. I have more than thirty-five Google Alerts set up for the names of our clients or topics they are interested in, or even keywords like "organic food." Three times a day, we get e-mails that tell us what reporters are working on, so I track that for our clients. I check my RSS feeds to see what happened overnight. Then I send that information out to our various account managers and senior strategists, asking them what they want me to do with it, if they want it sent to the clients, for example. We are trying to become a B Corporation (B stands for beneficial), a label that helps customers sort out a genuinely good company from one that merely has good advertising. One of my jobs is finding ways in which we can change our policies to become a B Corporation. I might edit a proposal or a press release. I prepare a plan for how we'd reach out to media for potential clients. I do a great deal of research, and it's different all the time. I do take time to cook my lunch. I try to get out of the office by five P.M. I have a column for *Edible San Francisco,* which I may or may not be able to keep with my new job. A few months ago the magazine hired me to plan an event, so I did a quiz, Edible Pursuit, which is a little side project.

How many hours a week do you typically work?

Forty hours.

What are your specific responsibilities?

To support all our account managers. I track and filter what's going on in the media. We don't do generic press releases. We try to connect very specific reporters to specific stories from our clients. My job is trying to see what the reporters want to hear and how our clients want to reach the media, like through blogs or corporate reports. For one client, we do trend-watching of the organic industry, what's going on in China, studies, etc. We write a monthly summary for them. I do the monthly reports, tracking how many impressions we got so that we can show results of our work to the clients. I don't have to answer phones or photocopy clips— I'm administrative support but I don't have to do too much administrative work. I get asked to do a lot of research, such as for potential clients. I participate in conference calls with clients. Much of what we do bleeds into the clients' overall business strategy. We do some short-term projects as well and are getting more and more into social networking.

What do you like most about what you do?

I love that all our clients are helping make the world better and that we are helping make that happen. I get to think about what reporters are writing about and what our clients are doing that's amazing and connect the two. We do a lot of creative strategy work to see how we communicate our ideas so that they don't get drowned out by the wash of sustainable-food news.

What skills are most important for you to do your job well?

Organizational skills. Both big- and little-picture thinking. We joke and call it poised communication. You have to be personable with everyone, whether it's a reporter or a client. You have to be strategic in your thinking, to see if what your clients are pursuing is carrying them toward or away from their goal. Writing skills are important for sure—being concise, using very few words to communicate what you want to say. Networking. Curiosity. Dedication to the overall cause of making the world better through our clients.

What skills would you like to develop to help further your career?

I'd love to get better with social networking and online media, with technology. There's so much to learn there; that's really the way it's going. People who are going to do well in the future are those who will integrate technology in their service offerings.

BEN FINK

As a freelance photographer, Ben Fink works on both books and magazines as well as on personal exhibitions around the country. He has photographed for *Food & Wine, Bon Appétit, Scientific American,* Random House, and Artisan Books, among others, and is a regular contributor to *Saveur.*

CURRENT POSITION: Photographer and owner, Ben Fink Photography, since 1986 (food photographer since 1994), www.benfinkphoto.com. ★ **EDUCATION:** Course work in painting and graphic design, Memphis College of Art, Memphis, TN; course work in art history, graphic design, and photography, University of Memphis. ★ **CAREER PATH:** Graphic design department, University of Memphis; photographer's assistant, Memphis. ★ **AWARDS AND RECOGNITION:** Addy winner, Art Directors Club of New York (1998 and 2000); Print Regional Design Annual (1998); Award of Excellence for *Artisan Baking Across America,* James Beard Foundation (2001); *Communication Arts* and *Photo District News*'s Photo Annual (2005); finalist, Critical Mass Photography (2006); worked on several books that won James Beard and IACP awards. ★ **MEMBERSHIPS:** Who's Who in American Photography; Woodstock Center for Photography; Silver Eye Center for Photography; the International Center for Photography; Texas Photographic Society; Los Angeles Center for Digital Arts; Griffin Museum of Photography; Provincetown Museum of Art; Photographic Resource Center in Boston.

Salary notes:

Depending on experience, it can range from $400 to $1,000 a day for magazine work, $1,200 to $2,500 for book work, and $3,500 to $25,000 a day for advertising work. My income varies from year to year.

Words of advice for people considering a similar career:

Try to find your own voice, your own visual language. Don't copy other people's work. It's a good idea to start as a photographer's assistant, but don't get stuck there. It can show you a lot about the industry, but it's important, at the same time, to work on your own photography. Don't mimic whoever you are working for—be different. That's what's going to ultimately allow you to succeed.

How did you start photographing food?

I lived in Memphis and worked for *Memphis* magazine, shooting local people for articles. They asked me to do a food article at one point, for which I worked with a writer, Mary Ann Eagle. We became a team: She would write articles and I would photograph them. It turned into a monthly feature. After about a year and a half, we decided to try to do it nationally. We pitched a story about soul food to *Saveur* and heard back the following week. It was 1995 or so—early in their publication. They came down for the story and said that they also needed a Thanksgiving article, so we did both. Mary Ann and I were both very green. I was used to working with corporations that paid fairly well and was taken aback when I realized what magazines paid.

Describe a typical day.

It depends if I am shooting in the studio or on location. I'm in the studio between eight and eight thirty A.M., then prop and food stylists show up. I shoot using natural light, so I'm in the studio until six or seven P.M., depending on how many shots we have to do. This week I'm mostly on the phone trying to get estimates out, to make things happen for the rest of the month. I might have an advertising job in Chicago later this week—advertising is always very last-minute. Next week I am booked on a book. My schedule is not always regular. I might shoot on weekends or travel to or from a shoot on a weekend. It depends on the year also; last year I was working seven days a week nonstop for six months. I like multiple-day shoots, because you can really wrap your head around someone's project. It allows you to develop something. For those, people will wait for you to be available.

How many hours a week do you typically work?

Between fifty and sixty hours, in a normal week.

What are your specific responsibilities?

My biggest responsibility, and the one that I always try to keep in the forefront of my mind, is to have an open mind and listen to each project that I am working on. I got the shooting down—I can do that without thinking. I have to approach things with a fresh eye, be alert and not stagnant. When you are working for someone else, there's always going to be a fresh angle, someone's point of view. That's what you try to get across: their point of view with their food, with their environment, with how they do things.

What do you like most about what you do?

Working with other people. Being in other people's world is almost a drug, a way of not dealing with your own world. You are kind of a voyeur. I'm really tuned in and enjoying what I'm doing and capturing something that is out of my realm. It adds an exciting element to my life.

What do you like least about it?

Conflict. I don't like to feel like I'm not relating to something I'm doing. There's conflict and resolution on a shoot. You have to have some empathy or common thread with the other people involved. There can be an element of disconnect. Rather than getting angry, I think about why that is and then resolve it.

What skills are most important for you to do your job well?

Being able to relate to other people and to listen. I am ultimately there to bring something to the table that enhances the story that someone is trying to tell.

What skills would you like to develop to help further your career?

I would like to develop public-speaking skills and be comfortable with it, so that I could lecture, for example. I also would like to learn about shooting motion, to work on movies and commercials—I shot my first commercial this year.

Describe your creative process.

I listen to the art director. I have preconceived ideas. When someone talks to you about a certain project, you sort of glamorize it—things have a certain romantic aspect to them—and when you arrive at the shoot it's a bit different. Sometimes it's good different, and sometimes it's "Good God, how am I going to do this?" Someone shows me elements; sometimes I can see what they want right off, but sometimes I have to see the photograph on the computer to make adjustments to the setup. My creative process is to see it on the two-dimensional screen. It tells the story; it romanticizes it. Editing is a big thing—it's editing out part of the environment. If you show the whole thing it becomes boring.

"My biggest responsibility, and the one that I always try to keep in the forefront of my mind, is to have an open mind and listen to each project that I am working on. I got the shooting down—I can do that without thinking. I have to approach things with a fresh eye, be alert and not stagnant."

13. ASSORTED BUSINESS SERVICES

We decided to call "assorted business services" all the jobs that surround the operations of a food business but might not fit neatly into one category. They are essential to the running of the operations, varying from staffing to design to investing. Many of the people who work in the positions detailed here do so away from the

spotlight. Few people know the name of a chef's assistant or kitchen designer. As the interest in the behind-the-scenes world of the restaurant business grows, however, even these jobs are attracting attention and will likely become even more competitive to obtain.

Some of these professions require specific training in areas such as design, finance, and human relations. People tend to come to these jobs through non-food-related previous experiences or educational backgrounds and find themselves involved in the culinary world because of a specific job they take on. James Feustel's training as an engineer was what allowed him to start designing kitchens, even though he also has a culinary degree (page 303), while Rachael Carron became a chef's assistant thanks to her previous experience in public relations (page 313). You will

not become the controller of a restaurant group without some finance background. However, a strong interest in the culinary world, and experience in it, will be key in obtaining the jobs outlined in this chapter. You will have to find the right balance between rigorous training in a field and spending enough time in the culinary industry. If you are thinking about a career as a restaurant controller while working on your undergraduate degree in accounting and are not yet working in a restaurant, go fill out applications immediately. Start as a busboy or a dishwasher, depending on whether you prefer working in the kitchen or on the floor. It doesn't matter much as long as you obtain experience with the running of a restaurant. Work hard and well so that you are promoted. Aim for a general manager, food and beverage manager, or purchasing director position, depending on the type of establishment where you work. Even if as a controller or in a related position you will sit in an office most of the day, you need to make sure that you enjoy dealing with restaurant people. At the same time, make sure to keep working on your finance background. Perhaps you will find time to intern at an accounting firm in town. Or by the time you graduate, look for an entry-level accounting job. Eventually, you will be able to parlay both sets of experience into your dream job on the accounting side of a restaurant group. In some cases, a strong corporate background will be seen as a plus.

Restaurant consultants at the operations level come to the job with years of proven experience behind them. The range of possible consulting assignments includes real-estate location analysis, menu development, kitchen design, point-of-sale systems, purchasing, and lighting and music design. If this is your ultimate career goal, plan on spending at least ten years in the industry before launching your consultancy business, which will give you time to work for the best, learn everything you can, and build a solid résumé that will garner the trust of potential clients. You might be successful starting sooner, of course, but then would not have as much experience to sell to prospective clients.

Chef's assistants come from all walks of life. Some take such jobs right after college and move on after a couple of years, whereas others work in other sectors of the food industry before deciding to work closely with chef-owners. Some chefs keep their assistants for years, particularly if they work with people who have tested other careers before. You may not make much money as a chef's assistant but will usually be able to accompany the chef to events and generally get to make many contacts in the industry. These jobs can comprise much variety: In one eight-hour day, you may handle press calls, test a recipe, plan a trip for your boss, and even cook on the line during the peak lunch hour.

Investors often have full-time jobs in sectors that are much more lucrative than the food industry, and they decide to invest in a restaurant or food company because they believe in its potential and are passionate about food (see "Investing in Restaurants," page 72). They might do so for years or get burned with their first investment and never do it again (see "Lessons Learned," page 70). If you are in a position to invest in a restaurant, be aware that it is unlikely that you'll make much of a return, if you are fortunate enough not to lose money.

JAMES FEUSTEL

James Feustel is the director of design at Gary Jacobs Associates, a New York–based firm that designs professional kitchens for restaurants, which launched in 2008.

CURRENT POSITION: Director of design, Gary Jacobs Associates, New York, NY, since 2008. ★ **EDUCATION:** BA, mechanical engineering, Cooper Union, New York, NY; MA, food studies, New York University; core skills block at New York Restaurant School. ★ **CAREER PATH:** In New York: coordinator of event operations, French Culinary Institute (January–October 2005); kitchen equipment consultant/project manager, Sam Tell and Son Inc. (January–December 2006); managing director, Studio e Design Group (December 2006–June 2008). Teaching experience: adjunct instructor, Kingsborough Community College (January 2006–present); adjunct instructor, NYU (June 2005–May 2006); math and design technology teacher, the Dwight School (September 2003–August 2004); adjunct instructor, Mathematics, Temple University (January–December 2002).

Salary notes:

For an entry-level draftsperson, $40,000. When working on the sales side, it's really easy to move up and get to six figures when working on commission. On the consultant side, you rarely make that much. I make $70,000.

Words of advice for people considering a similar career:

It's important to try new things. So it's important to work for a dealer, for a consultant, for a restaurant owner, just to have the food-service experience. But what's most important for this sector of the industry is to have passion and motivation for it. It's easy to teach the food side, the construction side, the technological side. But I think the people who will have the most success in this sector are those who actively develop an interest in it by becoming a low-commission salesperson or entry-level draftsperson.

Describe a typical day.

I work eight A.M. to five P.M. at a minimum. It's great to be on that schedule, but if I send a set of plans to a chef, he might not get to look at them until after service. So I have to pick up my phone if it rings at seven P.M., check my e-mail at ten P.M., etc. We're specifically geared toward restaurant design. Other companies might work for corporate cafeterias, schools, hospitals. It's pretty well segmented. I spend probably about half of my day actually designing. The balance of my day is preparing bid documents and answering RFI [request for information] forms for projects that are in construction. When a job is designed and everything goes smoothly on paper, equipment is ordered. We sometimes run into issues in the field, so I spend a part of my day coordinating construction projects. My engineering background comes in very handy. It can be learned, but I came in day one already speaking that language. The rest of the day is spent in meetings and conference calls with engineers, owners, chefs, architects, discussing designs that I've done.

How many hours a week do you typically work?

Fifty-five hours, typically eight A.M. to five P.M. three days a week and two crazy days.

What are your specific responsibilities?

I'm responsible for designing kitchens, for coordinating construction projects with architects, engineers, all the trades, chefs, and owners. I also have to put together drawings and specification standards. When I get my staff in place, I will be responsible for staff training and management. I have to be current on new products and new technologies out there. Sales representatives come to the office and tell me about the latest ovens, exhausts, etc. I go to many trade shows. I have to know about Energy Star and how much money will be saved by using these products.

What do you like most about what you do?

I like the variety; every kitchen is different. I'm dealing with different spaces and different concepts all the time. The space is going to be very different for a four-star French restaurant than for a gastropub. I like being able to say that we can do, with the same chef, fast-food or upscale concepts. They are both equally challenging.

What do you like least about it?

There's not very much that I don't like about the job. It can get frustrating at times, when I put a lot of time and effort into something and big changes are made.

It can be frustrating when I have to change a lot because the project is over budget or suddenly you don't have as much space as you thought you did. It can be something as stupid as basement storage space, and they say, "You no longer have your wine and liquor room because we didn't excavate under the kitchen." You can't get really mad at those things because often nobody has that information until they break ground on a project. All you can ask for is that everyone does their due diligence.

What skills are most important for you to do your job well?

Being organized and paying attention to the littlest details, because that little detail will end up costing someone down the road. It could be $1,000 per detail. On one of the first jobs I worked when got in the industry, I was to verify all the measurements of a U-shaped, custom-made refrigerated counter. All my dimensions worked perfectly. The one I forgot to check was the width of the door to the restaurant. We had to have a stainless steel fabricator come to the warehouse, cut the counter in half, and come to the restaurant afterward to weld it back together. It cost $1,600 that we couldn't ask the restaurant to pay for. The company ate it up. You also have to have the willingness to learn about all the new stuff that's out there. I think that's what's going to separate a draftsperson from a designer.

What skills would you like to develop to help further your career?

Sales skills. Even as a consultant, on some level you have to be a salesperson. I have to be able to sell my services.

What are your long-term goals?

I haven't really thought in terms of long-term goals because this is a startup company, and I am just thinking about getting out of the weeds I'm in now. But long-term, I don't want to design anymore; I want to manage designers who are managing draftspeople. I want Gary Jacobs Associates to be an industry resource, a recognizable name that's well known and respected across the industry, and not just for restaurants but for hotels, casinos, and at the corporate level. I made this move because this is it for me for a while. I've had one job a year for the last eight years, looking for a good fit. I want to do work that's well done, that people recognize.

What keeps you challenged?

The nature of the work. Even though I'm rolling out a chain of a certain restaurant, they're not all the same. The sheer variety of the work is challenging. Almost every week, some manufacturer is finding a way to make his product better. It's challenging just to stay on top of the trade magazines in my mailbox. I work with a dozen different architects, contractors, and more—people who approach tasks differently.

Describe your creative process.

Sometimes I'll draw boxes for the elements I know I need, and a lot of it is to put together the pieces of a jigsaw puzzle. Every kitchen will have a hood, a dishwasher, a refrigerator. If every kitchen were four thousand feet, my job would be easy. The creative process really starts when you have to squeeze things in small places. I always enjoy having to design custom pieces. It's like a thousand-piece jigsaw puzzle. Taking my cues from Gary, I started to do my design on paper. I print a blank room, take sheets of tracing paper, and start drawing.

CYNTHIA BILLEAUD

As head of human resources for the Dinex Group, Cynthia Billeaud handles recruiting and personnel issues for Chef Daniel Boulud's ten restaurants.

CURRENT POSITION: Director of human resources, Dinex Group, New York, NY, since 2005. ★ **EDUCATION:** Preparatory studies, HEC Paris (business school); MBA equivalent, human resources management, Institut Supérieur du Commerce de Paris, France. ★ **CAREER PATH:** Human resources assistant/internal communications, Carlson Wagonlit Travel, Paris (2000); human resources recruiting consultant, Expectra Group, Paris (2001–2002); human resources manager, Alain Ducasse Group, New York (2003–2005).

Salary notes:

Entry-level to two or three years of experience, $35,000 to $40,000. For an executive position, between $50,000 and $150,000 depending on the size of the operation. There can also be a bonus system, depending on the employer.

Words of advice for people considering a similar career:

Pugnacity and passion are the keys to success.

Describe a typical day.

I take care of the bulk of my e-mails on my BlackBerry while in public transportation. I schedule candidates every hour, each interview lasting thirty to forty-five minutes. I see five or six candidates a day. Every day we have a managers' meeting with one of the restaurants, in person at the restaurants in New York and by phone with Las Vegas and Palm Beach. Those last about an hour and a half at Daniel, forty-five to sixty minutes in the other restaurants. At Daniel, Chef Daniel is with us. We have 150 salaries to manage there; it's much larger, and that's also where his office is. His general manager, assistant, sommelier, executive chef, and executive pastry chef are always there. There's also always someone from special events, someone from operations, HR, and marketing. Then the executive body of the restaurant. I also take care of the payroll. On a weekly basis, I monitor the proper coherence of pay when there are promotions or raises, to ensure that this is done correctly.

How many hours a week do you typically work?

Fifty to sixty hours. I work from nine A.M. to seven or eight P.M. If I am at Daniel and I need to stay later, I stay later. But I also have much more autonomy in this position. I manage my department with an American management style, which is that if you have things to accomplish, the most important is to finish.

What are your specific responsibilities?

Because the group is constantly growing, recruiting occupies 99 percent of my time. We have 750 employees right now. For the ten restaurants, I handle visas for all the personnel who come from abroad, green cards, personnel relations, staff evaluations, internal promotions, setting up systems to evaluate employees repeatedly throughout the year, rectifying miscommunication, unhappy employees, termination. I handle staffing budget systems for the new openings. We are trying to intensify our relationships with schools more and more, to bring people into our organization early on. We are trying to put in place a management program. We are also working on redesigning the HR page on our website to help with recruiting. I train my assistant to be able to conduct interviews so that she can be part of the active recruiting process.

What do you like most about what you do?

My area of work. The relationship I have with my own boss. I have a passion for this sector, for food, for details. I like feeling that I am a source of support for our employees. I have two bosses: the employees and my boss; I am accountable to both. I have to balance the two so that we can grow.

What do you like least about it?

The instability of visas, the nonpermanent aspect of that, of having to continuously start the process again. Fifteen to 20 percent of our employees need visas. That's complicated.

What skills are most important for you to do your job well?

First of all, listening. Understanding that each restaurant is different from the others, thanks to its concept and its culture. Understanding the person I am talking to, his or her expectations, to know who will be the best candidate. When I meet a candidate, I can then say which restaurant will be the best fit for him or her. Answer everyone's expectations to a maximum. I have to be creative, available, able to think outside the box. A chef has many things to think about; I approach my role as being an assistant to his department and his job, to relieve him as much as possible.

What skills would you like to develop to help further your career?

I would like to have a greater knowledge of wine, to be able to evaluate sommelier candidates from a technical perspective as well.

What qualities do you look for in a new hire?

They have to have passion for the profession. They need to have a mind that is open to the restaurant world and understand how the kitchen functions. They need to understand how human resources helps in the process, what role we play. Then they need to be able to communicate with our interlocutors with simple messages. They have to be motivated, able to work long hours. A degree in HR is not necessarily mandatory. My specialization is more commercial than HR, thinking about selling a product, doing market research.

ELIZABETH BLAU

Elizabeth Blau is the founder and CEO of Blau and Associates, a strategic restaurant planning and development company that works with restaurants and hospitality companies worldwide. Her consulting tasks include developing original restaurant concepts and business strategies, helping companies solve problems in nonperforming restaurants, creating and implementing marketing strategies, and providing management training and operational support. She is also the owner of three restaurants in Las Vegas and one in Los Angeles.

CURRENT POSITION: Founder/CEO, Blau and Associates, Las Vegas, NV, since 2002, www.elizabethblau.com. ★ **EDUCATION:** BA, government and international relations, Georgetown University, Washington, DC; master's degree, Cornell University School of Hotel Administration. ★ **CAREER PATH:** Starting in 1995 in New York, opened Osteria del Circo, then reopened Le Cirque 2000; Las Vegas: senior vice president of restaurant development for MGM/Mirage Resorts (responsible for the design, development, integration, and promotion of new restaurant concepts for all MGM/Mirage Resort properties); opened own restaurant in 2003 with chef Kerry Simon; now has Simon's at the Palms Place, Society, and Cat's Lounge, and, with partners, Simon LA at the Sofitel Hotel in Los Angeles. ★ **AWARDS AND RECOGNITION:** Simon Kitchen and Bar named one of best new restaurants in America in 2003 by *Esquire;* Hospy Award from the Las Vegas chapter of Network of Executive Women in Hospitality; Gold Plate Award from the International Food Service Manufacturers. ★ **MEMBERSHIPS:** CIA board of trustees; on the boards of the President's Council of Cornell Women, Southern Nevada Make-a-Wish Foundation, the Jean-Louis Palladin Foundation, and the University of Nevada–Las Vegas dean's advisory board; member of James Beard Foundation and Women Chefs & Restaurateurs; on the advisory boards of *Hotel F&B* magazine, *Wynn* magazine, and *Vivmag.*

Salary notes:

Anywhere from entry-level to several hundred thousand.

Words of advice for people considering a similar career:

It takes a great deal of hard work and dedication. Make sure you have a lot of good, strong, solid operations experience before doing it.

What prompted you to start your own business?

I had worked for so many years for other people. After five years in Las Vegas, it was time to go out and build my own place. It was a difficult decision because I loved working with my mentors. But having my own business has allowed me to be more entrepreneurial and be in control of my own destiny.

How large is your staff?

Ten employees.

Describe a typical day.

There's absolutely no typical day. We have clients all over the world—Europe, Asia, the Middle East, Mexico—so I travel somewhere at least two weeks a month. We also own three restaurants here in Las Vegas, so some days I'm doing tastings. On other days I'm in the office.

How many hours a week do you typically work?

At least a hundred hours.

What are your specific responsibilities?

I oversee all the business operations of our company and the business operations of our restaurants. My husband, who is the president of the company, has the responsibility of the operations part of the business. I'm not involved in the day-to-day operations of our restaurants.

What do you like most about what you do?

I love that it is different every day. I love this industry, the people in it.

What do you like least about it?

The travel. That's both the good and the bad, but it gets to the point where it is almost excessive.

How do you find your projects?

They find us. We're lucky to be at a point where our reputation is out there. We're always referred through a network in the food industry, sometimes kitchen designers or past clients.

What skills are most important for you to do your job well?

There are so many. In the restaurant industry, if you go back to the basics there are many nontechnical skills that are impor-

tant. But it's important to know computers and other technologies to stay on top of your game, whether it's operating a POS system or using all the technological advantages of your BlackBerry or your laptop.

What are your long-term goals?

Building the consulting and continuing to expand in other complementary aspects of the business. There are so many areas to work in: cruises, airlines, etc. Right now we work with about twelve clients at a time, usually during preopening and opening, but sometimes after the opening as well.

What qualities do you look for in a new hire?

Great operational experience. I like to see some job stability, but I don't mind if somebody has moved around, because it's also important to have worked for various people. They have to have a special something.

What keeps you challenged?

The clients and the projects. We love when we take on a new client, because we get to see different aspects of the hospitality industry. We just started with a company that sells partnerships in private jets. It's different from cruise ships, from casinos, from hotels; they all have different variables.

Describe your creative process.

There's a strategy-assessment period when I see what needs to be done. Then we move to concept development and then to project management. Those are the three main steps in typical projects.

JOHN CHITVANNI

John Chitvanni founded National Restaurant Search as an executive search firm that specializes in the restaurant and hospitality industry. Companies at both the national and international levels hire National Restaurant Search to find them executives using very specific criteria based on the needs of the position. He was a contributing author to *Dining in America.*

CURRENT POSITION: Chairman and founder, National Restaurant Search, Atlanta, GA, since 1981, www.restauranttheadhunter.com. ★ **EDUCATION:** BA, political science, Boston State College, MA. ★ **CAREER PATH:** Brigham's, MA (ten years); Dunkin' Donuts (three years); fast-food desk, search firm; restaurant desk at another search firm (one year).

Salary notes:

There are two types of search in this industry: retaining search and contingency search, which is district managers and managers. Someone working for the latter will make $50,000 to $125,000. Someone at a retaining search firm who works at the executive level makes between $100,000 and $500,000 a year. Sometimes you have really good years, sometimes really bad years. You have to be able to handle the ups and downs and know how to manage your money.

Describe a typical day.

I spend my marketing time on the telephone. You have to continuously sell, even if you are busy. It all goes in a cycle. Once a client is interested, I fly to visit them and establish parameters. Once we establish we have a deal, we set up position specs with the exact criteria that they want. We highlight the company, position, and experience they are looking for. That way we know that we are both looking for the same thing. The information we compile is what I use to do my search. Then I narrow it down further and go through candidates. We go through forty to sixty people, searching through résumés and narrowing down the pool. We have a database of about forty thousand people. When we sit with the client we ask if they would like someone to come from a specific company. We look for the right personality, chemistry, and style. I narrow the selections down to ten to fifteen people and then I speak with the candidates on the phone. I narrow further to six to eight people whom I interview in person if I haven't already done so for another position. My staff and I then do a very thorough reference check. We present two to three candidates to the client; that way they see the best that we put forward. All three should be qualified; it's a matter of which one they prefer.

I know many key people in the industry. I go to a couple of conferences where I can see a lot of people. I don't have to travel as much as someone who hasn't been doing it as long or doesn't know the industry as well, so I travel 35 to 40 percent of the time, as opposed to 75 to 80 percent. Modern technology makes it so much easier.

How many hours a week do you typically work?

On the average forty to forty-five hours. That's when I am in the office. I don't count the days when I travel.

What are your specific responsibilities?

I am the spokesman for the company. I coordinate who does what search. I do the majority of the selling. I go to the most conventions; I'm continuously out there contacting people. I'm the name in the company that people recognize because I've been in it for so long.

What do you like most about what you do?

The restaurant industry is such a fun industry; it's a people's business; it's constantly changing and evolving. I talk to people all over the United States and internationally, so I see many different concepts. I can see what's going on, be in the know, talk to presidents and CEOs of companies, and see them grow (or crash and burn).

What do you like least about it?

The executive-searching industry is a respected industry, but through the years, people haven't wanted to pay for the executive search. So we often say that the restaurant industry is five years behind others in terms of accepting the fees and process of executive search. Now it's better. They view us sometimes as a necessary evil. They sometimes want to negotiate, nickel-and-dime us.

What skills are most important for you to do your job well?

Common sense, discernment, integrity. So many times, chemistry is the most important factor to decide which person will fit best with which company and which organization. You have to understand who your client is and discern what type of person will fit there. There are plenty of skeletons in the closet. I might go to a client and realize they might be hiding problems from the past. If I realize that, I pull out. Integrity: Once you work with clients, you don't steal employees from your clients. A lot of my competition will do that. It upsets clients. We've drawn the line there, which gives us an excellent reputation. It's always been our philosophy. You work hard for your client; you are honest with them; you discern what's going to work—that's going to make you successful. Many times the client will tell you what they want, and of course we agree because they pay us, but it might not be what's best for them. I tell them, "If you like, I'll make recommendations; if you don't that's fine, too." We are paid to manage the search, and they make the final decision.

What skills would you like to develop to help further your career?

When working with my staff, the key point on which I focus is that it is a relationship business. If you can't build and maintain relationships, you won't be successful. Much development and training is based on that. You have to have face time with clients to build relationships and trust. If you do that, over time, you will keep enough of your clients long-term, or they will take you along when they move to a different company.

How large is your staff?

We have four executives who do searches, and then administrative and research staff (right now two; it goes up and down with the economy).

What qualities do you look for in a new hire?

I look for people who know the industry, because that's instant credibility. People who are people's people and can build relationships. I will look at clients they worked for in the past. When checking references, I ask, "Would you hire them if I brought them to you?" I look for people who are well set emotionally. You have to be able to accept rejection, just like any commission sales position. You have to continuously pick up the phone, have a strong work ethic and drive.

Describe your creative process.

You're only as good as your last search. You cannot afford to lay down on it. You're always out there. It might not be called creative, but it's true that we have to be innovative. During the last recession, a company wanted a CEO based in Hall, Iowa, population eighteen hundred. We filled it. General Mills said they needed a director of marketing who was American but spoke Japanese to go work in Japan. That was one of the toughest ones I filled, but I eventually did it. You have to work hard for those projects, but when you close them it's really neat.

What keeps you challenged?

An individual drive. People in the restaurant industry are very passionate. It's long hours and hard work. Once that gets in your blood, you never seem to lose it. It's a drive and a passion that is in you. From this perspective, that's what drives me. I want to be successful. I don't have to be the richest person in the world, but I am in a place in the industry where we have a good reputation; I call presidents and CEOs and they take my call, and they call me to talk strategy regularly.

RACHAEL CARRON

Rachael Carron became chef Wylie Dufresne's assistant because she has a background in public relations and was able to provide assistance when the need arose—but also because she is married to Dufresne's father, with whom she was a partner in the restaurant 71 Clinton Fresh Food.

CURRENT POSITION: Assistant to Chef Wylie Dufresne, wd~50, New York, NY, since the late 1990s, www.wd-50.com. ★ **EDUCATION:** BA equivalent, English, Trinity College, Dublin, Ireland. ★ **CAREER PATH:** In New York: employee, small PR company that dealt with art galleries and small art institutions; partner, 71 Clinton Fresh Food.

Salary notes:

This is totally dependent on how the restaurant is doing, as does the salary of all the principals in that restaurant.

Words of advice for people considering a similar career:

Pick your boss. Because of the nature of what you do for this person, and what they do for their career, you have to have some kind of rapport. I couldn't do this for someone whose ethos and product I didn't respect. It's very personal.

Describe a typical day.

When I come in, I look at the reservation book for the next three days or so. We use OpenTable. In a tough economic climate in particular, I think most restaurants are dependent on this tool, because you can use it to encourage more people to come in. I communicate information such as VIPs and special needs to the kitchen. I pick up flowers for the restaurant before I come in. E-mails are a huge part of the day. I book the private dining room—our wine cellar—for fourteen diners, so I do anything in relation to that. If reservations are really low, we fax all the concierges to remind them of what we're doing, such as a wine list special. I communicate Wylie's schedule to him. I work on menu descriptions. Because of the nature of the food, it's very important for the staff to know the details inherent in each dish. I update the website; I can do all the text stuff myself but not the programming. I write up recipes that are requested for press and also for our own records. I attend certain events.

How many hours a week do you typically work?

I work a four-day week, thirty-five to forty hours. But I might have to do something on my days off.

What are your specific responsibilities?

I do all sorts of communication work and PR; I oversee reservations; I am an assistant to Wylie; I organize and schedule all of his stages. I do anything that is administrative, communication related, and anything as a personal assistant. He never crosses the line; he's an excellent boss. I don't do his personal schedule. He's independent. It started at 71 Clinton Fresh and then evolved. Someone needed to handle the press. Wylie needed more and more help with daily letters, e-mails, and communication; it evolved pretty organically. Much of it is detail oriented, but I get to learn a little about what he is doing.

What do you like most about what you do?

The camaraderie. It is like a family—a dysfunctional one, but there is a nice social aspect to dealing with people all day long. I like the variety of the tasks I have to do. I like working somewhere where I believe in what they are doing. I really admire what Wylie does, the tenacity he has for his own vision. It's taught me that if you believe in something you keep straight ahead.

What do you like least about it?

Since I'm so attached to what is going on in that restaurant, I deal very poorly with diners' criticisms. I shouldn't be attached. I don't read online comments anymore. Some of our floor managers do, to see if there are changes that we should consider. I think it's changed also. A restaurant evolves; we're at the point where diners come in and know what we are doing. At the beginning, they didn't. They were conservative. It's nice to see the evolution of the customer base, of regulars who have become incredibly faithful. I like the relationship with them; they become part of that family.

What skills are most important for you to do your job well?

Communication; being detail-oriented; mastering kitchen language, for everything from press releases to menus. You

have to be somewhat gregarious. You're not working in a corner office with the door closed. You're probably working in a very small office that is filled with things, has no windows, and is intruded upon by fifteen people a day asking the weirdest questions. And in a small business you end up being like a therapist to the staff. You have to enjoy people.

What skills would you like to develop to help further your career?

I would like to learn more about food photography. I think it would help us get photos onto the website more rapidly as new dishes are created.

What is the outlook for your type of job?

Regardless of the economy, I think there'll be more jobs like mine. Chefs are kind of the rock stars of the twenty-first century. They are traveling, on TV, giving talks, on the radio. Someone has to manage it all.

How large is your staff?

About forty in total, including porters and servers. We have eight full-time chefs/cooks, plus four interns (three savory, one pastry). They answer to Wylie, but I handle HR tasks, such as gathering résumés and getting them set up for payroll.

What qualities do you look for in a new hire?

With the résumés, it varies. It's important that the kitchen remain familial. There are a bunch of really nice people working here already, so they have to fit into the environment. They need an incredible work ethic and to be passionate and imaginative, because Wylie is looking for people's input. As well as experience, it's a personality thing. I'm not a gatekeeper for the kitchen, but I can usually tell from a cover letter if they are going to fit.

Describe your creative process.

I aim to convey the information as briefly and precisely as possible. You're just a convoy of information; you make it as accessible as possible. What they are doing at wd~50 sometimes appears cold to people, so you want to make it appear less so. If I can get a journalist in the kitchen, they can see how collaboratively it works. It's not a cold lab environment. It's trial and error, and the food does taste good. While there is a scientific aspect, you want to convey that it's not that removed from the cozy aspect that people want.

14. NUTRITION AND NONPROFIT

Opportunities in the fields of nutrition and nonprofit have increased substantially in recent years. Nutrition is a long-standing field with established training and certifications. Typically, however, registered dietitians worked in hospitals and private practices. This has changed, as stricter nutritional guidelines are being

passed by city and state legislations around the country. Many restaurants and food companies find themselves in need of nutritional analyses for their menus or specific dishes. As such, people with a nutrition background are now in demand for projects that involve enjoying food rather than restricting it. Nutrition and nonprofit positions are also important aspects of the industry since they provide valuable educational services, in addition to helping produce and provide better food for all. Many jobs are also available for those who wish to specifically work in the nonprofit sector, such as working for food banks and other service providers for those in need of food. Like other businesses, restaurants are constantly solicited for donations, and chefs lend their help and food to multiple causes all around the country. This tradition of giving is not

limited to donations of food itself, but also extends to food education and sheer labor—whatever it takes to make a difference.

nutrition

Increased federal and local government regulations on the nutritional content of food have created opportunities for nutritionists, since they can calculate the number of calories in a food item and provide a company or restaurant with that information. Even smaller operations that might not be required to abide by the regulations have taken an interest in offering lighter dishes and seek out nutritionists to assist them in creating lower-calorie dishes. Such recipe nutritional analyses are often completed on a per-project basis and might even allow dietitians to work from home.

Food allergies is another area that requires a nutritionist's expertise, as food professionals and companies aim to prepare dishes that are low in sodium, gluten free, or vegan. Developing an expertise in food allergies can become a profitable niche for a nutritionist, as they can then offer their services to magazines, newspapers, and websites as well.

Many nutritionists, if they do not wish to work on staff in a hospital or private practice, work as consultants. They might work on a monthly retainer for one company if it sends lots of work their way or charge hourly and project-based fees. As always with such positions, these fees vary widely based on your location, your experience, and the size of the project. A nutritionist can decide not to work for less than $250 per recipe analysis project or be happy with $50, as Rebecca Cameron explains (page 319). Teaching classes at local cooking schools, working as an adjunct in a university's nutrition program, writing about nutrition, and developing recipes are all ways through which business may be developed and income expanded.

A college degree in nutrition is required in order to practice as a nutritionist. Having additional culinary experience will greatly help when dealing with restaurant operators and cooks, since it will be easier to understand the techniques and ingredients they use and work with those when developing dishes or nutritional analyses for them, but it is not necessary for a hospital or clinical practice.

nonprofit

Working in the nonprofit sector is truly a labor of love, because salaries are low and the hours are long. However, it can be immensely rewarding because these jobs allow people to make a real difference in someone's life.

Nonprofit jobs tend to have an educational component, as they might involve teaching cooking skills to people who will then use those to gain employment and income, as Ryan Farr does (page 324). If working in a soup kitchen or a similar program, knowing how to cook food cheaply and in large quantities is essential. Nonprofit programs suffer greatly when the economy is poor, since donations dry up just as needs expand. As such, being able to create tasty food with very little is a valuable skill to have—and one that will be appreciated by those eating the meal. Having experience cooking in a restaurant makes it easier to develop such dishes, even when dealing with a very different supply of ingredients. People skills will be valuable as well as you manage a team that might vary widely from day to day, if it is volunteer based, and deal with customers who are eating your food not because they want to spend a night out with friends, but because they are hungry and might not have eaten another warm meal that day.

It is not necessary to know how to cook to be involved in the nonprofit culinary sector. Planning, managing sites and projects, fund-raising, and communications are all areas of work available at nonprofit organizations large and small. While some organizations, such as Share Our Strength, are national, many operate at the state and city level, but all depend on federal and state funding as well as donations. Writing grants, managing budgets, organizing fund-raisers, and promoting the organization and its events are thus essential aspects of a nonprofit's operation.

Moving from the for-profit to the nonprofit world might require adjusting to the change in organizational culture. Such a change is possible regardless of your background, as the staff of City Harvest, New York City's largest and highly regarded food rescue organization, exemplifies. Its administrators include former executives from Merrill Lynch, Estée Lauder, Hertz, Polaroid, and Doubleday.

With a lot of stamina, it is even possible to start your own nonprofit organization from the ground up, as Christine Carroll did with CulinaryCorps (page 322). Obtaining nonprofit status requires a great deal of paperwork in order to obtain a 501(c)(3) classification, which makes receiving tax-deductible donations permissible. If you choose to do that, you will need help from a lawyer for this process but might find one willing to help you on a pro bono basis. This step is important, because some donors are unwilling to give if they will not be able to claim that money in their tax deductions. Some foundations also reserve their money for nonprofits. It will likely be necessary to hold another job in the early days to secure an income, and paying staff will be impossible. Fortunately, volunteers and interns will be happy to participate in an effort that combines their love of food with their eagerness to help.

Going after grants and foundation money can be a better way to spend your time than organizing fund-raising events (such as galas), which require a lot of logistical arrangement, have high costs, and yield a smaller return on your effort. A combination of both elements might be the best way to go in a tighter economy, when foundations themselves are suffering and not able to give out as much money.

REBECCA CAMERON

Through her nutrition culinary consulting company, Haute Nutrition, Rebecca Cameron combines her culinary background with her dietetics training to provide services to restaurants and food companies, such as nutritional analyses of dishes or products.

CURRENT POSITION: Chef, registered dietitian, and owner of Haute Nutrition (nutrition culinary consulting), Seattle, WA, since 2005, www.hautenutrition.com. ★ **EDUCATION:** BS, food and nutrition with emphasis on dietetics, Seattle Pacific University (1997); culinary arts degree, Culinary Institute of America (2005). ★ **CAREER PATH:** Dietetics internship, Sea Mar Community Health Center, Seattle, WA; quality-control supervisor, Briaze (about three years), Seattle, WA; while in culinary school, restaurant work in the New York area on weekends. ★ **AWARDS AND RECOGNITION:** Management Award, CIA. ★ **MEMBERSHIPS:** American Dietetic Association; Washington State Dietetic Association; Greater Seattle Dietetic Association; Washington Restaurant Association.

Salary notes:

As a dietitian, the starting salary can be anything from $20 to $40 an hour. In my line of work, it varies widely, generally from $50 to $150 an hour, with some people charging $250 for each recipe nutritional analysis completed, and others $30.

Words of advice for people considering a similar career:

Having my background in nutrition, immersing myself in that world, has been very valuable. When I was in college, I worked for one of my professors who had a private practice. I really encourage people to get experience with private-practice work and then strike out on their own. On the culinary side, working for a corporate manufacturer, learning about product specifications and processing, has been very valuable. I also think that people don't stay current enough, so staying on top of industry trends enough is my number one piece of advice.

Describe a typical day.

My day is never typical. Much of my job is focused on nutritional analysis for restaurants. I may sit in front of the computer to complete a nutritional analysis with a computer program, or I might work with one of my clients in his or her kitchen, weighing different foods, making sure that I have the right weight. Sometimes I'm at a food manufacturer, taking photos of all of their products and taking down the nutritional analysis on all of their labels. I function as a nutrition expert for some of my clients' companies, so I do interviews for them on TV or in newspapers. Occasionally, and since it is an area where I want to grow, I might work on developing new food products.

How many hours a week do you typically work?

Forty to sixty. It depends on the time of year and the number of projects. As of January 1, 2009, King County had to do nutritional analysis for any restaurant that had more than fifteen establishments nationwide, so that kept me busy.

How many clients do you work with at a time?

After doing this for a few years, I've learned to space them out. If a project is very involved, I try to focus on one at a time. I'm always scheduling another client for when I am done with that project. Sometimes I'll do something for one of my regular clients while working on another project.

What are your specific responsibilities?

For myself, just running my business and performing all the functions it requires. I learn about public relations, research how to accept credit cards, research labeling laws, etc. For my clients, it's my responsibility to complete the nutritional analysis as accurately as possible.

What do you like most about what you do?

I really like working with restaurants and business owners in a nontraditional way. Most of the time, you graduate from culinary school and think you're going to work in restaurants, which means dealing with long hours, working on weekends, etc. I am still able to work with restaurants, but on my schedule and my time. Most dietitians are employed by hospitals and in health-care settings, so I am also doing something different.

What do you like least about it?

Nutritional analysis is not an exact science, so being forced into that is hard. I also have all these ideas, and I never seem to have enough time. There's always something more I could be doing. Having enough time for all of that is frustrating for me.

What skills are most important for you to do your job well?

Having a very broad knowledge of food and nutrition. For consulting, the RD [recipe development] skills I have are great and give me credentials in that area. You have to understand the recipe development process, which is what I learned as part of that large corporation. There, I worked with people in marketing, operations, the chef, and that's helped me tremendously in this job. And I rely on my cooking techniques on a daily basis.

Could you do this job without a culinary degree?

Yes, I think you can, but for credibility, a background of culinary education, associated with being a dietitian, makes clients feel better. It would be a lot harder working with these chefs and business owners without such credentials.

What skills would you like to develop to help further your career?

During my bachelor's studies, I was required to take accounting and HR management courses. The more business-management skills you have, the better. I would like to gain more skills in that area. I'd also like to do media training.

What are your long-term goals?

I really want to grow my business into the research and development area. That's been a love of mine in the past. I also want to position myself as a food and nutrition expert in the media.

What is the outlook for your type of job?

It's fantastic. More and more cities are requiring nutritional analysis. More and more restaurants are having menus devoted to more nutritious offerings. More hospitals are also employing chefs, bringing culinary into health care.

What keeps you challenged?

Staying on top of the current research on nutrition. Health care is rapidly changing, with more research coming out every day. Staying on top of that is very important to me and probably the most challenging. Also, since I'm not working with food every day, keeping my culinary skills at the top.

CHRISTINE CARROLL

Christine Carroll founded CulinaryCorps in 2006 with the aim of creating a world-class service organization for culinary professionals. CulinaryCorps designs, organizes, and launches volunteer outreach experiences—currently focused around the rebuilding efforts of New Orleans, LA, and the Mississippi Gulf Coast—for culinary students and professionals to assist communities through food, cooking, education, and exchange.

CURRENT POSITION: Founding director, CulinaryCorps, New York, NY, since 2006, culinarycorps.org. ★ **EDUCATION:** BS, the College of William and Mary (2000); grand diploma in culinary arts, the French Culinary Institute (2007). ★ **CAREER PATH:** Americorps VISTA (Anchorage, AK); research assistant, Harvard University Burden of Disease Unit, Cambridge, MA; strategic alliance analyst, Pfizer; executive sous chef, Fitzbillies, England; chef-instructor, Williams-Sonoma, New York; culinary center director, Whole Foods Market Bowery, New York, NY. ★ **AWARDS AND RECOGNITION:** WCR Women Who Inspire Nominee (2008); Black and Green Fund Grant Recipient (2008); CyWorld Community Grant Recipient (2007); Geoffrey Roberts Award Recipient (2007); TASTE 3 2008 presenter. ★ **MEMBERSHIPS:** Women Chefs and Restaurateurs; Slow Food.

Salary range:

$0

Words of advice for people considering a similar career:

Never underestimate the power of your ability; cooks *can* change the world.

How many hours a week do you typically work?

During a CulinaryCorps trip, we execute about fifty hours of volunteer service, which can include feeding hundreds of Habitat for Humanity volunteers and teaching dozens of third-grade students how to cook a healthy farmers'-market lunch.

What are your specific responsibilities?

As the founding director of a grassroots nonprofit, I do it all: from head recruiter to grant writer before the trip, to trip driver and kitchen expediter during. Hopefully, as the organization expands and thrives, I will be able to delegate these tasks to others who believe in our mission.

What do you like most about what you do?

I love connecting with people who understand the powerful change that can take place at the intersection of food and community, and then connecting them with each other.

What skills are most important for you to do your job well?

Believing in our vision. Caring about the communities we serve. Effectively networking. Listening well. Communicating clearly. Leading with compassion. Being a confident cook. Never letting no get in the way of your next yes.

What skills would you like to develop to help further your career?

Fund-raising: I need to get comfortable walking into a room and asking for money!

What are your long-term goals?

To create and launch short-term and long-term CulinaryCorps experiences across the globe. I would also like to pay the generosity I have received forward by starting a grant program for Culinary-Corps alumni who would like to launch their own nonprofit project when they return to their home.

What is the outlook for your type of job?

If someone reading this has a vision that they think can change their community, their city, their world, the outlook is entirely in their hands. If they have the insight to dream it, they just need to find the courage to do it.

What qualities do you look for in a new hire?

When I recruit for a CulinaryCorps team, I look for a balance of kitchen expertise and willingness to give back to the community. I need people who know how to cook on a professional level, but I also want cooks who can check their ego at the airport and open themselves up to the entire experience.

"I love connecting with people who understand the powerful change that can take place at the intersection of food and community, and then connecting them with each other."

RYAN FARR

Ryan Farr works as a butcher, caterer, and educator in San Francisco. At CHEFS, he teaches cooking skills to homeless people as part of a six-month program, the goal of which is to provide the participants with permanent jobs in the food industry. He also conducts special events that are centered on butchering and sells meat products through his company, 4505 Meats.

CURRENT POSITION: Assistant instructor, CHEFS (Conquering Homelessness Through Employment in Foodservice); chef-owner, Ivy Elegance (catering company) and 4505 Meats (artisanal meat products), San Francisco, CA, since fall 2008, www.4505meats.com. ★
EDUCATION: Culinary arts degree, Institute of Culinary Education, New York, NY (2001). ★
CAREER PATH: Cook (for several years, in the United States and abroad, before culinary school); Aquagrill, New York; in San Francisco: sous chef, Charles Nob Hill; interim executive chef, Fifth Floor; chef de cuisine, Orson. ★ **AWARDS AND RECOGNITION:** Amuse-Cochon Award for Most Creative, as part of Taste Network. ★ **MEMBERSHIPS:** James Beard Foundation; Slow Food.

Words of advice for people considering a similar career:

Taste everything. Leave the kitchen feeling fat and full because you've tasted everything you served. Be in touch with the community. Do what you love. Work with the best, to be the best. And whatever that is for you is fine; it doesn't have to be the best for anybody else as long as it's the best for you. Learn how to plan. Plan your work and work your plan. Go to the market and make friends there.

Describe a typical day.

At CHEFS we teach the homeless. It's a six-month program. They spend three months in class with us, during which we teach them culinary arts. We have about five students every day, and we work with them hands-on to create a lunch every day. Then we eat the lunch, with the whole staff, and somebody is the critic of the day. They critique the food, the meal, say what they thought. Then we discuss the Word of the Day, like "hollandaise," "consommé," "sabayon." Then the lecture class starts. I do this four or five days a week, in the morning. I'm also doing a lot of butchery and involved with other nonprofits. I do events, such as one last week where I butchered a pig in the middle of the party. I'm also focusing on Ivy Elegance, my private catering company. I skip all over the place doing events. I focus on higher-end unique parties, on working closely with the client. I want to create a feeling for the guests that the host was involved in creating the dish themselves.

How many hours a week do you typically work?

I'm always working. In restaurants, I was working sixty to seventy hours a week, and now it's just constant. At CHEFS, it varies, about thirty to forty hours a week. The rest of the projects are things that people contact me for, such as classes.

What are your specific responsibilities?

Working with the students one-on-one and the chefs with whom they are doing their internship. I'll talk to the chef and ask how our student is doing. If he says that the student needs to work more on knife skills, then I'll work on knife skills drills and develop the skills they need to excel as a cook and as a student. The student comes first, and we are really nurturing that growth. The other part is being in the school with other students and figuring out what the best method is for teaching other classes. I work with a select number of students every morning. Then they do three months in the field. We constantly have classes coming in. The last class had about an 85 percent success rate. It's challenging to make sure that our students are fully committed to it and stay on task. Finding a job is difficult, too, because they are not always in an internship that will have an open position for them afterward. So then we focus on the skills that they need to get a job out of their externship. If the chef says, "I'd hire them if they had more breakfast skills," we work with the students on developing that.

What do you like most about what you do?

I really love walking out and feeling like I've helped somebody. That goes a long way. It's a good thing to have as part of your day-to-day life.

What skills are most important for you to do your job well?

Patience. Knowledge that there is more than one way to do something and adapting to each different situation or emotion that a student or client or situation might throw at you. That comes from dealing with restaurants, where you have to be changing things last minute.

What are your long-term goals?

To have a successful business. I'd like to have a family- and community-oriented restaurant in the future. I was born in Kansas City, grew up in Denver, lived in the Caribbean, in Napa Valley, and now in San Francisco for seven years, and I don't envision leaving any time soon. I always left after a year or two, but once in San Francisco, I couldn't figure out where else to go that would offer me something better than here.

How did you get into butchering?

I couldn't get all the parts or cuts that I wanted and had to jump through so many hoops that I decided to get the whole animal and do it myself. I never really had anybody teach me; I watched people butcher whole animals; I referred—and still do—to really good books, old and new. Spending time in Japan and Spain and with farmers in San Francisco was the inspiration to figure out how to do it myself. I made mistakes and did it again until I did it right.

15. EDUCATION

Teaching others about food is a career path with increasing opportunities, thanks to the growth the culinary education market has seen over the last two decades. It can be a full-time occupation, such as when teaching in a high school or college, or one where the instructor sets the number of hours that he or she wishes to

teach each week or month. Some chefs teach a few recreational classes a year, for example, or might be adjuncts for professional programs. Kitchen stores and gourmet supermarkets often hire people to give demonstrations, which is another way to teach part-time. Some chef-instructors also take on personal chef projects, including teaching private clients how to cook.

professional programs

Chef-instructors who work in professional programs do so at high schools, colleges, and culinary schools that typically offer formal credentials such as a diploma or degree. Full-time instructors need to obtain a teaching license; employers will offer guidance for the process. Certain programs also require their instructors to have additional certifications and titles,

such as those offered by the American Culinary Federation. In order to maintain those certifications, chef-instructors will often have to take continuing-education classes and obtain a certain number of credits per year, through attendance at trade shows, for example. A chef-instructor's schedule will vary widely depending on where he or she teaches. At a high school, the schedule typically runs Monday through Friday, from early in the morning until the mid-afternoon. A college might offer evening and weekend classes, as do private institutions. Some schools, like the Institute of Culinary Education, offer morning, afternoon, and evening programs, which provide opportunities for night and weekend work. Because these schedules can be somewhat flexible and sometimes offer summers off, many instructors use their time off to take on additional work on a part-time basis, such as catering or making specialty cakes, or to spend a day here and there working in a restaurant to keep their line-cooking skills and industry knowledge fresh.

In high schools and colleges, assignments and grading are part of an instructor's duties. Grading papers and preparing for lessons, for example, will add to the workday. It is important that instructors keep current on techniques and trends in the industry, which requires an active consumption of culinary knowledge in the form of books, trade and consumer magazines, meals out, and general contact with current chefs, cooks, and other people working in the food industry. Some schools, particularly at the high school and college level, require instructors to perform some form of academic service, such as sitting on committees.

The best chef-instructors will have high-level cooking skills and experience working in the food industry—typically in restaurants, hotels, and bakeries. Their skill sets extend for beyond cooking, however. Being able to explain how to cook in a clear, inspiring manner is just as essential. A great instructor will be a clear and efficient communicator—communicating not only in the sense of sharing his or her knowledge but in being able to hear what students are saying (or not), such as questions, concerns, personal problems, and difficulties with career choices. An educator becomes a mentor and a trusted figure in the life of many of his or her students, who might share things they may not have anybody else to tell. Being engaging is also an important trait, since it will make students much more likely to listen and to learn.

recreational programs

Recreational instructors focus on teaching cooking to people who do not seek to work in a professional culinary environment. Recreational classes typically last just a few hours, or a week at most, rather than months or years. Instructors work out of established culinary schools, their home kitchens, cooking stores, and other similar facilities.

Recreational instructors who teach full-time generally teach in only one school, since few schools exist that offer a high enough volume of recreational classes to provide such employ. The Institute of Culinary Education, which offers more recreational classes than any other school in the country, provides such opportunities for instructors, who get to teach their own classes as well as the school's proprietary courses. But there are many smaller schools and organizations that regularly employ instructors. Overall, it is a good idea to be somewhat of a generalist, since it makes you much more flexible and appealing in the eyes of the person booking instructors. Teachers need to be qualified to lead the curriculum as it is designed by the school for that particular class, be it knife skills, Cooking 101, pasta making, or bread baking. Some schools might let you teach one of their own classes before they let you create your own, or take the opposite approach and try you out on your own curriculum before entrusting you with their branded program.

Most recreational cooking instructors work part-time at more than one school. They might even travel around the country to teach at cooking schools and kitchenware stores. Some of those places require you to teach hands-on cooking classes, while others prefer that you do demonstrations with tastings for the students. For instructors who do not teach exclusively for one company or school, having a niche is helpful, because an instructor will become known as the chocolate, bread, dumpling, Korean, Italian, historical-cooking, or wine-pairing expert. Choose your specialty carefully, though, as it could limit your opportunities if it is too specific.

A website is a great tool for a recreational culinary instructor to showcase themselves, since it can be used to post sample courses and menus, a bio, press mentions, and praises from former students. Approach the person in charge of scheduling at a culinary school with a list of classes you would like to teach, including sample menus. Spend some time researching their current schedule; if you only offer classes that they already have available, it is likely that you will not get booked there. Being prepared will gain you the trust of the director, since it indicates that you will arrive for the classes you teach ready to go.

Running a cooking-class business out of a home in the United States or abroad is another opportunity for recreational teaching. The most successful programs, particularly abroad, combine hands-on classes with visits to local producers, markets, and stores. This makes them a one-stop destination for travelers seeking to do culinary tourism. As an owner and instructor, you will get to share your cooking knowledge as well as your love for a city, region, or country that inspires you. Some people renovate their kitchen or put a second kitchen in their garage, in order to run cooking classes out of their home. While it is an expense, it is usually a cheaper option in the long run than having to rent space to run your classes.

salaries

For professional instructors, salaries start around $40,000 for a beginning educator and can go up to more than $100,000 for instructors at private institutions who work multiple shifts and might take on additional private or recreational teaching on the side.

Most recreational instructors are paid per class that they teach. Some schools and stores around the country will pay for travel expenses to get you there, but overall that has become a rarity. Pay rates vary widely from location to location, school to school, and store to store, but they typically start around $200 for a one-day class. Before approaching the programming director, ask other people who have taught at that location what the range is, and prepare to quote a fee accordingly. Private cooking lessons can command more money, as do events. Part-time recreational instructors combine teaching with other sources of income—such as catering, personal-chef work, private events, and writing—to make a living.

BOB PERRY

As part of his role with the University of Kentucky's College of Agriculture, Bob Perry works with local food growers and producers to help them expand their market access. He functions as a bridge between producers and the university's researchers, conveying questions from the farmer and answers from the latter. He also teaches.

CURRENT POSITION: Special projects manager, Sustainable Agriculture and Food Systems, University of Kentucky College of Agriculture, Lexington, KY, since 2006. ★ **EDUCATION:** BA, sociology and philosophy, Murray State University; some hospitality courses, University of South Carolina; MA, sociology, University of Louisville, KY; currently pursuing PhD, sociology, University of Kentucky. ★ **CAREER PATH:** Professional bartender; private yacht chef in Caribbean and off the coasts of New England; chef-owner of Farmer's Hall Restaurant, Pendleton, SC; consultant for high-speed ferries in Japan and on the Great Lakes; general manager of the oldest steamboat in America, the *Belle of Louisville;* general manager/ executive chef of My Old Kentucky Dinner Train in Bardstown, KY; director of food service and the commonwealth executive chef for the Kentucky Department of Parks. ★ **AWARDS AND RECOGNITION:** Kentucky Cattlemen's Association Service Award. ★ **MEMBERSHIPS:** Board of overseers, Chefs Collaborative; board of Partners for Family Farms (local group); Slow Food; Community Farm Alliance (local group).

Salary notes:

$50,000 to $75,000

Words of advice for people considering a similar career:

Get a good liberal arts–based education. And get a foundation in culinary arts. The reason I've been successful in this position is because I can act as a translator between chefs and farmers and researchers. I attribute that to the fact that I've been a chef and I have a degree in philosophy and sociology.

Describe a typical day.

There is none. My week is divided into teaching and nonteaching days. On a teaching day, I teach the capstone course for nutrition, dietetics, and dietetics management. Two days a week, the students run a café with three-course meals for $10.

I give a short lecture and assign them their task for the day. I supervise the students and teach the whole morning as we go. My goal is not to teach them the specific dishes they cook that day but to give them cooking skills for the rest of their life. Some will go to culinary school, but most will not—they'll become dietitians. On a nonteaching day, I research topics and issues on the Web and in library and journal databases, books, articles, and magazines, and I pull everything together. The biggest part of my job is to assist food producers in Kentucky. One of my tasks is to directly connect researchers on campus with any food producers in Kentucky. It can be about food storage, agricultural engineering, marketing assistance, explaining to people how to expand their business through direct retailing, CSAs, farmers' markets. I give many lectures on food systems both in the College of Agriculture and in other disciplines around campus. I support researchers in different ways by taking part in their research. I serve on a number of sustainability-related committees around the university. And I do whatever the dean needs me to do. I work directly under the dean of research in the College of Agriculture, not as part of a department.

How many hours a week do you typically work?

Fifty to sixty hours.

What are your specific responsibilities?

To be the front door for the College of Agriculture for research questions from the general public.

What do you like most about what you do?

Helping people. I'm an altruist. I really enjoy helping people reach their full potential, both out in the world and as students. Plus I get to eat some great foods.

What do you like least about it?

There are not enough hours in the day, not enough days in the week. Either that, or the commute, which is about forty-five minutes. We live on my wife's family's historical 160-acre farm. We can't move it and we'd never want to leave it. My children will be the fifth generation to own it.

What skills are most important for you to do your job well?

Communication. The ability to speak and write and understand other perspectives, whether I am dealing with undergraduates, graduate students, chefs, researchers, or the administration. Being a true born-and-bred southern boy, I can put on an accent with people or turn it off. I can have it when talking to farmers and turn it down a bit when I'm giving a presentation.

What skills would you like to develop to help further your career?

Computer skills, and just knowledge in general.

What is the outlook for your type of job?

I think that the opportunities in sustainable agriculture are going to grow significantly as the public comes to realize the shape that the food system is in and looks for more local foods. I use the term "neoagriculture" instead of "sustainable agriculture" because many people will lambaste the latter for going back in time. But that's not the point; it's taking the traditions of the past used to raise food naturally but using all the science that we've learned since. I've read about the decline in organic-food sales in this economy, but I haven't seen any decline in local-food sales. When you taste the quality of local foods, you can't go back. The last census that came out showed an increase in the number of farms and in younger farms.

How large is your staff?

It's just me. I don't have a staff, but we have a committee of twelve people, including myself, with a representative from each department within the College of Agriculture.

What keeps you challenged?

The lack of infrastructure. And the public's agricultural and food illiteracy. That's the biggest challenge. It's not only that people don't have a clue where their food comes from, but they don't have a clue what it should taste like. I encounter that a lot. We try to pin it down. People have really forgotten what food is supposed to taste like. I'm trying to educate people on taste. I have to get them to understand what it's supposed to taste like, because real food is not covered in salt and sauces.

"The reason I've been successful in this position is because I can act as a translator between chefs and farmers and researchers."

MELINA KELSON-PODOLSKY, CMB, CEPC, CSC

Melina Kelson-Podolsky is a chef-instructor in the pastry and baking division of the Kendall School of Culinary Arts at Kendall College in Chicago, IL, which offers associate's and bachelor's degrees and certificates.

CURRENT POSITION: Chef-instructor, pastry and baking, Kendall College, Chicago, IL, since January 2005. ★ **EDUCATION:** BA, English, Ithaca College, NY (1994); baking and pastry certificate, Cooking and Hospitality Institute of Chicago (1996). ★ **CAREER PATH:** In Chicago unless indicated otherwise: baker, Original American Scones (1987–1992); pastry chef, Spiaggia Private Dining Rooms (1995–1996); pastry assistant, Brasserie T, Northfield, IL (1996); pastry chef/sous chef, Just Imagine Dining Enterprises restaurants (1996–1998); baker/pastry chef, Spare Time Bakery (1998–1999); pastry chef, Laura's Café and Patisserie, Linconshire, IL (1999); sous chef, Fritz and Zoe's Distinctive Events, Evanston, IL (1999–2001); baking and pastry instructor, Cooking and Hospitality Institute of Chicago (2001–2005); baking and pastry faculty, Chicago Botanic Garden (March 2008–present); chef-owner, the Edible Complex (catering company), Skokie, IL (1999–present). ★ **AWARDS AND RECOGNITION:** Certified executive pastry chef and certified sous chef, American Culinary Federation (2003); certified master baker (2007); high honors, Cooking and Hospitality Institute of Chicago; numerous media mentions. ★ **MEMBERSHIPS:** Board member, Bread Baker's Guild of America; member, Retail Bakers' Association; Les Dames d'Escoffier International.

Salary notes:

There's a huge range, into which credentials and certifications factor. It ranges from $40,000 on the low end to $80,000 at the high end.

Words of advice for people considering a similar career:

Be prepared to work hard and constantly challenge yourself. Never settle. Not settling on the job, but on the quality of your own job. Learn from the people you respect the most.

Describe a typical day.

I have office hours before my class, at five A.M. I want to come into my classroom and get it set up—write my lesson plans on the board—before office hours. Class starts at six A.M. Students are expected to be in at five thirty or five forty-five so they can get ready. It's just like in the industry, where you have to be ready at the beginning of your shift. My class is six hours long. I think the length is a good thing. I teach a variety of classes, but my favorite is artisan bread, which sometimes lasts even longer because of the nature of the beast. Afterward I might be revising or refining a lesson plan, seeing how a class has changed, if it's still relevant, because the industry is constantly changing. Even though the foundations are always the same, there are seasonal changes, etc. I often have meetings—curriculum-development meetings, meetings with students, other meetings after class. And I'm always trying to improve on my skills and continue to grow. With three friends who are also instructors, we work one day a week on improving our skills, on things like breadmaking and sugar pulling. It's our own faculty-development side job.

How many hours a week do you typically work?

The nice thing about teaching is not working twelve-hour days. I usually work eight to ten hours, so forty to fifty hours a week.

What are your specific responsibilities?

Curriculum development, assessment, committee work at the school. I'm chair of the Green Committee, so sustainability is very important to me. We highlight ways in which the school can be more eco-responsible, as this industry can waste a lot of water and food. It's important that students understand the cycle from seed to plate. With respect to that, I've started many related projects at the school, such as the large organic garden I helped plant at the school and am responsible for. I help peers with curriculum development as well as do my own. I'm responsible for ordering the food for my classes. I may be asked to oversee or produce food for a benefit. Daily assessment, grading, quizzes, portfolios. I help students be successful with internship placements and jobs. They contact me years after for job advice and to tell me about their successes.

What do you like most about what you do?

Flipping on switches, getting students excited about things they thought of as mundane. It's really gratifying to watch somebody evolve and be stimulated and challenged by new ideas.

What do you like least about it?

Increasingly, with the popularity of Food Network, many students are coming to school and don't understand the real culinary world. No one is going to scale your ingredients for you. It will be a mix of failure and successes, of hard work, every day. Those who don't realize that don't succeed, in the program or in the industry.

What skills are most important for you to do your job well?

Patience. Being measured, being encouraging while truthful. Like in all facets of the industry, stamina. You have to come in and be excited every day or students won't be excited about what they are learning.

What qualities do you look for to predict success in a student?

Energy, open-mindedness, seriousness, proactiveness. Kitchen skills are important, of course, but I would take a hard worker over pure talent any day, because those are the people who will continue to grow and offer you 110 percent every day.

JAMES BRISCIONE

James Briscione is a chef-instructor in the professional culinary arts program at the Institute of Culinary Education in New York. He remains with a class for a full module, which corresponds to a section of the curriculum that takes six to eleven months to complete. He has also appeared on the Food Network, where he won his episode of the cooking competition *Chopped,* and is writing a cookbook with his wife, author Brooke Parkhurst.

CURRENT POSITION: Chef-instructor, Institute of Culinary Education, New York, NY, since August 2007. ★ **EDUCATION:** BS, nutrition, Samford University, Birmingham, AL. ★ **CAREER PATH:** Dishwasher, fine-dining restaurant, Pensacola, FL (as a teenager); lead cook, kitchen manager, then chef de cuisine, Highlands Bar and Grill, Birmingham, AL (six years); sous chef, private dining room, Restaurant Daniel, New York (about a year). ★ **AWARDS AND RECOGNITION:** Winner, *Chopped* episode, Food Network (2009); winner, Star Chefs Cook-Off at the Chef's Garden's Food & Wine Celebration (2009); videos on delish.com; ABC News Now segments; Beard House dinners; cookbook, *Just Married and Cooking,* to be published in February 2011. ★ **MEMBERSHIPS:** James Beard Foundation.

Salary notes:

$75,000 to $120,000 at the very upper end.

Words of advice for people considering a similar career:

Make sure you want to do it. Really think about it, about everything that it means. You have to decide if it's something you want to do for the rest of your life or if it'd be a fun hobby. It can be a very expensive process to learn that you just want to cook as a hobby.

Describe a typical day.

I come in an hour before class starts; I go through notes and through the lesson, making sure that I got all the material together. The students have to act just like they would in restaurants and arrive at least fifteen minutes early. I view classes like a restaurant: if your shift starts at nine, you need to be working at nine, not walking into the restaurant. When the setup is right, you are ready for a successful day. If you're not set up, nothing ever goes right. They put stocks on the stove and pull things out of the freezer. Then when the room is ready, I'll do my lecture and we go over new techniques, new material for the day that they need to be familiar with. We review the recipes that they will be cooking that day, make sure that everyone knows what they'll be doing, that they are clear on the instructions. That requires having read the recipes and knowing what you'll be doing. We do knife skills or some kind of cutting drill. Then we get into cooking. While they are cooking, my job is to make sure that everyone is doing what they are supposed to, but also to make sure that they are keeping clean, organized, that they know what's going on and are working as a team. I try to keep the classroom environment as close to that of a restaurant kitchen as I can, fostering an atmosphere of professionalism. I walk around, watch what everybody is doing, making sure everyone is safe. The hardest thing to do is to make people think about what they are doing. I don't care if the recipe says fifteen minutes—if it starts burning after nine minutes, pull it off the fire. At the end, we set a presentation of the dishes, which becomes like a plating deadline. We have to be done by this set time; everything has to be out. Then we taste everything and talk about the food, about what was good about it. I do a daily evaluation of each student, which ranges from how well they executed the recipes to how well they worked and were part of the team. All those things are important, to me at least. Periodically we have practical examinations where they are cooking without me watching or saying anything, and I evaluate them wholly on the finished product. There are written tests also.

How many hours a week do you typically work?

The schedule always varies. Classes last four hours inside the class, and I put five and a half hours into each. Usually around fifty hours a week. That's an average; it's sometimes less, sometimes more.

What are your specific responsibilities?

It's equal parts educator and manager. A big part of doing this job successfully is not just knowing about cooking and knowing about the Xs and Ys of what happens in a classroom and why, but also managing what happens in the classroom as a whole.

When people do things for the first time, they tend to be slow and methodical. So it's managing the time. A huge part of that is motivation. You have to create motivation for many people.

What do you like most about what you do?

I love everything about food and cooking, and I've enjoyed working in this field. I really enjoy teaching; I love when you see that "aha" moment happen, when someone sees that magical thing happen in an oven or sauté pan for the first time. I've always been passionate about food, so it's a great way to see passion and excitement.

What do you like least about it?

What I like least is when you get students who you don't know what they are doing here. It's a vocational school—no one is forced to be here—and they show up like it's the last place they want to be. One person like that in the room, with that negative energy, can affect the atmosphere of the whole class.

What skills are most important for you to do your job well?

Communication is definitely way up on the list, to make sure we communicate very clearly to the students what's expected and what's to be done. Right after that is organization. Certainly for yourself—if I walk in and I'm not perfectly organized, if I can't go through step by step in complete thoughts, the students are completely lost. That goes back to one of the hard things: remembering that no one has ever done this before. I've taught each lesson sixty-seven times; I know them backward and forward. But everything has to be fully in context, with an explanation behind it. It's easy to forget that. I'm so used to being a chef. It's easy to say, "Take that to the back burner, sear it, make a sauce," for something that takes twenty steps, but you can't assume that the students will know the twenty steps that are required by three instructions.

What skills would you like to develop to help further your career?

I know that I can always improve on organization. It's not necessarily a skill, but knowledge is something that I'm always looking to improve on and stay very current with. I go out and spend days in the kitchen with my friends in different restaurants in the city, to see what's really going on in the restaurant scene. All knowledge in general—I still have classes often enough where I get a question I don't know the answer to. It pushes me to go look

for an answer. That's what draws people to cooking—there's always more to learn, and no one knows everything.

What qualities do you look for to predict success in a student?

Work ethic. A certain amount of common sense. Someone who wants to work hard, who wants to know and do more, and makes good decisions in every way—in what to do with their time, how they read a recipe and interpret it, etc. When you start out with a really strong work ethic, employers are going to be a lot more willing to invest their time in you. Even if you're not that good, with the right attitude and work ethic, they'll work with you. Every chef is going to want specific things done differently. Especially starting out, you have to have a serious lack of pride—not in what you're doing, but you can't be too proud to pick parsley, shell shrimps, and sweep the floor. You'll see every executive chef at a table picking parsley if he has to. No one in the kitchen is above anything.

JOE PITTA, CCE, CEC

Joe Pitta works as a chef-instructor in a vocational culinary high school program in eastern Massachusetts. This involves being in charge of the school's kitchen, which is open to the public.

CURRENT POSITION: Chef-instructor, Minuteman Career & Technical High School, Lexington, MA, since 1986. ★ **EDUCATION:** Marine Cooks and Stewards Training Center, Santa Rosa, CA (1970); Berkeley School of Bartending, Berkeley, CA (1974); hotel and restaurant management program courses, Golden Gate University, San Francisco, CA (1980); certified professional chef, California Culinary Academy, San Francisco (1980); certified vocational instructor in culinary arts, Occupational Education Certification Program, University of Massachusetts, Boston, MA (1989). ★ **CAREER PATH:** Second cook and bartender, Marine Cooks and Stewards Union (1970–1971); cook, waiter, bartender, Giovanni's Café, Berkeley (1972–1975). In Oakland, CA: food specialist, National Railroad Passenger Corp. (1975–1979); sous chef, Women's Athletic Club of Alameda County (1978–1979); chef, Via Veneto Restaurant (1980–1981). Restaurant chef, Ritz-Carlton Hotel, Boston (1981); executive chef, Stouffer Bedford Glen Hotel, Bedford, MA (1981–1986). In Boston: examiner for vocational teachers testing in culinary arts, Commonwealth of Massachusetts (1986–present); chef de partie, Aramark at Fenway Park, owners' private suite (1999–present). ★ **AWARDS AND RECOGNITION:** National Restaurant Association work/study grant; Teacher of the Year, Minuteman Tech; Certified Executive Chef and Certified Culinary Educator, American Culinary Federation. ★ **MEMBERSHIPS:** American Culinary Federation (since 1982); Massachusetts Chefs Association; Massachusetts Teachers' Association; adviser for Skills USA (a network of extracurricular clubs at vocational high schools that sponsors a yearly student competition; advisers prepare students to compete every year at regional, state, and national competitions).

Salary notes:

It depends on the school district for which you work. I work in one that pays very well. A beginning instructor will make $40,000 to work 180 days a year, eight hours a day. At the high end, if you are department head at a vocational high school, it's not unheard of to make $80,000 and higher. We also have full health and dental benefits and a great retirement plan.

Words of advice for people considering a similar career:

This is something I tell our culinary students before they go spend $35,000 to $40,000 on culinary school: Go work in the industry first. Go out and get an entry-level job. The competition is tough—that's good. Learn how to handle yourself in the kitchen; there is a whole different set of skills you'll need to learn. See if that's what you like to do.

Describe a typical day.

Our culinary arts department has three different kitchens: a student-run bakery, a student-run restaurant, and a skill kitchen where they learn product identification, knife skills, etc. I'm the chef-instructor of the student-run restaurant. The restaurant is open Tuesday through Friday. Tuesday and Wednesday we offer à la carte meals, Thursday and Friday a buffet. On Mondays we research and cost recipes, place orders, make prep lists (the menu changes weekly), plan the rest of the week, what we will be doing and who will be doing it. Between seven and seven thirty A.M., I start with homeroom, which is usually senior culinary arts students. By eight the students change into chef uniforms. At eight ten we sit down in the dining room. On Monday, we receive produce. Tuesday through Friday, we go over operations, prep lists, assignments, getting students started in their tasks. There is another full-time instructor in the restaurant and a part-time dining room instructor. We open for lunch. At the end of lunch, we critique the food and the day that we had, how the restaurant operated that day, then we clean up and the students leave by two thirty P.M. Between two thirty and three thirty I have meetings; I provide extra help for the students, maybe do some ordering. I'm done around three thirty or four.

My contract is for 180 days a year. Since I've been teaching, I've always had a second job. As an instructor, it's good to keep current; I do that by continuing to work in the industry. When I first started teaching, I took a considerable pay cut, close to 40 percent. I did a lot of catering. For the past ten years, I've been cooking for the owner of the Red Sox on game days. Now I don't need the extra income, because I make good money as an instructor after twenty-two years, but I like to do it.

How many hours a week do you typically work?

Forty hours a week, but I also work at home, correcting papers, planning.

What are your specific responsibilities?

My number one responsibility is to teach our culinary students the restaurant business and how to cook. To ensure that they are all safe. The kitchen can be a very dangerous place, with cuts, burns, and falls, which I am always trying to prevent. High school students always fool around, but the kitchen is not the place for that. My immediate priority is to keep them safe. Second, to teach them. I try to keep them professional, in uniform, so that they look the part, that they are all performing and acting as professionals. Other things are hopefully giving them that love of food. Making sure that we follow the curriculum. Grading papers. We have performance exams that academic students have to take; now we're creating standardized tests for vocational students also, with competencies that every culinary high school student has to pass to graduate. Over twenty-two years, I've seen everybody teach different things, so it's good that they are standardizing.

What do you like most about what you do?

When students come back and thank me or I see what they've accomplished. It makes me feel proud about what I do, that I gave them a tool to be successful. On a daily level, it's also rewarding to see kids get the immediate gratification of seeing somebody enjoy their food. In a vocational high school, kids are there for different reason: Some really want to learn this trade, which is great; others are here because their parents don't think they'll make it as an academic. It's great to see kids whom people may have given up on becoming successful and learning a trade that will bring them success.

"My number one responsibility is to teach our culinary students the restaurant business and how to cook. To ensure that they are all safe. The kitchen can be a very dangerous place, with cuts, burns, and falls, which I am always trying to prevent."

NAAM PRUITT

Naam Pruitt, who grew up in Thailand, started teaching cooking while in college. She now offers recreational Thai cooking classes at schools around the country and out of her home in St. Louis, MO. She is also the author of *Lemongrass and Limes*.

CURRENT POSITION: Recreational cooking instructor, St. Louis, MO, www.naampruitt.com. ★
EDUCATION: Horticulture Studies, Thailand; Wilton School of Cake Decorating. ★
CAREER PATH: Dining room, including doing fruit and vegetable carvings and ice sculpture, Texas A&M, College Station, TX; catering company. ★ **MEMBERSHIPS:** International Association of Culinary Professionals; Women Chefs and Restaurateurs; James Beard Foundation.

Salary notes:

Out of town, $250 per class; in town, $150 per class; for parties at my house, $500. Events can be four digits a day.

Words of advice for people considering a similar career:

Be patient. Be willing to work on different things. It might not be what you're dreaming of doing now, but you have to be flexible to do those things before your true dream ones.

Describe a typical day.

I teach about once a month right now at a kitchen store that offers cooking classes. I tweak my menu toward seasonal items. Last week, I started teaching about noodles. The hands-on classes are for around thirteen people, who make about five courses. My day-to-day work is so varied. Tomorrow I'm making an appearance on a local TV channel, and on Monday on another one. I am working on a Thai cooking show concept. I'm hoping that I'll have a cooking show this year. Most of my time lately has been working toward that. We should be taping a pilot very soon. Since

this isn't an eight-to-five job, I don't do the same thing every day. I went to someone's home last week to do a cooking class/dinner party. And if my kids are sick, I stay home and don't make any money.

How many hours a week do you typically work?

I work on promotion and business development a lot, and I am not getting paid for that. Half of my work throughout the week is consulting without being paid. I am thrilled to death when somebody contacts me and asks my advice. Now I don't get paid for it, but maybe six months from now it will pay. I work about ten paid hours per week, I'd say.

What are your specific responsibilities?

Students want to learn to cook whatever I teach, and they want to have fun. My responsibility is to provide them with an environment where they will gain knowledge, where they feel like they can go home and think that this was the best Thai food they've had. I teach them all the tips and tricks that have been beneficial to me over the years, that I have learned through experience. I try to pass that on to the students.

Describe your creative process.

A lot of times an idea just comes to me. If I am eating a chicken wrap at a restaurant, it might dawn on me to do a Thai version. Tortillas are not Thai, but all the flavors inside the wrap are Thai. I start writing what might go in it, then I start cooking it, and I tweak it until I can give someone the recipe. I create things daily. I entertain on a weekly basis and love doing it. Any time I entertain, I need to come up with a menu. Many times I end up creating a whole new recipe, and my friends are guinea pigs— which they love.

What do you like most about what you do?

I love it all. I love passing information on to people. It is rewarding that people are learning and having fun. Teaching feels good when you know that your students are learning something. I like creating recipes for a company as a consultant. I'm working on material for a second and third book, and I am constantly adding on to those. I love doing that; I love creating things. I love anything having to do with food.

What do you like least about it?

Writing, because that's not my gift. My husband is really good at it; he's my ghost-writer. For me, it's a chore, not an enjoy-ment. I write my tips and tricks for the cookbook, and then I give it to my husband for him to improve it. But I couldn't write for a living.

What skills are most important for you to do your job well?

Organizational skills. That's one thing that I am good at. You need good knife skills, good knowledge of ingredients, and great knowledge of what you are teaching. If I didn't have my organizational skills, I don't think I could accomplish as much as I do now. I have a lot of energy and get a lot of things done. If you are organized, you are able to do more—that doesn't just apply to cooking.

What are your long-term goals?

I have so many. One, perhaps more short-term, is to have a cooking show. Last year, I was working on launching a line of Thai sauces. With the poor economy, I'm just putting it on hold. With everything that I do, I want to provide excellent Thai food. I want to be the one to bring up the level of prepared Thai products on the market. I don't feel like what's available is of a high-enough quality. I'm also thinking about a line of Thai frozen foods. I'd love to do more books.

What is your proudest accomplishment?

My cookbook. It's my third baby.

What keeps you challenged?

Creating. Continuing to do what I do. Always working on new projects. I'm busy, and I like to be busy. My mind is always going a hundred miles an hour. When you are creative, you need an outlet. Also, when you teach, you have to assume many roles and solve problems.

GINA STIPO

Gina Stipo left the United States for Tuscany in 2000 and opened her cooking school, Ecco la Cucina, a year later. There she offers hands-on one- or multiple-day cooking classes or weeklong culinary vacations.

CURRENT POSITION: Owner, Ecco la Cucina (cooking school and culinary tours), Siena, Italy, since 2001, www.eccolacucina.com. ★ **EDUCATION:** BA, business, University of Nebraska (1983); culinary arts degree, Institute of Culinary Education, New York, NY (1997). ★ **CAREER PATH:** Health care, Kansas City (thirteen years); extern and cook, San Domenico, New York. In Atlanta, GA: manager, Veni Vidi Vici, cook then manager, Babette's Café. ★ **MEMBERSHIPS:** International Association of Culinary Professionals.

Salary notes:

It depends on how hard you want to work. I charge 150 euros per person. You could make $50,000 to $100,000 working for yourself, but you can't get in this for the money because there are no guarantees.

Words of advice for people considering a similar career:

Be prepared and have the courage to do what you want to do and what makes you happy. And if you fail, so what? Don't be afraid to try it, to stand on your own two feet and just do it. It takes hard work; you have to spend a lot of time studying and being prepared.

What prompted you to move to Italy and open your own business?

I moved to Italy in winter 2000. First I was working for an estate there, to put together a culinary program for their guests. I didn't think I'd open a cooking school in Italy, but one thing led to another. I left for another estate and was doing cooking classes for both estates. Then, in 2001, I built a website. After about three years my business got to the point where I didn't

need to work for anyone else anymore. It just happened. When I tried to go back to the States there were all kinds of roadblocks, so I stayed.

You have to have a level of creativity to have your own business. I'm not trying to be the wealthiest person in the world. I'm not trying to do so many weeks of culinary classes in a row that I can't see straight anymore.

Describe a typical day.

When I have a culinary tour in session, they arrive on Saturday and leave on Saturday. We spend two days outside of the kitchen, seeing sights, going to farms, to towns, doing wine tastings. I'm responsible for making sure that everybody is on time. It's difficult with a group that is on vacation but paid you a lot of money to make sure that everything goes smoothly. Then four days out of the week, we are in the kitchen half the day, cooking lunch or dinner. The other half we are out at a restaurant, doing a tour. There is so much to see and do; I try to relate it to the history of this particular region. When I don't have a group, I spend my time finding new things and learning. I talked my sister out of corporate America four years ago; she was in consumer products and marketing. I needed somebody to help me—the business has grown quite a bit. She does all the marketing and organizing for it on the States side. She lives in Dallas and comes to Italy when I have a culinary week to help me.

How many hours a week do you typically work?

When you work for yourself, there's work that you can do all the time. You can scatter it or do it all at once. I typically run classes from April to November, and I can do three or four classes a week. There are many little things that take time, like washing and ironing all the linens. And there are whole weeks when I don't have to do anything.

What are your specific responsibilities?

I'm responsible for everything. People come over and they pay me, so my main responsibility is that they get what they pay for and feel good about the experience. A lot of people have written and say this is the best thing they've done on vacation. That's how my business has grown, through word of mouth. I've never had someone blow me off. We do a three-hour class, all hands-on. I want them to enjoy themselves in the kitchen. Another responsibility is to answer e-mails on time and deliver the product that they are paying me for. If you can do these things, people will talk about you. I have set my classes and tours in a way that I would want to take them.

What do you like most about what you do?

All the wonderful people. I love learning about food and talking about food, sharing the information that I found. I spend a lot of time reading and learning about it, and I have a captive audience with whom I love to share that information. I love being able to rid people of their cooking anxiety. They're all different people, and not all American. I've had guests from South Africa, Australia, Great Britain, and northern Europe, for example.

What do you like least about it?

Anything that becomes drudgery. I get bored very easily, so it's important for me to keep changing things up. One of the things I like least is that people come in and out of my life. I meet many people but I don't live near any of them. I suppose what I like least is to do this work in a country where it's not easy to do it. My job would be easy if I could just run to the nearest Whole Foods.

What are your long-term goals?

My long-term goal is to own my own estate, because I don't have any property in Italy. I'd like to have a place where I could run a bed-and-breakfast and run classes.

How large is your staff?

It's small and it's part-time. I can't offer anyone a full-time job. This week we have four classes; next week we might have one. And my cooking weeks are in the spring and fall. I have a couple of friends, people I know who are responsible and will be there when I need them.

CULINARY AND HOSPITALITY PROGRAMS

Among other sources, ShawGuides, Peterson's, StarChefs, and AllCulinarySchools provide listings, with websites, of various culinary, baking, management, and wine programs, from degree granting to recreational. For food service, the Institute of Food Technologists provides a list of universities with programs that meet its standards.

www.shawguides.com
www.petersons.com
www.allculinaryschools.com
www.ift.org/cms/?pid=1000426
www.starchefs.com

USA AND CANADA

L'Académie de Cuisine
Gaithersburg, MD
www.lacademie.com

Arizona Culinary Institute
Scottsdale, AZ
www.azculinary.com

The Art Institutes
National
www.artinstitutes.edu

Baltimore International College
Baltimore, MD
www.bic.edu

Branford Hall Career Institute
Six campuses in MA, CT, and NY
www.branfordhall.edu

California Culinary Academy
San Francisco, CA
www.baychef.com

California School of Culinary Arts
Pasadena, CA
www.csca.edu

Cambridge School of Culinary Arts
Cambridge, MA
www.cambridgeculinary.com

Cascade Culinary Institute
Bend, OR
culinary.cocc.edu

Cook Street School of Fine Cooking
Denver, CO, France, and Italy
www.cookstreet.com

Cooking and Hospitality Institute of Chicago
Chicago, IL
www.chic.edu

Cooking School of the Rockies
Boulder, CO
www.culinaryschoolrockies.com

The Cornell School of Hotel Administration
Ithaca, NY
www.hotelschool.cornell.edu

Culinard
Birmingham, AL
www.culinard.com

Culinary Institute LeNôtre
Houston, TX
www.culinaryinstitute.edu

The Culinary Institute of America
Hyde Park, NY
www.ciachef.edu

The Culinary Institute of America at Greystone
St. Helena, CA
www.ciachef.edu/california

L'Ecole Culinaire
Saint Louis, MO, and Memphis, TN
www.lecoleculinaire.com

Florida Culinary Institute
West Palm Beach, FL
www.floridaculinaryinstitute.net

The French Culinary Institute
New York, NY
www.frenchculinary.com

The French Pastry School
Chicago, IL
www.frenchpastryschool.com

The Institute of Culinary Education
New York, NY
www.iceculinary.com

International Culinary School at the Art Institute of Vancouver
Vancouver, BC
www.artinstitutes.edu/vancouver

The Italian Culinary Academy
New York, NY
www.italianculinaryacademy.com

Johnson & Wales University
Providence, RI; North Miami, FL;
   Denver, CO; and Charlotte, NC
www.jwu.edu

**Keiser University Center for
Culinary Arts**
Melbourne, FL
www.keiseruniversity.edu/
   culinary/school_melb2.html

Kendall College
Chicago, IL
www.kendall.edu

Kitchen Academy
Sacramento, CA, and Seattle, WA
www.kitchenacademy.com

Liaison College of Culinary Arts
Hamilton, ON
www.liaisoncollege.com

Louisiana Culinary Institute
Baton Rouge, LA
www.louisianaculinary.com

Natural Gourmet Institute
New York, NY
naturalgourmetinstitute.com

New England Culinary Institute
Montpelier, VT
www.neci.edu

Oregon Culinary Institute
Portland, OR
www.oregonculinaryinstitute.com

Orlando Culinary Academy
Orlando, FL
www.orlandoculinary.com

Pacific Institute of Culinary Arts
Vancouver, BC
picachef.com

**The Penn State School of
Hospitality Management**
State College, PA
www.hhdev.psu.edu/shm

Pennsylvania Culinary Institute
Pittsburgh, PA
www.pci.edu

Professional Culinary Institute
Campbell, CA
www.professionalculinary
   institute.com/

**Robert Morris University Institute
of Culinary Arts**
Chicago, IL
www.robertmorris.edu/culinary/

**Les Roches School of Hospitality
Management at Kendall College**
Chicago, IL
hospitality.kendall.edu

San Diego Culinary Institute
La Mesa, CA
www.sdci-inc.com

**The School of Culinary Arts at
Yorktowne Business Institute**
York, PA
www.yorkchef.com

Scottsdale Culinary Institute
Scottsdale, AZ
www.chefs.edu/scottsdale

**Secchia Institute for Culinary
Education at Grand Rapids
Community College**
Grand Rapids, MI
www.grcc.edu

Sullivan University
Louisville, KY
www.sullivan.edu

Texas Culinary Academy
Austin, TX
www.tca.edu

**University of California–Davis,
College of Agricultural and
Environmental Sciences**
Davis, CA
caes.ucdavis.edu

Western Culinary Institute
Portland, OR
www.wci.edu

OTHER COUNTRIES

At-Sunrice GlobalChef Academy
Singapore
www.at-sunrice.com

**Australian School of Tourism and
Hotel Management**
Perth, Australia
www.asthm.com.au

Capsicum Culinary Studio
Cape Town, South Africa
www.capsicumcooking.co.za

**Christina Martin School of Food
and Wine**
Durban, South Africa
www.christinamartin.co.za

Le Cordon Bleu
Eight international locations
www.cordonbleu.edu

**DCT European Culinary Arts and
Pastry & Chocolate Center**
Lucerne, Switzerland
www.culinaryschool.ch

Ecole Hotelière de Lausanne
Lausanne, Switzerland
www.ehl.edu

Ecole Ritz Escoffier
Paris, France
ritzparis.com

Glion Institute of Higher
Education
Glion, Switzerland
www.glion.ch

Hotelschool The Hague
The Hague, Netherlands
www.hotelschool.nl

HRC Culinary Academy
Dobrich, Bulgaria
www.hrcacademy.com

IMI-Luzern—International Hotel,
Tourism, and Events Management
Institutes
Lucerne, Switzerland
www.imi-luzern.com

Institut Paul Bocuse
Lyon, France
www.institutpaulbocuse.com

International School for Culinary
Arts and Hotel Management
Quezon City, Philippines
www.iscahm.com

Italian Culinary Institute for
Foreigners
Asti and Turin, Italy
www.icif.com

Istanbul Culinary Institute
Istanbul, Turkey
www.istanbulculinary.com

Mausi Sebess International
Institute of Culinary Arts
Buenos Aires, Argentina
www.mausisebess.com

Northern Sydney Institute—Crows
Nest College
Sydney, Australia
www.nsi.tafensw.edu.au/HTML/
    About-US/crows_nest_college.
    html

Oxford Brookes University
Oxford, UK
www.business.brookes.ac.uk/bs/
    departments/hltm

Les Roches International School
of Hotel Management
Crans-Montana, Switzerland
www.lesroches.edu

Silwood School of Cookery
Cape Town, South Africa
www.silwood.co.za

Swiss Hotel Management School
Montreux and Leysin, Switzerland
www.shms.com

Thames Valley University—The
London School of Tourism,
Hospitality & Leisure
London, UK
www.tvu.ac.uk/hospitality/
    London_School_of_Hospitality_
    and_Tourism.jsp

University of Gastronomic
Sciences
Bra and Colorno, Italy
www.unisg.it

CONTINUING EDUCATION AND CERTIFICATION PROGRAMS

Along with the programs mentioned in Chapter 2, these courses can help you hone specific skills.

BEVERAGES
Beer

American Brewers Guild
Salisbury, VT
www.abgbrew.com

Craft Beer Institute Cicerone
Certification Program
Chicago, IL
www.cicerone.org

Coffee

The American Barista Coffee
School
Portland, OR
coffeeschool.org

Coffee Fest
Issaquah, WA
www.coffeefest.com

Specialty Coffee Association of America
Long Beach, CA
www.scaa.org

Wine

American Sommelier Association
New York, NY
www.americansommelier.org

Court of Master Sommeliers
Devon, England and Napa, CA
www.mastersommeliers.org

Institute of Masters of Wine
London, UK
www.mastersofwine.org

International Wine Guild
Denver, CO
www.internationalwineguild.com

Kevin Zraly's Windows on the World Wine School
New Paltz, NY
www.kevinzraly.com

The Society of Wine Educators
Washington, DC
www.societyofwineeducators.org

United States Sommelier Association
Pembroke Pines, FL
www.ussommelier.com

Wine and Spirit Education Trust (WSET)
London, UK
wsetglobal.com

CERTIFICATIONS AND SKILLS

American Culinary Federation Certifications
St. Augustine, FL
www.acfchefs.org

International Association of Culinary Professionals
Atlanta, GA
www.iacp.com

ProChef—Culinary Institute of America
Hyde Park, NY
www.ciaprochef.edu

ServSafe
Chicago, IL
www.servsafe.com

CHEESE

Murray's Cheese Certificate
New York, NY
www.murrayscheese.com/edu_
    cheeseubootcamp.asp

University of Vermont's Vermont Institute for Artisan Cheese
Burlington, VT
nutrition.uvm.edu/viac

University of Wisconsin Master Cheesemaker
Madison, WI
www.cdr.wisc.edu/programs/
    masters/

ICE AND ICE CREAM

Academy of Ice Carving and Design
Fresno, CA
www.academyoficecarving.com

Carpigiani Frozen Dessert University
Winston-Salem, NC
ww.carpigiani-usa.com/fduophp

Ice Cream University
West Orange, NJ
www.icecreamuniversity.org

Penn State Creamery
State College, PA
www.creamery.psu.edu

PASTRY

Albert Uster Imports
Gaithersburg, MD
www.auiswiss.com

Center for Advanced Pastry Studies at ICE
New York, NY
www.iceculinary.com/professional/
    caps.html

The French Pastry School
Chicago, IL
www.frenchpastryschool.com

The Notter School
Orlando, FL
www.notterschool.com

PROFESSIONAL ORGANIZATIONS

Below is a list of national professional associations, trade groups, special interest groups, and nonprofit organizations that is included in America's broad culinary world. Many have local chapters, and most large cities also have local organizations of their own for culinary professionals. Your employers and mentors can help you locate the best ones among those for your purposes.

Action Against Hunger USA
New York, NY
www.actionagainsthunger.org

American Bakers Association
Washington, DC
www.americanbakers.org

American Culinary Federation
St. Augustine, FL
www.acfchefs.org

American Dietetic Association
Chicago, IL
www.eatright.org

AIB International (American Institute of Baking)
Manhattan, KS
www.aibonline.org

American Institute of Wine & Food
Carmel, CA
www.aiwf.org

American Personal & Private Chef Association
San Diego, CA
www.personalchef.com

American Society of Baking
Petaluma, CA
www.asbe.org

BCA
New York, NY
www.bcaglobal.org

La Chaîne des Rôtisseurs
Madison, NJ
www.chaineus.org

Chefs Collaborative
Boston, MA
www.chefscollaborative.org

Club Managers Association of America
Alexandria, VA
www.cmaa.org

Council of Hotel and Restaurant Trainers
Westfield, NJ
www.chart.org

Council on Hotel, Restaurant, and Institutional Education
Richmond, VA
www.chrie.org

Cruise Lines International Association, Inc.
Fort Lauderdale, FL
www.cruising.org

Culinary Arts Museum
Providence, RI
www.culinary.org

Les Dames d'Escoffier International
Louisville, KY
www.ldei.org

Feeding America (formerly America's Second Harvest)
Chicago, IL
feedingamerica.org

Food Institute
Elmwood Park, NJ
www.foodinstitute.com

Foodservice Consultants Society International
Rockwood, ON, Canada
www.fcsi.org

Foodservice Educators Network International
Chicago, IL
www.feni.org

Institute of Food Technologists
Chicago, IL
www.ift.org

International Association of Culinary Professionals
Atlanta, GA
www.iacp.com

International Cake Explorations Societé
Wyoming, MI
www.ices.org

International Foodservice Editorial Council
Hyde Park, NY
ifeconline.com

The James Beard Foundation
New York, NY
www.jamesbeard.org

National Association for the Specialty Food Trade Inc.
New York, NY
www.nasft.org

National Association of Catering Executives
Columbia, MD
www.nace.net

National Ice Carving Association
Oak Brook, IL
www.nica.org

National Restaurant Association
Washington, DC
www.restaurant.org

National Restaurant Association Educational Foundation
Chicago, IL
www.nraef.org

Network of Executive Women in Hospitality
Shawano, WI
www.newh.org

Oldways Preservation & Exchange Trust
Boston, MA
www.oldwayspt.org

Professional Association of Innkeepers International
Haddon Heights, NJ
www.paii.org

Research Chefs Association
Atlanta, GA
www.culinology.org

Retail Bakers of America
McLean, VA
www.rbanet.com

Share Our Strength
Washington, DC
www.strength.org

Slow Food USA
Brooklyn, NY
www.slowfoodusa.com

Society for Foodservice Management
Mount Laurel, NJ
www.sfm-online.org

United States Personal Chef Association
Rio Rancho, NM
www.uspca.com

Women Chefs & Restaurateurs
Madison, AL
www.womenchefs.org

Women's Foodservice Forum
Bloomington, MN
www.womensfoodserviceforum.com

SCHOLARSHIPS

The first step when looking for a scholarship is to ask the school where you wish to apply to provide you with a list of available opportunities. Most of the large culinary schools, such as ICE, partner with national organizations to offer scholarship programs specifically designed for their current or aspiring students. Overall, however, the culinary and hospitality fields do not offer a plethora of scholarships. We list here some of the most commonly available national scholarships that are specific to the food industry. Many national programs are not restricted to the food industry: Depending on the institution where you study, you might also be eligible for more general state and national scholarships. Several free online scholarship search engines exist that list those, such as www.fastweb.com and www.scholarships.com.

AIB International
www.aibonline.org

American Academy of Chefs, the honor society of the American Culinary Federation
www.acfchefs.org

American Hotel & Lodging Educational Foundation
ahlef.org

The Art Institutes Best Teen Chef Culinary Scholarship
www.artinstitutes.edu

C-CAP, Careers Through Culinary Arts Program
ccapinc.org

Chefs4Students.org
chefs4students.org

Coca-Cola Scholars Foundation
coca-colascholars.org

Les Dames d'Escoffier Scholarships
Each chapter typically runs its own scholarship program. Visit ldei.org to find resources for your location.

Institute of Food Technologists
ift.org

International Association of Culinary Professionals Foundation
theculinarytrust.org

International Cake Exploration Societé
ices.org

International Foodservice Editorial Council
ifeconline.com

International Food Service Executives Association
ifsea.com

James Beard Foundation Scholarships and Education
www.jamesbeard.org

National Restaurant Association
Each state's chapter runs its own scholarship program and/or lists available scholarships. Visit www.restaurant.org/states to find resources for your state.

National Restaurant Association Educational Foundation Scholarships
nraef.org

ProStart
prostart.restaurant.org

Women Chefs & Restaurateurs
womenchefs.org

ACKNOWLEDGMENTS

It's our strong belief at The Institute of Culinary Education that if you get a comprehensive, inclusive education, it can serve as the foundation for many different culinary career paths. It has been thrilling to see so many of those options highlighted in *Culinary Careers.* I owe thanks to many people for helping to make this happen.

I'd first like to thank my coauthor, Anne McBride. Her intelligence, energy, and spirit have always impressed me, and I'm thankful for the many hours she spent collecting this book's great interview profiles. Also, thanks to the many professionals we interviewed; their advice and perspective forms the majority of the content of this book.

On the publishing side, I'd like to thank our agent, Angela Miller, who brought Anne and me together with Clarkson Potter. And at the publisher, we have benefited from the guidance of editors Rica Allannic and Ashley Phillips. Thanks, too, to Doris Cooper, Lauren Shakely, Jenny Frost, Jane Treuhaft, Stephanie Huntwork, Natalie Mansfield, and Alexis Mentor.

Many thanks to the people I am and have been privileged to work with at ICE, including the talented chef-instructors, past and present, and the former students profiled in the book. Over the years I have learned much from ICE's school director/ director of education, Richard Simpson, and his team, which includes Nick Malgieri, Andrea Tutunjian, Mike Handal, and Stephen Zagor. I appreciate the unyielding care they take in making great programs even better. In our career services department, Maureen Fagin and her team, Jessie Craig, Adrienne Haeberle, Amy Quazza, and Deanna Silva are responsible for our job placement and externship programs. They gave much valuable input on the myriad of career paths in this book. And finally, thanks is due to my resourceful and always positive assistant, Alexandra Olsen, and our director of student affairs, chef Andrew Gold.

Above all, thanks to my family. Though my father is not an entrepreneur in the classic sense, he (and my mom) certainly instilled in me many values and traits that have been invaluable in my entrepreneurial journey of building ICE. It's easy for me to have an affinity and appreciation for all the culinary entrepreneurs in this book (and there are many) because I have travelled a similar road. And at home, I am grateful to my wife, Debi, and our kids, Charlotte, Anna, and Griffin. They provide encouragement, support, love, and laughter.

—RICK SMILOW

It is an understatement to say that this book would not have been possible without the dozens of people who agreed to be profiled or interviewed for it. They were very generous with their time and knowledge. We must also thank the numerous assistants and publicists—many of whom went above the call of duty—who helped make the interviews possible.

Rick Smilow first hired me at ICE in 2004. We have been fortunate to enjoy a productive collaboration since then, one filled with agreements and disagreements that have always made for a better end product. I am thankful for the opportunities he has afford me and look forward to continue working with him.

At Clarkson Potter, Rica Allannic and Ashley Phillips were perfect editors, trusting and trust-inspiring, with the balance of kindness and toughness that any writer needs. Their changes and suggestions undeniably made for a better book. Our agent, Angela Miller, made a wonderful match.

At ICE, many thanks go to Alexandra Olsen, who provided research and much needed support throughout the process—always with a smile—and to Maureen Drum Fagin and her team. Kelly Ann Hargrove,

Kate McCue, and Daniel Stone were patient and supportive when work on this book superseded work on our course newsletter.

In the department of nutrition, food studies, and public health at New York University, I am thankful for the understanding of my professors and mentors, Krishnendu Ray and Amy Bentley, and department chair, Judith Gilbride. The drive, intelligence, and friendship of my classmates, particularly Sierra Burnett, Jackie Rohel, and Damian Mosley, were constant sources of inspiration even if they were not aware of it.

Thanks to my kind friends who never tired of hearing me talk about this project: Geraldine Blattner, Rebecca Cole, Tae Ellin, Kristin James, Courtney Knapp, Elizabeth Matthews, Christine McDonald, Diana Pittet, Meryl Rosofsky, and Kiri Tannenbaum.

My family in Switzerland withstood long lapses between phone calls, e-mails, and visits, and yet never expressed anything but love and support. To my husband, Ron, thank you will never be enough to describe what I owe you and the love I feel for you.

—ANNE E. McBRIDE

INDEX